DANGEROUS LIAISON

DANGEROUS LIAISON

The Inside Story of the
U.S.-Israeli Covert Relationship

ANDREW AND LESLIE COCKBURN

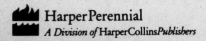
HarperPerennial
A Division of HarperCollins*Publishers*

A hardcover edition of this book was published in 1991 by HarperCollins Publishers.

First HarperPerennial edition published 1992.

Designed by Irving Perkins Associates, Inc.

The Library of Congress has catalogued the hardcover edition as follows:

Cockburn, Andrew, 1947–
    Dangerous liaison : the inside story of the U.S.-Israeli covert relationship / Andrew and Leslie Cockburn. — 1st ed.
      p. cm.
    Includes bibliographical references (p.   ) and index.
    ISBN 0-06-016444-1
    1. Israel—Foreign relations—United States.   2. United States—Foreign relations—Israel.   3. Intelligence service—Israel—History.   4. Intelligence service—United States—History.
I. Cockburn, Leslie. II. Title.
DS119.8.U6C64   1991   90-55949
327.7305694—dc20

ISBN 0-06-092145-5 (pbk.)

92 93 94 95 96 PS/MB 10 9 8 7 6 5 4 3 2 1

for Chloe and Olivia

Contents

Acknowledgments

We express our thanks to our editor, Terry Karten, who combined patience, encouragement, and a ruthless attitude toward redundancies and lack of clarity that has served us well. Charles Elliott, our editor at Bodley Head, also provided support when it was needed.

Most importantly, for the third time in our collective literary experience, we have had the great fortune to have had Andrew Wylie as our friend and agent. Without him, not to mention Sarah Chalfant at his right hand, this book would not have happened at all.

Washington, March 1991

DANGEROUS
LIAISON

1. The View from the Kirya

ON A SPRING DAY not long before the war against Iraq, a convoy of fifty red buses set out from the beachfront hotels of Tel Aviv and headed north. Each of the buses carried an identical slogan: "Philadelphia—Mitzvah," mitzvah being a Jewish religious term meaning a duty owed to God alone and performed in his honor. The 980 pilgrims were not, however, on their way to a traditional religious celebration. Their destination was the Barak battalion base of the Northern Command of the Israeli army on the Golan Heights.

The passengers on the buses, mostly middle-aged and all wearing identical blue windbreakers with insignia declaring "We are with you" and "We fly El Al," were in the country for a week of sightseeing and "identification." Today was the high point of their trip. They were going to see the Israeli army in action.

Up at the base the troops were in readiness for a major operation; jeeps and wagons milled about, tanks rumbled into position, while officers supervised the erection of signs in English. Particularly evident were a number of female soldiers from the army public affairs office, some of them sporting photogenic fireproof overalls.

The visitors in whose honor this operation was being arranged climbed down from the buses and immediately began photographing the tanks and other symbols of Israeli martial prowess, not to mention the female soldiers in their overalls.

As the last buses unloaded, the loudspeakers abruptly switched from Hebrew patriotic songs to announcements in English: "Ladies and gentlemen, the show will begin in fifteen minutes. In the meantime you can take pictures of the boys and girls, these nice Jewish soldiers and their equipment."

The sightseeing was soon interrupted by the introduction of General Yossi Peled, head of Northern Command. Peled, looking every inch a tough combat soldier, spoke in halting English about his childhood during the Holocaust and his consequent understanding of the need for Jewish solidarity. He gave way to the minister of defense himself, Yitzhak Rabin, who had just swooped down in his helicopter and was also sporting a blue windbreaker—though without insignia.

Rabin, a hero of the War of Independence, chief of staff in the Six Day War, prime minister, and now minister of defense, addressed the reverently attentive crowd on the special need for solidarity in these trying times. He referred to the Palestinian Intifada in the occupied territories, which was at that time receiving considerable coverage in the American press, explaining that he had just come from Gaza, where he had told a group of Palestinians that a solution to their problems could be found "only through negotiations" and that stones would not achieve anything. This line generated applause from the Americans and some cynical remarks from English-speaking Israelis in attendance.

After a ceremonial presentation of gifts to the senior officers, the time for action had arrived. The loudspeakers relayed the final battle orders to the troops, in English: "This is a command. Go to your positions. Good luck. Over."

Tanks fired from all directions, with plenty of noise and billowing columns of smoke. The soldiers darted about purposefully. The "enemy," represented by piles of barrels, attacked and was beaten back. Barrels flew in the air. The volume of fire redoubled. The loudspeakers announced with offhand melodrama: "I would not advise you to be on the other side of these tanks . . ." Finally the enemy was pronounced beaten. "Now," promised the master of ceremonies over the loudspeaker, "we will show you Israel's secret weapon." On cue, the young soldiers climbed out of the tanks and lined up, looking somewhat embarrassed, like actors at the end of a performance. They smiled at the applause, some of them even bowing slightly in acknowledgment.

Until recently, groups of visiting Americans like those who witnessed the "battle" on the Golan Heights could be found in the big hotels along the Tel Aviv seafront most mornings of the year. Even if their party was not large or prominent enough to warrant a full Israel Defense Force firepower demonstration, they were likely to have spent a good part of their trip visiting various way stations of the security tour: the Golan, from where, before 1967, the Syrian gunners could target Israeli settlements on the plains below; the old front line through Jerusalem; or the desert fortress of Masada on the edge of the Dead Sea, where the last Jewish resistance to Roman rule went down to defeat in A.D. 70.

Though Jews of the Diaspora may have found such excursions moving, they tend to evoke a different reaction from Israelis. Gideon Levi, a reporter for the Hebrew-language *Ha'aretz*, the most highly regarded newspaper in Israel, went along on the firepower demonstration in the Golan.[1] "I would have thought," he wrote afterwards, "that this sort of thing no longer happened in the real world and exists only in satire skits, that the Americans had matured and we had matured, and the nature of our relationship had become deeper, as befitting adults. It seems not.

"The PR officer of the event," wrote Levi, "came over to me and asked me not to forget to mention the fund-raising. 'Yes,' he added, winking, 'this evening they have four free hours and we hope they will spend some money.'"

As a sophisticated Israeli, Levi was appalled by the spectacle of soldiers performing like seals, furnishing vicarious excitement for Americans in the hopes of extracting donations. Yet the sad fact is that this was as important an operation for Israeli security as a bombing raid into Lebanon, for Israel is totally dependent on American largesse.

What Levi called the "masses of women with blue hair and . . . pseudo-athletic men" and many others like them back in the U.S. contribute at least $1 billion a year in private donations to Israel. These donations are tax-deductible. The state raises another $500 million a year through the sale of Israel Bonds. U.S. commercial banks lend an additional $1 billion.

Such generosity is dwarfed by the contributions of U.S. taxpayers overall, which amount to almost $4 billion in military and economic aid, at least, even in peacetime. All this adds up to well over $6 billion a year, or $1,300 for each and every Israeli. Israel's gross national product amounts to some $24 billion a year, so the country is receiving one-quarter of its total income in the form of gifts from U.S. citizens, acting either as philanthropists or taxpayers. Professor Yeshayahu Lie-bowitz of Hebrew University, editor in chief of the Encyclopaedia Hebraica, puts it this way: "For two thousand years the Jewish people survived without any help from the goyim. Now, the Jewish people in Israel are held captive in the velvet fist of the Americans."

Given the vital importance of this financial lifeline, it should come as no surprise that the Israelis devote so much care and attention to impressing or otherwise influencing the donors. If the young soldiers of the Barak battalion must go through the motions of a training maneuver that has nothing to do with actual warfare, it is a small price to pay. The middle-aged Americans for whom the show was staged could watch "Israel's secret weapon" and remember with pride the heroics of the War of Independence and the even more spectacular triumph of the Six Day War. As the *Ha'aretz* report sardonically noted of the audience's reaction to the firepower demonstration: "Many shivers shook backs. The bent stood tall. Here, this is the real IDF [Israel Defense Force], attacking the Syrian enemy, faultlessly, even if it was only a stack of flying barrels."

Israelis don't have to be doves to resent an attitude that treats their homeland as a living myth rather than as a real country and society. Even those Israelis publicly most strident in their invocation of inter-national Jewish solidarity in the face of the Arab threat can be sur-prisingly offhand about this semisacred topic, even as they pander to the myth. A few years ago Ariel Sharon, the famous general turned right-wing politician, was conducting a group of major donors, defined as individuals in the habit of contributing more than $250,000 a year to Israel, on the traditional security tour. He took them up to the old "green line" behind Tel Aviv, the border from where before 1967 the Arabs stood poised—he described in dramatic terms with the help of an elaborate map—to cut Israel in half. The threat that Israel might be forced to withdraw from the occupied territories was ever present, he declared, adding that if such an event were to occur Israel would once again be in mortal peril. Coming to this place, he proclaimed with emotion, always filled him with foreboding for his country's future.

As the donors, suitably impressed, climbed back on their luxury bus, Sharon dropped his careworn demeanor, turned to one of the present authors who had come along for the ride, and remarked, "I love this spot; it's so peaceful. Wouldn't you love to build a summer house here?"

Cynics like Sharon and many others in the Israeli ruling elite understand that Israel has built itself up into a regional superpower for reasons that go far beyond simple fear of the Arab enemy. They also know that there is a lot more to the relationship between the United States and Israel than the United Jewish Appeal and other uncomplicated manifestations of American-Jewish solidarity.

To find the Israel that is more than just a lobby, however, it is necessary to leave the route of the tour buses. Sharon's tour and the "Philadelphia—Mitzvah" contingent were shepherded to many sites the length and breadth of the little country, but one area not on the itinerary lies only a few blocks from their hotels.

If the visitors really wanted to understand Israel's security system and the true nature of its relationship with the United States, they could have done worse than to ask their guides to take them off the direct route from the Tel Aviv freeway to the beach and along a broad thoroughfare called Rehov Shaul Hamelech.

Coming in from the west they would have seen a high blank wall topped with barbed wire. Most of the pedestrians on that side of the street are soldiers, many of them toting American M-16 rifles.

For the most part, all that can be seen of what lies behind the wall are the tops of scattered buildings. At one point, however, a concrete needle soars over the rooftops, so high that it is visible from all over the city and beyond. In January 1991 it served as the aim-point for the Iraqi missileers as they launched their Scuds. At various levels the edifice sprouts electronic antennae, an array paralleled only by the similar adornments on the roof of the American embassy a few blocks away.

The spire conveys an ecclesiastical impression, which is only fitting. Behind the wall lies the headquarters of the most potent and revered manifestation of the modern state of Israel: the Defense Forces. Local wits claim that the elaborate electronic apparatus on the spire was built only so the generals below could "talk to their sons-in-law doing business in China" and that malfeasance by the contractors who built it means that the whole edifice is tilting.

Such irreverence is kept within the family. In public—meaning so far as foreigners are concerned—Israelis are proud of their military machine. "We believe in two things," Foreign Minister David Levy told an audience of applauding French Jews in 1990, "the Jewish God and the Israel Defense Forces."

The entire complex is known as the "Kirya," which simply means "place." It includes the offices of the minister of defense and his civilian staff, who deal with such matters as the defense budget and weapons buying; the headquarters of the chief of staff, who has overall operational command of the uniformed armed forces; and the office of the Military Intelligence service, dedicated to purely military matters and distinct from the more famous Mossad, of which Military Intelligence is a powerful rival.

Like most Israeli government offices, the Kirya is generally rather dingy in appearance and appointments. The other side of Shaul Hamelech, however, presents a different look. Modern high-rise buildings, featuring glass-fronted lobbies and wide plazas, line the street. America House, the IBM Building, or Asia House would not look out of place in a prosperous American downtown. However, it is not a coincidence that Tel Aviv's smartest office buildings are right across the street from defense headquarters. Most such business centers in the U.S. do not devote the bulk of their efforts to the arms trade. The men who own the corporations on Shaul Hamelech do just that.

Shaul Hamelech is the Main Street of what Israelis call the "security system," a network that comprises high-ranking military and intelligence officials, both active and retired, defense contractors, and arms dealers wielding enormous economic and political power in Israel.

While Americans are accustomed to reading and hearing about Israel, the world of the security system is largely unknown to outsiders. Though the dealings and private lives of its denizens are chronicled in the lively and relatively free Hebrew press, such knowledge rarely passes through translation to the English-speaking world. It is even more uncommon for outsiders to come to know this world on a firsthand basis.[2]

One man who has done so does not officially exist: an American sent to spy on the Israeli security apparatus. His employers placed a high priority on his mission because, as we shall see, the world of the Kirya and Shaul Hamelech is as fundamental a part of the U.S.-Israeli relationship as the bus tours and the United Jewish Appeal.

The Colonel, as we shall call him, was a veteran both of obscure operations in assorted hot spots—"Did I tell you about the time we blew away that Viet general in his outhouse?"—and a familiar figure at shadowy offices in and around Washington where unacknowledged policies that sway the fate of countries are formulated. As a true professional, he views his world in a dispassionate way, never letting a personal relationship interfere with the main mission of espionage or covert violence. Such attributes made him a good choice for his assignment to Israel in the 1980s. "My mission," as he explains it in a Southern drawl, "was to spy on the state of Israel, and that's what I did. The Israelis soon knew I was doing it. I knew they knew I was doing it, so everything was aboveboard, so to speak."

When word circulated around the Kirya in 1982 that the Colonel had ended his tour of duty and was finally going home, the then head of Military Intelligence, a rugged general named Yehoshua Saguy, threw him a good-bye party. At the conclusion of the festivities Saguy, surrounded by other ranking intelligence officials, rose to his feet and toasted the American with a telling tribute: "We like you. You are more Israeli than the Israelis. Now go away and don't come back."

The guest of honor took this as a great compliment. "They knew I didn't swallow any of the bullshit, and they respect that." He, too, made trips to the Golan Heights, but he was not there to "identify." He recalls how he was arrested for trespassing in a closed military area on the Golan. "I claimed that I was up there checking on how they'd changed the plaques on the trees according to which American donor was on his way." (Paying for a tree in Israel has long been a popular form of contribution for American supporters. Donors are supposed to have "their" tree forever identified by a plaque.)

Among the nooks and crannies of the Kirya and its neighborhood in which the Colonel took a particular interest was a small building just off to the side of the main complex. Outwardly unprepossessing, 8 David Elazar Street is one of the most important addresses in Israel. It is the head office of an organization known as Sibat.

The weapons trade accounts for almost 40 percent of Israel's export earnings—$1.5 billion a year. Whoever works in the arms-sale business, whether a large firm making major weapons systems or a small operation selling specialized expertise, has to come to David Elazar Street for clearance from the director of Sibat. For most of the 1980s the director, who reports directly to the minister of defense, was a graduate of Military Intelligence named Zvi Reuter.

The Colonel claims that there is a memorial to his visits to Sibat in the form of a video camera above the front door. "In the old days you could just walk straight into the reception area, and Zvi's office was right off there on the ground floor. I made it my business to do that just to see who I would catch him talking to. Some very interesting people indeed. Zvi finally got fed up with me busting in on him, so they locked the door and put that camera out there."

On personal acquaintance Reuter turned out to be a stocky individual with a pockmarked face, an affable manner and a job that made him one of the most powerful men in Israel. (He retired in 1990.) His command of defense exports meant that he controlled the fate of Israeli businessmen from Guatemala City to Singapore. Barrel-chested, he walked with enormous strides whether he was surveying a line of tanks with visiting American defense contractors or making his way through a crowd at a fashionable Tel Aviv soiree. When something needed to be arranged or fixed, he had a way of summoning minions with the gestures of a man accustomed to having things done his way, and quickly. A telephone call from him opened doors to places that were otherwise inaccessible or that, in the case of one military research institute, did not officially exist.

Reuter speaks excellent English, though his guttural discourse is occasionally interrupted by a fierce stutter. The Colonel's theory is that this denotes the Reuter conscience grappling with the necessity of telling a lie. "Zvi, you fat crook, you're stuttering. I know you're lying to me again," he would roar into the phone. Reuter's response was usually to chortle embarrassedly, and continue to stutter.

Reuter and the Colonel typify what one might call the nonsentimental side of the relationship between the United States and Israel, a link apart from and unknown to the eager pilgrims on their tour buses. The origins of this liaison go back a long way.

Once upon a time Israel needed powerful allies in an unfriendly Washington, and it found them at the CIA. The young country had pitifully few resources to trade, but it did have the loyalty of Jews behind the iron curtain who could be put to work on behalf of American intelligence. For the cold warriors at CIA headquarters in Langley, Virginia, this was a precious asset, and they were prepared to be generous in return.

As the struggle between East and West spread to cover the entire Third World, the secret agencies of the two countries found that there was much business they could do together. If the U.S. Congress balked at arming an unwholesome dictator, it was useful to have a friend across the sea who could take on the task without problems or scruples. If Israel needed help in building a nuclear weapon, it was a boon being owed favors in Washington. When Israel's enemies, such as the pro-Soviet regime of Egyptian Gamal Abdel Nasser, also became America's enemies, the secret liaison could be put to work in a very efficient way. If it came actually to starting a full-scale war, as in June 1967, then the Israelis would have to consult their senior partners in Washington and convince them that it was in everybody's interests that the opponent of the moment be crushed. But as time went by, less convincing was necessary.

Living by the sword seemed good for Israel, or at least for those Israelis who had a stake in the arms business. That business, of course, came to depend on the indulgence of the Americans, but the Americans were grateful when the Israelis helped out by testifying to the merits of U.S. military ideas and products, whether they were telling the truth or not. When the American arms business hit hard times, then there was additional gratitude for Israeli assistance in convincing the U.S. public that their products were still needed. If the Israelis were caught helping themselves to a few more secrets of U.S. military technology than was officially permitted, the Americans might get angry, but they were not really surprised. After all, the partners did not have to actually like each other to work together. In the world of arms and intelligence and money, there is not much room for emotion and sentiment.

From its small beginnings the relationship grew, and everyone prospered. When Russia threw in the towel and gave up on the Cold War, it seemed that perhaps Israel would have to find another role for itself and that the old partnership might break up. Then Saddam Hussein invaded Kuwait, and a new game began.

Reuter and the Colonel were therefore not just friendly antagonists. They were representatives of the two sides of the partnership, working with and needing each other, without being under any illusion about what each party was expecting to get out of the liaison.

Reuter was the second man to head Sibat. His predecessor had moved over to the other side of Shaul Hamelech to run a business that is well worth a visit for anyone interested in an unofficial tour of the security system.

The corporate offices of the Eagle Corporation, on the tenth floor of the distinctive IBM Building, do not at first give the impression that the company is engaged in really lethal affairs. The area behind the reception desk has a display of such relatively benign articles as bullet-proof vests, tents, and combat boots. It is not until the chief executive appears that a visitor gets the idea that Eagle is not just an army surplus store in a high rise, but a major player in the arms business worldwide.

Shapik Shapiro likes to confer with guests from behind a long and highly polished conference table. In keeping with the best traditions of Israeli informality, he is usually to be found in shirtsleeves, but the shirt is silk and his eyes are hidden at all times behind expensive sunglasses. A long talk will allow him to consume most of the one Havana cigar he allows himself every day.

Shapiro understands the strategic relationship between the U.S. and Israel as well as anyone, because he knows how deeply it is grounded in the arms business. The Eagle agents making deals from Central America to the Far East are essentially products of this relationship, forged over the years by people such as Shapik Shapiro.

Shapiro's early experiences were a long way from the silk shirts and Havanas. In the late 1940s he worked with Teddy Kollek in the United States. Today Kollek is known as the avuncular mayor of Jerusalem, but back then he was in charge of the semicovert and vitally important Israeli military purchasing office in New York. At that time the U.S. administration was loath to send military aid to Israel. It was the job of Kollek, Shapiro, and others to get their hands on whatever the military machine back home needed. Later on, as military links between the U.S. and Israel gradually became extensive and official, Shapiro helped negotiate the terms for the first big purchases of American fighter planes by Israel. Ultimately, he set up and ran Sibat, always paying careful attention, as the Colonel noted, to the desires of the Americans.

Despite his years of operating in the United States and unlike the rough-hewn Reuter, Shapiro cultivates a European air. This aura is indeed fairly standard, not only among members of his profession but across the whole class of those who in Israel are called Wasps. Wasps occupy roughly the same position in Israeli society as their counterparts in the American social system. Israeli Wasps are not, of course, White Anglo-Saxon Protestants. They are White Ashkenazi Sabras with *Proteksia*.

The Ashkenazis are the Jews from Eastern and Central Europe who built up the Jewish settlement in what was then Palestine, brought the state into being, and ruled it without challenge until the Sephardis, immigrants from North Africa and other parts of the Arab world, elected the first Likud government (made up of Ashkenazis like Menachem Begin) in 1977. A sabra, less common and more distinctive in the early days of the state than today, is someone who was actually born in the land of Israel. *Proteksia* is an almost untranslatable term, meaning in essence "influence" or "pull."

Wasps are snobbish, especially about what they consider to be the more vulgar manifestations of the American-Jewish connection. "Of course there are links between Israel and American Jewry," conceded Shapiro, wincing slightly at a description of the Philadelphians' excursion to the Golan Heights army base, "and of course America gives a lot of money to Israel. So much is well known, but I think you must take into account the intangibles." He waved his cigar in a delicate motion that encompassed the immediate neighborhood of Shaul Hamelech, the Main Street of Israel's side of the partnership.

Some of the inhabitants of this neighborhood are better known than others. Had the guides on the buses pointed out the headquarters of Sibat, the tourists would probably not have been impressed. But everyone has heard of Mossad. Ever since the kidnapping of the Nazi war criminal Adolf Eichmann in 1960, Israel's counterpart to the CIA has been a byword for deadly efficiency in the business of espionage and covert action. A glimpse of the unprepossessing, putty-colored, modern building a block up Shaul Hamelech would certainly have sparked an even bigger thrill than the exploits of the Barak battalion. Of course, no Israeli guide would dare point out Mossad headquarters to a group of foreigners, however much they loved Israel.

It is a lot harder for outsiders to penetrate the Mossad offices inside the featureless Hadar Dafna building than for them to visit Sibat or even the defense minister's office inside the Kirya. A casual visitor to the bank in the ground-floor lobby or to the public cafeteria on the second floor would not know that other floors house an espionage headquarters. The men and women who work there understandably prefer to remain anonymous. It is only when they retire that they can assume public faces and identities and, in many cases, profitable positions in the commercial side of the security system, often without having to leave the neighborhood.

Just round the corner from Mossad, for example, a block down Weizmann Street, is Asia House. One of the more elegant buildings in Tel Aviv, its flowing lines testify that someone had the money and the taste to hire an expensive architect. A few yards down from the elevator on the third floor is the office of a mild-mannered individual who wears a toupee and expensive bifocal spectacles and speaks in an accent that wavers between British and South African.

David Kimche's benign manner does not suggest that he is one of the most formidable intelligence operators Israel has ever produced, but that is what he is. Even better than Shapiro, he understands the basis, and the subtleties, of the covert relationship between Israel and the United States. In a world where intelligence intersects with diplomacy, where unlikely alliances are forged and wars are planned, everyone knows "David."

He joined Mossad in the 1950s and made his name on the agency's Africa desk, supervising an extensive and very successful operation to penetrate the newly independent black African governments. Later he graduated to other "accounts," such as the Kurdish insurrection against Iraq that began in the mid-1960s, not to mention covert diplomatic initiatives the world over.

After leaving Mossad in 1981 (bitterly disappointed at not being made head of the spy agency), Kimche became the director general of the Israeli Foreign Ministry. Retaining his old covert habits and associations, however, he made his mark by acting as the chief liaison with the Reagan White House, not only with regard to the operations that became known as Iran-Contra, but also in connection to others that escaped the headlines. He recalls this period as a time when "we maintained a very, very intimate dialogue on various parts of the world. We used to discuss what one should do in Third World countries, in the Middle East, et cetera. We'd give our opinion and they would give theirs. It was a *very* intimate dialogue."

Kimche officially left full-time government service in 1986. Though he is still a familiar and perhaps welcome figure in foreign ministries, intelligence headquarters, and presidential palaces around the world, he now appears as the representative of the man who owns Asia House: Shaul Nehemiah Eisenberg.

To understand Israel it is necessary to know about Eisenberg. There are many rich Israelis, but by common assent he is the richest of them all. He represents the ultimate confluence of arms, intelligence, and political power. Kimche, a man who spoke on equal terms with heads of the CIA and national security advisers to American presidents and who still has the official post of Israel's ambassador-at-large, is quick to run when the boss's buzzer summons him to the next-door office. Zvi Zamir, who ran the Mossad from 1968 to 1973, also works for Eisenberg, as does Amos Manor, the first chief of Shin Beth, Israel's equivalent of the FBI. "The big question," as an Israeli journalist once noted, "is whether the state of Israel owns Eisenberg or Eisenberg owns the State of Israel."[3]

Born in Galicia, a province of Poland whose inhabitants prided themselves on being entrepreneurs, Eisenberg moved to Germany in the 1920s and from there to Shanghai, where refugees from the Nazi persecutions found it easy to get visas. From Shanghai he made his way to wartime Japan, where he prospered in ways that remain murky to this day, purportedly thanks to marital connections with an influential Japanese family. After the war Eisenberg fostered mutually profitable links with the revolutionary Communist Chinese regime, and expanded his operations around the Far East. Today his business interests are worldwide, from cement plants and chemical factories in Korea to mines in Chile and extensive operations in Central America.

In 1968 Eisenberg moved to Israel and became a citizen. His arrival was commemorated by passage of the so-called Eisenberg law, specially tailored to give tax relief to his operations. While he swiftly became involved in all areas of the Israeli economy, the arms business was and remains central to his operations.

Keeping a close eye on Eisenberg's activities was one of the American Colonel's duties. "Every time I went through Ben-Gurion," he recalls, "I would check to see whether that 727 he used to use as an executive jet was in its parking spot next to the Israel Aircraft Industries hangar. That thing was his second home. If he was away, it was a good bet he was off in China, because he brokered big, big arms deals with the Chinese." These deals included artillery rounds, crucial technology on reentry warheads, ground-to-ground and ground-to-air missiles, avionics for warplanes, plus an upgrading of the entire Chinese tank force. Indeed, the Chinese "Eastwind" ballistic missiles sold to Saudi Arabia, whose defense purchases from the United States have always met with strenuous Israeli objections, had actually been improved by Israeli technicians in a deal arranged by Eisenberg.[4]

The people of Shaul Hamelech tend to pride themselves on their cultural sophistication. Derisive of the fanatical obscurantism of ultra-Orthodox Jews, they like to patronize the theater, eat good food without regard to religious dietary regulations, and collect art. A profitable trade in arms in various Central American countries, for example, has led to the acquisition of some very impressive collections of pre-Columbian artifacts in the fashionable suburbs of Herzliya and Savion. (Export of such items is for the most part forbidden from the countries of origin, of course, but experts at shipping guns in have scant trouble shipping pottery and sculpture out.)

Such collections have historical reverberations beyond their merits. David Kimche's study in his home in Ramat Hasharon, for example, provides an instructive visual chronicle of his role in Israeli covert foreign policy. A beautiful Zairian oil painting hangs on one wall—"Mobutu gave me that." An assortment of African carved wooden sculptures was, according to our host, a gift from a grateful "Emperor" Bokassa of the short-lived Central African Empire. Another wall is adorned with exquisite Persian miniatures, presents from the late Shah of Iran.

But Kimche's wall does not tell the whole story. The African artifacts are indeed a testimonial to the tremendous political success of operations on that continent. Not to be found on the wall, however, is any recognition of who actually paid for it all.

Israel has always enjoyed the support of American Jews, who have deployed a formidable lobby on its behalf. But the success of Israel in using American power and money to advance its position has depended on far more than just a lobby. It has been one result of a symbiotic relationship between the two countries that functions in ways of which the public knows little but that has helped mold the world and change the fate of nations and peoples. That is why Shaul Hamelech is as instructive a place to visit as Masada. It is also why a lonely memorial to one man a twenty-minute drive out of Jerusalem can tell the visitor much about the relationship that helped build all those smart offices along Shaul Hamelech, and much else in Israel besides.

2. Friends All Over

EVERY YEAR, tens of thousands of people make a pilgrimage to Yad Vashem, the museum that serves as a somber memorial to the victims of the Holocaust, on Herzl Road in West Jerusalem. There they gaze at the images and relics of a barely imaginable act of mass murder, a crime that still conditions the world's attitude toward Israel and its people.

Just past the museum, a road off on the right winds down a hill and eventually, after passing through the picturesque village of Ein Keren, continues into the Jerusalem forest. This forest is no ancient growth. The trees are conifers, not native to this part of the world. Here and there the original growth, olive trees untended now for decades, interrupts the light green glades. Ancient terraces crumble amid the roots, mute reminders of the Palestinian farmers who once lived here.

Like the museum on Herzl Road, much of this forest is also a memorial, though here the dead were heroes of the young state of Israel, commemorated in individual glades. Handsome granite plaques in English or Hebrew bear the names of the young men who died in Israel's wars.

After a few miles the forest glades thin out. But a short distance to the north on a road that leads off to join the Jerusalem–Tel Aviv highway there is one more plaque. The inscription reads, in English and in Hebrew, "James Jesus Angleton. 1917–1987. In Memory of a Good Friend."

The tribute, duplicated on a wall overlooking the Old City of Jerusalem, was unveiled in 1987 in the presence of some of the leading lights of Israeli intelligence, past and present. They came to honor a colleague from their world, a man who for nearly a quarter of a century was one of the most powerful and mysterious figures in the CIA.

Angleton was involved in many strange and secret dealings in the world of intelligence, but the Israelis like to talk of him as having been especially close to them, which is why they paid public homage to his memory.

Once upon a time it would have been inconceivable that an American espionage chief would be honored by Israel in this way, or indeed that the fact would be welcomed, as it was, by his former colleagues and friends in the U.S. At the time when Angleton first went to Israel, the infant state was by no means regarded as a loyal ally of the U.S.; on the contrary, it had strong ideological and even political ties to the Soviet Union and its system.

Isser Harel, a former chief of Mossad who was present at the creation of Israel and its intelligence services reflected in an interview with the authors how unlikely it had seemed that such a friendship would be forged. "Why should they have trusted us? We were a bunch of Russians, socialist Russians."

Israel has for so long been considered an ally of the United States that it is hard to remember how different things seemed at the time when the state was born. Most of the founding fathers of the country were born within five hundred miles of the city of Minsk. They came to Israel in the early years of this century, driven by the renewal of anti-Semitic pogroms and the failure of the 1905 revolution in Russia. They brought with them not only a burning faith in Zionism—the necessity for the Jewish people to have a state of their own—but also a belief in social revolution. David Ben-Gurion, who arrived in Palestine in 1906, was one of the founders of Poalei Zion, the Hebrew Social Democratic Party. Its first platform was a Zionist echo of the Communist Manifesto: "The history of mankind is the history of national and class struggle. . . . in the revolutionary process (in Palestine) an important role is played by the productive forces among the Jewish immigrants."[1]

After the First World War another tide of immigrants from Russia and Eastern Europe poured into Palestine. Many were devout believers in the distinctly anticapitalist concept of collective farming, the so-called kibbutz movement first established in the nineteenth century (and kept alive by subsidies from the Rothschild banking family).

As the kibbutz movement grew, the settlers set up a trade union federation, the Histadrut, which combined Zionist ideals with the socialist aim of "establishing a Jewish workers' society in Palestine."[2] This organization soon became the major economic power in the Jewish community in Palestine. The Histadrut was indissolubly linked with Mapai, the Hebrew acronym for the Land of Israel Workers' Party. The party, founded in 1930, soon controlled not only the labor movement but also the main political arm of the Palestinian Jewish community before independence, the Jewish Agency. (The Agency was a worldwide organization with many functions, including fund-raising. In Palestine itself it gradually assumed quasi-governmental status.)

David Ben-Gurion swiftly emerged as the dominant figure in this political machine. Born in the Russian town of Plonsk (now part of Poland) as David Gruen, he renamed himself, once he arrived in Palestine in 1906, taking the name of one of the last ancient Jewish defenders of Jerusalem against the Romans. An atheist who refused to attend a synagogue, he adopted Zionism as his religion.

By the time he wrote the Israeli declaration of independence four decades later, Ben-Gurion had steered the Zionist movement to victory with an iron simplicity of purpose. For most of his political life he acted on the assumption that he knew best what was good for the state. His domination of Israel's politics in the decades both before and after the achievement of statehood meant that the Israel that exists today still reflects his personality and plans. His chief objective in the period of the struggle for independence was to set up a Jewish state, however small, in the expectation that it would grow much bigger later on. That was why he was initially prepared to settle for less than what he considered to be the ancient Jewish homeland in its totality. As he explained in a letter to a friend in 1947, the plan was to bring into this state all the Jews it could possibly hold, to build a Jewish economy and organize a first-class army; if this was accomplished, he was "certain that we will be able to settle in all the other parts of the country, whether through agreement and mutual understanding with our Arab neighbours or in another way."[3]

Like many of his colleagues in the Zionist movement, Ben-Gurion was cultured, liking nothing better in his infrequent moments of free time than to browse in secondhand bookshops or discuss Greek philosophy. These traits, however, could not obscure the dominant characteristic of the man, the essence of his being: a total and absolute ruthlessness in pursuit of his chosen cause. Despite his benign air and informal manner, which sympathizers in Europe and America found so attractive, his passions and hatreds ran deep. Long after he had become prime minister and a respected statesman, he sought out the grave of former British Foreign Secretary Ernest Bevin (who had attempted to frustrate Ben-Gurion's plans for statehood) and stamped on it.

Ben-Gurion and Mapai faced political opposition before as well as after independence, both on the left and right. To the right there were the so-called Revisionists. The ideological ancestors of today's Likud government in Israel, they did not share Ben-Gurion's affection for socialist egalitarianism and despised what they considered his insufficiently militant attitude toward the Arabs.

To the left of Mapai there was Mapam, which Ben-Gurion himself described as "Jewish Communism," as opposed to the "Socialist Zionism" of his own party.[4] With strong support in the trade union movement and among the kibbutzniks, Mapam, together with other smaller groupings on the left, looked to the "forces of tomorrow," by which they meant the Soviet Union. The leader of the Mapam party declared in May 1949, "For us the USSR . . . is our second socialist homeland . . ."

The political divisions in Zionism before independence were reflected in military organizations. As head of the Jewish Agency from 1935 onward, Ben-Gurion had responsibility for the Jewish defense forces in the struggle against the British administration and the local Arab population. This armed force was called the Haganah. For the purposes of the struggle against the British, Mapam militants fought under the general direction of the Haganah, though they had their own separate formation, known as the Palmach, which was considered the elite of the armed forces.

The Revisionists had their own distinct military organizations: the Irgun, under Menachem Begin, and the even more extreme Lehi, Yitzhak Shamir's group. Lehi had split from Irgun on the issue of opposing Hitler during World War II. (In 1941 Lehi had written to the German Foreign Ministry proposing an alliance. Lehi, said the letter, was "of the opinion that common interests could exist between the establishment of a New Order in Europe in conformity with the German concept and the true national aspirations of the Jewish people . . .")[5]

Ben-Gurion's unswerving ambition was the establishment of a Jewish state, but he was prepared to adopt flexible tactics in getting there. Hence, his decision to accept temporarily the UN plan to partition Palestine into separate Jewish and Arab states. He was also prepared to take his allies where he could find them. Though he officially denounced the terrorist tactics of Irgun and Lehi, such as blowing up the King David Hotel and hanging British prisoners (an act of retaliation for the execution of Lehi gunmen), Ben-Gurion was quite prepared to take advantage of the extremists' military vigor. One sympathizer noted that he "seemed to want to have it both ways, to remain within the letter of the law . . . and to tolerate terror as a method of bringing pressure on the [British]."[6]

Given this kind of tactical flexibility, it is hardly surprising that Ben-Gurion and his supporters were anxious to keep their options open with both of the superpower blocs that emerged after World War II. To create a Jewish state, three resources were necessary: arms, people, and money. The leadership was prepared to seek these out wherever they could be found. In April 1947 a leading member of the Mapai Central Committee stated that "Zionist orientation [must be one of] 'casting its bread' upon humanity's vicious waters—wherever it reaches, so be it . . . No room exists for partisan positions. There is only the wretched position of a dependent nation [which] must follow any power willing to accept it."[7]

At the time these words were uttered, the power apparently most willing to accept Israel was the USSR of Stalin. Many decades and a whole Cold War later, Andrei Gromyko raised his hand and declared, "With this hand I created the state of Israel." Gromyko was referring to his vote, as the Soviet ambassador to the United Nations, in favor of the UN partition plan in 1947. His speech, endorsing the "aspirations of the Jews to establish their own state" and lamenting that no Western European country had "been able to ensure the defense of the elementary rights of the Jewish people," has been called the most eloquent statement of the case for the existence of Israel ever made in an international forum.

Gromyko's eloquence was deployed at the direction of Joseph Stalin, who was unlikely to have been swayed by emotion over the establishment of Israel. Immediately after World War II Stalin had taken steps to smash the Soviet Jewish organizations set up during the war as part of the general anti-Fascist front. His own solution to Jewish aspirations for a homeland was to create one—in eastern Siberia.

Nevertheless, there seemed to be sound reasons for the Russians to support both the armed Jewish resistance to British rule in Palestine and the creation of the Zionist state. The Arab world, after all, was firmly in the Western sphere of influence. The British in particular controlled puppet regimes in Egypt, Iraq, and Jordan, and the Persian Gulf states. Saudi Arabia had looked to the United States ever since Standard Oil of California had secured the lion's share of Saudi oil rights in 1933. Syria and Lebanon were the preserve of the French.

Diplomatic support, crucial though it may have been, was not the only encouragement granted by Stalin in the struggle to achieve and maintain Israeli statehood.

The Haganah, Palmach, and other fighting units were scouring the world for military supplies, calling on Zionist sympathizers to collect even the most obsolete weapons for the cause. Such efforts later became the stuff of legend, as desperate amateurs cajoled and bribed arms suppliers around the world to provide even a small shipload of guns or ammunition to Palestine. But such ad hoc arrangements were no substitute for the help of a friendly government. Fortunately, just such help was forthcoming from the Communist regime that took power in Czechoslovakia in February 1948, a regime on which Stalin kept a watchful and attentive eye.

In the months before Israel declared independence in May 1948, U.S. military intelligence began to chronicle what amounted to a regular shuttle of planes carrying arms between Prague and the Middle East. The planes were landing at isolated airfields either in Palestine itself or in Lebanon. By the end of March cargo planes carrying as much as seven tons of munitions were flying regularly out of Eastern Europe, and landing their loads under the noses of the British in Palestine itself.[8]

The CIA, which had been established less than a year before, also noted this traffic, though its reports were less detailed than those of military intelligence. As the director wrote in April 1948 in a memorandum for the president, the arms smuggling augured consequences unfavorable to U.S. national security, including "furtherance of the objectives of unfriendly nations."

As the CIA also duly noted, the Czech government was closely involved in the shipments, with cargos being loaded under the supervision of the security police. On at least one occasion the arms were flown part of the way by Czechoslovak Airlines. By August the CIA reported that Czechoslovakia had become "the main operational base for the extensive underground organization engaged in clandestine air transport of war materiel to Palestine."

From this source came all the World War II fighter planes, Messerschmitts and Spitfires, that were to form the nucleus of the Israeli air force. By the fall as many as five thousand Israeli military personnel were being trained at various bases in Czechoslovakia, and when they eventually departed for Israel their unit was named for Klement Gottwald, the Czech Communist leader. The Communists' military assistance went beyond arms. Officers of the Czech and Soviet air forces were also training pilots of the new Israel Defense Force.

This collusion continued in full swing through 1948 and beyond, with up to two planeloads of weapons a day being sent to Israel. U.S. Army Intelligence estimated (and somewhat exaggerated) the total value of this trade at as much as $300 million a year. The Czechs were of course being paid for their supplies in hard currency and gold, but payment was also rendered in an equally valuable currency—military technology.

At this time, it may be recalled, Europe was settling down to the long confrontation between the military forces of East and West. Although the Americans claimed that they were vastly outnumbered by Stalin's forces, the U.S. military felt confident that it had the lead in technology, particularly aircraft and electronics. U.S. authorities were interested to note that on at least two occasions in 1948 the Israelis shipped samples of modern American weapons into Czechoslovakia. In the spring of 1948, according to a declassified FBI report, the Czechs were the grateful recipients of an advanced BT-13 training aircraft. At the end of the year, in a transaction monitored by the U.S. air attaché in Prague, a large transport craft delivered a mobile early-warning radar system, an area in which the Soviets were severely deficient. Where and how these presents to the Soviets of Western military technology had been obtained by the Israeli suppliers remains unknown, but for the Israelis it was obviously a price worth paying.[9]

As vital as arms supplies may have been, they were no more important than another resource urgently needed by the Jews in Palestine: people. Here again, the potential supply was largely to be found behind borders controlled by Stalin, a fact not lost on Ben-Gurion. Zionism, he wrote not long after independence, had to seek an understanding with the Soviet Union, a "great and growing world power, controlling a number of states not hostile to us . . . and in it and its satellites lives the second part of the Jewish people."[10]

In the years immediately before and after Israel came into existence, the Soviet Union was prepared to help stock the fledgling state with citizens. In the first three years after the war, for example, nearly two hundred thousand Polish Jews who had escaped the Holocaust by spending the war in Russia were permitted to leave for the West and Palestine. Thousands of others followed from satellite countries such as Rumania, Hungary, and Bulgaria. Israeli representatives in Eastern Europe were informed in mid-1948 that the whole bloc was interested not only in helping Jews to emigrate, but also in giving them military training before they left.[11]

Arrangements for all these Jews to get out of Soviet-controlled territory, however, was up to the Israelis themselves, and they constructed an extraordinary organization to do it. Confusingly, the organization was called Mossad Aliyah Bet, or Institute for Immigration B (meaning illegal immigration). Nowadays, of course, the world understands "Mossad," which simply means Institute, as referring to the Israeli intelligence service analogous to the CIA, which was not set up until after the first Mossad was disbanded.

The earlier Mossad can best be described as a combination espionage unit and travel agency, a network dedicated to moving tens of thousands of people across thousands of miles. The operation not only required fleets of ships and aircraft, safe houses, forgers, and other tools of the contraband business, it also involved the corruption of officials and governments—particularly in Eastern Europe. Though the Kremlin had endorsed the principle of Jewish emigration, the local governments were apparently given latitude in extracting whatever price they could, either for state treasuries desperate for hard currency or for officials eager to supplement their personal incomes. The Mossad operatives referred to this latter activity as "lubricating expenses." Either way it was expensive. "In Rumania you can't do anything without money," Ben-Gurion grumbled in his diary. "From top to bottom. Even the [Communist] Party wants money."[12]

In 1946 hard bargaining with the Rumanian government led to an agreement under which fifty thousand Jews were to be allowed to emigrate. The Rumanians insisted that they leave all their property behind. The Mossad agreed to pay a set fee for each emigrant. The exodus began, but in December 1947, the commander of the Turkish Border Guard in control of the Bosphorus, through which the ships had to pass, signaled that he would not let them through without being paid off. The official got his money. One of the operatives involved in this operation later wrote: "In retrospect, one smiles at the naivete of the bold youngster travelling to Istanbul in Turkey carrying a suitcase laden with some $50,000 intended for bribes while at the same time, to save a dollar, sleeping in a dubious hotel that possessed no safe and therefore required him to tie the suitcase to his hand and to his flea-bitten bed."[13] (Despite this touching example of financial rectitude, there appears to have been a certain amount of internal lubrication within Mossad B. When the organization was closed down, for example, its fleet of ships was sold to the Israeli national shipping line, Zim, for considerably less than the true value. Subsequently some of Mossad B's senior officials became directors of Zim. It was not the last time that an Israeli underground operation had a personal financial angle for those involved.)

None of this effort in Eastern and Central Europe would have been possible without the third essential requirement—money. Millions of dollars were needed to buy the arms, transport the immigrants, and pay the bribes, as well as care for the fighting forces and administration in Israel itself. The only place where that kind of cash could be found was the United States.

The U.S. was a latecomer to the Middle East. Russia, England, and France had been intervening in the affairs of the region since the nineteenth century. The British, for example, were tormented for decades by the fear that someone, probably the Russians, would seize control of the Middle East and thus cut their route to India. The Americans did not become involved in the area until the 1930s, when the sterile sands of Saudi Arabia were discovered to conceal vast pools of oil. In 1945 President Franklin Roosevelt had met on an American warship with King Ibn Saud, who turned up with a medieval entourage of food tasters, wives, and bodyguards. The two got on well together, and Roosevelt presented the king with his spare wheelchair as a present.

Thereafter, control of the Saudi oil fields became a vital interest that the American national security establishment was loath to endanger. Saudi Arabia, one American official said in 1948, was "probably the richest economic prize in history." Both the State Department and the military were united in decrying any official support for the Zionist cause, not because of any concern for the fate of the Arab inhabitants of Palestine but because it might upset valuable allies such as the Saudi monarch.

President Harry Truman later recalled that Defense Secretary James Forrestal "spoke to me repeatedly about the danger that hostile Arabs might deny us access to the petroleum treasures of their country." This position was fervently echoed by State Department officials such as Forrestal's friend Robert Lovett, who also feared that "the admixture of European races in Palestine offers a unique opportunity for Soviet penetration into a highly strategic area." Attitudes like these on the part of powerful forces in the government led to policies that the Israelis regarded as hostile, such as the official U.S. embargo, introduced in 1947, against shipping arms to Palestine.

On the other side of the debate there was the American Jewish community, some 3 percent of the U.S. population—more in electorally important states such as New York. By the time the battle for Palestine was joined, this community was extremely well organized into various groups. Many (though by no means all) of these groups were supporters of a Jewish state in Palestine and were prepared to spend money for the cause. The American-financed Joint Distribution Committee, for example, paid for most of the huge Mossad B operation in Eastern Europe, including the purchase prices negotiated by the Mossad's agents with local governments. American money met the bills from the Czechs for their vital arms supplies; from the Iranian prime minister, who exacted a price for his country's recognition of Israel; and, not least, from the fledgling administration in Israel itself.

American Jewish support was not limited to writing checks; many individual American Jews gave more active assistance. For example, the airline that delivered the American radar into the hands of the Czech Communist government in December 1948 was called Service Airways, an organization set up by a Jewish/American arms smuggler named Adolph William Schwimmer. Better known as Al Schwimmer, he was to achieve rather wider notoriety many years later as a leading Israeli player in the Iran-Contra scandal. Schwimmer was a former TWA flight engineer who combined a devotion to Zionist ideals with boundless energy, a gift for motivating others and, as was later to become obvious, a nose for spotting the business possibilities in working for the security of Israel.

Hank Greenspun, later famous for his battles with McCarthyism and Howard Hughes as publisher of the *Las Vegas Sun*, recounts how, just when he was getting his business off the ground in Nevada in 1947, Schwimmer turned up unannounced and enlisted his services as an arms smuggler. Greenspun, a Jewish army veteran, had had no previous contact with organized Zionism of any sort.

Schwimmer told Greenspun that he must drop everything and fly immediately to Hawaii to inspect a consignment of war-surplus material needed by the Haganah in Palestine. Greenspun, feeling it was his duty as a Jew to do as he was asked, left at once. After getting hold of the guns, he loaded them on board a yacht, which he then hijacked at gunpoint when the owner balked at the dangers of the expedition. With the yacht on the verge of sinking, he shipped the weapons to Mexico, bribing Mexican officials along the way. In addition to the bribes, Greenspun had to produce papers, which he forged on the spot, "proving" that the guns were really destined for the Chinese. Finally, Greenspun loaded the weapons on board a cargo ship and dispatched them to Haifa before returning to a mystified wife and a faltering business.[14]

Thanks to the embargo, American supporters and others working for the Jewish state had to work underground. Mayor Teddy Kollek happily reminisces how, as the man in charge of covert arms buying and shipments in New York, he dispatched agents such as Al Schwimmer to bribe Latin American presidents with briefcases full of cash, and how he secured the cooperation of the Mafia in moving illegal supplies on the waterfront.[15] These tales make for exciting stories, part of the legend of the founding of Israel. On the other hand, they pale in significance when compared to the most important area in which Zionist money and influence was deployed—at the very top.

"The Democrats are always poor," noted a political commentator at the time, "they're always scrounging around for dough, and this makes them much more vulnerable."[16] Harry Truman knew the truth of this.

His early career in politics had been financed by the corrupt machine of Tom Pendergast, the machine boss of Kansas City and much of Missouri. (This rough-and-ready political upbringing seems to have colored Truman's view of world leaders; "A man more like Tom Pendergast I never met," he exclaimed on first encountering Joseph Stalin.)

Despite personal sympathy for the sufferings of the Jews in Europe, Truman was not overly enthusiastic about supporting a Jewish state in Palestine.[17] He felt that such a state would become a racist, theocratic entity and had no desire to overrule the policy of his own State Department. But it was not long before both his personal impressions and the dictates of diplomacy had adjusted to more pressing political considerations.

As an Israeli historian of the president's role in the creation of Israel has noted: ". . . during Truman's first term, there grew up a small, almost clandestine circle of wealthy Jews . . . who had entree into Truman's inner sanctum [who] fancied themselves as informal, substitute ambassadors for the official Zionist representatives, subtly pulling strings behind the scenes and, by virtue of their influence at the White House, enjoying positions of prestige in the fledgling State of Israel."[18] The foundations of this connection had been laid down in Truman's 1944 vice presidential election campaign, which was financed in part by a wealthy Zionist, Dewey Stone. The influence of this group was amplified by key presidential aides like Clark Clifford, who were well aware of the political and financial arithmetic of the Democratic Party's election fortunes.

The crucial battle for Truman's mind on the issue of Israel came in November 1947, as the United Nations moved to vote on the plan to partition Palestine into Jewish and Arab states. Anti-Zionists, led by the State Department, were adamantly opposed to the plan. The Zionists and their White House allies lobbied hard for U.S. support for partition.[19]

Harry Truman's public image of bluff and plucky independence belied his true political instincts, which as often as not were flexible to the point of timidity. His initial response to the dilemma of the partition vote was that the U.S. should itself vote in favor, but would not order countries under U.S. influence to follow suit. Thus, he would appear to have fulfilled his obligation to his Zionist donors while appeasing the State and Defense departments. At the last minute, however, the Zionists caught on to the stratagem and successfully pressured Truman to issue orders that quasi-colonies such as the Philippines, Haiti, and Liberia should switch their votes, which they did. The French were threatened with a total cutoff in U.S. aid, and capitulated. Most of the Latin American republics were equally willing to do as they were told (though some of their officials held out for hefty bribes), and the crucial resolution passed.

Truman's reward came in the 1948 election. As the campaigning commenced he told his advisers: "Boys, if I can have the money to see the people, I'm going to win this election. If I had money, I would put my own money in first. Now, you all go . . . and see what you can do about it."[20] His faith was not misplaced. Abe Feinberg, an ardent Zionist who had built up his fortune during World War II, coordinated a fund-raising drive that pulled in $100,000 (big political money in those days) within two days of the president's appeal. This support from Feinberg and others, such as jewelry store magnate Ed Kaufman, continued throughout the campaign. Stephen Smith, brother-in-law of John F. Kennedy and a veteran of Democratic Party back rooms, claimed that "two million dollars went aboard the Truman train in a paper bag, and that's what paid for the state of Israel."[21] After his second inauguration Truman formally recognized Israel, something he had previously avoided doing.

Maneuvering Truman into the pro-Israeli camp had been crucial, but this by no means ensured that Israel would forsake its links with the East and swing wholeheartedly into the Western bloc. That notion was anathema to many Israelis, who felt that Israel should at least be neutral, however many dollars the American Zionist charities might be spending on their behalf. U.S. diplomats in Tel Aviv took gloomy note of the fact that the first Soviet ambassador to Israel was greeted by a large and enthusiastic crowd, even though he arrived in the middle of the night.[22]

Pro-Soviet sentiment was particularly strong in the elite Palmach military formations, which tended to give their political loyalty to the leftist Mapam party. Therefore, once the war against the Arab countries—which began immediately after independence—had been won, Ben-Gurion swiftly abolished the Palmach.

Even before Ben-Gurion rid the military of what he regarded as unwholesome political tendencies, he had shown signs of favoring a military alliance with the United States.

During the fighting that immediately followed independence, the infant Israel Defense Force was bolstered by many professional soldiers who had learned their trade in the Allied armies during World War II. Some of these were attracted by the prospect of pay, others by idealism. The best known of the idealists was an American named David Marcus, a former colonel in the U.S. Army, who rose to become commander of the Jerusalem front before being killed by a sniper.

Less well known, but far more important at the time, was another American Zionist named Fred Grunich. Grunich had also been a colonel in the U.S. Army and had served on Eisenhower's intelligence staff. He went to Israel in June 1948 at the suggestion of Teddy Kollek.

Ben-Gurion took to the 32-year-old American and increasingly turned to him for military advice. Grunich, the former staff officer, took a dim view of the general deportment and discipline of the IDF, despite its stunning successes in the field. "I saw at once that the army was not worth much, professionally speaking," he said later. Grunich relayed his impressions to the prime minister, who insisted he attend General Staff meetings, even though the American spoke no Hebrew and had to have the proceedings translated.

Grunich was not a popular figure with the actual Israeli forces, especially when Ben-Gurion brought him along to meetings with the Palmach and sat him in the front row. "It was a serious error," Grunich said later. "I stood out like a red cow, and as an American I stood for everything they loathed." Specifically, the Palmach command believed that Grunich was a spy sent by Washington in order to draw Israel into the American strategic system. They were not entirely wrong. As Grunich later told an Israeli journalist, "I certainly did hope that as a result of the advice I gave Ben-Gurion the Israeli army would be so organized, trained, and equipped as to be able to fit into the overall strategic system of the United States in the future. I believed that it would serve the interests of Israel as well as those of the United States, because Israel would be unable to stand alone. It did not belong in the Communist bloc, and France was not to be relied on. West Germany was yet to be [a world power]; Britain was an enemy. That left the United States."

Grunich was not speaking for himself alone. His hopes for the future found a sympathetic echo in some quarters of the Pentagon. During his eighteen-month stay in Israel, he went home twice in order to persuade the administration to send military advisers to Israel. He found some support for the idea within the high command, but the Army chief of staff, General Lawton Collins, vetoed the scheme. Grunich was a little too far ahead of his time.

While in Israel Grunich had operated under the cover of a pseudonym: Fred Harris. When it leaked out that Ben-Gurion had been in close consultation with an American intelligence officer, the Communist Party paper *Kol Ha'am* declared that "General Harris" had been sent to "harness our army to the aggressive chariot of the American imperialists and to investigate the conditions prior to establishing American military bases on the soil of our country."

Later, in a court case, Ben-Gurion was asked: "Does not the presence of a foreign espionage officer in the General Staff headquarters of the army, and the passing of secret information to a foreign power by this means, constitute treason?"[23]

Ben-Gurion always defended Grunich, insisting that the fact that he was American should not disqualify him as a Jewish patriot—but the "Old Man," as he was known, was being a trifle disingenuous. As leader of the state of Israel, he was faced with a simple but profound dilemma. The most active and committed citizens of the new state were fervently opposed to linking the fate of their country with that of the Western camp. Indeed, only a minority were earnest partisans of a Soviet alliance; the majority favored a neutralist course.

The problem was that though Israel wanted both money and access to the two million Jews in the Soviet Union, it did not appear possible to get both at the same time, and the money was needed immediately. The American Jewish community had contributed enormous sums out of its own pockets for such causes as Czech arms and "lubricating expenses" in various countries, but private largesse was not going to pay for the ongoing upkeep of Israel. In 1949, for example, the government planned for the arrival of no less than 230,000 immigrants, principally from Eastern Europe but also from Arab countries such as Iraq. Since each immigrant cost the state at least $2,000 to resettle, this meant that the country would have to spend almost $500 million— more than the entire government budget the year before—just to take care of the new arrivals.

Israel's resources were pitifully inadequate. The total value of its exports in 1949 was only $40 million, most of which was accounted for by citrus fruit and cut diamonds. Unemployment stood at 10 percent, higher among new immigrants. In the course of the year Israel received about $100 million in contributions from the American Jewish community. But private generosity would not suffice. Only a government, specifically the U.S. government, could provide the necessary financial lifeline. Ironically, it was the very strength of Socialist sentiment in Israel that provided the first excuse for official American aid.

At the end of 1948 Israel was preparing for its first elections to the Knesset. Although Truman had not yet formally recognized the state (due to last-ditch pressure from the State Department), there was a U.S. envoy already installed in Tel Aviv. James MacDonald, an ardent Zionist who had been carefully selected by Israel's friends in the White House over bitter objections from the Foreign Service, had arrived some months before and had been hard at work lobbying Washington on behalf of the Israeli administration.

MacDonald seized on the prospect of the elections, and on the potential strength of the leftists, to warn his government that it had to send aid to Israel in the form of a guaranteed loan from the Export-Import Bank. "The Soviets may be planning some election tricks of their own," cabled the emissary. "The Soviet Union enjoys widespread public sympathy in Israel." Such aid would, he pointed out, benefit Ben-Gurion's Mapai party at the expense of the more leftist Mapam. "Mapam is equally aware of the need for this loan," MacDonald pointed out, "but it will object to any political strings that may be attached to it. It is therefore highly important for Mapai that the announcement should emphasize that the loan does not entail any political commitments."[24]

MacDonald was right about the Israeli left's reaction to the loan. One Mapam leader outlined a melodramatic scenario: "The first stage is aid, the second is subjugation, the third stage is military bases, and from here on the road is open for the final stage: a world war."[25]

Ben-Gurion himself loathed Mapam, whom he regarded as much too close ideologically to the Soviet Union. One of his supporters in the government put the matter in terms that President Truman's Jewish advisers might have found uncomfortably blunt: "In our relations with the U.S.A. we have in that country a fifth column, whereas in our dealings with the Soviet Union they have a fifth column here."[26] This concern, however, had to be weighed against the fact that the Soviet Union still controlled vital sources of arms and immigrants.

Official Israeli histories have always striven to conceal the fact that the Czechs (with Soviet approval) went on supplying arms to Israel well after the War of Independence. But declassified archives of the Israeli foreign minister show that in 1950 alone, one-quarter of the weapons bought for the IDF came from Czechoslovakia. The government in Jerusalem had no desire to shut off this flow of military hardware, certainly as long as no other country was prepared to supply weapons on the same scale. The Israelis did ask the Americans, but were turned down. An emissary in Washington reported to Jerusalem, "The main stumbling block for our arms request are the Joint Chiefs of Staff, who are uncertain about our attitude in a third world war."[27]

Getting the people was, if anything, even more important. Ben-Gurion said in January 1950, "Our security is entirely dependent on immigration. We cannot give up so easily on hundreds of thousands of Jews. There is still immigration from Poland, Czechoslovakia, Bulgaria. If there is any chance of bringing Jews from the East, and especially from Rumania, we must not abandon them."[28]

The trouble was that while the Soviets were content to see Israel stay neutral in the Cold War, the Americans were not.

In June 1950, the Korean War broke out, and the issue of Israel's international loyalties came to a head. As North Korean troops swept down the peninsula the U.S. mobilized a coalition to denounce and defeat what it considered naked aggression. Foreign Minister Moshe Sharett hoped that Israel could survive the Korean conflict with its officially neutral policy "unaffected . . . As hitherto we don't intend to identify ourselves with one bloc against another."

Sharett and the majority in the cabinet who supported him were behind the times. Ben-Gurion had resolved that Israel was going to become aligned with the West. He was determined to prove that Israel, which had received no further financial aid from America since the Ex-Im Bank loan, deserved to be considered a worthy ally of the U.S., and possibly receive a reward in the form of U.S. aid. Lack of Israeli support for the American position could have dire consequences. As Israel's deputy UN delegate Arthur Lourie pointed out in a dispatch, the U.S. Congress would give or withhold aid in the future on the basis of each country's willingness to support and perhaps assist the American war effort. "Our fate," concluded Lourie, "is inescapably bound up with the West." In a hint of things to come, the State Department had responded to Israel's vacillation on Korea by freezing some low-level loans already approved for water development and sewage treatment in Jerusalem. As the Israeli embassy in Washington warned its government, the U.S. action "is certainly a political reaction to Israeli neutrality and stand aloofishness [sic] regarding the U.S.A."[29]

Ben-Gurion was at this point prepared to go all the way and send a token force of Israeli troops to the war. Sharett, habitually more dovish than the fierce Ben-Gurion, persuaded the rest of the government that sending troops was a foolhardy notion, and the prime minister was voted down. This prompted Ben-Gurion to remark that sometimes the majority made a mistake. Nevertheless, the cabinet did agree that Israel would at least vote in favor of the U.S. position at the United Nations.[30]

Even then the Israelis endeavored to keep a low profile, continuing to adopt neutralist positions on various international issues for fear of terminally antagonizing the Soviets. They were caught in a dilemma. On the one hand, they did not dare make too open a commitment to the Americans for fear of cutting all links with the East (and outraging a lot of people at home in the process). On the other hand, Israel faced the problem, as one of its leaders explained at the time, of "how to keep on milking the [American] cow when we are not prepared and not able to give her anything."[31]

That, however, was not entirely the case. There was something Israel could give to the American "cow," but it had to be kept a secret.

The brilliant success of the Israelis in establishing a state in Palestine owed a great deal to intelligence and what would today be called "covert action," both activities heavily reliant on Jews of the Diaspora. Hank Greenspun was a good example of this kind of volunteer work; others were more discreet about their activities, such as the "two officials on the staff of the U.S. delegation to the UN" recalled by Teddy Kollek as key informants at the time of the partition vote.

At the heart of Israel's intelligence effort before independence was a secret organization called Shai. It had three main areas of operations inside Palestine itself: against the British administration, against the Arabs, and against Ben-Gurion's rivals within the Zionist organizations.

This underground intelligence effort had been highly successful. It penetrated the British civil administration in Palestine, which included a large number of Jewish officials, accounting for the fact that the British were never able to capture or seriously frustrate the activities of the Haganah fighting force. Shai was also involved in operations that went beyond simple intelligence gathering to political manipulation. When, for example, an Anglo-American commission of parliamentarians and judges came to Palestine in 1946 to judge between the claims of Jews and Arabs to the same land, they were immediately impressed by a charming and unassuming guide named Boris Guriel, supplied by the Jewish Agency to minister to their needs.[32] The helpful Mr. Guriel was in fact head of the Political Department of Shai. As soon as the commissioners had retired to bed in their hotel each night, their obliging assistant would hurry round to Ben-Gurion's headquarters and go over the ground covered that day in the inquiry. If Guriel detected that a witness had made an unfavorable impression, a new one would be supplied for the following morning in order to set matters right. Unaware how skillfully they had been manipulated, the commissioners (including future U.S. envoy James MacDonald) turned in a report that favored the Zionist position.

It was typical of Ben-Gurion's style of operation that Guriel should have come round to report to him personally on the progress of the commission. The Zionist leader liked to run things himself, using a small circle of young and trusted aides and bypassing high-ranking colleagues such as Moshe Sharett, the foreign minister. This was particularly true in the area of "security," meaning defense and intelligence. For most of the first fifteen years of Israel's existence, Ben-Gurion, through his personal control of both military and intelligence affairs, was able to conduct his own foreign policy without much regard to the niceties of parliamentary government.

Once the British had left and Israel became an independent country, intelligence priorities changed. Shai itself was abolished. In its place Ben-Gurion created three separate organizations. Military Intelligence, primarily concerned with the Arab armies, came under the Ministry of Defense and was also responsible for censoring the local press. Foreign Intelligence, headed by the veteran Guriel, became the Foreign Department and was subordinated to the Foreign Ministry. The Department of Jewish Affairs, which had monitored dissident Zionist organizations such as Irgun and Lehi, now became much more important. Reconstituted as Shin Beth, this organization, headed by a tiny Russian Jew with piercing brown eyes and huge ears named Isser Harel, was now responsible for all internal security and counterintelligence, a secret police.

Reuven Shiloah, Ben-Gurion's chief adviser on intelligence in the formative years, is a figure unremembered in most historical accounts. Yet his influence on the fate of the infant state was enormous. Shiloah had been one of the founders of Shai in the early 1930s. A schoolteacher, he had studied in Baghdad and was far better acquainted with the Arab world than most of his peers. During the war he had organized a Jewish Brigade to fight as an integral part of the British army, thereby training a cadre of future Israeli soldiers. At the end of the war the Brigade was stationed in the Netherlands. According to a CIA officer who had much to do with this unit's alumni in later years, "They were a very important way station on the emigration route. Later on, when the Brigade got moved to Italy, the route switched overnight. Make no mistake about it, they were very, very important. Shiloah was brilliant." During the war, Shiloah also began to forge links with Allied intelligence services in Cairo, working with them to drop some of his own operatives into occupied Europe.[33]

Shiloah is remembered as a conspiratorial individual who subsisted on a diet of amphetamines to keep alert, alternating them with sleeping pills when he needed to sleep. By all accounts he had a subtle and fertile mind, seeing intelligence not just as a system of gathering secret information but as a means of fostering secret alliances for Israel.

During the War of Independence and the subsequent war with neighboring Arab countries, Shiloah had played a key role in one of the least known but most important Israeli covert operations of the time. Despite the traditional perception that all Arab countries united to crush Israel at birth, King Abdullah of Jordan was by no means unalterably opposed to the Jewish state. In fact, secret negotiations with the king, involving Shiloah, Moshe Dayan, and others in Ben-Gurion's inner circle, resulted in a secret agreement, lubricated by bribes, that Abdullah would collude with Israel in order to ensure that the independent *Palestinian* state envisaged by the United Nations would never come into being. Instead, with Israeli assent and encouragement, Abdullah seized Arab Palestine in defiance of his fellow Arab rulers and ruled it as the West Bank.

Shiloah himself did not take an official position in the reorganized intelligence setup that followed independence. (His supposed job was acting editor of a Mapai party newspaper.) In 1951, however, following a series of internecine disputes, Israeli intelligence was made over yet again. Instead of the Foreign Department, which had been part of the Foreign Ministry, a new and separate agency was created that was to report directly to the prime minister. This was the Mossad, the agency that was to become legendary. Shiloah was put in charge of it. He had had no doubts in the great debate regarding Israel's loyalties in the Cold War. Soon after the end of World War II, in a secret report prepared for Ben-Gurion, he had recommended that a Jewish state ally itself with the Americans. Once the crucial decision to support the U.S. position on Korea had been made, Shiloah pressed for a further commitment. Ultimately, he argued, Israel should aim for a strategic military alliance with the United States. As a first step toward this goal, he said, the Mossad should forge a connection with American intelligence.

At first glance U.S. intelligence might not have seemed a particularly propitious prospect for Israeli courtship. Israel's covert activities and alliances had not gone unnoticed. American intelligence officers had dourly noted the Czech link, for example, including the traffic in sensitive military technology in exchange for arms. They also knew that there had been collaboration between the Israeli government and the Czechs in an especially sensitive operation: the protection of a gang of political assassins.

The original UN partition plan had led to open warfare in Palestine between Jews and Arabs. Count Folke Bernadotte, a Swedish diplomat who had spent the war years getting Jews out of occupied Europe, was accordingly dispatched to devise an alternative arrangement that might bring about peace. The plan he produced in September 1948, however, caused intense upset to the Israelis, who complained that it gave too much to the Palestinians. On September 17, the day after his report was released, Bernadotte was gunned down in Jerusalem in what was obviously a meticulously planned assassination. The terrorist team that carried out the murder were members of Lehi, the extremist group whose leaders included Yitzhak Shamir.

(Many years later, when Shamir became foreign minister of Israel, he greeted UN official Brian Urquhart by saying that he had "never dealt with anyone from the United Nations before."

"Oh, but you have, Foreign Minister," replied Urquhart. "You dealt with Count Bernadotte, did you not?")[34]

Ben-Gurion's government expressed shock and dismay at the assassination and quickly arrested several members of Lehi. That, as the State and Defense departments quickly learned from intelligence sources in Jerusalem, was not the whole story.

The day that Bernadotte was killed, no fewer than thirty Israeli passports were delivered to Czech consulates in Israel with a "recommendation" from the government that the owners be granted visas. All of the passports had valid Israeli exit permits dated that day.

These passports belonged to members of Lehi who were reportedly involved in planning and carrying out the murder of the unwelcome UN mediator. By the end of the month most of the owners had flown to Prague, including three who had been arrested hours after the killing but had somehow managed to escape Israeli police custody.

All this convinced high authorities in Washington that at least some in the Israeli government had been involved in the assassination and had received help from a Communist government in covering it up. Robert Lovett, acting secretary of state at the time, commissioned a special team within State Department intelligence to investigate further.

The Lehi members arrested in Israel were all released within two weeks. Subsequently Ben-Gurion became close friends with one of the killers. The State Department intelligence report has never been released. [35]

Zionist activities within the United States were no less closely monitored by U.S. intelligence agencies, though the most intensive scrutiny was the responsibility of an organization so shrouded in secrecy that very few officials had access to its reports.

During the war the U.S. Army had built up an enormous organization to listen in on the enemy's communications and break its codes. This organization, the Army Security Agency, continued to exist after the war. Sometime in 1945 or 1946 a special unit, even more secret than the rest of the code-breaking agency, was set up to monitor the activities of Israeli agents and their sympathizers in the U.S. and elsewhere. The men who ran this organization held the view that because of the use made by the Israelis of sympathizers from the Jewish community, no Jew, however apparently loyal a U.S. citizen, should be permitted to work in the special unit or even be told of its existence. All reports from the unit carried the code name "Gold," signifying that they were not to be shown to anyone of Jewish origin.

"We had them cold," recalls one former intelligence official who was cleared to see the Gold reports. "We knew who was shipping the arms, who was paying for them, who was being paid in this country, every illegal thing that was going on in this country. Because of politics, very little was ever done with [this intelligence]. But so far as I know the NSA [National Security Agency, successor to the ASA] still has a group like that, buried somewhere deep."[36]

Among those that did not have access to Gold was a young organization with a grandiose title. As the Korean War stirred up fears that the Cold War would turn hot, the Central Intelligence Agency was having trouble living up to its name. The CIA traced its institutional descent from the Office of Strategic Services, a wartime creation of an energetic Republican lawyer named William Donovan who had ambitions to be the supremo of U.S. intelligence. (Roosevelt may have originally encouraged his ambitions because, prior to Pearl Harbor, the president had need of Republicans like Donovan who wanted the U.S. to enter world war.)

Despite subsequent legends fostered by Donovan and others, however, the OSS had achieved little apart from publicity. Successful intelligence in World War II had been largely the product of breakthroughs in communications intelligence. The British broke the German codes and the Americans broke those of the Japanese. Both of them broke the secret systems of the world's neutral countries, as well as those of foreign corporations. But in the U.S., the army kept jealous control over anything to do with this extraordinary resource (apart from naval intelligence, which belonged to the navy). The OSS was permitted to use information obtained from German intelligence messages ("to stop them hiring quite so many German agents," jeers a graduate of the military effort), but despite strenuous efforts Donovan failed to get any further access to the fruits of the code-breakers' labors.

This being the case, the OSS did not rank high in the estimation of other agencies. Colonel Carter Clarke, the chief of what became the Army Security Agency and the custodian of Gold, later remarked scornfully, "The OSS did superb work in rescuing downed pilots and other unfortunates in Burma, but if it ever produced any intelligence worthy of the name, I was unaware of it."[37]

Thus derided and outmaneuvered by military intelligence, the OSS turned its energies to what later became known as "covert action"— aiding resistance movements in Europe and the Far East. Although there is little evidence that this activity discommoded the Germans and Japanese to any great degree, it did give its American practitioners a taste for underground intervention in foreign countries.

Donovan also nourished hopes that old-fashioned spies could produce intelligence as valuable as the enemy secrets being spewed forth by the code-breakers with their computers. Late in 1944, for example, the OSS chief excitedly informed the American high command that his people in Rome had penetrated the Vatican diplomatic service. They were receiving copies of dispatches from the papal nuncio in Tokyo— an invaluable source of information. The president and senior commanders took notice. It seemed that the OSS had justified itself at last. Sadly, it turned out that the Vatican spy was actually a journalist and pornographer—though author of the best-selling "Amazons of the Bidet"—who was concocting his seemingly credible reports on the basis of an intelligent perusal of the local newspapers.

So embarrassing was this discovery that Donovan concealed it for a time, continuing to pass on the intelligence as genuine. Even when the fraud was admitted, the OSS counterintelligence chief in Rome, a gaunt young man named James Jesus Angleton, kept the inventive pornographer on the payroll at $500 a month (a fortune in wartime Rome) in an esoteric quest to discover for whom the con man was really working.[38]

After the war a bitter bureaucratic battle broke out in Washington over the control of intelligence. The OSS had been abolished as soon as peace broke out, but the Pearl Harbor experience had left a general impression that the U.S. needed a centralized intelligence organization under civilian control. After the failure of an initial effort to put this new agency under the supervision of the State Department, it was finally decided to set up a totally new organization: the CIA. It looked a lot like the old OSS, and in fact many alumni of that institution reemerged from a brief retirement to join the new agency. Some had never left, since part of the OSS had been retained in a rump organization known as the Strategic Services Unit.

There were other similarities between the CIA and its lately departed predecessor. The military was in no way inclined to cooperate and made very sure that its monopoly on communications intelligence remained undisturbed. R. Jack Smith, in charge of Current Intelligence at the early CIA, recalls how members of the military agency would allow him to read only intercepted signals—selected by them at their headquarters—under guard "in a cage" and would never allow him to take anything away.

For a supposedly "central" intelligence agency, this state of affairs was a serious impediment. For example, the Soviet Union and its armed forces had the highest priority as intelligence targets. The military communications intelligence organization devoted extraordinary resources to this area, with some success. By the late 1940s, according to one former employee, the Army Security Agency was intercepting a large part of all long-distance domestic telegrams (because they were sent by radio) in the Soviet Union. "There were rooms full of them," he recalls, "everything from people announcing the birth of a grandson to Communist Party messages about collective-farm production. It wasn't military secrets, but they could have told you what was going on in the Soviet Union if anybody had bothered to read them."

Cut off by institutional jealousy from such potentially useful material, the CIA found itself turning, as had the OSS, to covert action as a major pursuit while simultaneously searching for its own sources of information on the Soviet Union and its Eastern Bloc allies.

In the best of all possible worlds the CIA would have had its own secret agents placed at advantageous spots inside Soviet society and its ruling apparatus. But with rare exceptions this proved impossible to achieve. The alternative was to look for friends who could help.

One such resource ready to hand was the recently defeated enemy. Long before the final German collapse, General Reinhard Gehlen, the Nazi regime's most senior intelligence officer on the eastern front, had begun planning to safeguard his freedom and a future career by turning over his organization and its files to the Americans. This was successfully accomplished. The Gehlen organization became a wholly owned subsidiary of the CIA, supplying copious data on Soviet military deployments in Eastern Europe. Gehlen had, or at least claimed to have, an extensive apparatus of agents in place deep behind the iron curtain. The Americans had sufficient faith in the value of his services to pay him up to $100 million by 1955.[39]

It should not be thought that the CIA insisted on, much less received, high-grade information from inside the Kremlin or the Soviet General Staff. There was always the hope that such a source might turn up, but in the meantime any information, no matter how inconsequential, from the Soviet Union or its satellites was worth reaching out and paying for.

If it was impossible to go and talk to the people of these and other places firsthand, then the next option was to find a country where there were a lot of people with recent experience of life in Soviet-controlled territory. If such a country also had extensive experience in underground work in that part of the world, in addition to a highly proficient intelligence organization that was anxious to cooperate, so much the better.

So Israel did have something to offer the "cow" in return for all that milk after all. Hundreds of thousands of immigrants who had only recently departed Soviet rule were already in the country. Israel also had a fully operational intelligence establishment, staffed by officers with firsthand knowledge of the languages and societies of the Soviet Union and its client states. The great operations of Mossad B in Eastern Europe were only in the very recent past. Until the beginning of 1951 Israel had a large military mission in Prague, closely liaising with the Czech Ministry of Defense and arms industry. Furthermore, there were personal and family connections with Communist governments, particularly in Czechoslovakia.

The problem with enlisting all such assets for espionage lay in the risk involved for the Diaspora Jews. Using even those immigrants already safely in Israel for intelligence purposes could endanger others still waiting to leave. As we have seen, the period of the founding of the state is replete with examples of foreign Jews dedicating themselves to the Israeli cause, a fact carefully noted by the secret unit in the Army Security Agency, but even so, Israel has always strenuously denied that its intelligence services have ever or would ever call on the services of Diaspora Jews in their own countries. It is not considered a fit subject for discussion. Thus, in the wake of the arrest and trial of Jonathan Pollard, a Zionist who spied for Israel while working for U.S. naval intelligence in the 1980s, it was considered especially scandalous that the relevant Israeli official had actually recruited a Jew as a spy. "The Mossad," as one Israeli paper restated the official position in 1990, "owing to understandable sensitivities, is not in contact with Jews in the Diaspora, for fear of making them targets of anti-Semitism or simply drawing the authorities' suspicion to them."[40] This official line was publicly discredited in 1990 when Victor Ostrovsky, a former low-level employee of the Mossad intelligence agency, wrote a book that shot to the top of the best-seller lists with an embarrassing amount of detail on his erstwhile employers' operations and methods. He made it very clear that the Mossad is absolutely dependent on foreign Jews, the so-called *sayanim,* and could not function without them.

We do not know how much the potential danger involved in putting foreign Jews at risk preyed on the minds of Ben-Gurion and the very few people, like Shiloah, whom he trusted on such matters. We do know that any such doubts were cast aside.

The moment of truth came in May 1951. Ben-Gurion made an official trip to the U.S. for the urgent purpose of launching a drive to raise no less than $1 billion from the sale of Israel Bonds. The public side of his visit was a great success. The huge Jewish population of New York turned out to greet him. The mayor granted him the freedom of the city. Ticker tape showered on his car as he rode down Broadway. It was no more than an Israeli prime minister might expect: an emotional celebration of the links between members of the American Jewish community and the state they revered from afar.

Ben-Gurion's business in Washington was of a more private nature, but hardly less significant for the future of his country. In a meeting with CIA Director Walter Bedell Smith and his deputy, Allen Dulles, the prime minister made a straightforward offer: the intelligence organizations of Israel would be enlisted in the service of the CIA. The arrangement was to be kept entirely secret. The two top CIA men expressed their appreciation and accepted the offer with alacrity.

Due to the secrecy of the arrangement, Israel had not formally cast aside its official policy of neutrality. But now Israel's international position had clearance, as it were. As Foreign Minister Sharett told the American secretary of state a few months after Ben-Gurion's visit: "It might be of help to the U.S. that the Soviet people should continue to feel free to talk to us . . . we were happy to have had recent evidence that this viewpoint is appreciated in certain governmental quarters in the U.S."

The month after Ben-Gurion's visit, Shiloah turned up in Washington to finalize the details of the arrangement, thrashed out in long meetings with Bedell Smith, Dulles, and James Jesus Angleton.

In October 1951, James Jesus Angleton arrived in Israel, the first of many visits. He was to be the CIA's principal liaison with the Mossad until the end of his career, a relationship that is now commemorated in that forest grove outside Jerusalem. As the memorial indicates, the sentiments expressed by this spymaster's Israeli peers are full of warm regard and respect. "Jim saw in Israel a true ally at a time when belief in a mission had become a rare concept" is one epitaph, typical of the genre, from Teddy Kollek. It is certainly true that Angleton had some close personal friends in Israel, such as Kollek himself and Amos Manor, a senior official in the Shin Beth internal security agency. An American friend recalls how he "adopted Israel. Certainly the way he talked about it made him sound almost like the [militantly pro-Israeli magazine] *New Republic*."

Angleton appears to have first come into contact with Israeli intelligence in the aftermath of World War II. It may be that, as some allege, he was moved by the sufferings of the Jews during the Holocaust and therefore helped the underground emigration effort that preceded independence. It is certainly true that Angleton was in Europe—in fact, in Italy—at this time. Like many in the OSS, he had been recruited at Yale in 1943, where he had displayed an interest in modern poetry, particularly that of T. S. Eliot and Ezra Pound. In late 1944 he was in Rome, where he involved himself, as we have seen, in the farcical episode of the fraudulent Vatican spy. When the OSS was disbanded, he stayed on with the rump organization, the Strategic Services Unit, as the main station officer for Italy and Switzerland. William Quinn, who ran the SSU, remembers him as having done good work, including the acquisition of a foreign country's code book—an achievement that, according to Quinn, brought grudging praise even from the overlords of the Army Security Agency.

Thus when the CIA was created in 1947, Angleton was already immersed in the espionage world of postwar Europe. It was very much the Europe of *The Third Man*. As nations that had just been fought over by massive armies struggled to survive and rebuild, the intelligence services of East and West plotted and intrigued. Old enemies became friends, as in the case of Gehlen and the Americans, and new friendships were forged, as was the case with Angleton and the underground Jewish network that ran down from Eastern Europe through Italy to the ports where shiploads of immigrants were loaded for Palestine.

At the time of the meetings in 1951 Angleton was not yet chief of CIA counterintelligence, a post he assumed in 1954. However, he was already occupying a far more important post, one he was to keep for the rest of his career. He was the official CIA liaison for all Allied foreign intelligence agencies. "That's the job that was so sensitive," a close friend of Angleton's recalls, "and that's the one that you don't read about. While he was liaising with everyone, he was getting them to do favors for either the CIA—things the CIA didn't want to carry out directly; like they've never killed anyone, right?—or for his own agenda. Even on a more mundane level, he could use his contacts with Israeli intelligence, which he kept to himself, as authority for whatever line he was trying to push at the CIA. You know, 'My Israeli sources tell me such and such,' and no one was going to contradict him, since no one else was allowed to talk to Israeli intelligence. I always had the impression that he used the Israelis in this way, getting them to say that the Russians had not really broken with the Chinese or whatever. They would be perfectly happy to do him the favor. On top of all that he felt that he was getting the benefit of Israeli networks and connections all over the place, not just in the Communist bloc."

A former high-ranking colleague of Angleton's supports this view. "Jim believed that the real exercise of power in and between countries occurs through networks of leaders. This was the importance of the liaison unit. It operated outside of the normal channels, which really irritated people like the State Department at times. A lot of it went back to relationships formed during and just after World War II. Jim cultivated these people, whether they were in or out of government."

One old CIA colleague of Angleton's saw him making early use of the networking possibilities offered by the Israelis. "Take Vienna in 1947. It was a real cowboy town—kidnappings, shoot-outs. No one really knew what was going on. We were there, the British were there, and the Russians, of course. The French were also very active, but so were the Israelis, very well organized. They worked out of a place called the Rothschild Kasern. Believe me, there was no closer relationship than that between the Israelis and the French there at that time. Now, in the French contingent there were some people who later turned out to be very key in French intelligence in whom Jim took a very close interest. That was the sort of world Jim lived in."

One very close colleague and friend of Angleton's, who by no means shared his attachment to the Israelis, altered the tone of a previously relaxed conversation to state with deliberate emphasis: "You have to understand that Jim's central dominating obsession was communism, something that for him was the essence of absolute and profound *evil*. For him nothing else really mattered, but he would use anyone and anything to combat it. Sure he liked Israelis, or at least the old-fashioned kind like Kollek who could talk about culture and things like that, but he was not a 'co-opted Israeli agent,' as some people in Washington used to call him."

On the other hand, conversations about Angleton with Israelis who worked with him reveal another element in the relationship. After effusive expressions of regard for their late friend, they tend to allow a little smirk to play around their weathered faces as the talk shifts to some of the more notorious aspects of Angleton's world view. He strongly believed, for example, that the Sino-Soviet split of the early 1960s was a cunning deception meant to fool the West. "Of course, Jim had some pretty weird ideas," said one former Mossad chief, "like that one about the Sino-Soviet split. But I think that he found himself a little more appreciated here in Israel than in Washington. We would listen respectfully to him [here the smirk] and his opinions."

So Angleton liked the Israelis, but used them for his own purposes. The Israelis may have liked Angleton, but they took great care to flatter him and bend a respectful ear to his interpretation of events in the shadowy world of intelligence and deception.

Given the complications and double meanings of this connection, it is worth taking a closer look at the public memorial to Angleton in the Jerusalem forest, a memorial created by his grateful friends in Israeli intelligence. Unlike the other memorial groves, the inscription here is not carved in stone, but is written on a sheet of plastic screwed to the stone itself. Within a year of the commemoration of the site most of the trees, tiny saplings, were dead or dying. The ground all around was covered in garbage: cans, rags, and, here and there, bones. There is nothing sentimental about this place.

3. Bumps on the Road

In 1952 the American voters swept Israel's Democratic friends out of the White House and installed General Dwight Eisenhower and his party in their stead.

This change confirmed Shiloah's wisdom in pressing for a covert connection with U.S. intelligence. The great virtue of the intelligence link was that it could withstand shifts in official U.S. foreign policy. For the next few years Israel was faced with an administration ominously inclined to look at both sides of the Middle East dispute, and even to flirt with the first really dangerous Arab opponent the Israeli leaders had to face. It is clear that throughout this period the Israelis used their relationship with the CIA to offset as best they could the unfriendly fire coming at them from elsewhere in the U.S. government.

Even though he had been the architect of the arrangement, Reuven Shiloah was not allowed much time to supervise it. Despite his brilliance, he was reportedly indifferent to the tedious business of administering the bureaucratic empire he had built. Waiting in the wings was another powerful intelligence official, who made sure that Shiloah's shortcomings did not go unnoticed by higher authority.

Isser Harel had run the Department of Jewish Affairs in the pre-independence Shai. After the reorganization of intelligence that took place when Israel achieved statehood, Harel was kept on in charge of an expanded Jewish Department, which had now become Shin Beth, the internal security service.

Born to a prosperous family in Russia, Harel had emigrated to Palestine in 1930, equipped with a gun and forged papers. His views on socialism had already been affected by the nationalization of his family's vinegar business during the Russian Revolution, and after a brief experience of kibbutz life he went into the orange-packing business. He might have gone on to become one of the new rich bourgeoisie of north Tel Aviv, save that he was recruited into the Haganah's intelligence service. There he found his lifetime calling.[1]

Even in old age Harel gives the impression of being an individual with whom it would be dangerous to meddle. An offhand remark from a visitor suggesting that not everything the old spymaster says is being taken at face value can ignite a dangerous flash from those sharp brown eyes. His interests appear confined to the subjects of intelligence (even today his bookshelves contain very little on any other subject) and Zionism.

In September 1952 Ben-Gurion fired Shiloah and appointed Harel to run Mossad, while simultaneously keeping him on as chief of the Shin Beth. Internal and external intelligence services usually coexist in a state of intense bureaucratic rivalry and antagonism. Governments tend to consider this a healthy state of affairs, as the alternative is to allow intelligence to become very powerful indeed. This was the reason that J. Edgar Hoover was balked in his bid to take over foreign intelligence in the United States after the war. Now Harel, already the Hoover of Israel, was also chief of the local equivalent of the CIA. Older Israelis remember how this period was marked by a vigorous crackdown on any form of dissent that remotely threatened the state or the political supremacy of David Ben-Gurion, which for Harel meant much the same thing. In January 1953, Mapam, the opposition party, found a bug planted by Harel's men in their central committee offices. The equipment had reportedly been supplied by the CIA.[2] "He really had a lot to do with creating Israel the way it is today, a society in which any serious dissent is marginalized," observes Professor Israel Shahak, a survivor of the Holocaust who combined a distinguished scientific career with a principled fight on behalf of civil rights in Israel. "The Shin Beth didn't go in for torture in those days; Harel was too smart for that. But with a few exceptions, anyone challenging fundamental assumptions about the way the state was being run found that they were pushed into obscurity, or in extreme cases just locked up."

Uri Avnery, for example, was in the 1950s and remains today the editor of a magazine called *Hoalam Ha'zeh*, a mixture of muckraking and high-society gossip. Avnery, who had fought in the Irgun, adopted in the 1950s what were, for the time, highly iconoclastic positions, such as advocating a separate Palestinian state. Needless to say, he was not popular with higher authority, especially when his widely read magazine started exposing corruption in the Tel Aviv police force, which was commanded by Ben-Gurion's son. Harel, lacking the legal means to close Avnery down, decided to start a rival and superficially similar magazine that would compete with *Hoalam Ha'zeh*.

A muckraking magazine edited by the secret police inevitably faced a conflict of interest. Readers stayed away in droves and the project failed. Harel then attempted a less subtle approach. He decided to place Avnery in administrative detention on the grounds of being a Soviet agent. As obligated by law, the security chief informed the Security Committee of the Knesset what he was about to do. Fortunately for Avnery, his old Irgun commander Menachem Begin was a member of the committee. "Begin, whatever his other deficiencies, believes in the law," explains Avnery. "He didn't believe that I was a Russian spy and was shocked that Harel was proposing to lock me up without any evidence whatsoever. He threatened to make my arrest a public issue and sent one of his aides to tell me what was happening." Avnery remained free.

Both his admirers and detractors agree that Harel has always possessed an almost terrifying power of concentration. His takeover of Mossad meant that he would have to be in close contact with the CIA. In preparation, he sat down and taught himself English, in six weeks.

The "connection," as he likes to call the liaison agreement with the Americans, is a matter of great pride for this formidable little man, as he makes clear with no suggestion of diffidence or self-deprecation. "At that time," he explains about the program, "the Americans were very hard up for intelligence about what was going on behind the iron curtain. They believed that the Israelis were a good and dependable ally and they told us that our contribution in this field was much greater than the whole democratic community in Europe put together."[3]

The immediate contribution was the debriefing of emigrés from the East European satellites and the Soviet Union itself. Although the Soviets allowed a grand total of only 131 Soviet Jews to emigrate between 1948 and 1955, they did permit, as we have seen, a large number of Polish Jews who had come to the USSR at the beginning of the war to go to Israel via Poland. In those same years just under three hundred thousand people from the Eastern Bloc turned up in Israel.

To carry out the "American program," as he sometimes calls it, Harel set up a special unit, composed of people from both Mossad and Shin Beth who were themselves from the Eastern Bloc countries. "It was very secret," he says, "even inside the service. We collected some of the best people who had come over from the other side. Russians—not only Russians, but also from the Socialist bloc countries. And so we found ourselves in a position that we were able to penetrate riddles that others couldn't."

It is fair to say that Harel is not enormously popular among many alumni of Israeli intelligence. There are those who feel he is overly inclined to take credit for other people's achievements. Left unmentioned in his account of the "special unit" is that it was run by Angleton's friend Amos Manor, whose responsibilities were nominally confined to Shin Beth counterintelligence. Among other services he rendered to the "connection," Manor took a close interest in Soviet efforts to collect military technology in the West.

The cooperation agreement was not popular with everyone in the Israeli government. Two years after it began one official, who thought that it was too dangerous to play these games with the Russians, recommended "the halting of interrogations of immigrants and the cessation of activity in Eastern Europe for the attainment of general information . . . Let the Americans deal with this [themselves] and pay the price for it."[4]

By that time, unfortunately, Jews in the East were already paying a price. Stalin had decided to abandon any semblance of neutrality toward Zionism and had moved to the attack.

It is an open question as to what degree Stalin's change of policy was affected by the fact that the Israelis were using their networks in the Soviet Bloc to spy on behalf of the Americans. The operation obviously put Jews at great risk, a fact that Harel insouciantly admits: "No question about it; in fact, they [the Russians] rather condemned us for it." On the other hand Joseph Stalin never felt the need to wait for an excuse to kill people. Jews in Russia itself, particularly the Jewish intelligentsia, had been under assault in the late 1940s, even as Stalin was giving support of various kinds to Israel. The turning point for the bloodthirsty old dictator probably came when Israel gave definite signs, after the outbreak of the Korean War, that it was aligning itself with the West.

Toward the end of 1951 Soviet propaganda began to take on a distinctly anti-Semitic edge. The most notable example came with the arrest in November of that year of the Czech Communist leader Rudolph Slansky and other senior members of the regime, eleven of whom were Jewish. This was the prelude to the famous Prague Trial, the last in Stalin's purge of those Communist leaders in Eastern Europe whom he suspected of harboring independent thoughts. The Hungarian leadership had been dispatched in 1949, but while they had been tortured and brainwashed into confessing to copious acts of espionage on behalf of the West, Israel had not figured in the indictments or confessions. With the Czechs it was different. The indictment against the accused stated: "After the State of Israel was established, the Americans used Israeli diplomats as spies . . ."[5]

Two Israelis were among those arrested in Prague: Mordekhai Oren, one of the leaders of the left-wing Mapam party, and Shimon Orenstein, former commercial attaché at the Israeli legation in Prague. They were compelled, after exposure to the working methods of the secret police, to confess to spying and to denounce Israel and Zionism.

The Prague Trial, as the episode became known, was not the first time that Stalin had cleaned out a satellite government using his preferred methods of torture and the rope, but it was the first time that "Zionism" had been employed as a specific term of indictment.

When Stalin providentially died in March 1953, the senior Jewish doctors on the Kremlin's medical staff were under arrest for the inevitably capital crime of spying for Western intelligence and Zionism. At the beginning of 1953 diplomatic relations between the Soviet Union and Israel were broken off. (They were restored a year later.)

However, while the Soviets had decided that Israel was now irredeemably in the Western camp, the new administration in Washington was apparently hesitant in showing its little ally the proper gratitude. Harel bitterly describes the departure of Truman and the Democrats as bringing about "a complete change in the relationship between Israel and the United States."

His thin forefinger poking the air in the impeccably neat sitting room of his house in Zahala on the edge of Tel Aviv, Harel bridles at the memory of how John Foster Dulles, Eisenhower's secretary of state, "proclaimed a policy of so-called impartiality. In fact, it was a direct pro-Arab orientation and unfriendly to Israel, to put it mildly."

Such grumbling takes the case too far. The actions of John Foster Dulles were motivated solely by his fanatical anticommunism. In 1948 he had advised President Truman to recognize the provisional government of Israel on the grounds that the new state's links with Eastern Europe might otherwise cause it to slip under total Soviet control.

It is nevertheless the case that Eisenhower and Dulles soon demonstrated that the U.S. was prepared to take severe measures against Israel when they thought it justified. In September 1953, Dulles informed the Israeli ambassador in Washington that all economic aid was being suspended immediately. Eisenhower had been infuriated by Israel's ongoing project to divert waters from the river Jordan for its own use, in defiance of a United Nations plan.[6] At first the cancellation of American aid was kept secret by both sides, but a month later a special unit of the Israeli army called Unit 101, commanded by a rising star in the IDF named Ariel Sharon, assaulted the Jordanian village of Kibya and blew up forty-one houses and a school. Fifty-three civilians sheltering in their houses were killed. Outraged, the president ordered that the aid cutoff be made public.

Israel's lobby in the United States reacted to Eisenhower's initiative with public outrage, while Ben-Gurion darkly hinted at Foster Dulles's supposed anti-Semitism. In the Truman days it had been possible to circumvent hostility from elsewhere in the bureaucracy by doing an end run through the White House. Those days were past for the moment. The Israeli government was not sure that pressure from the American Jewish community would be enough to bail it out, either politically or economically. Moshe Sharett, the foreign minister, recorded a gloomy cabinet meeting summoned to assess the damage two days after Dulles made the aid cutoff official.

"Pinchas Saphir [the finance minister] presented a program for a $50 million cut in the budget; $18 million would be raised in cash from Jews. Golda and Yossi predicted, 'The American Jews always give more in times of crisis.' I said to Ben-Gurion, 'It depends what caused the trouble.' Later Gus [an American who worked in Ben-Gurion's office as an economics adviser] confirmed that a crisis in relations between Israel and the U.S. government would not encourage American Jews to donate."

It took only eight days for the Israelis to cave in on the water project, whereupon aid was resumed. It was one of the rare instances when an American president had used the lever of American financial support. The effect had been immediate and devastating.

Such an event, which seems extraordinary in the light of subsequent U.S. indulgence toward Israel, was dictated by the shared belief of Eisenhower and Dulles that the spread of communism had to be checked, and that the Arab world was not yet a lost cause. They were therefore prepared to pay some regard to Arab sensibilities and to crack down on Israel when the occasion warranted.

Then, to complicate matters further, Israel suddenly found itself faced with a new and dangerous Arab leader. The Israelis had had a lot of help in their early years from the weakness and corruption of the Arab regimes facing them. The Iraqi prime minister had taken bribes, as had the King of Jordan and, possibly, the Syrian leader. The corpulent King Farouk of Egypt was an international byword for his less-than-diligent attitude to public office. However, in 1952 a group from the Egyptian army who called themselves the Society of Free Officers overthrew the monarchy and seized power. The titular leader of the officers' junta was a general, Mohammed Naguib, but it soon became apparent that the real power in the new government was a dynamic young officer named Gamal Abdel Nasser. In 1954 Colonel Nasser pushed Naguib into retirement and became the undisputed leader of Egypt.

Nasser at that time was first and foremost an Egyptian nationalist. His appeals to pan-Arabism were to come later. His main objectives were to oust the eighty-thousand-man army maintained by the British in Egypt for the ostensible purpose of safeguarding the Suez Canal, and to develop his country. These objectives did not at first unduly alarm Washington. The charismatic young leader professed no affection for communism and appeared anxious for good relations with the United States.

A dynamic Egyptian leader was not what the Israelis wanted at all. After the 1956 Suez War, Ben-Gurion said that he had "always feared that a personality might arise such as arose among the Arab rulers in the seventh century or like [Kemal Ataturk] who arose in Turkey after its defeat in the First World War. He raised their spirits, changed their character, and turned them into a fighting nation. There was and still is a chance that Nasser is this man."[7]

To make matters worse, Nasser had a close relationship with the CIA. Prior to the coup that overthrew the monarchy, Kermit Roosevelt, the covert troubleshooter who engineered the restoration of the Shah of Iran, had been dispatched to make contact with Nasser and his fellow plotters in the Society of Free Officers. They found, Roosevelt cabled back to Washington, "a large measure of agreement," so much so that the CIA assisted in the coup through which the insurgent officers took power.

Roosevelt's informal and close relationship with Nasser, as well as his readiness to disburse U.S. covert funds on a profligate scale, made the CIA the main U.S. link with the Egyptian leader. Initially at least, the news seemed all good. Not only did Nasser appear to have friendly feelings toward the United States, he did not even appear to harbor any special animus toward Israel. To Roosevelt, Nasser confided that even after the Israelis had thrashed the Egyptian forces in the war of 1948, he and his fellow officers directed their ire at "our own superior officers, other Arabs, the British, and the Israelis—in that order."[8]

Nasser, having negotiated an agreement on the withdrawal of British forces in October 1954, was anxious to get military aid from the United States, since his armed forces were no better armed than they had been at the end of the disastrous war of 1948. Roosevelt and his minions, reflecting the status the supposedly covert CIA station enjoyed in Cairo, carried on the negotiations. Even though the State Department, anxious not to irritate the British, was not wholly enthusiastic about the deal, the agency pressed ahead.

Endowed with his bulging covert budget, Roosevelt was keen to do well by Nasser. Among other endowments, he arranged for the CIA to construct a powerful transmitter to beam Egyptian propaganda across the Middle East. Later, when times and loyalties had changed, the CIA had to finance stations elsewhere in order to counter the overly successful effect of the "Voice of the Arabs."[9]

More straightforwardly, Roosevelt had decided that Nasser's affection for the CIA and America could be enhanced with cash, so he slipped $3 million in 1953 to one of the president's aides as a personal sweetener for the Egyptian leader. Nasser was less than gratified by the assumption that he was a hired hand, but instead of returning the money, he used it to build an ostentatious tower in the middle of the Nile opposite the Cairo Hilton, and called it "Roosevelt's erection."

Nasser was less offhand about a more practical aspect of U.S. assistance. He asked Roosevelt to help him build up Egypt's military intelligence and internal security squads. This was considered too sensitive an area for the CIA to involve itself in directly, so Allen Dulles, who had become CIA director on Eisenhower's election, arranged to have a surrogate do the job. There was, ready to hand, a team on the CIA payroll with ample experience in internal security intelligence work—the old Nazis of the Gehlen organization.

Gehlen took on the assignment and delegated responsibility for it to Otto Skorzeny, a wartime SS commando and personal favorite of Adolf Hitler. Skorzeny accepted the commission on condition that the CIA augment the slender stipend being offered by Nasser. To help do the job he recruited various luminaries of the Third Reich, including a former deputy leader of the Hitler Youth and Alois Brunner. Brunner had been Adolf Eichmann's expert on the deportation of Jews to the death camps and is estimated to have played a part in the murder of some 128,500 people. When the Egyptian mission came up he was serving as Gehlen's station chief in Damascus, partly as a way of keeping him out of the hands of the French, who had tried and sentenced him to death in absentia for war crimes.[10]

The presence of Nazi war criminals paid for by the CIA did not apparently affect Nasser's attitude toward Israel during his first years in power. He let it be known in conversations with influential Americans that he would be prepared to make peace with Israel if the matter were delicately handled.

Nasser was making all the right noises so far as the Americans were concerned, a trend that the Israelis found deeply disturbing. At this time, 1954, Israel was in the position of a desperate lover vying for the favors of an inattentive suitor. The government still hoped that the Americans would extend some sort of security guarantee and agree to supply arms. However, it could not or would not agree to the usual corollary of a military alliance with the U.S.—bases and a direct American presence in Israel's defense system. The internal political cost would be too high. As Moshe Sharett pointed out in January 1954: "We are opposed to humiliating [U.S.] military supervision . . . it would generate an internal dispute the likes of which we have not witnessed since the establishment of the state . . . it would mean the increase of dependency on the United States and the decrease of our independence."[11]

The problem was that the U.S. did not appear to have any particular interest in a special military relationship with Israel, being far more taken with the idea of building up an anti-Soviet Arab alliance. In April 1954, for example, the Americans agreed to supply arms to Iraq.

All Israel had to offer was the covert employment of the Jewish population behind the iron curtain. Sharett himself pointed out that this was "an asset to our foreign policy . . . As the only element in the Western world capable of attaining fraternal relations with a section of the population of the Soviet Union we . . . possess a monopoly which we dare not underestimate."[12]

When he wrote these words in a secret memorandum to his senior staff, Sharett was prime minister. In November 1953, Ben-Gurion had suddenly announced that he was retiring from public office and took himself off to a remote kibbutz in the Negev. Although this move was represented by his admirers as the action of a philosopher-king retiring for some peace and quiet, Ben-Gurion actually retired in the face of extreme popular discontent. His alignment with the West had not extended to permitting a free market internally. There was strict rationing and highly centralized control of the economy. The bourgeois General Zionist Party had done extremely well in recent elections, so Ben-Gurion thought it better to leave until better political times returned.

He was succeeded by Moshe Sharett (who immediately moved to reverse the Old Man's grim economic policies). Sharett, a veteran of Zionist politics and foreign minister since the founding of the state, has acquired something of a reputation as a dove. This image has been bolstered for historians outside Israel by the publication of a limited selection of translated excerpts from his diaries.[13] In these, he laments the bellicose attitudes of Ben-Gurion and Moshe Dayan, in particular their appetite for launching bloody "reprisal" raids, such as the one on Kibya, after alleged Arab sabotage operations.

As prime minister, Sharett made some effort to curb Israeli commando assaults into neighboring countries. He also agreed to enter into negotiations with Nasser, and even got the approval of the Knesset to do so. The proposals advanced by Sharett as a basis for negotiations included provisions for free passage of Israeli ships through the Suez Canal and an end to inflammatory statements and actions directed by either side against the other. There was no reference to the problem of the Palestinian refugees, then six years into their long exile—Sharett's dovishness was not that far-reaching. In fact, the deal that Sharett appears to have had in mind, which would have removed Egypt from any Arab coalition against Israel and left the problem of the Palestinian refugees untouched, is remarkably similar to what the hawkish Menachem Begin was to achieve with the Camp David agreement twenty-five years later. But while Begin was able to conclude his deal without significant political opposition at home, Sharett did not have as easy a ride.

In July 1954 a series of incendiary bombs caused minor damage in Cairo and Alexandria. Among the targets were the U.S. Information Service libraries in the two cities. It might have been assumed that the attacks were the work of militant anti-Western Egyptians venting their spleen at Nasser's friendly relations with the Americans and British. Those who ordered the attacks hoped both Nasser and the outside world would make exactly that assumption, because in fact the sabotage campaign had been set up and put into operation by Israeli Military Intelligence. The aim of this particular covert action was to destabilize Nasser's relations with the United States and Great Britain, and possibly compel the British to put off their planned withdrawal from their bases on the Suez Canal.

The actual operatives who laid the bombs were a group of Egyptian Jews in the service of the Israelis. (There was still a sizable Jewish population in Egypt. Even after the humiliating defeat of the 1948 war, there had been no reprisals against the Jewish community, which had been continuously resident in Egypt since the time of the Ptolemies.) But despite the towering reputation of Israeli intelligence, this operation was an amateurish affair. The group was badly equipped and made little attempt to maintain adequate security. Once one of them had been arrested (after his firebomb exploded prematurely in his pocket), nearly all the others were picked up without difficulty.

The precise background to the operation remains murky to this day. It became known in Israel as the "Lavon Affair," after Pinchas Lavon, a powerful Labor Party politician who had taken over the Ministry of Defense when Ben-Gurion retired to his house in the Negev. But the Old Man had left behind two of his acolytes in powerful positions, theoretically subordinate to Lavon, but in reality loyal to Ben-Gurion above all others. Moshe Dayan, who was already an Israeli military hero, was chief of staff of the IDF. Shimon Peres was director general of the Defense Ministry.

The scandal as to who had given the go-ahead for the Egyptian operation dragged on for years, mostly behind closed doors and with the press tightly censored. At first Lavon was made the scapegoat and was forced to resign. Prime Minister Sharett then had to ask Ben-Gurion to return as defense minister. It subsequently emerged that Lavon could not have signed the crucial order to launch the attack, and that documents indicating that he did had been forged. This laid the blame on the chief of military intelligence, an ambitious soldier named Benyamin Gibli, on Moshe Dayan, and possibly on Ben-Gurion himself.

There is a plausible theory that the Egyptian operation was orchestrated by Ben-Gurion and Dayan not only to create problems between the Western powers and Nasser but also to drive a spear through the heart of Sharett's peace negotiations. The chief of the team inside Egypt, who escaped and survived, has been quoted as saying that he believed the operation had been set up to fail and that it had been betrayed.

If this was indeed the case, the intrigue failed—for a time. Nasser's regime was not destabilized, the British stuck to their agreement to withdraw from the canal zone, the CIA found out almost immediately that the bombings were the work of the Israelis, and Nasser continued to believe that a peaceful solution to his dispute with Israel was possible. Furthermore, according to Isser Harel, Kermit Roosevelt came up with a scheme to use the affair to actually promote the peace negotiations.

In September 1954, as the pathetic team of Israeli agents were being interrogated by the Egyptian police (possibly with the assistance of the German experts so thoughtfully provided by the CIA), Roosevelt cabled Harel with a proposition. Nasser would be willing to start direct peace talks with Israel if Israel would let it be known that the Moslem Brotherhood had collaborated with the bombing operation. The Brotherhood was violently opposed to Nasser's negotiations with the British, and indeed nearly succeeded in assassinating him in October 1954.

Harel says that he agreed to the plan, which was code-named Operation Mirage, but told the CIA that if any of the Israeli agents were executed, the deal would be off. Nasser continued to indicate his interest in peace talks, so the settlement favored by Sharett was forwarded to Egypt. But while the proposal was "in the mail," as Harel puts it, the Egyptian court sentenced two of the saboteurs to death. Harel then cabled the CIA to say that Operation Mirage was off. Allen Dulles tried to get Nasser to commute the death sentences, but was told that there was nothing that could be done. Nasser had just hung six Egyptian Moslem Brothers for trying to kill him, so he was hardly in a position to be lenient toward Israeli spies. The CIA thought this reasonable. Harel, on the other hand, being an obstinate individual who never saw much point in talking to Arabs, did not.[14]

These were the glory days of the agency. In 1953 Kermit Roosevelt and other operatives (including H. Norman Schwarzkopf, whose son was later to play a prominent role in the affairs of the region) had engineered the restoration of the Shah of Iran. The following year a nationalist regime in Guatemala had been removed in a military coup organized by the CIA. Other covert operatives were hard at work setting up a client regime in southern Vietnam following the French defeat. These successes, in addition to the fact that the brother of CIA Director Allen Dulles was the secretary of state, meant that the agency had a remarkably free hand in covert initiatives and diplomacy around the world.

This freedom was particularly evident in the Middle East, where the CIA was attempting to get two of its most important assets to deal with each other. Both Egypt and Israel owed their status as allies, at least so far as the agency was concerned, to their importance in the struggle against world communism. The problem was that the slightest hint of deviance from the true path of anticommunism brought an instant and chilly reaction from Secretary of State John Foster Dulles. In 1954, for example, the Israelis were alarmed to hear from Washington that their basic loyalty to the West was still considered to be questionable. They hastened to assure the Americans that their fealty was unshakable.

The Israelis were able to survive the charge. Gamal Abdel Nasser was not so lucky. Blamed for the botched bombing operation in Egypt, Pinchas Lavon was forced to resign as minister of defense. Ben-Gurion then came back from the desert and took over the Kirya again on February 21, 1955.

One week after Ben-Gurion returned from the desert to take over the Defense Ministry vacated by Lavon in February 1955, Israeli paratroopers launched a bloody raid on an Egyptian army post in Gaza. They killed thirty-seven Egyptians and wounded many more before blowing up most of the camp and moving back into Israel. The raid, as the commanding officer of the local UN peacekeeping force put it, was "a critical event in the dismal history" of the Middle East.[15] It ensured that there would be no peace or disarmament so far as Egypt and Israel were concerned, but war.

Up until that point Nasser had aimed to expend his energies and money on development within Egypt. Only a few days before he had visited Gaza and assured the troops that there was no danger of war and that the border would remain absolutely quiet. Now the soldiers and the Egyptian population had had a sharp reminder that this was not the case. The Egyptian leader was going to have to do something to put his defenses in order.

Ultimately, and by indirect means, the Gaza Raid brought about the break between Nasser and Washington that those behind the Lavon affair had hoped to achieve. Moshe Sharett understood this very well. Asked later whether there was a connection between the intelligence operation in Egypt and the raid, Sharett replied: "The connection is this, that when Ben-Gurion returned as defense minister, he decided on the Gaza Raid. The Gaza Raid would not have been mounted if Ben-Gurion had not returned to the Cabinet."[16]

At this point Nasser still hoped that he might secure the required military aid from the United States. However, in April he attended the first conference of nonaligned nations in Bandung, Indonesia. Foster Dulles did not believe in the principle of neutrality, which he regarded as merely a fig leaf for Communist sympathies. The chances of Nasser getting any kind of military deal with the U.S. dimmed. The Egyptian accordingly opened negotiations with the Soviet Union. By May he had an agreement from the Russians that they would sell him arms, in exchange for cotton, but that the weapons would be "laundered" through Czechoslovakia.

The Israelis, who had won a war with Egypt and others only a few years before with the help of Czech arms, were outraged that Nasser had at last found his own supply. Given the size of the deal, it appeared that Egypt, for the first time, would be as well armed as Israel. On the other hand, there was the consolation that Mossad were the first to alert the Americans about what was happening, and to point out that this was further evidence of the perfidious Nasser's pro-Soviet sympathies.

In October 1955 Ben-Gurion summoned Moshe Dayan back from a

vacation in Paris and told him to start planning for a war with Egypt in the Sinai Peninsula.[17] The Old Man appears to have been determined that the problem of Nasser would be dealt with only by force. In addition, Ben-Gurion was set on forcing open the Straits of Tiran. This narrow outlet to the Red Sea had been blockaded by the Egyptians from their base at the end of the Sinai Peninsula since 1948, thus shutting off direct Israeli access to East Africa and the Far East, as well as hindering the development of the Negev. The slide to war was accelerating.

Strange as it may seem, the CIA continued to try and bring the two sides together. While the Israeli government was officially trumpeting the unrepentantly evil nature of Nasser's intentions, plans were going ahead for a secret deal by which Ben-Gurion and Nasser would meet and negotiate a peace agreement. The story is told in Moshe Sharett's diaries.

Most of Sharett's private journals remain untranslated from the original Hebrew, the equivalent of an enciphered text for most non-Israelis. Yet buried in these volumes are hints that, less than a year before the 1956 Suez War, the CIA actually attempted to broker a deal in which Israel would for the first time have been given official arms aid from the U.S. in return for accepting a lasting peace with Egypt. Sharett called it Operation Chameleon. For example, in October 1955, while on a fund-raising tour in the U.S., Sharett refers in his diary to a meeting in Washington with "Teddy," most probably Teddy Kollek, at that time the director of Ben-Gurion's office; "Jim—CIA man," almost certainly meaning James Angleton; and "Isser," which in this company must have meant Isser Harel. Under discussion was the "B-G [Ben-Gurion]–Nasser meeting."

The following month Sharett was commenting again on the progress of the operation. "The Americans sent a man [to Cairo]. Brother [by which he means CIA chief Allen Dulles, brother of Foster] briefed him personally. Upon his return Kermit and Jim met with him and he reported [that] N [Nasser] is willing to negotiate in principle, [but] expressed his doubts and does not believe in Israel's sincere desire for peace."[18]

Unknown to the Americans, the Israelis were themselves considering turning to the Russians for arms if they did not receive satisfaction from the U.S. Sharett recorded in his diary on February 14, 1956: "Am I doing the right thing by delaying an approach to the East for armaments? What is the correct line that we should follow? B-G once stated definitively that we must approach [the Soviets] immediately. I cannot consider such a hasty step so long as we have not lost hope in the United States."

Harel had had a better idea. When Allen Dulles had pushed Operation Chameleon on Sharett in October 1955, Harel told Ben-Gurion that he didn't trust Nasser, but that there still might be some advantage to be gained from the idea. "I suggested . . . that we make our agreement to the renewal [of Chameleon] conditional upon an explicit commitment of the West to supply us with defensive arms, particularly for our air force."

The scheme worked. In what Sharett delicately called "a political operation," the U.S. gave permission on February 24, 1956, for France to sell twelve fighter bombers earmarked for NATO to Israel. The possibility of Israel shifting back toward the Eastern Bloc for military support had gone away.

Up until this point the Israelis had been faced with the choice of relying on the good wishes of either the U.S. or Soviet governments in order to get arms. Although the Americans had had to be induced to give the French permission to transfer the NATO planes, Israel's military relationship with France was rapidly becoming a full-fledged alliance.

There was a strong basis for close ties between the countries in the early and mid-1950s. The French governments of the period included many veterans of the resistance who had shared the horrors of concentration camps with Jews. The Jewish underground after the war formed close links with French intelligence, such as in Vienna in 1947. But the bond that most closely tied the two countries together at this time was the Algerian War.

The Algerians had begun their revolt against French colonial rule on Halloween night 1954. Like most powers faced with a subject nation in revolt, the French could not believe that their major problem was the determination of the Algerian people to take their country back after 120 years of French rule. The real cause of the trouble, they reasoned, must be the poisonous agitation and support for the rebellion coming from Cairo.

The Israelis did not fail to note the possible advantages of this conviction. As Shimon Peres, the young apparatchik charged by Ben-Gurion with building up Israel's weapons arsenals, succinctly put it in

June 1955, "Every Frenchman killed in Algeria, like every Egyptian killed in the Gaza Strip, is a step toward strengthening the ties between France and Israel."[19]

In reality, Nasser's support for the Algerians' struggle was for the most part confined to rhetoric. As the guerrilla leaders themselves later made clear, the Egyptian leader sent them very little in the way of arms or money.

On the other hand, all parties involved chose to pretend that Nasser's support was vital. Nasser himself, seeing the advantages of burnishing his credentials as a Third World leader, boasted of how he sent help to the rebels. The Algerians kept quiet about the true situation, as their chief arms buyer later admitted, because "of the need for solidarity." The French wanted to be able to blame their problems on an outside cause. The Israelis were happy to supply the French with suitably tailored intelligence in order, as one former Israeli official has put it, "to increase French willingness to cooperate with Israel." (Subsequent accounts of the heroic cooperation between French and Israeli intelligence during the Algerian war should be read with this in mind.)[20] The Israelis were using intelligence, not for the last time, as a tool for maneuvering a potential ally in the desired direction. In this case they were persuading the French that arms supplied to Israel for use against Nasser was the best possible means to solve the Algerian problem at its source.

True to form, the essential arrangements between the French and the Israelis were handled in a covert manner. Bypassing both foreign ministries, Shimon Peres negotiated the arms deals directly with the minister of defense, General Pierre-Marie Koenig, and with the senior officials in the offices of the prime minister and the minister of the interior (who had responsibility for Algeria). When Foreign Minister Sharett told Ben-Gurion that he was off to Paris on a diplomatic mission in the fall of 1955, the old hawk snapped: "The only reason to travel is to go to France to buy arms."[21]

The French-Israeli relationship was essentially covert, concealed as much as possible from the Americans. Though the U.S. had officially cleared France's diversion of twelve NATO planes to Israel, the actual quantity of aircraft and other weapons sent was much greater. Tanks and artillery from France streamed into Israeli ports. This traffic was already in progress before Nasser attempted to even the equation with his Czech arms deal. Afterwards, the flow redoubled. In addition, as we shall see, there was a different and infinitely more potent type of weapons aid under discussion.

At the beginning of 1956, therefore, the Israelis were using a CIA-sponsored scheme for Israeli-Egyptian talks, Operation Chameleon, as an inducement for the Americans to agree to the French supplying arms to Israel. They were also supplying the French with the welcome intelligence that all their troubles stemmed from Nasser.

All this time, Israel was also, of course, diligently working away in the Soviet Bloc on behalf of the Americans. There is no clear record of any single great intelligence scoop yielded up by the operation in the first five years, just a steady trickle of otherwise unobtainable tidbits on conditions in the Soviet Bloc. Then, in the spring of 1956, the "connection" bore fruit with a tremendous prize.

On February 25, 1956, Nikita Khrushchev, first secretary of the Soviet Communist Party, delivered a sensational oration to a closed session of the Twentieth Party Congress. This was the famous secret speech in which he denounced Stalin, citing his crimes against the Communist Party, his execution of many innocent people, his disastrous reorganization of Soviet agriculture, and his criminal mistakes at the time of the German invasion. It has to be remembered that up until the moment Khrushchev spoke, reverence for the memory of Stalin and his achievements had been absolutely de rigueur for the entire worldwide Communist movement.

The speech was secret insofar as the press and all observers were excluded while the Soviet leader was speaking, but there were several thousand delegates in the hall, and word soon began to leak out that something extraordinary had occurred.

Naturally enough, the CIA was desperate to get its hands on a copy of the speech. Robert Amory, a decorated World War II combat veteran who since 1950 had served as the agency's deputy director for intelligence (which was separate from the covert department, then known as the Directorate for Plans), later remembered how Allen Dulles had offered him "half his kingdom" if he could get hold of a copy. Amory tried the Yugoslavs, but was turned down.

It seems strange that the Americans found it so hard to get hold of the speech. Since it signaled a sea change in Communist Party politics—a coup by Khrushchev against the Stalinists, who were still infesting every level of the Soviet bureaucracy—the text was widely disseminated. Communists sympathetic to Khrushchev's line had every interest in making sure the message got across. For example, the Polish Communist Party leadership alone printed and distributed over fifteen thousand copies.

Fortunately for the Israelis, the CIA did not appear to know that the speech was in mass circulation, because in April, two months after Khrushchev had delivered it, the Mossad was able to hand to the astonished and grateful Americans their first full copy of the "secret" address.

Isser Harel takes full credit for the achievement, and has at various times embellished the story with accounts of how he deputed the one Mossad officer stationed in the Soviet Union, who was normally under "strict instructions not to engage in any illegal activities," to come out of the shadows and obtain a copy from his sources, which he duly did. A more recent Israeli account, based on information from the many former intelligence personnel who do not like Harel, claims that in fact the speech was obtained by Amos Manor (Angleton's friend) from a counterintelligence source of his in the Eastern Bloc. Manor, in a crafty piece of bureaucratic gamesmanship, reportedly took it straight to Ben-Gurion rather than passing it to Isser Harel, his immediate superior. Ben-Gurion, according to this account, then ordered it to be given to the Americans. [22]

The Israelis were only just in time, since Frank Wisner, the CIA's deputy director for plans, got hold of another copy—almost certainly from a French source—at almost exactly the same moment. Still, as one agency alumnus of those days points out, "The Israelis were the first to walk in the door with the speech, and that's the one that gets the credit."

Angleton, who shared in the glory reflected by his friends' achievement, characteristically wanted to "exploit" the speech by feeding it to selected audiences. The clandestine operators at the agency, including Angleton, in any event wanted to keep the speech secret until publication could be tied in with a projected paramilitary operation in Eastern Europe that was not yet ready to start.

Allen Dulles was eventually persuaded that the sensible thing to do with the speech was to let people read it, so he authorized its release to the *New York Times*, which published it on June 5, 1956. The CIA also arranged for its broadcasting subsidiaries, Radio Free Europe and Radio Liberty, to beam the text back behind the iron curtain.

The *Times* attributed its scoop to the State Department. No one mentioned the Israelis at the time, and when Allen Dulles wrote his memoirs he confined himself to describing the acquisition of the speech as one of the CIA's greatest achievements.

General distribution of Khrushchev's electrifying revelations certainly had an explosive effect. In particular, their dissemination in Eastern Europe helped fuel popular discontent with resident regimes, most significantly in Hungary.

Harel piously insists that the Israelis asked for "exactly nothing" in return for their "services on behalf of the American people" (as represented by the CIA), and even that he personally resisted an unseemly initiative on the part of some in the Israeli government to get a quid pro quo. "It was well known that the highest levels in the United States were very grateful for our achievements, so they wanted to make a secret lobby at the top of the American administration." His face wreathed in earnest innocence, the aged spy chief insists that he opposed this idea "because I didn't want to involve the connection just to make pressure on the administration. I wanted to turn it into a strategic goal for Israel to create a situation [so that] the Americans, it didn't matter what administration, would conclude that Israel is a true and dependable ally."

The Mossad had banked its credit with the agency just in time, because Israel was about to provide evidence that it was not always so true and dependable.

As Operation Chameleon had faded away, Israel's French-supplied arsenal had steadily grown. At the same time, Washington was growing colder toward Nasser. In July 1956 John Foster Dulles, irked by Nasser's improving relations with the Soviet Union and his decision to open relations with Red China, formally reneged on a previous promise to finance Nasser's project of a dam across the Nile at Aswan. Nasser then nationalized the Anglo-French–owned Suez Canal, which he had every legal right to do. The leaders of Britain and France saw the Egyptian action, however, as a suitable casus belli for military action to liberate "their" canal and, more importantly, destroy Nasser in the process.

To provide themselves with an excuse to invade Egypt, the British and French made a secret pact with the Israelis. Israel would invade the Sinai and head for the canal. The two European powers would then intervene on the pretext of stopping the war.

All this plotting took place without the Americans being told what was going on. The close cooperation between Israel and the CIA did not extend at that point to advance warning of a war, although as the Anglo-French invasion fleet assembled it was photographed by the U-2 spy plane, the first time the new espionage tool was used.

On October 26, 1956, Robert Amory, the CIA's deputy director for intelligence, noticed a curious dispatch from the U.S. military attaché in Tel Aviv that had been passed along from the Pentagon. As Amory recalled it years later, it said, "Just thought you ought to know that my driver—a reservist with one arm and one leg missing and blind in one eye—has been called to the colors!"

The attaché evidently did not think that his news was particularly important, since he had sent it with a low-grade classification, but Amory thought it had momentous implications. "I read the message that Friday morning when I got into my office at about 7:30 and immediately realized it meant war. The Israelis were claiming that they faced a threat from Jordan at that point, but I knew that they didn't take the Jordanian army seriously enough to be calling up double amputees. This indicated to me that they were mobilizing to attack someone—Egypt. Since from sundown on Friday to dusk on Saturday was the Sabbath, I thought it meant they were going to go on Monday. I showed it to Allen Dulles and commented that it meant a general mobilization. He said we should call the Watch Committee [a joint crisis committee of the U.S. intelligence agencies]."

The committee met an hour later in Dulles's office. Amory presented his conclusions, which the other intelligence officials found convincing. According to Amory, "At that moment James Angleton suddenly burst out of a bathroom that connected Allen's office and the deputy director's office next door. We used it to keep people visiting the director from meeting each other outside. You wouldn't want the head of Pakistani intelligence to meet his Indian counterpart on the way out, for instance. Anyway, Angleton comes bursting in and says 'I can discount what Amory is saying. I spent last night with our friends and they have assured me that they are just carrying out protective measures against the Jordanians.'

"Well, I got mad at that. I said to Allen, 'The taxpayer lays out $16,000 a year to me as your deputy director for me to give you the best intelligence based on the evidence available. Either you believe me or you believe this co-opted Israeli agent here,' and I pointed at Angleton."

Despite this eloquent statement, the committee concluded simply that the situation should be watched carefully. The next day, a Saturday, Amory and both the Dulles brothers were at a State Department meeting to review a foreign policy speech that Foster Dulles was due to deliver that night. One passage stated that the U.S. could not guarantee a peaceful outcome to the crisis in the Middle East. Amory spoke up: "Mr. Secretary, if you say that and war breaks out twenty-four hours later, you will appear to all the world as parti pris to the Israeli aggression—and I'm positive that the Israelis will attack the Sinai shortly after midnight tomorrow."

Amory convinced Dulles to change his speech, but no one told the president. "Allen should have gone to see Ike and told him what was going to happen, but he didn't. After all, I thought I had convinced him. I found out later that Angleton went in to see Allen three times between then and the Sunday evening. Make of that what you will."[23]

Only on the evening of Sunday, October 28, had the picture become clear enough for Allen Dulles to be sure of what was about to happen, and of the fact that the Israelis had lied to him. He fired off a cable of complaint to Harel for having led him to believe that Ben-Gurion was opposed to war. He was especially irked, according to Harel's account, that when the fighting began, he had been called to the White House and had been unable to present a proper evaluation. Israel should have let him know at least two hours in advance, Dulles told Harel, "considering the special relationship between both of us, which was based on sincerity and mutual trust."

Harel's reply was a model of chutzpah. As he recounts it, his answer was: "My opinion is that those in charge of the United States, including yourself, have reached the conclusion that it is no longer possible to negotiate with Nasser. I would say that the differences in our approaches to this problem are no longer a matter of principle but of tactics, and they involve the best way of clipping his wings and eventually removing him from power."

It might be thought that being attacked as a "co-opted Israeli agent" would have put a crimp in Angleton's career. This did not happen, perhaps because the triumph of the Khrushchev speech was still fresh. Harel later claimed that he had deliberately not told "our man" (the Mossad station chief) in Washington what was being planned, thus providing Angleton with an excuse.

Reflecting thirty years later on Angleton's (probably) unwitting service as an agent of Israeli disinformation, a close colleague remarked, "The Israelis could get away with lying to Jim that once. I don't think they did it again."

From the Israeli point of view, the war itself went perfectly. Their troops smashed the Egyptian forces in the Gaza Strip without undue difficulty and then moved on through the Sinai. The only serious casualties occurred during an attack on the strategic Mitla Pass ordered by Colonel Ariel Sharon. He had ordered the assault in defiance of headquarters. His fellow officers on the mission never forgave him; as they, too, rose through the ranks of the Israeli security system, they provided a steady source of criticism of the arrogant general. Feuds last a long time in Israel.

Eisenhower was furious at what had happened. His supposed allies and friends had gone to war just days before presidential election day and at the same time as the Soviet Union was moving in to crush the Hungarian uprising. Ironically, the uprising had in part been touched off by the impact of the Khrushchev speech, which the CIA had disseminated in Eastern Europe after receiving it from the Israelis. Furthermore, the Soviets had actually been brought into the Middle East as major players for the first time. They spoke of using military force to help the Egyptians and later claimed they had helped bring about the cease-fire that stopped the fighting. Whatever the president's feelings about Nasser, he was determined not to allow the aggressors to retain any spoils from the war.

The British were swiftly brought to heel by the withdrawal of American financial support. It took somewhat longer for Ben-Gurion to be forced out of Sinai and Gaza. In the end Eisenhower and Foster Dulles had to threaten to support UN sanctions and withdraw the tax-deductible status of private contributions to Israel. "I am aware," Foster Dulles told one prominent American who had called him to lobby for Israel's continued occupation of the conquered territory, "how almost impossible it is in this country to carry out a foreign policy not approved by the Jews. I am going to try to have one."[24]

Despite these high-level fulminations, peace rapidly returned on the intelligence front. Harel notes with satisfaction, "In contrast to the crisis and hostile atmosphere on the political and diplomatic level, on the interservice [intelligence] level the relationship continued being satisfactory, correct, and even friendly . . . The Israeli side declared that it would continue the routine normally, regardless of what took place on the political level. The American side accepted this position enthusiastically.

"During the entire war and the crisis that followed, which continued for many months, the relationship carried on peacefully. The American administration preferred to use this channel as a substitute for the political and diplomatic ones, which had been seriously disrupted during the entire period of the Suez crisis."[25] In other words, the important issues between the U.S. and Israel were being settled not through the State Department and the Israeli Foreign Office, but via the CIA and the Mossad.

As it turned out, the Suez crisis ended up with Israel very much on the plus side of the ledger. Although Eisenhower forced a furious Ben-Gurion to give up the territory he had gone to war to conquer, Israel did gain the right to send shipping down to the Red Sea through the Gulf of Aqaba. More fundamentally, the episode eventually caused a change in American relations with the Arab world that was very much in Israel's interests.

The overriding objective of U.S. policy in the Middle East had been and remained to prevent the Soviet Union from gaining ground. The day after the shooting stopped Eisenhower dictated the first draft of what was to become the "Eisenhower Doctrine." Its central theme was the absolute necessity to "exclude from the area Soviet influence." The president proposed to "make certain that every weak country understands what can be in store for it once it falls under the domination of the Soviets."

Wilbur Crane Eveland, a Middle East specialist working for the CIA, was summoned to a meeting in the State Department to discuss the proposed doctrine. Eveland read the draft, which stated that "many, if not all" of the Middle East states "are aware of the danger that stems from international communism." He was shocked. "Who, I wondered, had reached the determination of what the Arabs considered a danger?" he wrote later. "Israel's army had just invaded Egypt and still occupied all of the Sinai Peninsula and the Gaza Strip. And, had it not been for Russia's threat to intervene on behalf of the Egyptians, the British, French, and Israeli forces might now be sitting in Cairo, celebrating Nasser's ignominious fall from power."

Suez had turned Nasser into the undisputed hero of the Arab world. Everywhere, nationalist forces were bolstered by his example and prestige. Wherever this happened, however, the U.S. saw the dark hand of Soviet Communist influence further extending its grip. The consequent U.S. reaction—a freezing of relations, causing the Arab country in question to move closer to Moscow—had the inevitable effect of a self-fulfilling prophecy. Harel claims, "The Americans admitted, both at the intelligence level and at the top political level, that forcing Israel to retreat from Sinai and the Gaza Strip had been a fatal error on their part, that things could have been completely different in the Middle East had they acted differently. Now they admitted that without their decisive intervention Nasser would have fallen, and with him the Soviet penetration into the Middle East and Africa would have collapsed."

So much in agreement was the CIA with the Israeli viewpoint on the Middle East that the agency set about trying to assassinate Nasser.[26] The operation had been set in motion following a remark by Eisenhower that he hoped "the Nasser problem could be eliminated." Foster Dulles later learned that the president had merely meant that perhaps relations with the Egyptians could be improved, and hurriedly told his brother to call off the projected killing. Just to make sure that everyone involved, which included the British and French as well as the Israelis, got the point, the secretary had to publicly emphasize U.S. hopes of "getting along with Nasser."

Other covert initiatives in the region were hardly more successful. A projected coup organized by the ubiquitous Kermit Roosevelt against a supposedly leftist government in Syria ended when the local "assets" walked into the office of the chief of Syrian intelligence and turned in their CIA bribe money, together with the names of the CIA officers who had paid them. A plot to get the Iraqis to threaten Syria was abruptly terminated when a pro-Nasser military coup (totally unforeseen by U.S. or Israeli intelligence) toppled the Iraqi monarchy. Millions of dollars and frantic intriguing across the Middle East had served only to make the U.S. ever more unpopular.

This steady flouting of the Eisenhower Doctrine could only serve to bolster and expand what Harel called the "connection." Reviewing recent failures in a meeting with Wilbur Eveland in 1958, Allen Dulles paused and said, "I guess that leaves Israel's intelligence service as the only one on which we can count, doesn't it?"

For this reason Dulles had decided, so Eveland records, that the CIA division dealing with covert operations in Arab countries would from now on work closely with James Angleton. "Not against the

Arabs, of course," he explained to Eveland, "but against our common target, the Russians."[27]

In the seven years since Israel had first offered to assist the CIA by debriefing immigrants from Communist countries, the covert liaison had survived bumps on the road and flowered to the point where Israeli intelligence was now to play a major part in assisting the U.S. to fight the Cold War in the Middle East and elsewhere.

Meanwhile, however, Israel was planning to get assistance from the U.S. in quite another area. Ben-Gurion, in a decision shared only with his most trusted advisers, had determined to arm Israel with the ultimate weapon. To build a nuclear bomb, Israel needed help from outside, and that in turn gave the covert allies in Jerusalem and Washington a terrible secret to share.

4. A Sword for Damocles

IN THE EARLY SUMMER OF 1989, a tall, fair-haired career bureaucrat chose an outdoor table on the Bethesda Metro-stop plaza, surrounded by the colorless urban sprawl of greater Washington. After ordering corned beef on rye, he began to talk, slowly and deliberately, about the ruin of his career. This dour middle-aged man was a casualty of secret policy. He had dangerously ruffled the composure of Washington's national security community by stumbling across evidence of nuclear espionage by a foreign government. James H. Conran believed it was his job to report it. He had not understood that the evidence had been carefully buried at the request of at least one president. The trouble was, the foreign government was Israel.

His ordeal began in 1975, when this serious-minded nuclear engineer was assigned the laborious task of compiling a history of nuclear safeguards in U.S. plants since the days of Atoms for Peace, when private enterprise had entered the nuclear business. Jim Conran's employer was the newly created Nuclear Regulatory Commission, born when the Atomic Energy Commission was dismantled by Congress on the grounds that one agency could not promote atomic energy while policing its own activities.

To do his job, Conran needed the old AEC files and, with his top-security clearances, he had access to the lot, except for one. When he requested access to that particular ultrasecret file, he was told flatly that he had no "need to know." The subject was a company called the

Nuclear Materials and Equipment Corporation of Apollo, Pennsylvania.

Conran badgered his superiors about the file, until the Chairman of the NRC requested a briefing on it from a top official of the CIA. Carl Duckett was the agency's deputy director for science and technology. He stood before an elite club of nuclear officials known as the "secret seven" and expressed the CIA's view that the Apollo, Pennsylvania plant had most probably provided bomb-grade uranium for Israel's nuclear weapons program. The CIA believed that program had been well under way in the 1960s.

There was indeed alarming evidence that the uranium had been methodically removed from the "NUMEC" plant over a period of up to ten years. But as Conran began turning up this evidence, the fact that the Israelis had heisted materials essential to their very secret weapons program shocked him less than the reaction of his superiors to his probing in such murky and politically charged waters. "They lied to me," he said. "I came to believe that some of them were involved." Conran concluded that there was an ongoing coverup of the very peculiar circumstances surrounding what looked like Israel's nuclear theft, and that the CIA was deeply implicated.

When he confronted Kenneth Chapman, the top safeguards official at the NRC, Chapman warned him that some of the documents relating to the case were "born classified." Even the "knowledge of their existence was classified."[1]

It is a sin in Washington to ignore the proper "channels" in venting complaints, and Conran was fully aware that he could be unceremoniously fired for doing so. But if Israel had looted a U.S. nuclear facility to build an arsenal, and members of his own agency had acquiesced, Conran had to talk to someone on the outside.

He went first to Charles ("Chick") Brennan, former head of domestic intelligence at the FBI. Brennan, it turned out, was quite familiar with the Apollo case. The FBI had accumulated vast files on what it called the DIVERT theft and had been consulted by the White House more than once to find out where the investigation stood and whether there were any leaks. Brennan took Conran with him to meet with a "very high-level" CIA official to discuss the fact that the Nuclear Regulatory Commission might have been compromised.

The CIA man expressed concern, but somewhat off the point, turned the subject of the conversation to Soviet moles at the NRC. He thought one particular NRC official might fit the profile. This was apparently of far more interest than any possible coverup of evidence pointing to Israeli espionage. The purpose of the meeting was never properly addressed, and Conran withdrew discouraged. He would have to take his story farther outside, though he knew he was running a greater risk of exposure. He turned to Capitol Hill, to try and get Congress to launch an investigation.

Conran was right about the risk. The NRC now accused him of trafficking in classified documents and dismissed him from his job. He was exiled to an office that set standards for nuclear power reactors. He had in the meantime been the subject of an internal report recommending that he see a psychiatrist. On April 4, 1977, he sat down and wrote an open letter to the NRC:

"Events and developments which I have observed or experienced during my safeguards involvement over the past eighteen months have been so consistently bewildering and deeply troubling and so totally out of character for NRC, as to suggest that something is indefinably but terribly wrong . . ."[2]

No one had bothered to tell Jim Conran that he had blundered into one of the biggest mine fields in U.S. policy, from which secrets of every administration since Eisenhower could be exhumed. Powerful men in Washington and in Jerusalem hoped that the secrets would remain buried.

When congressional staffers took over Conran's aborted inquiries they found a case in complete disarray: sloppy paperwork, grossly negligent security and evidence of ongoing nervousness in the Oval Office over what the investigators came to believe was an elaborate Israeli covert operation.

In July 1977 Congressman Morris Udall, chairman of the House Interior Committee, convened hearings and forthrightly billed the Apollo affair as a scandal in the same league with Watergate, Koreagate, and My Lai. By the summer of 1978, however, one year after promising to "get to the bottom" of how at least 206 pounds of highly enriched uranium had disappeared from the Apollo plant, Udall and his staff had still not overcome stubborn resistance from powerful quarters to the release of key classified documents. The FBI and CIA stalled.

Filling out the congressional trenches were the staff of the General Accounting Office, who had also been laboring for a year on the case, and who had also been firmly denied access to the relevant FBI and CIA files. Even so, the GAO did finally complete a voluminous report, which was then muzzled by these same agencies. By December 1978 it was gathering dust, stamped "secret."

John Dingell, the combative Democrat from Michigan who chairs the House Commerce Committee and who had commissioned the GAO report, now charged that the behavior of the FBI and CIA had caused "widespread suspicions of a government coverup." The FBI then revealed that there was an ongoing government investigation into the matter, commissioned by President Ford, which had priority over any demands from Congress. Any cooperation with "the Hill" would impede and interfere with this inquiry. (It was a neat Catch-22, echoed years later during the Iran-Contra affair.)

Congressman Dingell was not impressed. The FBI, he said, had been less than energetic in digging up the facts. After thirty months, he noted, the FBI had "still not interviewed some of the critical actors involved." According to the gagged GAO report, the FBI had neglected to interview "eight key officials." These included the chairman of the Atomic Energy Commission during NUMEC's prime; the loan officer of the Mellon Bank, who had approved a substantial loan to the company; and the "chief Department of Energy field investigator for NUMEC."

Whatever its shortcomings, the internal government investigation allowed official spokesmen to claim that the case was "inactive" but nevertheless still "open." Thus it could not be discussed. The CIA stated that the reasons for its insistence that the GAO report should be classified was itself "classified."

A top-secret FBI memo from May 14, 1976, filed under the code word DIVERT, provides an interesting insight into the attitudes in the Ford White House that led to the internal inquiry:

"The President is aware of instant matters and extremely interested in it. The President feels that it is necessary as best as possible to understand what happened at NUMEC and circumstances surrounding the situation. He is particularly concerned with any indication of a prior cover-up . . . At the White House only four people know of the investigation and it is the hope of the White House that the investigation will not come to the attention of the general public."[3]

That hope was not unique to the Ford administration. The case of the Apollo plant had long been regarded as a political grenade. Peter

Stockton, long a member of Congressman Dingell's Oversight and Investigations Subcommittee (a watchdog offshoot of the Energy and Commerce Committee), came to know the sorry history of official probes into Apollo extremely well. He states flatly, "Every administration through Carter investigated it and dropped it."

Ever since an American U-2 spy plane had photographed Israel's supposedly "peaceful" nuclear reactor in the Negev in 1960, U.S. presidents had questioned Israeli leaders about their nuclear plans. It had been a significant factor in relations between the two countries, although the subject was never discussed in public. In May 1961, ten years after his journey to Washington to arrange the original covert deal with the CIA, Ben-Gurion met with John F. Kennedy at the Waldorf-Astoria Hotel in New York. Ben-Gurion was worried about American pressure over the nuclear program taking shape in the Negev, but was determined not to yield. Kennedy offered to allay Israeli concerns about security by supplying sophisticated conventional arms for the first time, in exchange for an understanding that the Israeli bomb program would at least slow down. The program did slow down for a period (due mainly to Israeli concerns about the cost), and deliveries of advanced American weapons gathered speed, but the problem kept coming back to haunt whomever happened to be occupying the White House.

"In 1968," recounts Stockton, drawing on his investigation for Dingell, "Richard Helms [CIA Director at the time] told President Johnson that there had been a diversion of nuclear materials to Israel." Johnson's reaction was not "Get me the Israeli ambassador," but something far more telling about the complications of the U.S.-Israeli relationship. According to the former deputy director for science and technology at the CIA, Carl Duckett, Johnson responded to Helms's news by exclaiming, "Don't tell anyone else, not even [Dean] Rusk and [Robert] McNamara." The two men who were to be kept in ignorance were, respectively, Johnson's secretaries of state and defense.

Johnson had been assured by Levi Eshkol, Ben-Gurion's successor as prime minister, that the nuclear program was on hold. (There was some truth to this, as Eshkol was not as enamored of the program as the previous regime.) Johnson had seen no problem in accelerating the supply of conventional weapons. In 1968, the President agreed to sell F-4 Phantom fighter-bombers—fully capable of carrying a nuclear bomb—to the Israelis. Paul Nitze, then deputy secretary of defense, recalls that he told the assistant secretary of defense for international security affairs, Paul Warnke, not to authorize delivery of the planes until the Israelis were more forthcoming about their nuclear program. Soon after making this decision, Nitze, the number two man in the Pentagon, received a visit from "a Mr. Finkelstein from the Jewish Relief Agency. He told me I could not do that. I said, 'What do you mean? I've just done it.' He said the matter would go to the president and I would be overruled. It did. I was overruled."

The Nixon White House was equally sensitive to the need for "damage control" in the NUMEC affair. In February 1969, only days after Nixon had been sworn in as Johnson's successor, the new president told Attorney General John Mitchell to call J. Edgar Hoover. Hoover, the formidable FBI chief, was regarded as the keeper of Washington's most delicate secrets. After the call, Hoover sat down to write a memo for the record on the top priorities of Richard Nixon. One of them was "atomic espionage."[4] Mitchell had made it clear that the president wanted any material Hoover had on the matter. Hoover understood the power of such information and toyed with the new attorney general. "I advised the Attorney General that I did not know what he had [sic] reference to; that of course we have continuing espionage by the Russians. The Attorney General said he thought he [Nixon] was talking about another country involving some American nationals going back and forth . . . the Attorney General said he thought it was commonly referred to as the [deleted]. I told the Attorney General I would have a memorandum prepared on that case."

Three months later, a high-level National Security Council meeting convened at the White House. Among those present were Nixon's national security adviser Henry Kissinger, and CIA chief Richard Helms. The subject was the Apollo plant and the implications of the Israeli operation. Helms says he cannot recall the meeting. But Mort Halperin, then a National Security Council staffer, remembers it well. "It was an important issue, so you had to have a meeting," Halperin recalls. "For the record, the meeting was a charade." It was a charade because those in the room knew precisely what the Israelis were up to. "Kissinger saw nothing wrong with the Israelis having nuclear weapons. His view was, they have nuclear weapons, so what? It means we don't have to defend them." According to this former NSC staffer, it was common knowledge among his colleagues in the White House that

Kissinger was comfortable with the fact that Israel was building its own nuclear weapons. If they were stealing materials from Pennsylvania that was acceptable. Although Kissinger would certainly deny this interpretation of his views, he was still meeting with officials to discuss the NUMEC case as late as January 1971.

The White House discussions were not public knowledge. According to Halperin, the White House was not prepared to tolerate leaks. Politically, too much was at stake. "The concern was that if the diversion became public, it could jeopardize our relationship with Israel." But there was a leak, in an unlikely venue, that went to the heart of the NUMEC case.

On February 26, 1969, two weeks after J. Edgar Hoover wrote his memo for the record, a neighborhood newspaper called the *Advertiser*, distributed free to the residents of greater Pittsburgh, ran a curious "box" item by "Mack Truck, *Advertiser* staff writer." It was titled "Dr. 'X.' " The obscure column attracted the attention of few people, apart from the FBI. The bureau opened an urgent investigation into the source. Dr. "X," FBI people knew, was at the heart of the Israeli espionage case. What worried them was that someone at the *Advertiser* knew it too. (Why the story was planted and who did it has yet to be revealed by the FBI.) The item read:

Once or twice a month at Greater Pittsburgh airport, a Pittsburgh physicist takes off for JFK International airport where he then boards an El Al plane for Tel Aviv. Dr. "X" is one of the nation's best informed men on nuclear materials. He once worked at Bettis [an American nuclear facility] until he and a few others left to start in business for themselves. Now he's a "consultant" to several Israeli firms and the [U.S.] government on handling radioactive materials and related matters.

Dr. Zalman Mordechai Shapiro's FBI file was first opened in March 1949. Between the first report from the Cleveland office and the last memo from the head office in Washington in July 1974, Dr. Shapiro had been the subject of fifty-one FBI reports, forty-one of which were classified "secret." Before he founded the Nuclear Materials and Equipment Corporation of Apollo, Pennsylvania, in December 1956, Shapiro had been a successful chemist with the Atomic Energy Commission. His credits included some of the most prestigious programs from the early days of nuclear research. He had worked on the Manhattan Project, where seminal work had been done processing uranium into weapons-grade material for the first primitive bombs. He had helped develop the nuclear reactor for the Nautilus submarine, the first jewel of Admiral Hyman Rickover's nuclear navy.[5]

Zalman Shapiro was also a friend of Israel. His father was a Lithuanian Jew and Orthodox rabbi. Zalman joined the Zionist Federation and Friends of the Technion, which raised funds and collected equipment for Israel's MIT, the Technion Institute of Technology in Haifa. When Shapiro wanted to found his own business, he turned to a veteran of Israel's War of Independence, David Lowenthal, who gave Shapiro an old brick factory building in Apollo, thirty miles outside Pittsburgh. Lowenthal's Apollo steel company could spare the room for Zalman Shapiro's nuclear processing plant. Because of Shapiro's old government ties, his young company received a healthy flow of contracts to turn enriched uranium into fuel for naval reactors and an experimental space rocket. At one point, NUMEC boasted twenty-six clients, including Israel. In spite of what appears to have been an initially diversified client list, there are those who believe that Shapiro's company was set up from the first as an Israeli front.

Stockton found that at least one CIA official had a very clear idea of what the NUMEC affair was really all about. John Hadden had a good insight into the ways of Israeli intelligence, since he had been CIA station chief in Tel Aviv before retiring in 1974. Hadden told Stockton that "NUMEC had been an Israeli operation from the beginning, but the CIA had not been able to follow the money trail. The agency thought NUMEC had been financed by the owner of the Apollo steel mill, Israeli War of Independence veteran David Lowenthal."

Lowenthal was indeed the financier. A secret report from the FBI office in Pittsburgh named David Lowenthal as president of the Raychord Steel Corporation and an officer of Apollo Industries of Pittsburgh, "a company," the report noted, "which was instrumental in establishing NUMEC through investing a substantial amount of money in NUMEC stock." Apollo Industries was also financing Raychord, having made loans and advances of nearly $3 million by 1967. Apollo also held a good deal of Raychord stock. In 1960 the president of Apollo Industries was also on the board of NUMEC.

Hadden's belief that NUMEC was an Israeli front was not shared by all of his CIA colleagues, at least not when they talked to Congress. The assistant to the deputy director for (covert) operations, Theodore

Shackley, was vehement in disparaging colleagues in the agency who tied NUMEC to the Israeli weapons program. Stockton remembers Shackley saying that Hadden in his retirement "was contemplating his navel and getting bored and was therefore spinning stories." Carl Duckett, the CIA scientific intelligence chief who had alerted the NRC to the CIA assessment of NUMEC as a source for Israel's bomb-grade material, was dismissed, spuriously, by Shackley as an "alcoholic," while for good measure he referred to James Angleton as "a wacko." There had, insisted Shackley, simply been "no diversion." Yet it appears from reports of secret testimony to the Department of Energy by retired Air Force General Alfred Starbird, who went on to become a top-security official at the Energy Research and Development Administration, that there is evidence to suggest that in reality Shackley saw things quite differently.[6]

In Starbird's 1978 statement under oath, according to government sources, the retired general said he had been told by a CIA official that the agency had managed to obtain a sample of highly enriched uranium from Israel. The chemical "signature" specifically identified it as uranium that had been enriched at the U.S. enrichment plant at Portsmouth, Ohio, which was where NUMEC's enriched uranium came from. As his CIA source, General Starbird reportedly named none other than Ted Shackley. Carl Duckett had also told the NRC that CIA evidence from Israel itself had figured in the agency's assessment that NUMEC uranium had been diverted.

Asked about these varying reports of his views on the matter, Shackley would only say that he could not comment "one way or the other." John Hadden, asked about Shackley's derisive reference to his "spinning tales" from his place of retirement, laughed and said, "I can deny that. I spun no tales from here." On Shackley's denial that there had been a diversion, he observed: "Don't forget who it was who kicked off the whole Iran-Contra thing with a trip to Hamburg." This opaque remark was apparently a reference to a meeting held by Shackley in Hamburg in November 1985 with Manucher Ghorbanifar, the Iranian middleman in the initial phase of the arms deals between the U.S. and Iran that led to the scandal. According to Oliver North, Ghorbanifar "was widely believed to be an Israeli agent." As an old covert operator, Hadden chooses his words very carefully.

Hadden also observed that any suggestion that Angleton had actually helped the Israelis with the NUMEC operation was "totally without foundation. But on the other hand, he [Angleton] had no interest in stopping" the Israeli operation. Hadden, who knew Angleton well, puts it bluntly: "Why would someone whose whole life was dedicated to fighting communism have any interest in preventing a fiercely anti-Communist nation getting the means to defend itself?"

Hadden was impressed by the scale of it all. "This was a big operation," he says. "It was much more complex than the old arms-smuggling operation from the 1940s, where people like Al Schwimmer got their start. For this you needed money, you needed protection, you needed corporations, nuclear engineers, nuclear physicists."

Dr. Shapiro's processing plant had been under suspicion from various quarters of the nuclear establishment since as early as 1962. There were two glaring problems: complete lack of security for bomb-grade uranium supplied by the AEC to the plant, and an obvious and active Israeli presence. The combination of the two alarmed inspectors, who understood that such a plant was not just a source of uranium, but also a window on U.S. nuclear secrets that went beyond any specific activities at the plant itself. Apollo was part of a network of installations with top-secret clearance under the umbrella of the Atomic Energy Commission. Dr. Shapiro had access to a whole repository of knowledge on nuclear matters, including weapons.

On February 27, 1962, J. A. Waters, the Atomic Energy Commission's director of security, wrote a memo to A. W. Betts, the director of military application:

> Security inspections at NUMEC have disclosed numerous security discrepancies attributable to the lack of effort on the part of NUMEC management to establish and maintain an adequate and effective security program. Coupled with this is the information that NUMEC has the following known affiliations.
>
> 1. An agreement for cooperation with Israel under which NUMEC serves as technical consultant and training and procurement agency for Israel in the US . . .
> . . . We have informed you about the aliens working in the plutonium plant . . . One of them, an Israeli metallurgist, is a guest worker under the agreement . . .

AEC investigators found that although the company had classified U.S. government contracts, "aliens working at NUMEC are permitted in security areas without escort while working on plutonium." The

Israeli metallurgist, Baruch Cinai, had been a "guest worker" since March 1961. There were numerous visits to the plant by Ephraim Lahav, scientific counselor at the Israeli Embassy in Washington. Lahav's activities were the subject of at least one classified FBI report. According to a secret AEC memo, Lahav visited the Apollo plant as early as December 1961. Both the flow of foreigners and the cavalier attitude to security was causing alarm at the AEC, because this operation was ripe for espionage. A 1961 report said, "The level of security protection afforded AEC classified interests at NUMEC has become a matter of grave concern to the Division of Security." Yet no one made a move to shut down the plant.[7]

The "classified interests" went far beyond the quantities of highly enriched uranium on the grounds. NUMEC had approximately 2,400 classified documents on the premises, including 169 "microcards" with descriptions of secret U.S. government research and development programs. The FBI said, "There are no barriers to prevent uncleared individuals from having access to such classified information." NUMEC files were a feast of U.S. national security secrets. At Apollo, one could dip into classified technical blueprints while scraping together some bomb-grade uranium.

A dedicated uranium thief could have started by sweeping the floor. The secret GAO report published in 1978 interviewed one field investigator who said that on a visit to NUMEC in "1963 or 1964, he saw nuclear material deposited in the crevices of the stairwells and on the floor." The NUMEC management was in the habit of mixing "unclassified uranium materials" with highly enriched uranium in the same area of the plant without the "color code" one could find at other nuclear facilities. "All they had around the area was a "hog wire fence." Yet, in spite of the "grave concern," NUMEC carried on in its haphazard way without serious censure. Even the "trees and bushes," noted one top-secret FBI report, were "covered by a white residue."

The security staff at NUMEC left something to be desired. The title of "plant security officer" was regularly abused. AEC reports in 1961 said, "Two employees have had this assignment during the past year. Unfortunately, in both instances these individuals were assigned other duties which consumed the majority of their time and neither has had any experience in the field of security."

When in 1967 the Atomic Energy Commission found that a total of 572 pounds of highly enriched uranium had vanished from the stocks, the AEC generously chose to assume that 366 pounds had been lost through "normal plant operations," including a substantial amount of uranium that supposedly ran off into the Kiski River. This was received with some skepticism by the former staff director of the Joint Committee on Atomic Energy, who observed that such a loss was possible only if the Apollo plant had "run seven days a week, twenty-four hours a day since before the Revolutionary War."

NUMEC paid $929,000 in fines to the AEC as compensation for the loss. Business had fallen off in the mid-sixties, and NUMEC was cash-poor. Yet the company managed to secure a swift million-dollar loan from the Mellon Bank. Shapiro had attempted to avoid the fine altogether, according to an internal memo prepared for the chairman of the AEC. After several months of questioning by the AEC about where the uranium might be (and after acres of ground were turned over in vain), Shapiro displayed breathtaking tactical initiative. He suddenly declared that the Atomic Energy Commission owed *him* money, not the other way around. He had been covering up the real resting place of the uranium, which was a waste dump consisting of eight hundred barrels of "Kleenex" and "Kimwipes." He had withheld this vital intelligence because "the situation was embarrassing." Thus, workmen were dispatched to sift through mountains of glutinous Kimwipes, with no discernible result.

Charles Keller of the AEC later remarked, "I don't know what pressures were being brought politically and otherwise in Washington to keep that company operating. I wouldn't have given them any more [uranium or contracts] until they straightened up and flew right, but I guess I was a voice crying in the wilderness."[8]

One AEC case history in 1971 cited what the FBI investigations had found out overall about NUMEC and its associations: "very close ties with Israel and a highly organized effort on the part of Israel in this country to solicit substantial technical and financial assistance." Dr. Shapiro's "ties" went beyond invitations to Israeli technical staff and embassy officials to come to Apollo. In 1965, Shapiro went into partnership with the Israeli government. They founded a company called ISORAD—Israel Numec Isotopes and Radiation Enterprises. NUMEC and the Israeli government each held 50 percent of the stock and each provided four board members. The Israeli team was impressive, including the head of the Israeli Atomic Energy Commission and the commission's chief of research. A prominent banker and the head of Israel's citrus board were also on the letterhead. ISORAD was supposed to "conduct research involving irradiation of agricultural products." The idea was to stop oranges from spoiling and to "eliminate the transportation of live larvae of the Mediterranean fruit fly." But one FBI report noted that "ISORAD never accomplished anything beyond the experimental stage, and experiments were conducted in Israel."

The ISORAD venture gave Shapiro the opportunity to develop a "business association" with Joseph Eyal, the science attaché at the Israeli Embassy and the "purchasing commission [sic] of the Israeli government in New York." There were some irregularities on the matter of an export license. "While NUMEC's sale of goods to the Israeli government certainly must have involved a request by that government for certain products, NUMEC's acquisition of an export license from the Department of Commerce was on its own behalf rather than that of a foreign principal."

Shapiro had not registered as an agent for Israel. But that was how the U.S. government apparently regarded him. In a letter from the AEC to J. Edgar Hoover, NUMEC was described as a "sales agent for the Government of Israel through its Ministry of Defense, Division of Supplies," on Third Avenue in New York. When Hoover put Dr. Shapiro under surveillance in 1968, the FBI found it could not tap Shapiro's telephone. As the FBI told Congress, Shapiro was using an "encoded phone," in which messages were scrambled and unscrambled at the other end, for his conversations with Israeli officials in New York. The FBI failed to crack the code.

Shapiro apparently described himself as representing Israel, at a time when his top-security clearances precluded any chance of his legitimately being an agent for a foreign power. When the FBI debriefed one inspector of the Apollo plant, he described a meeting with Shapiro and his lawyer, Jack Newman. Shapiro, according to the inspector, "indicated that he was an agent for Israel. This apparently was used in a loose manner indicating possibly that he was acting in an official capacity for the Israeli government."[9]

After ISORAD was established, Shapiro began shipping large food irradiators and similar but smaller units called "howitzers" to Israel. The shipments were legal. One plant employee told the FBI that this took place just about the time that large amounts of enriched uranium disappeared. "It would have been a simple matter of placing the material in these food irradiator units in large quantities and [shipping them] to Israel with no questions asked . . . With a notice printed on the side of the container indicating that the contents contained radioactive material, no one would have opened or examined them." Other sources at the plant told of shipping containers that arrived late in the day and disappeared by morning. One such container (with heavy shielding for radioactive material) was stamped with a "pre-addressed stencil" to Haifa, Israel. Another NUMEC employee observed strangers loading cans of the right dimensions for high-enriched uranium. A guard with a gun ordered the employee to leave.

There were other peculiar incidents at NUMEC. One night a witness discovered a flatbed truck backed up to the Apollo loading dock with men stuffing "stovepipes"—storage containers for high-enriched uranium—into steel cabinets, after being wrapped with "a brown paper insulation." The "stovepipes," he said, came from the "high-enriched vault area." The cannisters inside them were marked with nuclear fan symbols. He, too, was asked to leave the area. "An armed guard ordered him off the loading dock."

There were threats the following day. "[Deleted] of NUMEC threatened to fire [deleted] 'did not keep his mouth shut' concerning what he had seen on the loading dock the night before . . . [deleted] claims he was visited by [deleted] and again told to keep his mouth shut." There appears to have been intimidation further up the line on the NUMEC matter inside the Atomic Energy Commission. One AEC staffer, according to the FBI, "received a call from William Riley, who was director at that time, requesting [deleted] to appear in his office. Riley then began to chew [deleted] out about discussing the NUMEC affair in a social gathering, and swore him to secrecy. Riley stated something to the effect that he didn't want [deleted] to talk about NUMEC to anyone, since he wanted the matter of NUMEC 'shut up once and for all' . . . Riley told [deleted] that the matter of NUMEC was bigger than they were."

One senior congressional staffer who was deeply involved in the NUMEC investigation believes the affair was very big because it went beyond the diversion of uranium for the Israeli nuclear weapons program. When the FBI began its surveillance at the request of CIA Director Richard Helms, it uncovered the rest of the operation. "The FBI wasn't looking at the diversion of material." That, by 1968, was past history. "They cared about the other stuff—this ring—just like Pollard."[10]

Jonathan Pollard, now serving a life sentence in the United States' top-security prison in Marion, Illinois, was convicted in 1985 of spying for Israel. In the course of his prodigious efforts to collect top-secret documents, Pollard photocopied thousands of pages of highly technical data on weapons systems, secrets which the Pentagon had no intention of sharing with its ally. Pollard was run as an agent by LAKAM, a shadowy intelligence agency dedicated to collecting sensitive technology for Israel. Its very existence had remained a secret for years (even from the CIA for two decades) until the operation was forced into the open by the capture of its overzealous American spy. The chief of LAKAM in Pollard's time was Rafael Eitan. It had been Eitan who paid a visit to Apollo, Pennsylvania, on September 10, 1968.

"Rafi" Eitan is one of Israel's most celebrated spies. By the age of ten, he had found his calling in espionage after being captivated by the Mata Hari figure in the film *Fräulein Doktor.* "Stinking Rafi," as he came to be known in the army, fulfilled his ambitions in 1951 when he was recruited by spymaster Isser Harel. While serving in Shabak, Israel's domestic intelligence agency, and later in Mossad, Eitan was regarded as particularly talented. He was dispatched with the select group of agents who successfully pursued and kidnapped Eichmann and assisted in the capture of Soviet agent Israel Beer. Eitan even hunted for Mengele. Physically, Eitan seemed badly suited for such missions. Squat and nearsighted, Eitan inhaled vitamin pills (up to forty a day) and was nearly stone deaf. He was never without a hearing aid after being wounded while sabotaging a British radar station in the late forties, on an operation with the elite First Brigade of the Palmach. He was also wounded while releasing illegal Jewish immigrants from a British detention camp in Atlit.

At the time of his visit to Apollo in 1968, Eitan was acting as an agent for Mossad on special assignment to LAKAM. LAKAM was born in the 1950s, with the express purpose of acquiring nuclear technology, by any means. Israel was already determined to have the bomb. Ben-Gurion was personally fascinated by the idea and used Israel's close military alliance with France to negotiate for a suitable reactor. Dimona, the towering reactor complex in the Negev Desert, became the hub of the secret weapons program. Even now, one can easily be arrested for lingering in the desert opposite the Dimona fence. One former Defense Intelligence Agency spy said he had more flat tires outside Dimona than anywhere else in Israel.

Francis Perrin, the French high commissioner of atomic energy, had first visited Israel in 1949. By 1953, the two countries had signed a nuclear cooperation agreement. Israeli scientists packed their bags and headed to Saclay, outside Paris, a complex of reactors known as the Institute of Nuclear Science and Techniques. (In the early eighties a visitor to Saclay could see serious young scientists from Iraq filling the tables at the cafeteria. Iraq's Osirak reactor, bombed by Israel in June 1981, was a replica of the Osiris model at Saclay.) The Israelis were granted access to French technical data that proved extremely useful in their pursuit of the bomb. The French, as part of the exchange, were given the patent to an Israeli chemical process for producing "heavy" water.

When France agreed to ship a 26-megawatt reactor to Israel in 1957, the decision to go nuclear was by no means unanimous. Six of the seven members of the Israeli Atomic Energy Commission resigned in protest. The chairman, Dr. Ernst David Bergman (a friend of Zalman Shapiro's), became a one-man commission. The other positions were simply terminated. Bergman later commented on the opposition during a lecture in Tel Aviv. "With two or three exceptions," he said, "the leaders of the country opposed the new nuclear policy, which they regarded as irresponsible." But there was only one leader in Israel whose opinion mattered. The decision had been railroaded through, declared Bergman, "thanks to Ben-Gurion's visionary genius."

Shimon Peres, who was busy making secret weapons deals with French Defense Minister Pierre-Marie Koenig, later mused that critics of the nuclear option had called the reactor project "an act of political adventurism that would unite the world against us." A leading member of Ben-Gurion's own political party, Mapai, called it "a political, economic, and military catastrophe."

Some of Israel's best-known military strategists were equally vocal in the opposition. Yigal Allon, the hero of the War of Independence and commander of the elite Palmach commandos, fought the nuclear weapons program. Yitzhak Rabin, who would go on to become chief of staff in 1964, was against it. Even Ariel Sharon, then and now one of Israel's leading hawks, opposed the decision, preferring, as did many of Israel's military men, to rely on conventional force. Nonetheless, Ben-Gurion prevailed.[11]

The French reactor was constructed on a desolate site in the Negev Desert, near the dusty, unappealing settlement of Dimona. Ben-Gurion, on various occasions, called it a "textile plant" or a "pumping station." As late as 1963, Shimon Peres, then deputy minister of defense, said that Dimona's purpose was to turn the Negev Desert into a "garden." A billion cubic meters of seawater, he said, would be desalinated annually at the plant. At this pronouncement, Aharon Weiner, director of Tahal (the Israeli water company), was taken aback. The story, he said, was "unfounded."

The CIA knew precisely what Dimona was and regarded Ben-Gurion's reluctance to consult his cabinet as indicative of his autocratic management style. In a 1961 memo, CIA Director Allen Dulles wrote:

> . . . Ben-Gurion, without the knowledge of his Cabinet gave the order sometime in 1956, to begin construction of a second nuclear, plutonium-producing reactor which would permit, if necessary, the manufacture of an atomic bomb. This decision was revealed to an extremely small circle of confidants.

The agency did not regard the decision to go ahead with the weapons program as a by-product of the Suez War, but rather as an example of Ben-Gurion's obsession with the "security of the State." It would appear that the weapons program was discussed as early as 1955. However, the Suez War may have been the critical factor that convinced the CIA to help secretly. According to former CIA official Wilbur Eveland, Ben-Gurion had refused to withdraw his forces from the Sinai and Gaza until the U.S. agreed to "provide Israel with means to protect its population centers from attack by the Russian ballistic missiles that, Israeli intelligence reported, would soon be furnished to Egypt and Syria. The CIA had therefore been secretly authorized to help Israel acquire the capability of retaliating against possible attack by advanced weapons in the hands of the Arabs." Unfortunately, Eveland is now dead and thus cannot elaborate on whether this secret cooperation agreement with the CIA stretched to nuclear technology, or indeed, enriched uranium from the Apollo plant, which opened its doors exactly three months after the Suez War.[12]

The Dimona reactor complex, with its dramatic silver dome shimmering in the heat of the Negev, was completed in 1963. "Kirya-le-Mehekar Gariny" soon employed 2,700 scientists and technicians. The sand inside its perimeter fences was swept each day to detect any intruders. Pilots knew that any aircraft flying overhead would be speedily shot down. The heart of the weapons plant was and is a six-story underground facility known as Machon II. It was Machon II that a technician named Mordechai Vanunu spent forty leisurely minutes photographing with his Pentax in 1985. This plutonium separation/reprocessing plant was part of the original deal with French Premier Guy Mollet in 1957. French engineers had bulldozed an eighty-foot hole in the desert to house the concrete bunker. Reprocessing technology, labeled "textile machinery," had been shipped from France. Charles de Gaulle, who had always maintained that French nuclear cooperation with Israel ended in 1960, lied, according to former French nuclear chief Francis Perrin. De Gaulle, he said, had allowed the construction of the separation plant, which, by reprocessing the reactor's spent fuel rods into weapons-grade plutonium, was one means of building a bomb.

Why the French were so generous with their nuclear technology may be explained by the story told by an American nuclear physicist who helped build nuclear weapons at Los Alamos.

The French government, according to the physicist, did not deliver the reactor out of charity. At the time, French scientists were having trouble perfecting small, efficient nuclear warheads, a breakthrough that had occurred previously in the United States. The U.S., however, was not forthcoming with the critical data, and France, alleges the physicist, struck a deal with Israel to steal it. The means would be Israeli agents in the United States. In light of the physicist's story, it is interesting to note that NUMEC had a close association with the French and received a stern warning about violations of the espionage act with regard to information passed along to the French. In February 1962, Lawton Geiger, from the Atomic Energy Commission division of naval reactors, wrote to Zalman Shapiro:

I consider the NUMEC relationship with the Société D'Application Industrielles de la Physique a matter of serious concern calling for increased security vigilance. The failure to comply with security regulations may be punishable as provided by law including the Atomic Energy

Act of 1954 (sections 221–227 inclusive) and by the espionage laws, Title 18, United States Code, Sections 793 and 794.[13]

The threat of an espionage charge was, according to an internal congressional report, inserted at the request of Admiral Rickover.

Between 1957 and 1960, Israelis worked with technicians from the French Dassault Corporation to design a Mirage bomber that could carry nuclear weapons. Israelis had joined the French to observe nuclear tests in the Algerian Sahara. When Ben-Gurion made a trip to the White House in 1960, Eisenhower, ever cautious on Israeli matters, told the prime minister that nuclear weapons would not improve the balance of forces in the Middle East, because the Russians were unlikely to give such weapons to Egypt. In the summer of 1960, the CIA briefed the president on Dimona, saying it would enable the Israelis to produce at least one bomb per year.

The Eisenhower administration was not entirely innocent with regard to the weapons program. The Weizmann Institute, where much of Israel's nuclear research was carried out, was in large part funded by the U.S. government. The U.S. Air Force, as well as the navy, funded classified nuclear physics research at the institute. Washington also knew that Israel's "peaceful" nuclear program was entirely controlled by the Ministry of Defense.

In December 1960, when President-elect Kennedy's transition team was settling into Washington, it received a background briefing on the Dimona situation. Eisenhower was worried about Arab reaction to the Israeli nuclear program. It was now Kennedy's problem, one which the president-elect called "highly distressing."[14] Early in 1961, when Ben-Gurion had embroidered his "textile plant" explanation of Dimona with the phrase "research in problems of arid zones and desert flora and fauna," Kennedy wrote the prime minister a diplomatic letter, politely suggesting regular inspections by the International Atomic Energy Agency.

In May 1961, Ben-Gurion flew to New York for a crucial meeting with the newly installed president. He was extremely worried about the American pressure on Dimona. If Kennedy was unyielding on the matter, the domestic opposition to the project within Israel would probably take heart and get it killed.

At the meeting, in the Waldorf-Astoria Hotel, Ben-Gurion agreed to occasional inspections of the Dimona reactor (which did not include the

Dimona *complex*), on Israeli terms. Kennedy, in return, agreed in principle to Ben-Gurion's request for Hawk antiaircraft missiles, an advanced weapon that the U.S. had never previously considered supplying to Israel. Kennedy had to balance the roles of statesman and politician; at the end of the meeting he drew Ben-Gurion aside and stated, "I know I was elected by the votes of American Jews. I owe them my victory. Tell me, is there something I ought to do?" Ben-Gurion claimed to have been shocked by this invocation of crude political realities and said he replied: "You must do whatever is best for the free world."

Meanwhile, the specter of the "Arab Rocket" (the grounds for secret CIA cooperation with Israel, according to Wilbur Eveland) was unveiled to the world in November 1961, with shocking revelations of German scientists secretly working in Egypt. The Israelis had in fact known about the Germans for at least seven years, as had the CIA. But the "Affair of the German Scientists" was handy in promoting the nuclear program as the only deterrent against Nasser's missiles.

By March 1963, Sherman Kent, the chairman of the CIA's Board of National Estimates, the supreme body for U.S. intelligence analysis, had concluded that an Israeli bomb would do serious damage to the U.S. position in the Arab world. Kent wrote a memo for the CIA director outlining his misgivings regarding the "Consequences of Israeli Acquisition of Nuclear Capability."

> Even though Israel already enjoys a clear military superiority over its Arab adversaries, singly or combined, acquisition of a nuclear capability would greatly enhance Israel's sense of security . . . Israel's policy toward its neighbors would become more rather than less tough. [Israel would] seek to exploit the psychological advantages of its nuclear capability to intimidate the Arabs and to prevent them from making trouble on the frontiers.

The effect on U.S.-Israeli relations, predicted Kent, would not be good. He saw the Israelis exploiting the obvious Arab reaction, which would be to turn to the Soviets "for assistance against the added Israeli threat." The Israelis, he said, would then pressure the U.S., "arguing that in terms of both strength and reliability Israel was clearly the only worthwhile friend of the U.S. in the area. It would use all the means at its command to persuade the U.S. to acquiesce in, and even to support, its possession of nuclear capability."[15]

Kennedy had dragged his feet on supplying the Hawks promised to Ben-Gurion in 1961, so in April 1963, a month after Kent had submitted his gloomy predictions, Shimon Peres, Ben-Gurion's trusted aide on such matters, arrived in Washington to settle the matter. Meeting with the president in the Oval Office, the Israeli invoked the threat of the Arab Rocket, to which he ascribed vastly inflated capabilities. Kennedy, in turn, pointed out that Israel's nuclear program would more than compensate for whatever missiles Nasser could deploy. Peres then produced the artful formulation that was to remain the official Israeli position on its weapons program: "I can tell you clearly that we will not introduce nuclear weapons into the region; certainly we will not be the first to do so." Since the U.S. had had nuclear weapons in the region as early as 1949, Peres was telling the truth, after a fashion.

Peres's parting line to the president was that he represented a "nation of doves who had come to buy Hawks." After further negotiations on the right of the Americans to inspect parts, but only parts, of Dimona, Peres got agreement for Israel to get its Hawks.

John Hadden, the former CIA Tel Aviv station chief, considers Kennedy to have been the last president to have really tried to do something about the Israeli bomb. In his judgment, "Kennedy really wanted to stop it, and he offered them conventional weapons (i.e., the Hawks) as an inducement. But the Israelis were way ahead of us. They saw that if we were going to offer them arms to go easy on the bomb, once they had it, we were going to send them a lot more, for fear that they would use it."

By 1964, Dimona had put the United States in a difficult position vis-à-vis the Arabs, as Sherman Kent had predicted. The State Department instructed the U.S. ambassador in Cairo to put the best spin possible on the issue. He was told to make an issue of the Arab Rocket, which everyone knew was militarily a nonstarter: "We particularly want you to emphasize mischievous role of UAR [Egyptian] missile program in pushing arms rivalry to new and dangerous levels. We recognize of course [the] thin line between ensuring Nasser understands and appreciates nature of this escalation and on other hand giving him [the] impression Israel [is] about to go nuclear with our understanding and tacit support." The ambassador was instructed to tell Nasser "this is a game he cannot win," thanks to Israel's "outside financial sources."[16]

U.S. scientists visiting Dimona that year said they found no sign of a plant to make bomb-grade weapons material. That did not mean, of course, that Israel was not getting the necessary material, such as enriched uranium, from somewhere else.

When Israeli spy Rafael Eitan arrived in Apollo on his mission for LAKAM in 1968, he was accompanied by the LAKAM station chief, Avraham Hermoni. Hermoni's innocuous title at the Israeli Embassy in Washington was "scientific counselor." Abraham Bendor was also along. Although he billed himself as a visitor from the "Department of Electronics, Israel" he was actually representing Shin Beth, Israel's internal security service. Bendor, like Abraham Shalom, went on to the top post at Shin Beth. He was subsequently forced to resign when it was revealed that he had ordered the killing of two Palestinian prisoners in captivity. (He then went to work for Shaul Eisenberg.)

The purpose of the Apollo trip was "damage assessment" on the progress of the American investigation of NUMEC. The large quantities of enriched uranium had long since vanished. But the FBI was, at the time, in the midst of its surveillance campaign and was more concerned with whether or not Zalman Shapiro was a spy. Not only would the thousands of classified documents at the plant have been a welcome boost to LAKAM's knowledge of nuclear matters, but Shapiro had his clearances and contacts throughout the nuclear industry. At one point Hermoni attended a meeting at Shapiro's home with eleven U.S. scientists. The FBI recorded at the time that Hermoni was "possibly an Israeli intelligence officer." The bureau found that Shapiro traveled throughout the United States, "soliciting advice from scientists who were friendly to the Israelis and who agreed to help solve technical and scientific problems confronting Israel."

Shapiro was also urging Jewish scientists to pick up stakes and move to Dimona. Around the same time, the *Jerusalem Post* described a "Home-to-Dimona" drive for "Israeli physicists working in the United States." The *Post* had reportedly been alerted to this campaign by Abraham Ben Zvi of the "Bureau for Israeli Professionals" in New York. Dr. Shapiro exhibited tireless energy on behalf of the Israeli nuclear program. He would certainly have proved a very attractive agent for his friends in LAKAM.

Shapiro met several times with another Israeli, Jeruham Kafkafi, whom the FBI believed to be an intelligence officer and an associate of LAKAM station chief Hermoni. According to a congressional report on the matter, Shapiro met Kafkafi in June 1969 (the 20th) at Pittsburgh Airport. Kafkafi had flown in from Washington, stayed for an hour, and flown back. The FBI men were taking notes. Shapiro later told investigators that the airport meeting was arranged "to discuss payment of a delinquent bill." The report goes on to say:

> An AEC document suggests the Department of Justice had under consideration a request to the Department of State that Hermoni and Kafkafi be declared persona non grata. The basis for this was presumably the belief that both were engaging in impermissible intelligence gathering activities.

Shapiro told investigators that he never shared classified information with his frequent guests (nor had he arranged to ship them uranium) even though they were spies and Zalman Shapiro was perfectly placed for their needs. In 1969, J. Edgar Hoover recommended that Dr. Shapiro and NUMEC should be barred from receiving any more classified contracts. The only problem with the FBI assessment was that the Atomic Energy Commission's penalty for espionage activities was a place on death row.[17]

Atlantic Richfield bought NUMEC in 1970. Dr. Shapiro was kept on staff for a few months before he was quietly fired. There were no further incidents of missing uranium or breaches of security. When the question arose of whether Shapiro should be allowed to keep his security clearance, the matter went once again to the White House. It crossed the desks of both Kissinger and John Erlichman, the president's Domestic Affairs adviser, and was reviewed by Secretary of State William Rogers. Shapiro wanted access to nuclear weapons data for his new job at Kawecki Berylco, a company in the business of making nuclear weapons components. With the AEC, the Justice Department, and the White House mulling over the wisdom of such a clearance, Shapiro eventually quit his job and landed a "less sensitive position" at Westinghouse. Whether Shapiro's relationship continued with, as an internal congressional report put it, "persons involved in Israel's nuclear weapons program and other Israelis who were up to no good," is not clear. Certainly, without his top-secret security clearance, this man who had received VIP treatment in Israel, even the aerial tour of the Sinai battlefield, was a less valuable friend.

Early in 1976, a group of aerospace executives gathered at the CIA to get a briefing from the agency's top technical analyst, Carl Duckett. He calmly announced that Israel had "ten to twenty" nuclear weapons. This sensational remark naturally found its way into the press. Duckett's boss, then-CIA Director George Bush, was compelled to apologize for the disclosure, calling it "unfortunate." Not long after, Carl Duckett retired, citing reasons of health.[18]

The intense effort on the part of five administrations to keep the lid on public knowledge of Israel's nuclear weapons program, and that ally's espionage inside the United States, strongly suggest that the U.S. was aiding and abetting the effort. It certainly looked that way to the British Labor Party politician Dennis Healey, who was his country's minister of defense from 1964 to 1970. As Healey wrote in his memoirs, "It is still unclear whether the assistance which Israel received from the United States in developing its nuclear weapons programme was obtained with the consent of the authorities in Washington. But they made clear to me at the time that they knew what was happening, whether or not they approved it. This is not the only issue in which America's commitments to Israel have contradicted its broader objectives."

The White House believed the American public had no need to know. The leadership in Jerusalem could not have agreed more. In July 1987, the technician who had worked in the most sensitive facility at the Dimona complex for eight years and had gone public with his story wrote a letter from Ashkelon Prison, where he had landed after Mossad agents kidnapped him in Rome. The letter reflected Mordechai Vanunu's resentment that the Israeli public also had "no need to know." It was in large part why he had risked photographing Machon II in 1985:

> Today the government still does not even admit the existence of nuclear arms in the country. They hint at their existence, yet they refuse to allow international inspection of the Dimona reactor. Because the citizenry here is not informed, people are unable to work in a coordinated way to prevent the disaster which may lie ahead. The danger is that in a future crisis Israel's leaders will be influenced by unreliable information or will mistake a false threat for a real one, and so will trigger off a nuclear holocaust.[19]

Vanunu, who will serve time for at least another decade for his act of treachery, is a strange and complicated man. His family were Sephar-

dic Jews from Morocco who suffered discrimination and forced reloca-
tion at the hands of the Israeli authorities. Although the family wished
to settle in Haifa, they were told under pain of arrest that they must
live in Beersheba, in harsh desert conditions that nearly broke Vanunu's father. The fancy appliances they had bought in France for their
new life in Israel rusted in the sand. Conditions were so crowded and
so primitive that there was no room for such luxuries. The formerly
prosperous shopkeeper was forced to do manual labor. Vanunu grew
up surrounded by despair. His bitterness at the treatment of the
Sephardic community as second-class citizens (a fact that Menachem
Begin had made campaign promises to redress) caused Vanunu to
befriend Israeli Arabs, Israel's "third class." In fact, Vanunu was active
in pro-Palestinian politics for three years before Shin Beth, Israel's
internal security service, realized this might be a problem for a worker
in a top-secret plant. Vanunu actually stood up and called for the
creation of a Palestinian state during a rally where a huge PLO flag,
illegal in Israel, was unfurled.

Vanunu had already taken fifty-seven damning photographs, including a full-scale model of a hydrogen bomb and the "Golda balcony," where Golda Meir had stood to admire the main production
hall, a chemical laboratory for the separation of plutonium to make
nuclear weapons. He had snatched the key to the elevator on Level
5, where the bombs were actually made, from a supervisor who
regularly dropped it on a shelf in an open locker. He photographed
glove boxes, where plutonium disks were machined into spheres and
round copper sheaths to house bombs. What Vanunu saw on Level 5,
known as MM2, left no doubt in his mind that Israel had a good-sized
arsenal.

The stunning lack of security evidenced by this photo spree by a
man who had even flirted with the Israeli Communist Party was
compounded when Vanunu was allowed to leave the Dimona complex,
(he was honorably "laid off"), set sail from Haifa, and soon after spend a
night in Moscow en route to Bangkok. Although Vanunu did not trade
Israel's secrets with the Russians, he certainly could have. Instead, he
wandered rather aimlessly around the world with his two rolls of film,
trying to interest his occasional companions in his unlikely tale. He
bared his soul to one woman, the daughter of a British journalist,
whom he had picked up in Burma. She dropped him. Finally, when
Vanunu landed in the midst of a well-meaning Christian community in

Australia, he fell victim to a Spanish-speaking hustler who happened to be painting the church.

Oscar Guerrero, apparently a seasoned con man, saw in the Vanunu story riches beyond his wildest dreams of avarice. But even when Guerrero rushed over to the Israeli consulate in Sydney thinking that the intelligence officer might pay him for the tip, neither Mossad nor Shin Beth picked up Vanunu. When the intelligence officer Avi Kliman contacted Tel Aviv, the Atomic Energy Commission assured Mossad that a control room technician would pose a minimal threat, as he undoubtedly understood little about the Dimona weapons program. The small matter of the photographs did pique enough interest to warrant a tail of seven agents to watch Vanunu. They followed Vanunu, now a cabdriver, through the streets of Sydney. The seven Mossad men even sat in on St. John's Church workshops.

In fact, Mossad did nothing about Vanunu until he had spent the better part of a month spilling his story to the staff of the London *Sunday Times*. Having promised Mrs. Thatcher that he would not be seized in Britain, Mossad only managed to capture him because the editor of the paper spent so much time mulling over the decision of whether or not to publish. Vanunu nearly went mad with frustration. It took nothing more than a very average Florida-reared blond to fill the "honey trap." "Cindy," a part-time Mossad agent, smiled at Vanunu as he gazed, bored to distraction, at a London shop window. He finally noticed. In fact, "Cindy" had been trying, without success, to catch his eye for days. When this badly made up plant offered Vanunu a free ticket to Rome, he gratefully accepted, in order to escape the tedium of the endless sessions in the offices of the *Sunday Times*.

Once the bait (whose real name was Cheryl Hanin Bentov) had drugged Vanunu and relinquished her catch to seasoned kidnappers, he was spirited off to Tel Aviv. Mossad was duly proud of this successful, if somewhat flawed, operation, and gloated over the obvious failure of Shin Beth to stop Vanunu from boarding a boat in the first place. Shin Beth took its revenge, leaking the story of the kidnapping to the London *Financial Times*.[20]

The Vanunu affair rendered all of the elaborate trappings of security surrounding Dimona superfluous. Yet little changed. As for a public debate on nuclear weapons, none ensued. Israeli politicians still maintained that Israel would not be the first to introduce nuclear weapons into the Middle East. That would have been impossible in any case, as the U.S. had kept nuclear weapons at its Saudi Arabian base, Dhahran, as early as the 1940s, as a convenient launching pad for a nuclear raid on the Soviet Union.

With American nuclear weapons in the region, Israel could never be "first." The oft-repeated litany was a clever deception, but the men in the White House and at the CIA were themselves too deeply involved to challenge the deceivers.

Israel's nuclear weapons stockpile, immune from American criticism, has been the ghost at the feast whenever succeeding administrations have calculated the risks in the Middle East. In 1973, as Egyptian and Syrian tanks crashed through Israeli defenses in the first days of the Yom Kippur War, the White House knew that the covers had come off the nuclear silos in the Negev. American resupply planes began to pour into Israel.

The shadow of the Israeli bomb lengthened over the Middle East, and beyond, as the range of the weapons increased. Early in the Reagan administration, Richard Burt, then director of the Political-Military Affairs Bureau at the State Department, confided to the authors that the government believed the Israelis had targeted the Soviet Union. The Israeli "SIOP," as nuclear targeting plans are known, was thought to include cities such as Odessa in the southern USSR.

As the Bush administration plotted its strategy in the lead-up to the war with Iraq, the Israeli nuclear factor was central to its planning. In the fall of 1990 an urgent call went out from the White House to the CIA: intelligence on the Israeli nuclear stockpile and SIOP was of the utmost priority. Saddam Hussein had his chemical arsenal. If he used it against Tel Aviv, what would the Israelis do in response? Israel's nuclear arsenal hung like a sword of Damocles over the whole affair.

5. Dirty Work on the Mountain

THE SHARED SECRET of the Israeli bomb was to provide a bond, all the tighter for being inadmissible, between the two countries down through the years. But as successive White Houses and the CIA pondered the lengthening shadow of Dimona, they also knew that Israel was doing good service in the Cold War struggle across the Third World.

Allen Dulles had told Wilbur Eveland in 1958 that Israeli intelligence was now the only ally against the Soviets in the Middle East on which the CIA could count, a notion which Eveland thought was akin to "depending on a fox to guard the henhouse."[1]

In July 1958 Dwight Eisenhower dispatched fourteen thousand marines to Beirut. This massive intervention, the largest U.S. military expedition to the Middle East until the 1991 war with Iraq, had in fact been partly caused by Eveland himself. In May of that year a civil war had broken out in Lebanon in response to the blatant rigging of the country's elections by the CIA, with Eveland himself delivering the cash. The troubles had soon spread into neighboring Jordan, with the possibility that King Hussein would be deposed by his angry subjects. Hussein was the cousin of King Faisal of Iraq, who decided to help his relative in Amman by dispatching an armored brigade across the border to lend assistance. The commander of this rescue force, however, Colonel Abdul Qarim Qassim, opted instead to storm the royal palace in Baghdad, physically eliminate Faisal and his ministers, and declare a republic loyal to Nasser. The day following the Iraqi coup Eisenhower, fearful that Lebanon would now go the way of Iraq, gave the order to land the troops. (Due to a lack of proper field sanitation, most of the force camped on the Beirut beach was incapacitated by dysentery within two weeks, but this did not affect events.)

"'We are in historic times," Ben-Gurion noted in his diary four days after the marines arrived, "and this opportunity will not repeat itself."[2] He had just heard that the Turks, unsettled by tumultuous events in the region, had asked for closer relations with Israel.

Three days later, on July 24, 1958, Ben-Gurion sent a personal letter to Eisenhower expressing grave concern for the future of Jordan, Lebanon, and Saudi Arabia. These were in danger of falling into the hands of Nasser, as were Libya and even Iran. "With the purpose of erecting a high dam against the Nasserist-Soviet tidal wave," he wrote, "we have begun tightening our links with several states on the outside perimeter of the Middle East . . . Our goal is to organise a group of countries, not necessarily an official alliance, that will be able to stand strong against Soviet expansion by proxy through Nasser."[3]

What Ben-Gurion had in mind was a "peripheral" strategy. The notion was a simple one. The Arab countries surrounding Israel would remain enemies. On the periphery of the Arab world, however, were countries that had no direct quarrel with Israel, had reason to fear Communist subversion, and were staunch allies of the U.S. The potential allies he had in mind were the Turks and the Iranians, who were ideally placed to box in Iraq and Syria, as well as the ancient empire of Ethiopia, bordering the Arab territories in Africa.[4]

It seems that Eisenhower and Foster Dulles reacted warmly to the Israeli initiative and informed Turkey, Iran, and Ethiopia that the idea had their endorsement.

As so often in Israeli diplomacy, it was the spooks who led the way, with the arms salesmen following not far behind.

Isser Harel, with characteristic immodesty, takes full credit for the idea of a peripheral alliance, although other Israeli sources give credit for the original notion to the eclectic Reuven Shiloah. "My purpose," he declares, "was to create a dam to stop the Nasser-Soviet flood . . .

For this reason I invested great effort in helping these countries organize for themselves effective intelligence and security services, as well as military and police striking forces, which would be able to withstand any sudden attempt of revolution . . . The countries which we helped in this manner came to have full trust in us and our intentions, and we did everything to justify this trust."

A secret CIA review of Israeli intelligence written in 1976, and declassified by the Iranian students who occupied the U.S. Embassy in Tehran three years later, notes, "A formal trilateral liaison called the Trident Organization was established by Mossad with Turkey's National Security Service (TNSS) and Iran's National Organization for Intelligence and Security (SAVAK) in late 1958 . . . The Trident Organization involves continuing intelligence exchange plus semiannual meetings at the chief of service level."[5]

This dry little history, though informative about some interesting facets of Israeli intelligence—"The Israelis select their agents almost exclusively from persons of Jewish origin"—is reticent on the subject of its relationship with the CIA. Thus there is no mention of the fact that arrangements such as Trident formed part of a larger pattern in which the Mossad, for money, worked on behalf of the CIA throughout the Third World. If there were countries where the CIA found it hard to gain access, or particular activities that the agency preferred to leave to someone else, the Mossad could take on the job, to the benefit of all. The CIA's internal code name for this operation was KK Mountain.

The CIA was and is in the habit of handing out "subsidies" to friendly foreigners. The Gehlen organization was financed in this way. King Hussein of Jordan was on the payroll from 1957 to 1977, to the tune of several hundred thousand dollars a year. In those cases, however, the subventions, or bribes, were paid out of the budget of the relevant subdivision of the clandestine services. King Hussein, for example, got his money through the CIA's Near East Division.

KK Mountain was different. The Israelis got their money straight from the top. In addition to the normal agency operating budget, the CIA director had his own special contingency fund, money that could be released on his signature alone. "It was basically money under the mattress," one former high-ranking official recalls. "It would normally only be called on for some super-secret one off operation where you needed a lot of money fast. KK Mountain was the exception. Year after year that money would be in the fund for Israel. You have to remember that the relationship wasn't as open as it is now. Paying the Israelis to do operations for us was a very sensitive subject."

According to cognizant former officials, KK Mountain had a budget of between $10 million and $20 million a year during the 1960s. "That was quite a big item," remembers one. "The whole agency budget was only $650 million at the end of the 1960s, and we were fighting a war in Southeast Asia at the time. Of course the Israelis were making extra money on the deal, too, above and beyond what they got from the fund. To get the total figure you would have to include whatever money was generated by proprietaries [commercial companies, possibly profitable, secretly owned by an intelligence agency], which could have been a whole lot more."

One such example of a U.S. subsidy for Israel was the way in which the "Reynolds Construction Company" garnered multimillion dollar contracts to build secret communications intelligence facilities in Iran and Turkey, as well as five airfields in Ethiopia. The contracts had originally been awarded to the CIA-backed Vinnell Corporation, but had then been switched and given to Reynolds. Reynolds was in fact secretly owned by the Israeli Labor Party through its trade union organization Histadrut. In order to qualify legally for U.S.-taxpayer-funded projects such as these, the Israelis had bought the charter of the defunct Reynolds Ball Point Pen Corporation and submitted the bids under that name. The legal work required was performed by Clark Clifford, who had done yeoman service on behalf of Israel as a political aide to Truman.[6]

Turkey, a non-Arab Moslem country in the good graces of the Americans, was an important catch for the Israeli "peripheral" strategy. Iran, however, as a non-Arab, oil-rich Moslem country regarded by the Americans as a key asset, fit even more perfectly into the scheme.

Israeli agents had been at work encouraging friendly forces in Iran since the early days of the state. In June 1950, for example, Iran had recognized Israel "de facto" (a diplomatic concept meaning something just short of full relations).

This act of friendship from the land of Cyrus the Great, who had freed the ancient Jews from Babylonian captivity, was the subject of much sentimental commentary in later years. The real reason for the recognition was more prosaic. The prime minister at the time was called Muhammed Saed. Like many political leaders the world over,

Saed had his "silent" partner to handle the business side of a states-man's affairs. This partner, a merchant in the bazaar, was approached by an American, who is referred to in the Israeli state archives only as "Adam." Acting on behalf of the Israelis, Adam wanted to know what it would take for Iran to recognize Israel. Saed's answer was short and to the point: $400,000.

This was an enormous sum for Israel at that time, and for a while the cabinet in Jerusalem balked at the price. Some purer souls in the Israeli Foreign Office protested the use of corrupt means to extend Israel's influence. Adam, however, proceeded on his own initiative and handed over a down payment of $12,400 to the prime minister's bagman. Saed kept the bargain. He immediately began to talk to the powerful religious leaders about the need to distinguish between global politics and religion. He then restocked the cabinet to ensure complaisance and obtained the Shah's authorization. The Israelis, moral qualms subdued, duly found the rest of the $400,000, and a thirty-year relationship began.[7]

However much the wheels of diplomacy might have been greased, the connection between the Shah's Iran and Israel rested on firm foundations. The two countries shared a suspicion and dislike of the Arab nations on their borders. Both had strong connections to the United States, in particular the CIA. Each had something to offer that the other needed. In Iran's case it was oil, which it began to ship to Israel in 1954. Israel, for its part, could offer valuable expertise in the fields of intelligence, defense, and domestic security.

In the eyes of the Shah, Israel had something even more valuable to bestow on its friends: the pervasive influence of the Jews in the United States and indeed the world over. David Kimche recalls with amuse-ment how "if there'd be any anti-Iranian article in any newspaper in the United States or even in Europe, the Shah would call us and say, 'Why did you allow this to happen?' We would in vain plead inno-cence, saying that we don't control the whole of world media, we don't control the banks as some people think we do." Chaim Herzog, now president of Israel, who had many dealings with the Iranian monarch while head of Military Intelligence, later said that His Majesty saw every Israeli as a link to Washington.

For the Iranian regime, the U.S. was the indispensable ally. The CIA (with considerable help from the British) had ousted the national

Mossadegh government in 1953 and put the Shah back on his throne. Following the success of the coup, the U.S. rewarded its client with a copious flow of economic and military aid. In return the U.S. had not only the benefit of a loyally anti-Communist ally between the southern border of the USSR and the Persian Gulf, but also a regime disinclined to challenge Western oil interests in the country.

Iran's role in American strategy came into sharper focus as a result of the readjustments that followed Suez. The Eisenhower Doctrine obviously put a premium on the stability of the Shah's rule as a bulwark against Russia. The leftist coup in Iraq in 1958, which substituted a pro-Soviet government for one that had been slavishly pro-British, naturally increased the importance of Tehran for Washington.

Part of the American aid went toward making sure that the Shah had an efficient secret police apparatus. In 1957 the CIA oversaw the creation of SAVAK, the Farsi acronym for the Intelligence and Security Organization of the Country. This organization was divided into a number of sections. The Second Department dealt with foreign intelligence collection, the Seventh was concerned with foreign intelligence analysis, and the Eighth was assigned the task of counter-intelligence.

It was the Third Department, whose task was internal security, which was to make SAVAK a byword for savagery and repression, and it was here that the CIA found a useful outlet for Israel's skills. Although Mossadegh and his National Front movement had been vanquished by the CIA coup plotters (with the ubiquitous Kermit Roosevelt at the helm), the Iranian Communist Party was still considered a significant force. The party, known as Tudeh, was crippled by mass arrests and executions in the mid-fifties. Although it operated mainly in exile until the late 1970s, the Shah and his American sponsors remained convinced that the Tudeh was a serious threat, justifying the most stringent measures by the internal security service.

CIA officials are always at pains to deny that they encouraged torture or other unpleasantness by SAVAK. If the Iranians required any expert tuition in that area, they suggest, the input came from the Israelis. It was the Israelis, so the agency story goes, who worked with SAVAK on "the hard stuff."[8]

The initial contacts between SAVAK and Mossad appear to have been established in the fall of 1957, when Isser Harel met in Rome with General Taimour Bakhtiar, the first chief of SAVAK. The two secret police chiefs reportedly reached full agreement on the dangers posed by both Nasser and the Soviets.

The arrangement was good for Israel. It was also good for Israelis, specifically those entrepreneurs who were ready to take advantage of the opportunities offered by Israel's strategic role in the Cold War. Yacov Nimrodi, a corpulent multimillionaire who now lives in a replica of the White House in the Tel Aviv suburb of Savion, was one who turned the Iranian connection very much to his advantage.

Nimrodi was born in Jerusalem in 1927 to a family that had emigrated from the Kurdish area of Iraq. At an early age he was recruited into Shai, the pre-independence intelligence service, by a senior official named Yitzhak Navon, who went on to become Ben-Gurion's private secretary and later president of Israel. Nimrodi was useful to the Eastern Europeans who dominated the Haganah and Shai, because he spoke Arabic. During the War of Independence he was put to work collecting intelligence on the Jordanians, and from there he graduated to the Military Intelligence service once the Israeli state was set up. In the early 1950s, while attached to the Southern Command of the IDF, he met and befriended a rising young army commander named Ariel Sharon.

The turning point in the young major's life came in 1955 when he was posted to Tehran, where he was to spend most of the next thirteen years. "When one day we shall be permitted to talk about all that we have done in Iran, you will be horrified," he told an Israeli journalist later. "It is beyond your imagination."[9] Sharon once described Nimrodi as the "architect of relations with far-reaching economic and political implications, including the Kurdish rebellion against Iraq."

Israeli intelligence operators had taken an interest in the Kurds ever since Reuven Shiloah had reconnoitered their remote mountain homeland in the 1930s. Spread across Iraq, Iran, Turkey, and the Soviet Union, several million Kurds lived in northern Iraq, a region that happens to contain the country's richest oilfields. The only time in modern memory they have enjoyed a semblance of autonomy was at the end of World War II, when the USSR granted them limited self-government in areas controlled by its troops. The Soviet retreat in that part of the world in 1946, however, left them bereft of support, and not for the last time.

In 1961 the Kurds began an armed revolt against Iraqi rule. They faced more formidable obstacles than most movements of national liberation, because their land is not only completely landlocked but is surrounded by countries with their own Kurdish minorities. Therefore a Kurdish success in Iraq would have posed awkward problems in Iran, Turkey, Syria, and the Soviet Union.

Nevertheless, the Shah was so perturbed by the threat of a militant Iraq next door that he agreed with the Israelis that sponsorship of a Kurdish insurgency in Iraq would cause the Baghdad regime problems that Iran and Israel might find useful. David Kimche recalls a trip he made to Kurdistan in 1965 as being the first time that an Israeli envoy actually visited the Kurds at home. The following year an Israeli cabinet minister trekked over the mountains on a mule. The envoy, Aryeh Eliav, later wrote of his romantic expedition to bring a field hospital to Israel's grateful clients. In addition to these high-level visitors from afar, Yacov Nimrodi was coordinating matters with his opposite numbers in SAVAK and the Iranian military.

The bulk of Israel's aid to these guerrillas was in the form of military advice and training. In June 1967, just before the outbreak of the Six Day War, an Iraqi military delegation asked for a cease-fire in order that the Zionist enemy should be presented with a united front. A "guerrilla" on the Kurdish side spoke up and denounced the notion. He was, in fact, one of the Israeli advisers.

Operational details of the Kurdish operation are still rigidly censored in Israel, and probably with good reason. The Shah certainly had no interest in the Kurds actually being successful, and it seems unlikely that Israeli sentiments were any less cynical.

The U.S. had always approved this effort at Iraqi destabilization. In the early 1970s, however, it appeared that the Kurds, who had some notable military successes, might be on the point of reaching some accommodation with Baghdad. At a meeting in Tehran in 1972, President Nixon and Henry Kissinger agreed with the Shah that the Kurds must be kept fighting. The CIA was ordered to get directly involved.

The point of the CIA support to the Kurdish operation, some $16 million worth over the next three years (the Shah was spending a great deal more), was to convince the insurgents that the U.S. would not let the Shah abandon them. On the American side the whole operation was cloaked in the deepest secrecy, mainly to keep the operation from reaching the ears of the State Department, which had consistently opposed any such venture. A CIA memo from March 1974 stated: "We would think that [the Shah] would not look with favor on the establish-ment of a formalized [Kurdish] autonomous government. [The Shah] like ourselves, has seen benefit in a stalemate situation . . . in which [Iraq] is intrinsically weakened by [the Kurdish movement's] refusal to relinquish its semi-autonomy. Neither [the Shah] nor ourselves wish to see the matter resolved one way or the other." As the censored report by the Pike Committee on U.S. Intelligence observes: "Even in the context of covert action, ours was a cynical enterprise."

In March 1975, the Shah made a deal with Saddam Hussein and immediately closed the border to the Kurds. Despite the romantic memories of Kimche, Eliav, and Nimrodi, the Kurds were abandoned forthwith by their foreign sponsors. (The Kurdish leader's wedding present to Nancy Kissinger of a gold-and-pearl necklace apparently stirred no chord within Henry, who remarked apropos of the betrayal of the Kurds that "covert action should not be confused with mission-ary work.")[10]

Nimrodi, meanwhile, while not ministering to the Kurds, was en-joying himself. In later life he referred to his thirteen years in Tehran as his "happiest hour." He was a new kind of Israeli envoy, not lurking in the shadows, but broadcasting his power and access to the mighty, even though Iran and Israel still did not enjoy full diplomatic relations. Israeli visitors were astonished and impressed to see Iranian generals waiting patiently in the corridors of his office for a brief meeting to ask him to intercede on their behalf with the chief of staff, or even with the Shah. Because of the semicovert nature of relations between the two countries, Nimrodi was meant to keep a low profile, something he found hard to do. On one occasion he printed visiting cards grandly inscribed "Israeli Military Attaché," which caused something of an upset when a specimen fell into the hands of the Egyptian military attaché. Fortunately for the round-faced colonel, the Iranian minister of defense issued a barefaced denial that the Israelis had any such representation in Iran.

Colonels in the IDF were not handsomely paid in those days. Nev-ertheless, an array of visiting Israeli dignitaries, including various chiefs of staff and prime ministers, were happy to enjoy Nimrodi's lavish hospitality, without raising awkward questions. He was also careful not to neglect more junior officers visiting from home who might be in a position to return favors later on. A less than flattering profile that appeared in the Israeli newspaper *Davar* in 1985 mentioned rumors of bribes and gifts. "Nimrodi denied it all and maybe these were only rumors which were spread by those who were envious of him. But we should mention that the man who replaced Nimrodi was removed from office after a few months under unpleasant circumstances and he claimed in his defense that what he did was done 'because that was the custom.'"

Nimrodi left Tehran in 1968. He had his heart set on becoming the military commander of the newly conquered West Bank, and he later claimed that he had been promised the job. When the appointment failed to materialize, however, he announced that "they are forcing me to become a millionaire," resigned from the army, and headed back to Tehran. He was now ready to turn the contacts and influence he had cultivated in his years of government service to his own account. In the decade before the Iranian revolution he became known as the indispensable master fixer for Israeli business in Iran. The leading Israeli military-industrial enterprises of the 1950s—Israel Aircraft Industries, Soltam (artillery and mortars), Israel Military Industries, Tadiran (electronics)—all found they had to pay Nimrodi a fat commission in order to do business. In addition to taking his percentage, Nimrodi set up a business marketing water-desalinization plants to the Iranian military and other agencies of state. One of them was for the Shah's private resort island of Kish, in the Persian Gulf, which later became a symbol of the regime's corruption.

As the years went by and the Shah's military ambitions grew ever greater, Israeli ambitions for the partnership kept pace. In the spring of 1977 Shimon Peres, who was at the time the minister of defense, signed an agreement for Iranian cooperation with Israel's ballistic nuclear missile program—"Project Flower." Iran would finance the project by supplying Israel with $1 billion worth of oil and would also provide a special airport, an assembly plant, and the site for a long-range test. In return, the Shah hoped that he would enjoy the fruits of Israel's weapons development.[11] When the Iranian revolution swept away Project Flower and the rest of the world that had made Nimrodi rich, he complained that he had lost $6 million. However, Nimrodi, like the Americans, was not finished in Iran.

In Ben-Gurion's original letter to Eisenhower proposing the "peripheral" alliance, he had specifically stated, "We have made contact with and have developed relations of mutual trust with . . . the Ethiopian Emperor." These relations, in fact, went back to the days of the covert airlift from Czechoslovakia. When the first arms deal was negotiated in Prague at the beginning of 1948, both parties wished to conceal the identity of the buyer, so the Israelis signed the deal as representatives of Ethiopia. Relations with the venerable emperor, Haile Selassie, remained warm thereafter. Staunchly anti-Communist, the feudal monarchy was an ideal spot for monitoring activities in the adjacent Arab Sudan, as well as along the Red Sea and in the former European colonies that began to achieve independence in the late 1950s in Africa.

In keeping with Isser Harel's desire to impart Israeli expertise in internal security, his advisers trained a highly efficient secret police for the emperor. When a coup threatened in 1960, a despairing call was heard from the palace: "Send for the Israelis." General Matityahu Peled, once a hawkish member of the General Staff who later became an outspoken dove, recalls that this Israeli assistance saved the emperor from coups no less than three times, though of course they ultimately failed in 1974, when he was overthrown.

In the days before it became a byword for starving refugees, Ethiopia was an exporter of beef. One of the more successful companies in this business was a Mossad-owned concern called Incoda. One of its directors later recalled, "Incoda was a station for Israeli intelligence in Africa. We had a huge arms cache . . . We were only a cover in Mossad deals. When they had to send someone to an Arab country, they did it through us . . . We transmitted mail to spies in Arab countries in our ships."[12]

Even after the Marxist military coup that displaced Haile Selassie in 1974, the Ethiopian connection was preserved. Among other reasons of state, the new regime was happy to use Israel as a conduit for communications with the United States. As late as 1990 the relationship was still warm enough for Israel to be shipping cluster bombs to the regime in Addis Ababa for use on separatist rebels. This caused some unhappiness with the U.S. State Department, which protested the traffic. However, such unhappiness was smoothed over in the preparations for war with Iraq. The Ethiopian government supported the U.S. position in the UN Security Council, and Washington blessed Israeli shipments of lethal military aid.[13]

It was, however, in the new countries of black Africa that KK Mountain really came into its own. David Kimche, the Mossad executive whose involvement with Africa goes back to those early days, becomes positively lyrical when discussing the natural affinity between Israel and the black rulers: "When they come to Paris or London or Washington or Bonn, it's for them like going to a different planet. These countries [are] wealthy; they've existed for hundreds of years. Here, they come to Tiberias and they smell the smells of the overripe melons and they see the market and they feel the heat . . . This means something to them."

It is indeed true that Israel was ready and equipped to advise countries struggling to develop their economies after years of colonialism. In that halcyon period Israeli agricultural advisers, irrigation experts, and other harbingers of benign aid poured into the continent, eager to pass on the expertise that had made the desert bloom.

Unfortunately, there was another agenda to hand. The independence of black Africa, released from the tight grip of the old European colonial powers, raised the possibility that the continent might slip into the hands of the Soviet Bloc. Although the United States had not had colonies in Africa, it was tarred with the brush of its European allies who had.

"The opposition [the Soviets] did a very good job of spreading the word that we were just the same as the colonialists," explains one former CIA official much involved with African covert affairs. "We needed help." Fortunately, help was available in the form of the Israelis, ready to act as surrogates in combating Soviet penetration.

"We knew very well how to talk to the black people," is Isser Harel's succinct summation of Israel's African entree. "The Europeans left Africa and the gate was open for everyone to enter. White people weren't able to get in, except for us. We managed it because they didn't suspect that we would be imperialistic. We were the only ones at that time to have a foothold there."

In other words, Israel was ideally placed to provide intelligence on Africa to the CIA and others. As Harel explained the arrangement, liaison with the CIA on this matter was part of the ongoing "connection" with the agency. The Europeans got less in the way of Israeli intelligence regarding Africa, "and they had to pay." (The Americans were, of course, paying through the nose with their annual subvention to Mossad for KK Mountain, but Harel does not like to discuss the fee, insisting that it was all done for love of "the American people.")

The value of Israel's penetration of black Africa was enhanced by the changing focus of its involvement. Despite Kimche's romantic memories of the smell of overripe melons, the focus of Israeli relations with the African states changed fairly early on. General Peled recalls, "At first the idea was to sell constructive know-how—to send instructors in agriculture, in fishery, in industries—but eventually all these governments showed much more interest in arms and the training of military units and establishing internal security machineries. Israel was very happy to change its role, and rather than send instructors in agriculture and fisheries they started sending experts in internal security, intelligence services."

The extent of Israeli interest in Africa in the mid-1960s can best be gauged from the record left by an influential IDF officer who toured some of his country's newfound allies in 1965 and 1966. Israel Lior was the military secretary to Prime Minister Levi Eshkol. The purpose of the earlier trip, on which Lior was accompanied by Avraham Tamir, the then adjutant general of the IDF (and whom we shall meet again), was to check up on the local IDF contingents in the various countries, and to see how to cultivate even closer relations with the black armies. As Lior later remarked, "The Israeli military and civil aid to the African countries was then at its height. In almost every one of the countries there were Israelis aiding the military and civil systems."[14]

When they reached Uganda, then a relatively prosperous former British colony ruled by President Milton Obote, they were welcomed by the Israeli ambassador, Uri Lubrani. Lubrani was no ordinary diplomat, having served as a close adviser on Arab affairs in Ben-Gurion's office. Later on he became ambassador to Ethiopia, ambassador to Iran, and in the late 1980s, "Coordinator for Lebanon."

Lubrani explained to his distinguished visitors that they had an important appointment with the assistant chief of staff, Idi Amin. The ambassador was frank about Amin's idiosyncracies, such as a lack of concentration and an inability to turn up on time. Lior, who seems to have been something of a stuffed shirt, was puzzled: "I was quite surprised. I did not understand why it was necessary to see him if this was indeed the case." Lubrani and Baruch Bar Lev, the head of the military delegation, explained all: Amin was " 'our man,' or if he was not yet 'our man,' he would be." The eventual meeting with Amin (who turned up late) left Lior with "ambivalent feelings about Africa, and more so about the Africans."

The following year Lior was back on the dark continent, this time in the company of his boss, Prime Minister Eshkol. There was great competition among the various military missions and embassies as to the honors the host governments would pay their distinguished guest. Bar Lev, the military representative in Uganda, wrote to say that Idi Amin was now chief of staff and preparing a lavish military ceremony for the arrival at the airport, and that an "entire regiment had received new uniforms for this purpose." Bar Lev also boasted that there would be tribal dancers and bands on hand.

The trip started well. In Senegal the head of state promised to do his best to work for peace between Israel and the Arabs and said that he expected to pay an official visit to Israel in the near future. In the Ivory Coast there was a satisfactorily impressive guard of honor at the airport, as well as the president. Eshkol, an astute politician but more used to the smoke-filled rooms of Mapai party intrigues, was not unmoved by the experience of the motorcade into town, in which he and his host were raucously cheered by tens of thousands of the local citizenry. "Even a PM is only made of flesh and blood," recorded Lior primly. Lior was disconcerted to discover that the people of the Ivory Coast considered the most impressive example of Israeli aid to be a luxury hotel built by a local Jewish family in Abidjan. Eshkol was required to open the hotel officially, which Lior thought to be somewhat beneath his boss's dignity.

When they got to Zaire they were presented with an awkward question of protocol. It seemed that Mobutu had just hanged four of his ministers, and Eshkol was concerned that he might appear to be endorsing the action. These qualms were speedily overcome, however, and the visit went ahead. A high point of the tour was an excursion to the parachute training school, run by Israelis, where Eshkol was received, as Lior noted, "with great affection, and enjoyed watching the exercises of the parachuting girls, aged fifteen and above." Lior, straitlaced as ever, considered the skydiving nymphets a waste of time and money. "I asked why Mobutu wanted parachuting girls and received an answer which did not delight me at all." It seemed that the girls were to be a star turn in the upcoming independence day parade. "Bread and circuses for the citizens," he records scornfully.

It was very well for Lior to sneer at Mobutu and the girls, but parachute training had helped cement the Zaire-Israeli relationship. One may recall that Zaire—or the Congo, as it used to be known—was a matter of grave concern in Washington in 1960. The White House was so alarmed by purported leftist tendencies in the country's first and last freely elected leader, Patrice Lumumba, that the CIA was ordered to kill him. Lumumba met his end soon afterwards at the hands (and boots) of disaffected rebel soldiers, before the local CIA station had had a chance to use the deadly poison dispatched posthaste from headquarters.

Lumumba's successor, President Joseph Kasavubu, was much more to the liking of Washington. Apart from his genial attitude toward Western interests in his country, he was well disposed toward Israel and paid a state visit there in 1963. That same year Israeli military experts were dispatched to Zaire to help set up a palace guard while about two hundred and fifty Congolese soldiers arrived in Israel. Accompanying them was the army commander, General Joseph Mobutu. Mobutu has been proud to wear the Israeli paratrooper's wings that he was awarded on that visit.

Mobutu already had a close Israeli friend, a Mossad agent named Meir Meyouhas. An Egyptian Jew, he first came to public attention as one of the Israeli agents ordered to firebomb American and British installations in Egypt in what later became known as the "Lavon Affair." Meyouhas's role in the operation may have been less than heroic. One source claims that a "Meir M." was to set up an explosives plant for the network, to which end he was given the equivalent of $1,500. No explosives appeared, and when his case officer demanded the money back the agent refused and indicated that if they continued to badger him they "would have reasons to fear" him.

Although arrested with the rest of the ring, Meyouhas got off with a relatively light sentence and was released in 1960. In no way ready for a quiet life after his experiences, he set off for the newly independent Congo, where he met and befriended Mobutu, who had risen rapidly from his rank of sergeant under the Belgians to the command of the army.

For at least the next thirty-five years, Meyouhas remained close to his influential friend. Once the general had seized power for himself in 1964 (assisted by the CIA) and changed his name to Mobutu Sese Seko, he proceeded to amass one of the world's larger private fortunes. Meyouhas's wealth increased in proportion, and in the 1980s he was still going strong. In the words of one Israeli commentator, he "will surely be remembered as one of Israel's most effective emissaries ever."[15]

If Lior had felt offended by the sort of people with whom Israel was allying itself in Zaire, his disapproval only deepened when the prime ministerial party arrived in Uganda, the last stop on the 1966 tour. Lior's least-favorite African dignitary, Idi Amin, was on hand.

At the end of a festive state dinner, complete with the obligatory tribal dancers, it came time for the presentation of gifts. The present selected by the Israelis for the newly promoted chief of staff was an Uzi submachine gun. In Lior's vivid recollection, "Idi Amin . . . took the Uzi in his hands and shouted wildly with joy. He was uncontrollable in those moments. His savage leaps and roars shocked me . . . I was even sorrier we had given him an Uzi machine gun; he seemed capable of anything . . . The next day we visited the local botanical park. I was told that most of the Tarzan movies had been shot in this park, and it seemed to me that this should have been Idi Amin's natural habitat."

Israel was not the only country that considered Idi Amin "our man." The British, who had launched his military career as a sergeant major in the King's African Rifles, considered him "intensely loyal to Britain," though "a little short on the gray matter." They had valued his services during the brutal suppression of the Mau Mau nationalist rising in Kenya in the 1950s, where his diligent efforts on behalf of his colonial masters earned him the nickname of "The Strangler."

By the end of the 1960s President Obote was arousing increasing irritation in London and Washington. It is unlikely that he was losing favor because of his repressive treatment of his own people, but rather because he had started to nationalize Western-owned companies and was taking the lead in African protests against warm Western relations with South Africa.

The Israelis had no desire to see Uganda drift to the left. In particular, they were worried for the future of their protege. Much of Amin's own Kakwa tribe lived over the border in the southern Sudan. From the late sixties on the Israelis sponsored a secessionist movement called the Anya-Nya in this region against the Moslem Arab government in Khartoum. This effort was coordinated, according to Israeli sources, with the CIA. As with the Kurds, it was a tactical employment of the peripheral strategy to weaken and destabilize an unfriendly Arab government.

In February 1971, Amin grew worried that Obote was about to dismiss him. He was encouraged to take preemptive action both by agents of the British MI-6 intelligence agency and by the Israelis. Colonel Baruch Bar Lev, the Israeli military attaché, has recounted how Amin told him that he thought that Obote loyalists might capture him before he could take Kampala. Bar Lev counseled him with sage advice on the necessity of moving up troops from his own tribe as well as from the tank corps, which was equipped with surplus American tanks bought from the Israelis the year before.

Meanwhile the British, whose agents were operating under the cover of aiding the Anya-Nya, moved seven hundred troops to neighboring Kenya, to be used, according to a report at the time, "if trouble for Britain and British interests starts."

The coup was a great success and Amin installed himself as president. Initially his sponsors were well pleased. Amin endorsed the principle of selling arms to South Africa, denationalized Western companies taken over by Obote, and welcomed an increased Israeli military presence in his country.

For master arms salesman Shapik Shapiro, this was a halcyon period. "We did a landslide business with Uganda," he recalls with happy nostalgia.

There have been many massacres both around the world and in Uganda itself since the departure of Idi Amin, so it is worth recollecting just who it was that the Americans, the British, and the Israelis were so enthusiastically sponsoring. Soon after he took power, for example, Amin carried out a purge of potentially disloyal elements in the army, killing hundreds of soldiers. Two Americans who attempted to investigate the massacre, free-lance journalist Nicholas Stroh and a sociology professor named Robert Seidele, were murdered by Amin's men. This did not apparently trouble the CIA, which preserved a friendly relationship with Amin for another year after the killings. Over the course of his rule, from 1971 to 1979, Amin is estimated to have killed up to three hundred thousand of his countrymen. Among other personal foibles, he is reported to have had the habit of eating portions of his victims' livers after he had killed them.

A year after the Israelis had helped steer Amin through his seizure of power, the honeymoon with "our man" was over. Amin nurtured dreams of an invasion of Tanzania, where his old enemy Obote had found shelter. To that end, he asked the Israelis to get the Americans to sell him Phantom jet fighters and other sophisticated equipment. The Israelis felt unable to oblige and were summarily expelled. However, the departure of the Israeli military delegation from Kampala by no means brought KK Mountain to an end in Uganda.[16]

One subsequent aspect of Israel's involvement in Uganda is very famous and inspired numerous books and movies: the so-called Miracle at Entebbe. In 1976 a Palestinian group hijacked an Air France jet with a large number of Jewish passengers on board to Entebbe Airport, outside Kampala. After considerable bickering inside the cabinet, the government of Israel authorized a military operation to free the hostages. For advice on the rescue operation, Shimon Peres, minister of defense at the time, was able to turn to Baruch Bar Lev; Yosef Soen, who had run the air force mission in the happy days of the Ugandan-Israeli alliance; and Moshe Bedichi, who had been Amin's personal pilot. Their intimate knowledge both of their old friend and the physical layout at Entebbe proved invaluable to the operation. Once the hostages had been successfully rescued and were in the air back to Israel, Bar Lev placed a call to his old friend in Kampala, giving him the first news of what had happened.[17]

No less important for the success of the mission, however, had been a British agent named Bruce Mackenzie, a close adviser to Kenyan President Jomo Kenyatta. The entire operation depended on the Israeli planes being able to refuel in Kenya, and Mackenzie secured the requisite permissions. Mackenzie was at the time engaged in a profitable trade in military communications equipment with Amin. A British writer on intelligence, Chapman Pincher, reported that he had met senior officials from Mossad, MI-6, the CIA, and even SAVAK in Mackenzie's home. There could be no better illustration of the usefulness, to Israel at least, of the covert relationship.

Mackenzie died when his plane was blown apart by a bomb (reportedly sponsored by a vengeful Amin) not long after the hostage rescue, but the trade in British electronics went on, as did the CIA-Mossad involvement in Ugandan affairs. At a time when Amin was becoming internationally notorious for the savagery and repression of his regime, the dictator continued to enjoy favors from the partners in KK Mountain.

The CIA trained Amin's thugs at the notorious International Police Academy "school for torture" opposite the end of Key Bridge in Georgetown, while other Ugandans were brought to the U.S. for training on the security equipment, including twelve police helicopters, sold to Amin by American firms.

Thanks to a deal between American business and Amin that fortuitously attracted the attention of the Securities and Exchange Commission, we have an insight into one particular CIA-Mossad operation in Uganda and Libya. The known details of the operation throw a vivid light on KK Mountain in action.

The story begins with the friendship that developed between Idi Amin and Muammar Qaddafi after Amin's Israeli alliance came to an end. Amin would frequently visit the Libyan leader and indeed accept lifts from him on his personal Grumman Gulfstream II jet.

One day in 1975, while the two leaders were aloft in the Grumman, Amin expressed his appreciation of the plane's amenities and said how much he would like one of his own. The conversation might have gone unremarked had it not been for the very peculiar nature of the plane in question.

Qaddafi had bought his jet from a Swiss company called Zimex Aviation. Zimex's ostensible business was the provision of aircraft and crews to various world leaders, particularly those of Arab countries. This was profitable for the company's president, Hans Ziegler. It was also good for Israel, because Ziegler was a Mossad agent and Zimex, in the words of one cognizant U.S. official at the time, was "one of the most ingenious and valuable operations by any intelligence agency in the last two decades."

Qaddafi's plane was crewed by Mossad operatives, and it was wired for sound, thus making the Israelis privy to the colonel's more intimate airborne excursions and conversations. So Amin's wish for a plane of his own swiftly became known to Herr Ziegler.

Ziegler took the news of Amin's interest to an American corporation known as Page Airways. The chairman and cofounder of Page was an Irish Bostonian named James Wilmot, who had built a large part of his extensive fortune through lucrative federal contracts. Page Airways, founded in 1939, had prospered from a federal civilian-pilot training program, while Wilmot's other main interest, a construction company named Wilmorite, specialized in large federal construction contracts. Both Page and Wilmorite received over $100 million worth of business from the U.S. military services and the CIA.

As is not unusual in the federal contracting business, Wilmot took an intense interest in the financing of political campaigns, particularly Democratic campaigns. For two successive years he was the cochairman of the National Democratic Congressional Dinner. He was at various times a key fund-raiser for presidential candidate Hubert Humphrey and Senator Daniel K. Inouye (both, as a matter of interest, great friends of Israel).

Page Airways's aircraft marketing overseas was lubricated by another form of political contribution, according to a 1978 civil lawsuit brought by the SEC. The company was charged with paying $200,000 to the president of Gabon and no less than $412,000 to the ambassador of the Ivory Coast in Washington. However, it is the matter of Idi Amin's silver-plated Cadillac Eldorado that concerns us here.

Initially, Ziegler simply told the Page Corporation that he might have a customer for a Gulfstream. Charles Hanner, a senior vice president of Page, flew to Zurich and learned that the customer was Idi Amin. Nothing daunted, Hanner flew on with Ziegler to meet the customer. According to Hanner's sworn deposition in the SEC suit: "Our first introduction to Idi Amin was at the Intercontinental Hotel. He came there to swim at a lovely pool, and Mr. Ziegler went over and introduced himself and then called us and we all went over and he introduced us to the president."

Hanner's sales pitch went down well with Amin, who agreed more or less at once to buy a Gulfstream II. Hanner was pleased at the news, as was Ziegler. Apart from any possible intelligence payoff to come, the Mossad agent extracted a $100,000 commission from Page for his introduction.

Amin not only liked his new plane, but he took an equal shine to Charles Hanner. For the next five years Hanner found himself spending up to one week every month in Kampala, attending to the burgeoning relationship between his company and the fearsome President Amin. Amin honored his friend in a ceremony appointing him "honorary consul for Uganda in the United States." Page Airways honored Amin by presenting him with a silver-plated Cadillac. It was this gift that helped cause later unpleasantness with the SEC, which took the view that it constituted a bribe. Wilmorite, Wilmot's other major interest, received a $6 million contract to build a new Ugandan UN mission building in New York.

Although his initial introduction to Amin had come courtesy of the Mossad, Hanner was reportedly soon also dealing with the CIA on the Ugandan matter. Not long after the Gulfstream deal, Page arranged to sell Amin a Lockheed L-100, the civilian version of the well-known C-130 military transport, and also contracted to supply flight crews and maintenance support for both planes. Page then turned round and subcontracted with another company to provide the personnel.

The company chosen was Southern Air Transport, based in Miami. From 1960 to 1974 Southern Air had been part of the CIA's huge airline proprietary Air America, notorious for its role in the secret war in Laos. The air-charter company was then sold, in a remarkably advantageous deal for the buyer, to the same man who had run it for the CIA. Despite profuse assertions that its intelligence connections came to an end in 1974, Southern Air retained very close links with its former owners. It resurfaced in the public eye during the Iran-Contra affair when its integral role in the shipment of arms both to Iran and to the contras came to light.

The two planes required the services of at least a dozen Americans in Kampala. All sources agree that at least some of the crews supplied by Southern Air were full-time CIA operatives.

The Israelis, meanwhile, had not dealt themselves out of the action. In 1975 Zimex sold a Boeing 707 cargo plane to Amin, along with a contract to supply crews and services.

The Boeing was one of several that had once belonged to Pan Am but had been sold, reportedly at the request of the CIA, to a company called ATASCO—Aircraft Trading and Services Company—based in Tel Aviv.

ATASCO had originally been set up by a group of executives from the state-owned Israel Aircraft Industries in 1971. Shortly afterwards, however, it was bought by a very prominent Israeli: Shaul Eisenberg. Eisenberg, it may be recalled, is the somewhat mysterious billionaire who made his money in the Far East after the war, has brokered arms deals with China, and is now one of the most powerful, among the most feared, and certainly the richest man in Israel. He is the present employer of David Kimche, former overseer of Mossad's African operations.

Eisenberg's aircraft company sold a Pan Am 707 to Zimex, which then sold it to Amin. The following year Zimex leased another 707 from a company called Ronair, which had the same office address as ATASCO. This plane was also leased to Amin.

Uganda is, of course, a landlocked country, so air transport was absolutely essential for the viability of Amin's regime. Much of the vital coffee export crop, the source of Amin's funds, was hauled out by air, while both munitions and consumer goods for the necessary delectation of Amin's henchmen came in the same way. By the mid-1970s Amin's entire air transport system had been constituted courtesy of the CIA and the Mossad. No doubt all the assorted spies were furnishing copious amounts of intelligence, for which their various headquarters were duly grateful. The most evident consequence, however, was that the companies that served as vehicles for the espionage operation were making a great deal of money. Mr. Wilmot's concerns grossed some $22 million from Idi Amin; it is not clear how much the Israelis took home, but it cannot have been much less.

While the companies profited, so did Amin. Not only were his commercial air transport requirements taken care of, but the intelligence agencies soon began to supply his military airlift requirements. Two of the Southern Air crew members told the SEC that they had been specifically ordered by their CIA overseers to transport munitions and take part in military operations for Amin. Furthermore, in order to aid in military parachute drops, the L-100 was fitted with an Airborne Deployment System ramp. According to one witness, the ramp had been supplied by a Southern Air Transport executive. When this one witness, a pilot, complained in writing to higher management at Page about what was going on, he received no reply.

To keep the CIA/Mossad intelligence triumph in perspective, it is worth quoting from the autobiography of Henry Kyemba, a former cabinet minister in Amin's government, who described what this regime, assisted in large part by the air operation, was meanwhile doing to the Ugandan population. Kyemba is discussing a place called Owen Falls, a popular spot for Amin's killers to dump the bodies of their victims. He wrote while this holocaust was still in progress:

"A boatsman at Owen Falls works full-time recovering corpses from the water. If he recovered twenty corpses a day between July 1971 and my departure in April 1977—a reasonable assumption—then, in round figures, this would amount to over 40,000 dead. But this figure doesn't include those that must have been eaten by crocodiles or swept through the dam—at least another 10,000. Moreover, Owen Falls was only one of three dumping areas. Multiplying the Owen Falls number by three gives a total of 150,000 by mid-1977. There were, in addition, many, many other dead, abandoned in forests and hidden in pits near barracks.

"The dead are literally innumerable: all their names will never be known, their numbers never counted. My own list is but a small indication of the true horror. And day by day the total grows."

In fact, 1977 was the year that former CIA official Frank Terpil, an unwholesome associate of Edwin Wilson—who was then supplying lethal goods and services to Qaddafi—signed a $3.2 million contract to furnish arms, explosives, and surveillance equipment to Amin. He soon became a familiar figure at Stanstead Airport outside London, supervising the loading of arms and other supplies aboard what became known as the "Stanstead Shuttle"—the Eisenberg/Mossad 707s en route to Entebbe Airport outside Kampala. Among those who noticed his comings and goings must have been the Mossad crews working on the planes, not to mention other CIA agents reportedly infiltrated into Amin's inner circle in Kampala. Nothing, however, appears to have been done to interfere with the "ingenious and valuable" joint endeavor. The private entrepreneurs, such as Wilmot and Eisenberg, did well; the American and Israeli governments knew more than they otherwise would have about the activities of Amin and his associates, such as Qaddafi. A CIA official who had enjoyed a close relationship with Amin memorialized the friendship by mounting a stuffed animal head presented to him by the dictator above his fireplace in Washington. It remained there until 1986, when reporter Murray Waas asked whether it had been reported to the Treasury, as required by law for all gifts to U.S. officials of more than minimal value.

In the end it took the lawyers and accountants of the SEC, hot on the trail of Page's alleged bribery routines around Africa, to put a crimp in the operation. The SEC charges themselves were easily disposed of; Page's lawyers in Washington simply issued a subpoena to the CIA for all records of the agency's dealings with Page over the years. The case was then dropped, with both sides referring cryptically to a secret matter of "national interest." Page passed to new ownership shortly afterwards. The party was over, in any case. Amin had been deposed by a Tanzanian invasion, while in Tripoli Qaddafi had replaced Zimex as his aviation contractor.[18]

The close cooperation between the agency and Mossad in Uganda was certainly not unique. John Stockwell, a professional CIA officer who served as station chief in Rwanda, recalls how Mossad officers would check in. "We were under instructions to treat them as friends and colleagues, which we did."

Stockwell had an opportunity to get a closer view of the fruits of

Israeli cooperation when he was put in charge of the CIA's task force on Angola in 1975. Portugal, having fought a long and bitter counterinsurgency war in Africa, had decided to withdraw following the anti-Fascist military coup in Lisbon in 1974.

Despite the considered judgment of CIA Director William Colby that there was little to choose from, ideologically, between the three guerrilla factions contending for power, Henry Kissinger decided that Angola should be a trial of strength for the U.S. The "Marxist" MPLA was to be prevented at all costs from taking power in Luanda. The CIA, whatever Mr. Colby's reservations, threw itself into the task with a will. Stockwell has recorded not only how arms were poured in, as well as a gang of European mercenaries of dubious antecedents, but also how an extremely sophisticated disinformation campaign was able to plant fictitious stories on the iniquity of the MPLA in the receptive U.S. media. For further assistance in this crusade, Kissinger turned to South Africa and Israel.

Although Israeli military instructors were present in South Africa in force at that time, Kissinger wished them to step up the scale of their African involvement by actually sending troops to join in the fight in Angola. Failure to stop the Russians in Angola, the secretary of state told Israeli officials, "could encourage Arab countries such as Syria to run risks that could lead to a new attack on Israel, backed up by the Russians." The Israelis, who had been using the Syrian threat to good advantage long before Henry Kissinger had been thought of, refused to commit troops. They were, however, prepared to send material assistance. John Stockwell remembers the occasion.

"I was told that the Israelis were going to help us. But it didn't come free. The idea was that our people would be using non-U.S. materiel, which was where the Israelis came in. In exchange for some Redeye missiles (a then state-of-the-art U.S. portable antiaircraft weapon) they were going to give us a consignment of Grails, which was a really primitive SAM. It was part of my job to make the exchange.

"I had some suspicions of what might happen, so I sent two of my best men over to Israel. I told them to check what they were being given very carefully, to make sure it was what we were paying for. That was what they did, but the Israelis pulled a box switch. When the boxes were unpacked in Angola every single one of those Grails was a dud. They were going off in people's faces, or flying all over the place. So after that I was less enamored of our gallant allies."

Although the Israelis refused to commit their actual forces, the South Africans were ready to oblige. The success of the initial South African armored thrust toward Luanda, however, brought an unpleasant response. Cuban troops landed in force and speedily drove the Boer forces back to their borders. Meanwhile, the U.S. Congress, more ready to question administration assertions about national security prerogatives in those days, banned further CIA involvement in Angola. The remnants of the anti-MPLA forces were therefore left to fight on without direct American support. But they were not alone. The South Africans, with discreet Israeli assistance, were ready and willing to step into the breach. KK Mountain had laid the groundwork well.[19]

In the beginning Israel had enjoyed an advantage in Africa, because the new countries welcomed Israeli emissaries and aid. That gradually changed as Israel's identification with the white supremacist regime in South Africa, which we will return to later, became more evident. The coup de grace for these overt friendly connections came during the 1973 Yom Kippur War, when no fewer than twenty-one African countries broke off diplomatic relations with Israel. The move was impelled both by disenchantment with Jerusalem's policies and pressure from the Arab oil states.

This did not, however, mean that the connections so usefully serving KK Mountain withered and died. As the Ugandan operation described above makes clear, Israeli intelligence could still be active in countries that had supposedly joined the other side. Meir Meyouhas remained close to Mobutu, and Zaire had no trouble in supporting the U.S. initiative to destabilize Angola.

In the early 1980s Israel embarked on a concerted effort to reestablish full ties with sub-Saharan capitals. It is striking how little the cast of characters in Israeli national security affairs changes. Thus the man spearheading the renewed offensive in Africa was David Kimche. Also involved in the effort was Avraham Tamir, whom we last met accompanying Israel Lior to Uganda in 1965.

Lior has remarked of those early excursions, "From the first moment we realized that the African leaders considered us omnipotent, a sort of monster with all-embracing arms . . . especially from the financial point of view. They had no doubt that we were involved in every bank and every money box in the world [and] controlled the U.S., too, and certainly all the media there."

Mobutu was very much of this belief, and when Tamir accompanied Arik (Ariel) Sharon, then minister of defense, to Zaire in late 1981, the president asked his guests to use their good offices to get the U.S. Congress to be more forthcoming with aid. This, to everyone's surprise, the Israelis managed to accomplish. "They thought we were miracle-makers," recalls Tamir happily. As a quid pro quo, Mobutu reestablished diplomatic relations with Israel.

Thus Israel helped Mobutu in Washington, Mobutu helped Israel with the recognition it wanted, and, of course, Israel worked with the Americans to further mutual interests. The sorry history of the desolate Republic of Chad in the last decade provides an interesting example of such cooperation. In 1982 a joint U.S.-Israeli operation installed Hissen Habre in power. The CIA, according to reports in the Israeli press, set up a "security and intelligence assistance" program for Habre, while the Israelis trained his secret police. His bodyguards were both Israelis and former U.S. marines.

The prime object of the exercise was Libya, which borders Chad to the north. The Reagan administration had early identified Libyan leader Colonel Muammar Qadaffi as an enemy marked for destruction, so the fact that Chad had a long-standing border dispute with Libya served as a perfect pretext to use Chadians against the flamboyant colonel. France was also persuaded to send troops to back up Habre's regime. Following the failure of the American bombing raid on Tripoli in April 1986 to kill Qadaffi, U.S. and Israeli instructors were deployed to train up a force of two thousand anti-Qaddafi "contras" recruited from Libyan prisoners. The training was conducted both in Chad itself and in neighboring countries, including Zaire. As with the Nicaraguan Contras, Israeli military expertise appears to have been complemented by financial help from Saudi Arabia. According to sources on the U.S. National Security Council, this whole operation, which passed without comment in the mainstream U.S. press, was properly cleared with Congress.

In December 1990, however, President Habre was overthrown by a rebel force that invaded Chad from Sudan. The turning point came when the French, tiring of their role in the anti-Libyan operation, ordered their troops not to intervene to save Habre, who then fled the country. The U.S. had to evacuate its fledgling contra forces in a hurry, flying most of them to Zaire in the hope of redeploying them as part of the UNITA forces in Angola.[20]

The operation against Libya shows that the U.S.-Israeli covert partnership in Africa was in full running order in the late 1980s.

However, various factors suggest that the great days of the partnership were over. With the end of the Cold War it became hard to postulate a Soviet threat on the dark continent, which may account for the apparent disinterest of the Bush administration in black Africa. The Middle East war that began in January 1991 seemed likely to set off a wave of hostility toward both America and Israel in the Third World. As the bombing of Iraq began, for example, there were rumors that Mobutu had disloyally turned over his Libyan contra guests to Qaddafi, in exchange for a promise of aid from Tripoli.

Like the Israeli bomb, KK Mountain was an unacknowledged secret that lay close to the heart of the covert relationship between the United States and Israel. It was easy to conceal, because the coups and wars it dealt in took place in out-of-the-way places. But its operations pale in significance compared with the world-shaking conflict that erupted in 1967. It was a very public war, which concealed some dark secrets.

6. Strategic Asset

THE VETERAN CIA OFFICER was reminiscing about battles against the Soviets and their Middle Eastern allies back in the 1960s, a struggle that for him culminated in the Arab-Israeli War of June, 1967. "That," he said firmly, "was the time that the Israelis really proved themselves as a strategic asset."

It seems strange to hear the 1967 war described in such terms. The traditional view of that war is that Israel's Arab enemies, led by Nasser, combined in an attempt to wipe Israel out, but were instead deservedly defeated and humiliated in just six days. In the subsequent decades, of course, the Middle East and the rest of the world have had to live with the consequences of that triumph, in particular Israel's unyielding occupation of territory conquered in that fateful week.

Why, then, should an old covert operator consider the war a job well done by Israel, on behalf of the United States? For the answer, we must return to the aftermath of the 1956 Suez War.

The Eisenhower administration had been furious at the Israelis for attacking Egypt without approval from Washington. Indeed, the Israelis had been foolhardy enough to lie to their colleagues in the CIA about their plans. Nevertheless, after the war, the U.S. had come to share the Israeli view that Nasser was a threat to Western interests in the entire region.

Nasser's successful defiance of Britain and France had amplified his appeal to "Pan-Arabism" across the Middle East. This, for Washington, was an especially ominous development. Since World War II the fundamental U.S. strategic interest in the region has been Saudi Arabia and its oil treasures, as President Bush has made abundantly clear. Pan-Arabism carried the implicit threat that the oil wealth enjoyed by a small number of feudal rulers under U.S. influence should be used for the benefit of the more numerous but poorer Arabs in Egypt and elsewhere, which were in the Soviet sphere of influence. That fact alone was sufficient to ensure that the U.S. would remain antipathetic to Nasser. As Eisenhower grumbled to Richard Nixon in July 1958, all the unrest in the Middle East came from the "struggle of Nasser to get control of those [petroleum] supplies—to get the income and the power to destroy the Western world."

The hostility evinced by the Eisenhower administration in its later years toward Nasser was mitigated, at least superficially, by the Kennedy regime. John Kennedy himself thought that it might be possible to entertain warmer relations with his Egyptian counterpart. Among other indications of improved relations, the U.S. began shipping grain to Egypt under the Food for Peace program.

Despite the exchange of friendly notes with Nasser and the provision of American wheat on easy terms to Egyptians, there was meanwhile a sharp escalation in American aid to Israel. For the first time the U.S. government officially agreed to send it sophisticated arms.

As we have seen, this decision was heavily influenced by American concern about the Israeli bomb program. Ben-Gurion had gone to New York in May 1961, specifically to discuss the matter with Kennedy. Kennedy thought that he had secured an agreement from Ben-Gurion to slow down the Israeli nuclear weapons program and to allow American inspectors into Dimona. Ben-Gurion asked Kennedy to supply Hawk antiaircraft missiles. Kennedy held out for some agreement on the resettlement of some of the hundreds of thousands of Palestinian refugees, in exile in neighboring Arab countries since the Israeli War of Independence. Ben-Gurion adamantly refused. Eventually, after a further trip to the White House by Shimon Peres, Kennedy agreed to supply Hawks without any agreement on the refugees.

This deal was a crucial breakthrough for the Israelis. The Hawks themselves did not make a significant difference to Israel's military position (enemy bombers could be easily dealt with by air force fighters), but once the deal had been concluded, in the words of General Motti Hod, air force commander in the 1967 war, "the barriers were down" so far as further military deals with the U.S. were concerned.

Despite lingering perceptions that Kennedy tilted toward Nasser, he expressed greater commitment to Israel than either of the two presidents before him. In 1962 he assured Israeli Foreign Minister Golda Meir that the U.S. and Israel were de facto allies.[1]

Meanwhile, also in 1962, in the faraway medieval kingdom of Yemen, an old ruler died, contrary to expectations, in his bed. Since Yemen borders Saudi Arabia, and indeed has a historic claim to a large slice of Saudi territory, this event was of great interest to Nasser, to the rulers in Riyadh, to the Israelis, and to the CIA. For all these people, Yemen was a very important piece of property indeed.

At that time Yemen was divided in two, and had been since the early eighteenth century. The British ruled South Yemen from their massive military port at Aden, the headquarters for the British military presence in the Persian Gulf. Up until 1962 North Yemen was under the control of Imam Ahmed. Ahmed, known as the "bulging-eyed tyrant," was a ruler of the old school who kept order in traditional ways. For example, he thought that the up-country tribes would pay more attention to their civic duties if prominent local tribesmen were confined at his court as hostages. Life was not too intolerable for these involuntary guests. When the Imam went to Italy for medical treatment, as he frequently did, he would take along his hostages as well—somewhat to the discomfiture of the Italian authorities.

Despite this hospitality, there was an opposition, centered in the army. Egyptian intelligence supported the dissidents and also made strenuous efforts to assassinate the Imam. CIA officials still smile happily at the memory of the intercepted phone call between a palace cleaning woman recruited to place a bomb under the Imam's bed, and her case officer. She had some difficulty in reading the instructions, and the panic-stricken officer was attempting to talk her through the exercise.

The plot failed and the Imam passed away peacefully in September 1962. His son had hardly taken over the throne when Nasserist officers staged a coup and declared a republic. The young Imam escaped to launch a civil war, drawing support from up-country tribes on the Saudi border and, more importantly, from the Saudis. The Saudi royal family were terrified by the events in Yemen, seeing them as the first stage in a plot by Nasser to displace them from their own kingdom.

The war quickly became a big power affair. The Russians immediately began a military airlift out of Cairo to aid the Republicans. "This was the first time the Soviets had long-range airlift capability, and it made a big difference," recalls one former CIA official who had been intensely concerned with these events.

He and his superiors in the agency were filled with the darkest forebodings about this further evidence that the Russians, through their proxy Nasser, were advancing steadily into the oil-rich region of the Middle East. The coup occurred just as a promising operation aimed at eliminating Russian influence in Egypt itself had gone wrong. Prince Faisal, the brains behind the Saudi throne, had been "persuaded" by the CIA while on a visit to Washington in 1962 to offer a deal to Nasser by which Russian aid would be replaced by Saudi money and the Soviets expelled. Unfortunately, on the way home the deeply religious prince happened to tune in to the "Voice of the Arabs," the radio station thoughtfully donated by Kermit Roosevelt to Nasser ten years before. The broadcast was so full of blasphemous abuse of the Saudi royal family that Faisal's disgust at the foul practices of Nasser was renewed and he called off the deal.

For Faisal, as a British historian of the House of Saud has noted, "Nasser rather than Israel was the devil incarnate, and the Egyptian leader's revolutionary creed as sinister a carrier of Marxist plague as Zionism."[2]

Whatever the CIA felt about Zionism, the agency was in full agreement with Faisal about Nasser and the Marxist plague. Not only were the Russians supplying the airlift for the Egyptians, but the CIA's radio intercept reports soon revealed that they were intervening directly in the fighting. "They were sending combat missions down from Cairo West [a major Egyptian air base] from November '62," recalls one official who had occasion to pay close attention to these events. "The planes were TU-16 bombers with Egyptian markings and one Egyptian on board to talk on the radio, but discipline wasn't that good and in moments of stress they would start chattering in Russian." These bombing raids were not only directed at areas actually inside Saudi Arabia, but the bombers brazenly flew over Riyadh on their way to their targets.

The Saudis, not unreasonably, were terrified of what was going on to the south of them. The CIA, equally worried by the Soviet offensive, resolved to do something about it. The problem for the agency was that its views were not shared in other parts of the U.S. government. "There was a lot of disagreement between us and the State Department and White House on this issue. Our government was quite sympathetic to the Egyptians at this time [1962–63]," recalls one key CIA official of the time, his voice inflected with the scorn of a hardened practitioner of realpolitik for starry-eyed do-gooders. "There was a mighty effort to cultivate 'new forces in the world' like [Indian leader] Nehru, Nkrumah [the President of Ghana], and Nasser. It was the view of our State Department that we should not sully the relationship [with Nasser] with intelligence activities. We felt that there was a very big issue at stake in the Arabian peninsula." CIA officials found that their alarmist and militant views were shared by British intelligence, which began a program of assistance to the anti-Nasserite Yemeni Royalists, and by the Israelis.[3]

Thanks to Israeli concern, the CIA had the means to provide help, through one remove, to the Royalists. Among the immigrants who poured into Israel immediately after independence were a people who presented a sharply medieval contrast to the refugees arriving from Eastern Europe. The Jewish community in Yemen had existed since biblical times, their way of life apparently changing little in the intervening millennia. From 1948 to 1950, however, approximately fifty thousand of them were brought to Israel in a celebrated airlift known as "Operation Magic Carpet."

Now, thanks to the CIA, some of the Yemeni Jews were going back. Having arrived in Israel lacking, in the words of Ben-Gurion, "the most basic and primary concepts of civilization," they were returning to teach their former fellow countrymen how to use modern weapons.

The operation involved not only the CIA and the Israelis, but also the Shah of Iran. The plan was to send both trainers and arms. The arms originated in Israel, but any sign of overt Israeli participation in what was supposed to be an inter-Arab struggle had to be carefully disguised. So the weapons were sent first to Iran, where they were repackaged so as to disguise their true country of origin. They were then sent on to the war zone. The trainers, naturally, took care to disguise their true nationality.

Faisal, who took over the throne from his brother Saud in a peaceful coup in 1964, posed an additional problem. However much he loathed Nasser, he was also a very committed anti-Semite. (He once expressed his sympathy for his hosts at an official dinner in France over the fact that it was the season of the Jewish Passover and that meant that all Christian children would be in danger.) The king, therefore, had to be kept in the dark about the Israeli role in the operation.

"We had the help of some practical-minded members of the Saudi royal family," smiles a CIA veteran of the affair. "The king never knew about it."

Despite all the panic in Riyadh, Tel Aviv, and Langley, Nasser had little hope of turning Yemen into an Egyptian puppet, still less of using his allies as a springboard for taking over Saudi Arabia. Even with Russian aid, the campaign was extremely costly, and it tied up seventy thousand troops—one-third of the entire Egyptian army. Despite lavish bombing, as well as the use of poison gas in large quantities, the Egyptians were bogged down.

From the point of view of the CIA and its allies, however, the situation appeared dire. Not only was a Soviet-sponsored army en-sconced close to a strategic interest vital to the U.S., but the highest levels of the administration appeared largely indifferent to the fact. Kennedy had taken a dangerously soft line on Yemen, while Lyndon Johnson soon became preoccupied with his own war in Southeast Asia. It was becoming harder than ever to get Washington alarmed about any Marxist tide advancing up the Red Sea and across the Middle East.

This did not prevent the CIA from exerting itself to the utmost in this bitter Cold War battle. In Iraq, for example, the leftist regime of General Kassem that had taken power in 1958 was overthrown in a Baath party coup in February 1963. This was considered a definite plus by the CIA. "That coup was better covered than any other in the Middle East," recalls one senior official with satisfaction at a job well done. "We really had the T's crossed on what was happening. We regarded it as a great victory." One reason the coup went over so well was that the agency helpfully supplied lists of Communists to the new regime, so they could be rounded up and eliminated. (Among the obscure revolutionaries who formed part of the ruling group in Baghdad at this time was a tough gunman from the provincial town of Takrit named Saddam Hussein.) Later that year a pro-Nasserite coun-tercoup ejected the Baathists, who then had to lie low until they reclaimed Baghdad in 1968.

For Nasser, however, the steady development of an engineering project in northeast Israel may have seemed more urgent and pressing than the bloody proceedings on the banks of the Tigris. Israel's plan for exploitation of the headwaters of the Jordan had caused Eisenhower to temporarily cut off aid in 1953. The dispute had been smoothed over, and the Israelis had proceeded with work on the "National Carrier" for the next ten years. It was a massive scheme by which water from the Sea of Galilee and the lakes above it near the Syrian border was to be pumped through a conduit down the length of Israel to irrigate the Negev Desert.

The scheme was the basis for the familiar Israeli claim that it was "making the desert bloom." The country's Arab neighbors, however, were of the opinion that they would pay the price of seeing their farmland, deprived of water by the Carrier—77 percent of the Jordan's waters came from tributaries arising in Arab countries—turn into deserts.

The Syrians felt particularly discomfited by Israeli activity close to their border on the Golan Heights. Sovereignty was undecided in three distinct areas of this region, territory occupied by Syrian troops in 1948 but demilitarized under the armistice agreement that ended the war. Over the years, the Israelis had made periodic efforts to take possession of the land by sending in soldiers disguised as farmers. The Syrians would fire at them, the Israelis would retaliate. Anytime, therefore, that Israel wished to provoke a military incident on this northern border, it could do so simply by dispatching an armored tractor for a morning's plowing. This, at least, in the opinion of the Swedish General Carl Von Horn, commander of the UN Truce Supervision Organization, was the deliberate Israeli policy.[4]

The imminent completion of the National Carrier in 1963 generated particularly vociferous demands from the Syrians that Nasser, the hero of the Arabs, do something to stop the Israelis. This posed an awkward problem for the Egyptian leader. However ready he might be to deploy his military against tribesmen and mercenaries in Yemen, he was in no condition to take on the Israelis, and he knew it.

Accordingly, Nasser summoned a general Arab summit conference in Cairo at the beginning of 1964 to decide on policy toward Israel. His purpose was by no means to mobilize a jihad, but rather the opposite: to make sure that unruly elements such as the Syrians would not start anything rash and thus draw him into a conflict. To the same end, he got summit support for the creation of a Palestine Liberation Organization. Contrary to appearances (and later developments), this was not intended by Nasser to be a spearhead for the liberation of Palestine, but rather a means by which Palestinian aspirations could be kept safely under control.

Nasser held several more summits, but they became decreasingly successful at keeping the troops in line. Some of the Palestinians, derisive of the posturing lawyer Ahmed Shukeiry selected by Nasser to lead the PLO, formed guerrilla groups to take the fight to the enemy. One of these, Fatah, carried out its first action from Syria on New Year's Day 1965. It was a bombing attack against the Israeli water project.

While Nasser struggled to contain what he considered unwise provocations of Israel, his hitherto unchallenged position as the guiding hand of Arab radicalism was slipping away. For example, the Movement of Arab Nationalists, which he had used as a counterweight to the Baathists in political struggles outside Egypt, repudiated his leadership in 1965. Nor were things going well for him farther afield. His friend Ahmed Ben Bella, the leader of the Algerian revolution, was overthrown in the summer. In October the old alliance of Mossad and French intelligence had cooperated with the Moroccan secret police in the capture and death by torture of the Moroccan revolutionary Mehdi Ben Barka—also a friend of Nasser. President Sukarno of Indonesia had been overthrown by a CIA-assisted clique of reactionary generals.

Adding injury to insult, Lyndon Johnson cut off the food aid to Egypt initiated by Kennedy. To make matters even worse, the Soviet officials who succeeded Khrushchev in 1964 were far less interested in the Third World than their former colleague had been. In April 1965, Nasser had been told in Moscow that the Russians were cutting back sharply on their economic aid to Egypt, though they did insist that he continue with his costly intervention in Yemen.

Nasser's woes did not affect the view of the CIA, more so than the rest of the U.S. foreign policy apparatus, that the Egyptian leader and his Soviet sponsors posed a serious threat to the vital strategic prize of Saudi Arabia. It was a problem that would have to be dealt with. One place the agency found emphatic agreement with this view was Israel.

Meir Amit, who had succeeded Isser Harel as head of Mossad in 1963, made frequent trips to Washington to lay out the Israeli view of the world for his counterparts at Langley. "Amit's strategic studies were big stuff," recalls one official who needed little convincing. "The Israelis were really getting worried. Because of the Yemen business, they could see the Russians getting hold of the southern Red Sea, which was out of range of their planes. In fact, they tried and failed to get landing rights in Ethiopia at that time."

What Amit proposed, according to agency officials who took part in the meetings, was a "practical military alliance" of Israel, Jordan, and Saudi Arabia, sponsored by the U.S. and directed against Communist encroachment. To some degree this alliance already existed, but only on a covert level, as shown by the maneuvers necessary to get Israeli military aid to the Yemeni Royalists. American participation would have involved a military presence, including the dispatch of naval forces to the Gulf. The scheme, which had apparently originated in the Reuven Shiloah Institute, the Mossad think tank, foundered on the administration's increasingly exclusive absorption with Vietnam.

While the mind of the president may have been far away on the banks of the Mekong, responsible officials at the CIA, at least, were taking the Israeli warnings to heart. So grievous did the situation appear that James Angleton was prevailed upon at this time to liaise more closely with agency officers responsible for Arab countries—a group he was normally inclined to keep at arm's length.

In February 1966, two events occurred that appeared to confirm the possibility of a Marxist plague spreading through the Middle East. The British government announced that it was abandoning its old imperial outpost in Aden, next door to Nasser's outpost in Yemen, and would have all its forces, naval and military, out of the area by 1968. With them would go Britain's traditional position as the "policeman of the Gulf."

Within a day of the British declaration, the turbulent and bloody politics of the Baath party in Syria produced a coup by younger military officers. The new leaders, among whom was Hafez al-Asad, were more leftist than their predecessors. They had long ago lost their devotion to Nasser as the standard-bearer of radical Arab nationalism, and indeed regarded themselves as his competitors. They appeared to take Syria resolutely into the Soviet camp. Indeed, for the first time in its history, the Syrian cabinet had a communist member.

Ominous as all this may have appeared in Meir Amit's briefings, there was less to the communist encroachment than met the eye. The austere group of officers now in power in Damascus had a traditionally Baathist suspicion of communism, and the one communist cabinet member was given the less-than-elevated position of minister of communications. While the head of the Syrian Communist Party was allowed home after years of exile, he was strictly enjoined from holding meetings or making speeches.[5]

Observers who chose to disregard these finer details and see the Syrian coup as a Soviet gain, however, could point to the warm relations struck up by the new regime with Moscow. The Russians, after some hesitation, declared their support for the leadership and promised a limited amount of military and economic aid, including money for a cherished Syrian project to dam the Euphrates.

In May 1966, Soviet Prime Minister Alexei Kosygin visited the Middle East. What looked to some like a further and sinister Soviet offensive in the area may in fact have been merely a lackadaisical effort to shore up pre-Soviet regimes against the threat posed by the U.S. and its Israeli and Saudi surrogates. If this was the Soviet aim, the means deployed to achieve it were lacking in diplomatic finesse.

Kosygin urged a socialist union between Egypt, Syria, Algeria, and Iraq. Syria and Iraq were already at odds, due to the bitter rivalry between the wings of the Baath party ruling the respective countries. Furthermore, Soviet support for the Syrian Euphrates Dam project (miserly though it was—one-tenth of the amount lavished on the Aswan Dam) was hardly calculated to foster closer relations between Syria and Iraq, since Iraq would thereby be deprived of a considerable part of its water resources. Egypt and Syria were very much at odds, while Nasser felt less than close to the regime in Algiers, which was keeping his friend Ben Bella under close house arrest.

The CIA, meanwhile, though attentive to the alarmist estimates coming out of Tel Aviv, knew perfectly well that the Arab unity being fostered by Moscow had little hope of success. The brief flirtation with Nasser during the Kennedy years had enabled the agency to revive some old contacts. CIA officials smile as they reminisce how "we were the beneficiaries of Jackie Kennedy's cultural interest in the antiquities at Luxor" and refer elliptically to "all those letters on perfumed stationery" she wrote. The benefit they appear to remember most fondly was a "real dialogue" with Salah Nasr, the head of Egyptian intelligence. After Kosygin had gone home, his hosts' heartfelt endorsements of the Soviet unity proposals still ringing in his ears, there was, so Nasr informed his American friends, "a good deal of snickering" at the idea.

Nasser knew that Soviet Middle Eastern policy was less than realistic. He was also well aware that whatever the radicals said, it was the

Israelis who held the initiative. At a meeting of the Palestine National Council in May 1965, the Syrians had complained about his "timidity" in "hiding" behind the UN peacekeeping force on his border with Israel, put in place after the 1956 war. Nasser answered frankly: "They say 'Drive out UNEF' [United Nations Emergency Force, set up as a peacekeeping force in the area in 1956; the Israelis had never permitted the peacekeepers on their side of the border]. Suppose that we do—is it not essential that we have a plan? If Israeli aggression takes place against Syria, shall I attack Israel? Then Israel is the one which determines the battle for me. It hits a tractor or two to force me to move. Is this a wise way? We have to determine the battle."[6]

Unfortunately for Nasser, the Syrian leadership that took power in February 1966 was happy to provide shelter and support for Palestinian militants launching armed attacks on Israel. Yasser Arafat, the leader of Fatah, the strongest guerrilla group at that time, seemed anxious to spark off an Arab-Israeli war before Israel became too powerful ever to be destroyed. The Syrians did not necessarily endorse this less than brilliant strategy. They knew that they were poor, starved for modern weapons, their officer corps decimated by repeated coups and purges, and in no condition to take on the powerful Israelis. But allowing Arafat and his fellow fighters to launch pinprick raids across the border was one way of relieving their frustration.

Even if Nasser had been successful in getting the Syrians to clamp down on the Palestinian guerrillas, this would not necessarily have had much effect on Israel's policy of retaliation, a point underlined by the fate of the Jordanian town of Samu on November 13, six days after the Egyptian-Syrian treaty was signed.

Unlike the Damascus regime, King Hussein of Jordan was doing his best to restrain guerrilla activity. A faithful client of the Americans, and willing recipient of CIA largesse since 1957, he wished only for the quietest and most secure life possible in a fractured and turbulent region. In October and early November 1966, however, Palestinian guerrilla raids from Jordan killed three Israelis and wounded eleven. The day after the last raid, an Israeli armored brigade—nearly four thousand men—swept across the Jordanian border and struck at the West Bank town of Samu. After ambushing a Jordanian army column rushing to the rescue, the Israelis drove the five thousand inhabitants of the town from their homes and then calmly set about blowing up a hundred and twenty-five homes, the clinic, a school, and a workshop, as well as damaging another twenty-eight houses and the local mosque.

Hussein's quiet days were over. His embittered Palestinian subjects rioted in protest at what they regarded as his subservience to the Israelis and unwillingness to protect them. There were shouts of "Down with monarchy!" and "Give us arms!"

The king was now under pressure to team up with the radical half of the Arab world. The PLO called on the Arab Legion [the Jordanian Army] to rise against the "traitor Hussein." Cairo radio heaped insults on the diminutive monarch, while the Syrian president called for a "holy war against the throne of treason." Amman radio lashed back with taunts at Nasser for hiding from Israel behind the UNEF peacekeeping troops, which had been on his border as a buffer since 1956. At home Hussein held to the line of noninvolvement, closing down the PLO offices in Jerusalem and throwing activists in jail.[7]

In the words of one acute commentator, Israel's massive assault on Jordan had "sharpened Arab divisions, radicalized opinion, and set its lamentably weak and hopelessly quarrelsome neighbors lurching amid mutual plots and accusations, to the very edge of the precipice."[8] It is difficult to believe that these consequences were accidental.

Throughout the winter of 1966, the Syrian front had remained tense. Then, on April 3, 1967, the Israeli press reported that the government had decided to cultivate all parts of the demilitarized zone, including a section that the Syrians insisted belonged to Arab farmers.

Four days later a solitary armored tractor began plowing a strip of the disputed land. Predictably, the Syrians mortared the vehicle, though without injury to the driver. The waiting Israelis struck back in force with artillery, tanks, and a large force of jet fighters. About a hundred Syrians were killed and six Syrian semiobsolete Mig 17s were shot down, without loss to the Israelis. Humiliatingly for the Syrian government, one of the Migs fell inside Damascus, which was then buzzed by the victors.

This military blow to Syria had immediate repercussions for Nasser, since his Arab enemies were quick to taunt him for passivity. The Saudis asked why he had not retaliated against Israel's southern front. Jidda radio made it clear that the question was rhetorical: "Anyone who imagines that Egypt will wage any kind of battle against Israel, to

defend Syria or anyone else, will wait a long time." The official Jordanian media asked why Nasser allowed Israeli shipping to pass through
Egyptian waters in the Straits of Tiran.

At the end of April the Egyptians received the first of several
warnings from the Soviets that the Israelis were contemplating a
massive attack on Syria. On May 8, a pair of highly agitated Syrian
envoys delivered the same message to Cairo, a war warning again
confirmed by the Russians.[9]

Whether or not the Soviets had any evidence for their warnings
has been a vexing question in the subsequent debate over the origins
of the war. It was clear that Nasser could not afford to stand idly by
while the Israelis went into Syria in force. If the Israeli buildup was a
fiction, then it follows that the Soviets were irresponsibly driving the
region to the brink of war—perhaps in hopes of actually liquidating
Israel. On the other hand, if there was valid evidence that the Israelis
were intending to attack, then the Soviets were indeed acting respon-
sibly in warning their shaky clients.

It has long been the contention of Israel and its supporters that no
major assault on Syria was being contemplated, notwithstanding the
admission in 1972 by Ezer Weizman, head of operations on General
Staff before and during the war: "Don't forget that we did move tanks
to the north after the downing of the aircraft." [He meant the shooting
down of the six Migs.][10]

If the tank movements caused alarm, Israeli rhetoric was not designed to calm things down. On May 11 General Yitzhak Rabin, the
chief of staff, announced on Israel radio, "The moment is coming when
we will march on Damascus to overthrow the Syrian government,
because it seems that only military operations can discourage the plans
for a people's war with which they threaten us."

The day after Rabin's crude threat, which was not repeated in the
Israeli press, his colleague General Aharon Yariv, head of Military
Intelligence, summoned the foreign press corps for an unprecedented
background briefing on the situation.[11] The peg for his pronouncements were the Palestinian guerrilla attacks coming out of Syria.
Despite the fact that these were hardly inflicting mortal wounds on
Israel—fatalities from such attacks in the first half of 1967 amounted to
one—the intelligence chief warned that ". . . we must make it clear to
the Syrians that they cannot continue in this way, and I think that the
only way to make it clear to the Syrians is by using force . . . I could say

we must use force in order to have the Egyptians convince the Syrians that it doesn't pay . . . I think that the only sure and safe answer to the problem is a military operation of great size and strength."

While threatening Syria, Yariv also made it clear that he understood very well what the possible effect might be on Nasser. "I would say that as long as there is not an Israeli invasion into Syria extended in area and time, I think the Egyptians will not come in seriously . . . they will do so only if there is no other alternative. And to my eyes 'no alternative' means that we are creating such a situation that it is impossible for the Egyptians not to act because the strain on their prestige will be unbearable."

It is interesting that despite all the alarums in the previous year over Soviet encroachment, Yariv in his talk appeared to discount the dangers of provoking a reaction by Moscow in defense of its Syrian friends. He pointed out that it had taken the Russians fourteen days to comment on the April 7 battle. Accepting that Israel could expect abuse from the USSR whatever action it took against Syria, and possibly a cutoff of Soviet Jewish emigration (which was running at record levels), the general stated, "If you look at it very closely, Russia is limited in their capacity to act against Israel—under certain, but not all, circumstances."

In essence, Yariv was repeating the same theme being simultaneously bellowed over the airwaves by Nasser's enemies in Jordan and Saudi Arabia: Nasser was weak; the "all-Arab leader," as the Israeli Military Intelligence chief derisively called him, would not intervene. Syria would be left to the mercies of Israel. Yet, "a military operation of great size and strength" would indeed leave Nasser with no alternative but to intervene, as Yariv and his intelligence colleagues must have understood.

General Yariv's background briefing quickly made headlines. United Press International reported a "high Israeli official" as threatening that "Israel would take limited military action *designed to topple the Damascus army regime* [authors' italics] if Syrian terrorists continue sabotage raids inside Israel." The *New York Times* reported that Israeli leaders had decided on "the use of force."

Assailed by threats and taunts from all sides, Nasser finally reacted to what he later called Israeli "impertinence." On May 14 he gave the order to move two divisions into the Sinai.

When members of the Israeli high command, gathered in Jerusalem for the Independence Day military parade, heard the news, they were apparently unconcerned. No general mobilization was ordered.

Despite his show of strength, Nasser was still open to the persistent gibe that he was sheltering behind the UN forces on the border. On May 16, however, the Egyptian chief of staff requested the UN commander to withdraw his men from Gaza. The request made no mention of the contingent stationed at Sharm el-Sheikh, far off on the mouth of the Gulf of Aqaba, whose symbolic presence guaranteed free passage for Israeli ships out into the Red Sea and the Indian Ocean. For reasons that have never been satisfactorily explained, UN Secretary-General U Thant insisted that if any of his forces had to leave their positions in Egypt, then all of them must leave. Nasser, with less and less political room in which to maneuver, had no choice but to ask them all to go.

While additional Egyptian troops on the frontier were not in themselves a casus belli—Nasser had reinforced Sinai once before, in 1960, without the matter going further—the closing of the straits to Israeli shipping was different. Significantly, Nasser waited three days before taking the fatal step of closing the straits. Perhaps he was waiting for some outside power to find a way to defuse the situation. But no word came, so on May 21 he occupied Sharm el-Sheikh, following up with an announcement suffused with bellicose rhetoric that he was blockading the Gulf of Aqaba to all ships carrying strategic cargo bound for Israel. The Israeli General Staff ordered mobilization of all remaining reserves and decided that they would attack on May 25, two days later.

So far as most of the world was concerned, little Israel was now menaced by an Arab "ring of steel." The Syrians, for their part, knew that this was far from true, given that half their five hundred tanks were out of action, their air force consisted of a hundred semiobsolete Migs, and their officer corps was wracked by plots and bloody purges. ("How can we fight with no officers?" complained a commander on the Golan front just before the war. "Promote the officer cadets," came the reply from Damascus.)[12]

Syria's most energetic military efforts at this time were, in fact, directed against Jordan. On May 21, the day that Nasser moved to control the straits, the Syrians detonated a car bomb at the Jordanian border post at Ramtha, killing twenty-one Jordanians. In response, Hussein broke off diplomatic relations with his Arab neighbor.[13]

Although the Egyptian army seemed impressively large (it had over two hundred thousand regular troops), a third of its forces were bogged down in distant Yemen. Nor did it fit the description of a "lean fighting force." In order to placate his officer corps, Nasser had further burdened the ramshackle Egyptian economy by putting officers in charge of various state-owned businesses. One of the first Israeli soldiers to enter Gaza during the war later recalled how "when we got to the Egyptian headquarters we found all the senior staff lined up in impeccable uniforms and [each] attended by a batman carrying a suitcase packed and ready for the prison camp—except for the commanding general, who had two suitcases. The only trouble came when we separated the generals from their servants." The Egyptian soldiery could hardly draw inspiration from the top: Field Marshal Abdel Hakim Amer, the commander in chief, had developed the habit of relieving the tensions of his post with hashish.

In contrast, the Israeli military machine had been honed and perfected over the years. All the senior commanders, such as Rabin, Weizman, Sharon, and others, were men of vast experience stretching back to the War of Independence and before.

The highly professional Israel Defense Force was well armed. Not only did it have the benefit of the military industries first built up by Peres, but foreign supplies had moved a long way from the scrambled efforts of the early days. The French were still selling arms, particularly the Mirages that spearheaded the air force, and in addition the Americans were allowing a limited amount of arms shipments, including ammunition.

Once Nasser had responded to the escalating pressures by closing the Straits of Tiran, the Israelis had a casus belli. These pressures were the result of Israeli actions on the Syrian and Jordanian front, so the small group of officials directing military policy must have known just where they were going. Nevertheless, as events moved to a conclusion in the last ten days of May, some of the Israeli leaders were getting nervous. On May 23, Chief of Staff Yitzhak Rabin had what amounted to a nervous collapse and told Operations Chief Ezer Weizman he wanted to resign. Weizman talked him out of the idea—"You'll be the victorious chief of staff . . . You'll reach the Suez Canal and the Jordan"—while saving the story for a snide rendition in his memoirs.[14] His self-doubts allayed, Rabin returned to work.

The generals knew that they could sweep in and smash the Egyptians whenever they wanted, but Prime Minister Levi Eshkol preferred to wait until he had a clear authorization from Washington. He was not going to repeat the fatal mistake made by Ben-Gurion in 1956 of attacking without permission and then having the paymasters in Washington cancel the fruits of victory. But, as Israel mobilized to smash Nasser's military machine, the White House appeared intent on fostering a diplomatic solution to the issue of the Straits of Tiran, thus depriving Israel of its casus belli.

Israel's supporters in the U.S., like indeed much of the Israeli population itself, were highly alarmed by the bellicose rhetoric and bloodcurdling threats coming out of Arab capitals. They feared that the little state would be crushed by the mighty Arab armies. Lyndon Johnson knew better. The CIA had made it clear to him in briefings that Israel was not in any mortal danger. The CIA also knew that Nasser had no intention of going to war. Just after Nasser had closed the straits, the agency had talked to its friend Salah Nasr, the Egyptian intelligence chief. " 'What's going on?' we asked him," recalls one former agency official. " 'You know you're going to lose [a war].' He leaned back in his chair and patted a pile of bound volumes on the shelf behind him. 'Don't worry,' he said, 'we're going to send the whole crisis to the Hague [the International Court of Justice].' "

Johnson, who had given scant attention to the Middle East before the crisis, now had to weigh the advantages of seeing Nasser crushed and the Soviets suffering a major setback against the possibly awkward consequences of a war in the Middle East launched by America's client, Israel. The Soviets, after all, might decide to intervene on the side of their clients. While he mulled the matter over, he placated the Israelis with a promise of a hundred armored troop vehicles, spare parts for tanks, technical data for Hawk improvements, and a $20 million loan.[15]

In order to shore up the international front, Foreign Minister Abba Eban, whose cosmopolitan manner and mellifluous speaking style had always gone down well in the West, was sent off to Washington. On the way he stopped in Paris, where President de Gaulle, knowing from his own intelligence reports that Israel was in no danger, told him that Israel would lose French support if it attacked first. But since Israel no longer depended on French military support, as it had in the fifties, such admonitions carried little weight. Eban next stopped in London, where the government, misinformed (deliberately or otherwise) by MI-6, fully agreed that Israel was on the brink of disaster but could offer little except moral support.

Eban finally arrived in the U.S. to find a cable from Jerusalem, dictated by Chief of Staff Rabin, instructing him to tell the Americans that Egypt and Syria were about to attack and that the U.S. should therefore pledge direct military assistance to Israel. The implicit corollary was that if it did not, Israel might have to attack on its own.

The U.S. administration, like the Israelis, knew that no such attack was pending. On the other hand, the Israelis had been careful not to share this appreciation of the situation with their influential supporters in the U.S., who were paying more attention than was wonted to the windy rhetoric coming out of Cairo. On May 26, for example, Nasser told an audience of trade unionists: "If Israel embarks on an aggression against Syria or Egypt, the battle against Israel will be a general one . . . and our basic objective will be to destroy Israel." Two days later he declared, "If Israel chooses war, then it is welcome to it."[16]

The beleaguered Egyptian leader (who had been told by the Russians a few days before that he was on no account to attack Israel) thus coupled his empty threats with a careful statement that he would not fire the first shot. These qualifications had less international resonance than the threats, however, leading to further pressure on Johnson.

Arthur Goldberg, whom Johnson had moved from the Supreme Court to the UN ambassadorship to make room for his crony Abe Fortas (another key lobbyist for Israel), had earlier painted Israel's vulnerability to the president in heartbreaking terms. Johnson responded by flourishing a CIA estimate that Israel would win any war with the Arabs in two weeks. Goldberg had refused to believe it, so Johnson commissioned another estimate. "We sat down on the evening of the 25th," one of the analysts charged with this duty later recalled, "licked our thumbs, and set to work. By the next morning we had the paper ready for the White House." It was a revision of the earlier estimate. Now the agency concluded that Israel would win in six days.

Armed with this intelligence ammunition, Johnson was able to fend off both Eban and the likes of Goldberg, and the foreign minister had to return to Israel without a specific endorsement for an attack on Egypt.

All this diplomatic dickering was making the Israeli warriors very restive indeed. Yigal Allon, a former chief of staff, harangued Eshkol, telling him that if he attacked now, he would go down in history "as another King David." Eshkol, a more cunning politician than the soldiers gave him credit for, told the importunate general to wait, and that he could still "get more out of LBJ."

This important point was lost on some of the eager war planners. As Ezer Weizman recalled later, "There were disagreements on the General Staff about how long to 'give' the government to try out all the possibilities of a political settlement for the crisis. Not that anyone thought of acting in defiance of the government, should it remain hesitant and continue to pin its hopes on a political solution, but there should be a recommendation, something like: 'Keep trying for a political solution for such and such a time longer. Beyond that, time will be against us, for the element of surprise, which is the basis of our plan, may disappear, or at least dwindle, and Egyptian military deployment will make things hard for us.' "

With this sort of sentiment abroad in the high command, Israel was edging closer to a transfer of power from the civilians to the military. When Eban returned with no specific commitment from Johnson, the cabinet decided to hold off the attack, perhaps for a matter of weeks, and consequently ordered that some of the reserves who had been mobilized should be allowed to return to civilian life. According to Eshkol's military secretary, the same Israel Lior who had been so shocked by Idi Amin the year before, the military simply ignored the order and in fact continued to call up more forces. Later that day, when Eshkol met with the General Staff and insisted that they must still wait for some kind of all clear from Johnson, the generals, particularly Ariel Sharon and Matti Peled, were outraged. Lior noted that the meeting had come quite close to a rebellion by the military.

Meanwhile Moshe Dayan, the hero of the 1956 war and the architect of the IDF, who had been out of power since Ben-Gurion resigned, was campaigning hard for the job of minister of defense. His main activity in this respect was to tour the military units in the south, where the senior officers, chafing at the delay imposed by the timid civilians, welcomed him as the lost leader. Editorials in the press were quick to take their cue, railing at the ineffective government of Eshkol and demanding a replacement.

On June 1, Dayan got his wish. Eshkol at last caved in and appointed the one-eyed general as minister of defense; he also brought the former terrorist Menachem Begin into the government.[17]

But the waiting and the rows went on. The tough young military and intelligence chiefs knew what they wanted and expressed it with steely determination. Watching a lecture by Yariv (the chief of military intelligence) to the civilians, Lior recalled later, "There was no doubt that Yariv was leading them on the way to war . . . As a detached observer I noted the words of the generals fell like hammers on the ministers' heads."

Even so, the ministers balked at the great gamble that the generals were urging them to endorse. What about the Russians? Rabin dismissed the problem: the Russians would not come in, and the fighting would last only a few days before the superpowers imposed a cease-fire. Wouldn't it be better to wait for a little longer? Sharon interjected that Israel would be better served by going ahead and winning the war without waiting for permission. A furious Matti Peled fumed at the politicians' lack of faith in the prowess of the IDF: "What must an army do besides win every battle in order to gain the government's trust?"

Again, Eshkol patiently explained that the IDF's strength, of which the generals were so boastful, had been obtained with help from outside. He ran through the list of arms that they had recently acquired. Victory would be no use without having an ally at the end of it who would help rearm the country, he said, "Because a military victory will not be the end of it. The Arabs will still be here."

The generals had some reason to be worried. On June 1, a special emissary of Johnson's, the oil man Robert Anderson, had talked with Nasser and had arrived at the basis of a compromise over the issue of Israeli passage through the Straits of Tiran—which was still deemed to be the cause of the whole crisis, even though Israeli military objectives transcended the opening of the waterway. The Egyptian foreign minister was due to arrive in Washington a week later for talks that might settle the dispute. The suggested compromise was that Israeli ships should revert to a previous practice of hoisting a neutral flag—the Liberian one, for example—while passing through the straits. The moment for dealing with Nasser might be slipping away, the war supporters countered. Eban's "scurrying about," as Sharon derisively termed the distinguished minister's travels, had failed to achieve an American promise of military support, and the signals coming out of Washington could not be considered a green light for war.

It was now time for the intelligence chief who had been briefing the

CIA for the previous three or four years to go to Washington. On May 30 Meir Amit, the chief of Mossad, set off to see his friends.

Amit was and is a tough representative of a tough institution. In 1989, in the middle of a conversation with one of the authors about the events of June 1967, he received a phone call informing him that a close relative had just been killed in a car crash. Observing that there was nothing he could usefully do about the tragedy, he returned to discussing his momentous visit to Washington all those years before.

Amit is circumspect about exactly whom he talked to and what they said, but he did have private talks with CIA Director Richard Helms and Defense Secretary Robert McNamara. Both men have strongly denied that they ever gave him the signal to go to war.[18]

On the night of Saturday, June 3, a select group gathered at Levi Eshkol's house in Jerusalem. It included Eshkol, Moshe Dayan, Yitzhak Rabin, Abba Eban, and of course the observant Israel Lior. In the heavy fog of cigarette smoke that usually attends Israeli meetings, especially when Yitzhak Rabin is present, they waited for the chief of Mossad to return from Washington.

"Around midnight," Lior recounted in his memoirs, reproduced here in English for the first time, "there arrived Meir Amit . . . Amit had been sent to Washington, because it had not been clear from Eban's visit what the real intentions of the Americans were.

"Now Amit was back, sitting on a sofa in the private residence of the prime minister. All eyes were upon him. It was clear that after his report, the final decision would be made: war or no war."

Part of Amit's assignment had been to check that U.S. and Israeli intelligence had come to the same conclusions about the current political and military situation in the Middle East. As he immediately stated to the tense little group in Eshkol's living room, there were "no significant differences" on that score. Nor were the Americans going to use their navy to break the blockade of the straits.

Amit kept the answer to the most vital question of all until last: How would Washington react to an Israeli attack on Egypt?

"I am given to understand," he said simply, "that the Americans would bless us if we were to break Nasser in pieces."

Lior recalled the effect this announcement had on the men in the room: "These last words of Amit were stunning. Our impression from the reports, cables, and public announcements had been that the U.S.

would not applaud if we were to go to war. Meir Amit had ascertained that this was not the case."

The moment that Amit finished his careful report, the group decided to tell the cabinet when it met the next day that Israel should go to war. Now that Eshkol felt he had obtained clearance from Washington to go ahead, the cabinet's endorsement was a formality.[19]

We may never know exactly what the Mossad chief discussed, and with whom, during his lightning visit to Washington. It would certainly have been strange if he had not talked with James Angleton, the official liaison with Mossad. Amit's remark that he had found "no significant differences of opinion" on the two countries' intelligence assessments of the situation is extraordinarily telling. As we have seen, the CIA was as certain as could be that the Egyptians did not plan to attack Israel, and that Israel would win any war with the Arabs in six days. Therefore, no one who was privy both to these estimates and to the Amit conversations could have been under any illusions as to what the suggestions about crushing Nasser would mean—an Israeli attack.

Meir Amit's earlier trips to Washington had been attempts to get the Americans interested in an overt coalition against Nasser. Sometime in the spring of 1966, according to a cognizant former CIA official, "The Israelis concluded that they were not going to get us [the United States] to join in an anti-Communist alliance in the Middle East. So they decided they were going to do the job on their own."

"The job," as this individual makes clear, was the destruction of Nasser as a political force—a reprise, in fact, of the 1956 campaign. On that occasion, the Israelis had launched their attack without clearance from Washington and had even, apparently, lied to their friend and liaison James Angleton about what was afoot. In consequence, Eisenhower had shown no hesitation in summarily ordering the Israelis to give up their conquests and go home. Eshkol had understood that the same mistake must not be made again. His intelligence chief had obtained the necessary green light. The 1967 war was launched with American permission to "break Nasser in pieces."

The question remains, however, whether the planners in Tel Aviv undertook the preparations for "the job" on their own. There is a body of opinion within the American intelligence community that Angleton had played a leading part in orchestrating the events leading up to the June 1967 war. One long-serving official at the CIA's ancient rival, the code-breaking National Security Agency, states flatly that "Jim Angleton and the Israelis spent a year cooking up the '67 war. It was a CIA operation, designed to get Nasser." Such a verdict, from a source inside an agency that had the inclination and the facilities to monitor both the CIA and the Israelis, must carry some weight.

A man who believed that the savage quarrel between Khrushchev and Mao Tse-tung was all a pretense to deceive the West would have had little trouble in accepting the proposition that the Soviets were sweeping all before them in the Middle East. Angleton, in the opinion of many who knew him, was a figure of some considerable intellectual vanity. To "do the job" on Nasser and at the same time present Israel as the threatened underdog fighting for its life involved, as we shall see, a psychological operation of enormous sophistication and subtlety. It would be a disservice to the Israeli planners in Mossad, Military Intelligence, and the General Staff to presume that they were incapable of constructing the plan on their own. But if it was indeed a solo effort, they would have lost little by letting Angleton presume that he had played a crucial role, even *the* leading role.

The question is, what agreements or understandings did Amit's interlocutors in those crucial meetings in the first two days of June 1967 carry away regarding Israel's actual war aims? While the breaking of Nasser's bones was fully in accord with U.S. national security policy, the dismembering of Jordan was not.

From the time of the Samu raid in November 1966, King Hussein of Jordan had done his best to keep his head above the turbulent political waters surrounding him. Relations with both Syria and Egypt, as well as with Nasser's surrogate Ahmed Shukeiry of the PLO, had grown steadily worse, and the airwaves had rung with blast and counterblast. The Egyptians routinely referred to the king as the "CIA dwarf" and the "Harlot of Amman," while Amman radio harped on Nasser's betrayal of the Palestinians by his sheltering behind the UN peacekeeping force.

Hussein had few friends, but the United States was apparently one of them—as evidenced by the cash-laden suitcases regularly delivered to the palace by the CIA station chief. Immediately after the Samu raid, the king had sent an anxious entreaty to the Americans. President Johnson cabled to reassure him: "Ambassador [Findley] Burns has informed me of Your Majesty's concern that Israel's policies have changed and that Israel now intends to occupy territory on the West Bank of the Jordan. While I can understand the reason for this concern, we have good reason to believe it is highly unlikely that the events you fear will in fact occur . . . The strong private representations we have made in Israel . . . make clear that should Israel adopt the policies you fear it would have the gravest consequences. There is no doubt in my mind that our position is fully understood and appreciated by the Israelis."[20]

Hussein may have been operating on the assumption that he had powerful protection from the Israelis, but as the tension rose in the Middle East at the end of May 1967, he was feeling more and more vulnerable in the face of his Arab enemies. The ferocious generals in Damascus, in particular, were moving beyond rhetoric to violent action, as the bloody explosion at the border post on May 21 vividly demonstrated.

Weighing the possibility of an Israeli invasion (which the president of the United States had told him would not be allowed) against the entirely unrestrained threats from fellow Arabs, who were lining up to defy Israeli "impertinence," Hussein decided to take a gamble.

On May 29, the king sent a message to his archenemy Nasser, saying that it was time that their two countries "coordinate means of defense against the Israeli threat." Early the next morning he flew to Cairo.

News of the visit had quickly spread to the Syrians. American communications intelligence intercepted a worried call from Damascus to Nasser asking what he thought he was doing dealing with the traitor Hussein. Nasser told the Syrians not to worry. "We will trap him," he said.

The CIA was worried for their little friend as he disappeared off to Egypt, but there was nothing they could do.

Late that night Hussein returned, relaxed and smiling. American diplomats in Amman were horrified and astonished to hear that he had come back with company. Right behind him on the aircraft steps was the PLO leader Ahmed Shukeiry, who not long before had declared, "The primary struggle is against the tyrant of Amman, Hussein, who has betrayed God, the Prophet, and the Palestine cause." But Shukeiry was not the only passenger to get off the plane. Right behind him was Egyptian General Abd al-Moneim Riad. Under a mutual defense treaty signed by Hussein and Nasser that morning, Riad would command the Jordanian armed forces in war. Hussein had indeed been trapped. Under the cover of the crisis with Israel, Nasser had succeeded in getting one of his archenemies in the Arab world, one who had been regarded as irredeemably in the grip of the Americans, to sign a treaty, express undying friendship, and accept not only the PLO but an Egyptian general to command his forces.

American Embassy officials in Amman scrambled to find out what on earth had happened. "Don't worry," said one of the king's entourage. "For the first time in weeks I can sleep easy in my bed. The whole Arab world is no longer against us." Hussein evidently thought that he had neatly deflected the greater danger to his throne. If there had been no war, it might have seemed like a wise move.

CIA Director Richard Helms has said that immediately after Amit's departure from Washington, he sent an "Eyes Only" message to the president, telling him that Israel would "probably" go to war "in a few days."[21] In fact, the CIA had more precise information, certainly by June 4. That evening the CIA station chief in Amman sought out Hussein. The king, in keeping with his newfound insouciance, was at a party. Taking him into the garden, the station chief gave him an urgent message: Israel would attack Egypt the following morning. It would be a short war. Israel would win. Jordan should stay out of the fight, but if Hussein felt he had to demonstrate Arab solidarity, he should confine himself to a pro forma demonstration. Jordan would be left alone by the Israelis.

Despite high-level assumptions in Washington that Jordan was protected, some American diplomats in Jerusalem, as well as the Jordanian military, were not reassured by the sight of Israeli forces "in offensive posture" drawn up on the edge of the divided city.

Hussein took the hurried conversation in the garden seriously. In fact, he went and phoned Nasser to pass on the warning. The Egyptian leader, apparently buoyed by his talks with Johnson's envoy Anderson and by the impending visit of his foreign minister to Washington, refused to believe that disaster was at hand.

As advertised by the CIA to Hussein, the blow fell on Nasser the following morning. The attack on the Egyptian air force was set for 7:45 A.M. Israeli time, because the Israelis knew that at that hour the Egyptian pilots would be relaxing from their early-morning patrols and senior commanders would be on the way to their offices. The Egyptians had anticipated the possibility of an Israeli air attack at some point, but not that Weizman and Hod would gamble on throwing their entire combat force into the assault, leaving only a scant dozen planes to guard Israeli airspace. In less than two hours, the Egyptian air force was wiped out—309 out of 390 planes—along with a third of the pilots. Motti Hod, the air force commander, later boasted that the attack had been planned for sixteen years. "We lived with the plan, we slept on the plan, we are the plan," he boasted. "Consequently we perfected it."[22]

Three-quarters of an hour after the first Israeli Mirage swooped down on the neatly lined up Migs at the Bir Gafgafa in Sinai, Lieutenant General Odd Bull, a Norwegian in charge of the UN Truce Supervision Organization, was summoned by a senior official to the Israeli Foreign Ministry and given a message for King Hussein: "We shall not initiate any action whatsoever against Jordan. However, should Jordan open hostilities, we shall react with all our might, and the king will have to bear full responsibility for all the consequences."

The official coupled this threat with an explanation of what was going on. The war had started, he said, when Egyptian planes had taken off against Israel and had been intercepted by Israeli planes. This, of course, was a deliberate lie.[23]

Hussein received the warning, but just as Nasser had chosen to deceive himself the night before, so now the king took hysterical claims of victory pouring forth from Cairo radio at face value. Dayan had cunningly instructed the public affairs office to keep quiet about what it had achieved "to keep the enemy camps confused."

So, for the second time in a week, Hussein fell into a trap. Four hours after the war began, his forces, which he had placed under the command of General Riad (not one of the great commanders of history), opened fire on Israeli targets. At the same time his tiny air force set off and strafed a small Israeli airfield.

The first reports of the initial Jordanian bombardment were not taken very seriously at Israeli military headquarters. As Ezer Weizman later recalled, "There was an inclination to make light of it: 'Hussein's just pretending, to keep in with Nasser; but he doesn't mean it.'" Weizman hoped that Hussein was in earnest. As he put it, he wanted the war to give him "the chance to write a wish on a slip of paper to be stuffed into one of the cracks in the Western Wall"; i.e., to take all of Jerusalem and the rest of what he regarded as the land of Israel—the West Bank. Weizman had never made much secret of his ambition to conquer the West Bank. While still head of the air force he would ask cadets at graduation ceremonies: "When you come to Hebron [a West Bank town then under Jordanian rule], will you come as a conqueror?"

A well-primed cadet would know that the correct answer was "No—as a liberator!"[24]

The Jordanian attack on the airfield was taken to mean that Hussein was in earnest. From his command post Motti Hod had only to utter a cryptic order, "Do the Jordanians," for the plan to swing into action. The Jordanian air force was immediately wiped out. One pilot demonstrated the ruthless professionalism of Military Intelligence by aiming his rockets precisely at Hussein's private office in Amman.

At the end of that day, Johnson's national security adviser, Walt Rostow, forwarded an intelligence report on the fighting to the president. "Mr. President: Herewith the account, with a map, of the first day's turkey shoot."[25]

Israeli troops moved to take the old city of Jerusalem that same night. Although they met stout resistance from the Bedouin soldiers of the Arab Legion, the West Bank militia was badly armed and barely trained—possibly because the king did not trust his Palestinian subjects. Hussein never had a chance of holding either the city or the rest of the West Bank. The king himself realized this by the second day of the war, so when the UN Security Council called for a cease-fire, he quickly accepted it. The Israelis, however, did not, and continued with the task of solidifying their conquest of Jerusalem and the West Bank, meanwhile driving out as much of the population as possible by such means as laying down liberal doses of napalm on refugee columns fleeing to the east. By noon on Tuesday, June 6, the U.S. Embassy in Amman was reporting, "IDF Air Force yesterday and again today hit many civilian targets on West Bank where there are absolutely no military emplacements."[26]

As Hussein surveyed the ruin of his kingdom on the second terrible night of the war, he summoned the CIA station chief to his military headquarters. The man had been a good friend of the king's, but colleagues recall him later describing his trepidation as he met with the king and a group of irate-looking Bedouin officers. "Didn't you tell me that Israel was not going to attack Jordan?" Hussein reportedly asked. The CIA man agreed this was so. "Have they not taken over half my country?" Again, the American agreed. "Well," said the shattered monarch, "what the fuck do I do now?"

There was not much he could do. On Wednesday, June 7, the Israelis completed the conquest of the Old City of Jerusalem. Moshe Dayan, who was reaping international glory for the campaign planned and fought by Rabin and his colleagues, announced, "We have united Jerusalem, the divided capital of Israel. We have returned to the holiest of our holy places, never to part from it again."[27] Israel now signaled its acceptance of the cease-fire. The next day the guns also stopped on the Egyptian front, which now lay along the Suez Canal.

The war was not over, however. On Friday, June 9, Dayan, without reference to the prime minister or his own chief of staff, ordered an immediate attack on Syria. Despite all the grave warnings about the dangers posed by Syrian-sponsored terrorism, which had sparked the prewar crisis, the opening of the northern front came as an afterthought. Rabin had argued against it the day before.

Taking the Golan Heights, from which Syrian guns had launched shells on the Israeli settlements below for so long (without, it must be said, much effect), took two days. The ill-equipped Syrian forces gave a good account of themselves until a false report that the enemy had occupied their line of supply caused a general panic and retreat. The war that changed the Middle East forever was over.

The plotting and lies that accompanied the 1956 Suez War have for the most part been exposed, thanks mainly to the political rifts the campaign caused among Western countries. The 1967 war, which in many ways followed the course of the earlier conflict—a premeditated attack to destroy Nasser's regime—has kept its secrets better concealed. Why, for example, did the Israelis attack the American intelligence ship *Liberty* off the coast of Sinai on June 8? It is clear that the Israelis knew that they were attacking a vessel of the U.S. Navy, especially as it was flying a large Stars and Stripes at the time. The fact that they spent six hours reconnoitering and executing the attack, which included machine-gunning lifeboats, attests to the deadly intent of the operation.

The fact that the U.S. government, then and since, has done its best to cover up the circumstances of an attack in which thirty-four Americans died suggests that the two countries share some very guilty secrets indeed. However, it is still unexplained why the Israelis did it. It has been suggested that they wanted to prevent the U.S. from discovering, through military traffic intercepted by the *Liberty*, that despite the cease-fire they were going to open another front against Syria. But the U.S. was by no means as solicitous of the alleged Soviet proxies in Damascus as it had been of King Hussein. Furthermore, while Dayan had only to give the go-ahead for the IDF northern commander, David Elazar, to swing into action on the Golan, the assault on the *Liberty* involved coordination with the air force and navy. Since Dayan did not consult Rabin about ordering the Syrian attack, could he have told the General Staff to attack the Americans without explaining why he was doing it?[28]

For whatever reason, the Americans on the *Liberty* were regarded as expendable, and Washington accepted the results of the June war with entire satisfaction. The American client had humiliated the Soviet clients. At a general Arab summit meeting in Khartoum that August, Nasser, in return for promises of vital cash from the Saudis, agreed that he would finally pull his forces out of Yemen. Israeli withdrawal from the West Bank, Gaza, and the Golan Heights is taking somewhat longer.

Israel had suffered for its failure to communicate plans and intentions to either the CIA or the White House in 1956. The 1967 war was better managed. The covert liaison had matured.

The Suez operation had been further marred by the deep unpopularity of that war in France and Britain, particularly Britain. Public relations were far better handled in 1967. So far as most of the world was concerned (the Arabs took a different view), the legend of David turning on Goliath took hold and lives on until this day.

In Israel itself, however, a little of the truth about the June war has seeped out over the years. In 1982, for example, Prime Minister Menachem Begin (who had been a member of the government in June 1967) declared, "In June 1967 we . . . had a choice. The Egyptian army concentrations in the Sinai approaches do not prove that Nasser was really about to attack us. We must be honest with ourselves. We decided to attack him."[29]

Begin admitted this truth in the course of justifying his own choice to go to war in Lebanon. But his bald assertion that Israel was not forced to lash out at the Arabs in 1967, but could instead have avoided a war entirely, is backed up by statements from three very unsentimental senior Israeli generals.

Ezer Weizman, who as commander of the air force and then deputy head of the Israeli General Staff did much of the operational planning for the war, said in 1972 that there was "no threat of destruction" in June 1967 but that the attack on Egypt, Jordan, and Syria was nevertheless justified so that Israel could "exist according to the scale, spirit, and quality she now embodies."[30]

Gen. Matityahu Peled, who before his metamorphosis into a dove had been a hawk among hawks on the General Staff, stated, "To claim that the Egyptian forces concentrated on our borders were capable of threatening Israel's existence not only insults the intelligence of anyone capable of analyzing this kind of situation, but is an insult to Zahal [the Israeli army]."[31]

Yitzhak Rabin, chief of staff before and during the war, echoed the military consensus when he stated, "I do not believe that Nasser wanted war. The two divisions he sent into Sinai on May 14 would not have been enough to unleash an offensive against Israel. He knew it and we knew it."[32]

The facts seemed obvious to these cold professionals. Although their remarks caused something of a furor in Israel when first expressed in the early 1970s, the matter is not considered a subject of dispute in their country today.

In the immediate aftermath of the war, the cold warriors in Washington (who knew the truth just as well as Begin and the generals) were highly pleased with Israel's role in punishing the Soviets in the Middle East. The relationship was now ready to move on to a different phase. In the 1960s America had made the first tentative steps toward meeting a long-held Israeli dream—a military relationship between the two countries—by supplying some arms. Now, with the world hailing the "miracle" of June 1967, it was time for that relationship to become overt. The consequences, both for Israeli society and the world, were to be profound.

7. The Weapons Business

THE MAN who gave his name to the only world-famous Israeli brand name lives a few hours' drive from Pittsburgh. The product he invented nearly forty years ago is still a best-seller, but Uzi Gal lives in a modest suburban house on a quiet street far from the country he helped make powerful.

The Uzi submachine gun is in fact the only product native to Israel that commands instant name recognition everywhere. (Jaffa oranges might count, but they were indigenous to Palestine before their cultivation passed into the hands of Israelis.) It was Israel that produced Mr. Gal, and it is the state-owned Israel Military Industries (IMI) that still profits, to the tune of tens of millions of dollars every year, from the sale of his product.

For the inventor of a supremely successful device for killing people, Uzi betrays no disquieting fascination with the end result of his work. A stocky and astonishingly well-preserved sixty-six-year-old with a neat goatee and a disarming manner, he talks about his profession with an engineer's detachment—"the human being is a very unstable weapons platform." A discussion with him leaves the impression that he would discuss lawn mowers with the same insight and absorption, were lawn mowers his obsession and Uzi lawn mowers Israel's only well-known export.

Such an eventuality was never likely. "I liked guns from the beginning," he says matter-of-factly, with a hint of an Israeli accent. He

155

absorbed his interest from his father, a veteran of the Imperial German Army who served as an aerial gunner on the Western front in World War I.

Born in 1926, Uzi moved to England with his family as a child to escape the Nazis. He mainly remembers England as the place where he acquired his first gun, an air pistol, with which he severely injured his thumb. From Britain his family moved on to the Kibbutz Yagour in Palestine, where the young Uzi started sketching his first gun designs. The kibbutz was a hotbed of Haganah activity, so much so that when the British army descended to search for arms, they found more than one hundred rifles. All the men were carried off to prison.

In jail, Uzi continued to think about the proper design of a submachine gun, and when he was released the local Haganah elevated him to the position of chief armorer. He set to work repairing the guns that the British had missed.

Like most underground armies, the Haganah was armed with a variety of weapons picked up wherever they could be bought or stolen. Uzi pored over the assortment of guns from around the world, noting their good and bad points. His dream of a perfect submachine gun slowly took shape.

The gun he eventually designed for the Israeli army was essentially the same weapon sought after and esteemed today, by everyone from the Secret Service men guarding the White House to the drug dealers guarding their wares a few blocks down the street. It had a bolt telescoped around the end of the barrel, which kept the overall length of the weapon short. The free-floating bolt itself was heavy, which made both for a diminished recoil and for a well-balanced gun overall. The magazine was in the handgrip, which also aided the balance. In addition, it was extremely rugged and reliable, and could be cheaply manufactured out of machine-stamped parts rather than requiring expensive machine tools.

Each of these concepts had been individually realized in other weapons, but it was Uzi's genius to know which were the best ideas and how to fit them together. Modest though he may be, he is careful to emphasize the significance of his achievement. "A good chef creates original dishes from ingredients that are there for anyone to use. That's what I did. Yes, I'm a good cook." He nods, satisfied with the analogy.

Uzi perfected the gun and the production techniques required to manufacture it in quantity at the workshops of Israel Military Industries, which had grown out of Ta'as, the underground weapons-making arm of the Haganah. By 1954 the gun was in production, and in 1955 it was unveiled to the world at the annual military Independence Day parade in Jerusalem. The high command, after prolonged cogitation, decided to officially name it after its inventor.

Most of the time Uzi eschews any outward manifestation of Israeli chauvinism, but he recalls the emotional reaction of his countrymen when they learned of his invention: "It was a great moment for the state of Israel, because never in two thousand years had there been such a thing, a weapon that the Jewish people had made for themselves, and I designed it from the ground up."

This last point is a sore one, because there have been rumors over the years that the original inspiration for the Uzi was actually a Czech submachine gun, and furthermore, that an important part of the final engineering work on the Uzi had actually been the work of Israel Galil.

Israel Galil is not a popular name in the Gal household. In fact, Uzi does not even care to utter it unless pressed. While not as ubiquitous or as famous as the Uzi, the Galil automatic rifle is also a well-known product of the Israeli weapons industry. However, its design has few pretensions to originality, being basically a copy of the Finnish AK-74, which is in turn an adaptation of the Soviet Kalashnikov AK-47. (Any possible Finnish outrage over the appearance of their gun under an Israeli imprint was doubtless mitigated by the fact that the Finnish manufacturer, Solomon Zabladowicz, was also the owner of Soltam, a prominent Israeli munitions manufacturer.) It is not hard to guess to whom Uzi is referring when he sniffs and talks of "modificators" who like to "call themselves inventors" and are really nothing better than "copyists."

Nonetheless it is Uzi who lives, unremarked by his neighbors, in the modest suburban home in the U.S., while Galil remains in Israel, an honored figure and a powerful force at Israel Military Industries. Despite the millions of dollars he has garnered for the state (an Uzi costs on the order of $50 to manufacture and retails for around $700), Uzi never received a shekel in royalties. Nor did he find IMI particularly grateful for the riches he had brought it. When it transpired that the only place he could obtain treatment for a gravely ill daughter was in the United States, he cashed in his pension and moved.

This affable man is as modest as his present surroundings, but he does exhibit a certain unself-conscious pride at the place he has earned in history. "When people talk about Uzi-ing a house," he says reflectively, "I guess I should feel proud that my name is in the language, but really, you know, I don't deserve such fame. I just made a good gun. It's crazy." He shakes his head in bemusement at the way it has all turned out. [1]

While the young Uzi Gal was pondering the beauties of a telescope bolt, another young kibbutznik, only three years older than the gunsmith, was also taking steps to make Israeli weapons famous around the world. Shimon Peres has never actually designed a gun or other instrument of war. His career was built on the business of arms—that, and an unwavering loyalty to his patron, David Ben-Gurion.

Peres's first steps to power came when he caught the eye of David Ben-Gurion in 1947. He was just the type of underling the Old Man liked—young, willing, and with no power base of his own. But unlike other Ben-Gurion proteges, such as Moshe Dayan, he was generally disliked by his peers. A sympathetic biographer later addressed the question of Peres's unpopularity among his fellow workers in the Zionist labor movement: ". . . as would be the case throughout his life, it was not just that he received no gratitude, but that he drew enmity and dislike. What was it then that turned them, and later, other comrades, against him? Possibly Peres himself had the best explanation when he wrote, many years afterward: 'I have to accept the fact that many people think I am the type who pushes to the front of the queue.' "[2]

Peres got a jump up the queue in the Haganah early on, when he was made the headquarters liaison with Teddy Kollek's covert arms-buying mission, headquartered above the Copacabana nightclub in New York. So, unlike most of the other men who were to emerge as Israel's leaders over the next forty years, Peres never carried a gun or wore a uniform—a fact his numerous detractors did not allow to be forgotten.

In 1950, at the age of twenty-six, he was posted to New York to take over Kollek's job. Although Israel was now a legitimate state legally empowered to buy arms, the mission remained a semicovert operation because the U.S. officially adhered to the May 1950 Tripartite Agreement with Britain and France, under which the three governments agreed to regulate arms shipments to the Middle East. Peres had to rely on the secondhand market, where he operated with some success. Ben-Gurion, an obsessive diarist, noted in his entry for September 13,

1950: "Shimon Peres arrived. He is working for the Defense Ministry and studying in the evenings. So far we have spent $1.7 million on arms in the U.S., $1.1 million on the air force (80 planes and spare parts), $0.41 million on the navy (a frigate, 12 landing craft, three launches, spare parts), $0.09 million on the infantry (explosives, .22 ammunition, shells, etc.)."[3]

Peres's duties included not only finding arms but also, on occasion, the money to pay for them. A trip to Canada at that time ignited in Peres what was to become a lifelong fascination with millionaires. He was trying to buy artillery from the Canadian government and approached the Jewish multimillionaire Sam Bronfman, founder of the Seagram liquor corporation, to find the necessary funds. Bronfman obligingly agreed to raise the $1.5 million required (having first beaten down the price by half a million), but made Peres buy a new pair of socks before allowing him to attend the fund-raiser with his fellow plutocrats.

Peres returned to Israel at the end of 1951. Although still only twenty-eight years old, he was "pushy" enough to reject the proffered post of chief assistant to the director general of the Defense Ministry, holding out successfully for the title of deputy director general. He had important support among the arms dealers. Al Schwimmer, the former TWA engineer who had lured Hank Greenspun into the smuggling business and flown military technology to Czechoslovakia, lobbied for Peres to be put in charge of a project to set up an Israeli aircraft industry. Schwimmer and Leo Gardner, another veteran arms smuggler, had been repairing secondhand planes for Israel in a run-down machine shop in Burbank, while living in Jeanette MacDonald's old house in Hollywood. Ben-Gurion personally approved the idea of their moving the repair operation to Tel Aviv, an enterprise that eventually grew into Israel Aircraft Industries.

In effect, Peres was now running the noncombat side of Israel's defense effort, putting himself in charge of arms buying, arms production, and administration. Over the next few years he organized and molded what was to become the country's military-industrial complex.

Back in 1947 Ben-Gurion had written to a friend about his plan to use the partitioned section of Palestine allotted to Israel by the UN to build a first-class army and a Jewish economy, before expanding into the rest of the neighborhood. His hopes for a properly developed economy were slow to materialize. The country was almost entirely without natural resources, apart from potash in the area of the Dead Sea. Agriculture was heavily dependent on expensive irrigation schemes. The Arab boycott of Israel as a trading partner meant that the country was excluded from its natural markets, and had to find an outlet for exports farther afield.

On the other hand, Ben-Gurion's dream of building up a first-class army was realized, and fairly quickly. Alongside the training of troops and the purchase of arms from abroad, this involved the creation of a local defense industry. Uzi's world-class gun was (and remains) the most significant product of this industry, but the dreams of Ben-Gurion and his closest aides, such as Peres, did not stop there. The decision, after all, to back Al Schwimmer in his scheme to build an aircraft industry, given Israel's economic position as a poor and under-developed country, was highly significant. Investment in a nuclear weapons program was an even more ambitious project for the tiny state, whether or not it was possible to cut corners through operations like NUMEC.

Hand in hand with Ben-Gurion's overriding interest in a foreign policy based on military force went a deliberate and steady investment in military industry that inevitably made the Israeli military-industrial complex the backbone of the country's economy. It was a fateful turning point for Israel. Nowadays some Israelis talk wistfully of how different things might have been if the country had invested its productive energies in high-technology civilian industry, like a prototype South Korea. That was not a realistic proposition. Once meaningful negotiations with neighboring countries over either territory or the fate of the million or more native Palestinians in unwilling exile had been ruled out, Israeli policy depended solely on arms and guile to maintain its position.

There is no evidence that David Ben-Gurion ever seriously contemplated any other course. Other leaders of the time, such as Moshe Sharett, considered the possibility of defending the Zionist state by peaceful means. But Ben-Gurion's control of security policy, with the help of capable underlings like Peres, Moshe Dayan (chief of staff from 1953 to 1957), and Isser Harel, ensured it was his hawkish policy that triumphed.

Nowadays, there is no better illustration of where this policy led than the naval shipyard in Beersheba. The town is, of course, in the middle of the Negev Desert, but that has not prevented the government from directing the state-owned IAI conglomerate to manufacture naval patrol vessels there. "We were pushed by the government to provide jobs in Beersheba," explained the chairman of the company in 1988. Overall, upwards of 120,000 Israelis work in the defense business, which means that about one in four families in Israel is dependent on it for their livelihood. In 1989, the country earned over $1.6 billion on the international weapons market, far more than for any other industrial export.

Success in the international arms market is as much a matter of foreign policy as commercial considerations. That is why the buying and selling of weapons—or, as it came to be known, "Uzi Diplomacy"—became early on a major consideration in Israel's overseas relations.

Although Israel was emerging in the world as an arms supplier as well as arms buyer, its way of doing business never quite lost a certain piratical edge. In March 1958, for example, Peres's arms-dealing friend Leo Gardner made an emergency landing at the small Algerian city of Bone, about two hundred and fifty miles east of Algiers, and immediately ran into trouble.

The problem was that Gardner and his crew were carrying a load of bazookas, part of a deal worth $15 million and destined for the blood-stained regime of Gen. Rafael Trujillo in the Dominican Republic. At the time Algeria was French territory, under bitter dispute with the rebels of the FLN. The airfield's security officer was duly suspicious. "What are you carrying?" he asked Gardner.

"Arms," replied the pilot, who had been assured that transit had been cleared with a contact of Peres's in the French prime minister's office.

"What have you been doing for the past eleven years?"

"In 1947 I smuggled American planes to Israel. In 1948 I flew arms from Czechoslovakia to Israel, and I bombed Cairo. In 1953 I flew Spitfires from Israel to Italy. In 1956 I flew arms from France to Israel."

Gardner was proud of his record, but for some reason the French official thought he was dealing with a professional arms smuggler. It turned out that Peres's friend in Paris had simply forgotten to pass the word along to Algiers that the Israeli plane was cleared for transit.

Things were smoothed over with the French, but the affair raised some interesting questions as to who was actually running Israeli foreign policy. The diplomats at the Foreign Ministry thought it bad for Israel's image to be selling weapons to the likes of Trujillo, not to mention Somoza in Nicaragua, and Peres had promised that he would stay out of those markets. He had promptly broken the promise, as Gardner's unfortunate appearance in Algeria made clear.

Peres laid down his principles at a meeting in his ministry in 1958: "By not selling an Uzi to a certain country, we are not implementing an embargo against that country, but against ourselves. It is absolute nonsense to embargo ourselves on an item that can be acquired elsewhere."[4]

The Foreign Ministry might complain at this unprincipled attitude, but it is clear that the true Israeli foreign policy was being framed and executed by the directors of the security system—Ben-Gurion and his faithful lieutenants.

This state of affairs is amply illustrated by the Franco-Israeli covert military alliance that burgeoned in the mid-1950s, an alliance based, as we have seen, on a shared antipathy toward Nasser. It was not the Israeli Foreign Ministry that supervised the liaison between the two governments, but Peres and Dayan. Peres also directed a massive campaign of what amounted to covert manipulation to garner support for the relationship within French society. A French journalist later described the Peres of those days as a "political seducer . . . haunting the corridors of power," his emissaries "infiltrating the French army at all levels, cultivating bonds of friendship with senior and junior officers . . . sticking close to all politicians, in or out of power, the underlings as well as the bosses," in an "immense effort, conducted in the shadows, to make sure that no chance, no opportunity was left unexploited."[5] As part of the effort the Israelis arranged to subsidize the newspaper of the governing French Socialist Party. Questioned about this initiative in later years, Isser Harel simply replied: "Ask Shimon Peres."[6]

The arrival of Charles de Gaulle at the Elysée Palace in 1958 removed the bloom from the France-Israeli military romance, but cooperation nonetheless continued. The two countries maintained consultation on nuclear matters, with Israeli scientists reportedly on hand to observe French nuclear tests in the Sahara, while on the Iles d'Hyeres off the Riviera the joint project to develop a medium-range missile continued undisturbed. The two intelligence services also maintained a fraternal cooperation, with Mossad lending a helping hand to the French SDECE (Service de Documentation Extérieure et de Contre-Espionage) intelligence agency in the kidnapping of the Moroccan dissident Ben Barka (for subsequent torture and murder by the Moroccan secret police) in 1966. The French arms industry, particularly the Dassault aircraft firm, was on extremely close terms with its Israeli counterpart. In fact, by 1960 Israel Aircraft Industries was producing French-designed jet trainers under license, many of which were used in combat in the Six Day War. Nevertheless, total defense sales in 1966 amounted to no more than $15 million.

The whole picture changed utterly for the arms industry after the 1967 war, as it did for practically everything else in Israel. The dazzling victory sparked a boom in immigration, in the economy, and in the defense business. Just prior to the war the economy had been stagnating, with immigration down to zero and unemployment running at 10 percent. In March 1967 there had been a riot by jobless workers in Tel Aviv, who stoned the City Hall.

After the war the economy surged ahead at over 10 percent a year. Immigrants, including a large number of Americans, poured in. The most spectacular increase was in the defense business. In the first three years after 1967 military industry quadrupled its output. Between 1968 and 1972 the number of employees in defense industry rose by twenty thousand. In those same years the Ministry of Defense increased its purchases of weapons from local industry by 86 percent, while the share of weapons in industrial exports went up from 14 percent in 1967 to 21 percent in 1968. In 1972 the Ministry of Defense created Sibat, headed by Shapik Shapiro, the man who today presides over Eagle from his office in the IBM Building on Shaul Hamalekh.[7]

This postwar boom was inseparable from the new and warm relationship forged with the Americans in 1967. Israel had indeed proved itself as a "strategic asset," and the Americans were prepared to equip and finance it accordingly. This was just as well, because Israel had lost the French connection forged by Peres. Thus, one military partnership was coming to an end and another, long sought after by Israel, was coming to fruition.

In January 1968 Prime Minister Levi Eshkol arrived for an official visit with President Lyndon Johnson. These two seasoned politicians had got on well since their first meeting in 1964. "The chemistry between them was fantastic," recalls one participant in their discussions. Once again Eshkol had come to ask for weapons. This time he wanted the F-4 Phantom, which was then the frontline U.S. fighter-bomber.

The Israelis were anxious to secure the Phantom, for both political and military reasons. At the time they were engaged in the so-called "War of Attrition" with Egypt. Nasser was bombarding Israeli positions along the Suez Canal with artillery, and the IDF was replying in kind. The F-4 Phantom could carry up to six tons of bombs, and the Israelis wanted to use it to bomb targets deep inside Egypt.

Politically, it was important to commit the U.S. to a highly visible demonstration of its military support for Israel. At that time the F-4 was being sold only to two close U.S. allies—Britain and Germany. True, the Americans had made the crucial break back in the Kennedy administration by agreeing to Ben-Gurion's request to supply Hawk missiles. Even so, the breach opened by the Hawk sale had remained a narrow one for the next few years. The Phantom deal was to change all that.

As he liked to do with intimates, Johnson invited Eshkol down to his ranch in Texas so that the two leaders could enjoy the pleasures of family life and drives around the extensive LBJ holdings. Eshkol and the press were even treated to the unveiling by the president of his appendectomy scar. The other guests included the president's military advisers and Motti Hod, at the time chief of the Israeli air force. Hod, a rough-hewn kibbutznik, was slightly overawed by his introduction to the leader of the free world, especially as he was munching on a handful of grapes when he first encountered the president and had to shake hands. Military discussions with Israelis were still a sensitive topic, so the Israeli air force chief had to be smuggled in the back door. Once inside, however, the Israelis were quite at home. Hod recalls how Eshkol chose to sit in the president's special armchair, replete with communications gadgets and buttons.

At the meeting, Johnson promised Eshkol that the U.S. would supply fifty Phantoms to Israel. Some officials in the State Department complained that the F-4 was far too potent a weapon to be introduced into the Middle East and suggested that the Israelis be sold the F-5, a supposedly less capable fighter on offer to the Third World market. But the era of restraint in arming Israel was coming to an end, and the professional diplomats' protests were swept aside, as was the attempt by Deputy Secretary of Defense Paul Nitze to require Israel to open up its nuclear program for inspection in return for the Phantoms.[8]

Shapik Shapiro, then in charge of all Israeli arms acquisitions in the U.S., eagerly awaited the news that Johnson and Eshkol had reached agreement. As soon as he got word, he called Sanford McDonnell, a famously mean Scotsman who owned and ran McDonnell Douglas, manufacturers of the F-4. "We talked for over half an hour," Shapiro recalls. "Later on people told me that the only reason we had talked for such a time long distance was that I was paying for the call."

While Shapiro and McDonnell proceeded on the (correct) assumption that the deal was set, Johnson declined publicly to acknowledge the commitment. He was apparently hoping that some sort of Middle East settlement could be arranged with the Soviets. Since 1968 was an election year in the U.S., the Phantom sale became a hot political issue. Israel's supporters argued that the sale was needed in order to maintain a "balance of power" in the Middle East—despite the fact that Egypt did not possess, and had no hope of acquiring, a bomber capable of inflicting comparable damage on Israel.

In fact, Johnson did not sign the final authorization for the Phantom deal until a few days before leaving office, and the first planes did not arrive in Israel until September 1969. The Israeli pilots were unimpressed with the F-4's capabilities as a fighter (they derisively nicknamed it the B-4, *B* standing for "bomber," a gross insult from a fighter pilot) and were disappointed that the USAF and McDonnell Douglas had exaggerated its range. Nevertheless, the new arrivals were put into action immediately, and by January 1970 the F-4s were attacking targets in the suburbs of Cairo itself.

Back in 1958 the administration had invoked the "Eisenhower Doctrine." In those days the threat to vital American interests, particularly the oil fields of Saudi Arabia, had been the radical Arab nationalism led by Gamal Abdel Nasser and allegedly backed by the Soviets. Now, twelve years later, despite the 1967 war, Nasser's bones remained unbroken. In 1969 an obscure Libyan army officer, Muammar Qaddafi, inspired by the aging leader in Cairo, had seized power in Tripoli and moved to eject the Americans from their military base there. That same year a radical group in Saudi Arabia called the National Liberation Front, which included several hundred army officers, attempted a coup. The plot failed, but both the U.S. and Saudi governments were seriously alarmed. An American firm, Interset, with CIA alumni on the payroll, now took over Saudi internal security.[9]

In the late 1950s the CIA had gone into closer partnership with

Israeli intelligence, to curb what was perceived as the Soviet-backed Nasserite threat to American interests in the region. That link had remained covert. Now, though the objectives remained the same, there was an overt connection between Washington and the Israeli military itself. Thus Yitzhak Rabin, who had gone from chief of staff to Israel's ambassador in Washington, claimed that he had been given the nod by the Nixon White House for an escalation in the bombing of Egypt with the new American planes. As an Israeli historian puts it, "It was clear to Israel that the Nixon administration would prefer to see Nasser struck down." Some things had not changed much in the Middle East.[10]

Whatever the intention, the bombing had the effect of driving Nasser farther into the arms of the Russians, who agreed to send combat troops to Egypt and set up a comprehensive air defense system in the country. In consequence, the Israelis found it was no longer possible to bomb at will, and in August 1970 the U.S. sponsored a cease-fire, bringing the "War of Attrition" to an end.

Richard Nixon and Henry Kissinger, undeterred by the experience, put the Israeli military to work again soon afterwards, this time in defense of an old friend of the U.S., King Hussein of Jordan. The Six Day War had not only cut his country in half and injected a further mass of refugees fleeing Israeli rule from the West Bank, it had also produced a new militancy in the Palestinian movement. The PLO was no longer a pliant tool of Nasser. Its military offshoots, well armed and buoyed by some limited military successes against the Israelis, had made Jordan their base.

By the beginning of September 1970 it appeared that Hussein was losing control of the kingdom to the guerrillas. While officials at the State Department were pessimistic about the king's chances of keeping his throne, the Hashemite monarch had more potent supporters in the White House and at the CIA. The local station chief, a tough Irishman named Jack O'Connell, thought the king could be saved. Richard Nixon and Henry Kissinger agreed.

On September 6 the Popular Front for the Liberation of Palestine, one of the more radical Palestinian groups, precipitated a crisis by hijacking three airliners to a remote Jordanian airfield and announced that they intended to hold the 421 passengers, including many Americans, hostage for the release of prisoners held by Israel.

For Nixon, the crisis presented not just a threat but an opportunity.

As Henry Kissinger later observed in his memoirs, the president decided that "the hijacking should be used as a pretext to crush the fedayeen [Palestinian guerrillas]" using an Arab proxy, the king. On September 16 Hussein, after consulting with the CIA station chief (who spent much of the ensuing crisis at the king's headquarters), decided that he would have to crush the Palestinians or risk being crushed himself. Two days later the Jordanian army went into action against the Palestinian camps.

Despite fierce resistance, the Palestinians were soon being driven from Amman. Their desperate cries for help went unheeded in most of the Arab world (not for the last time), except in Damascus. There, Hafez al-Asad, the strongman of the regime, dispatched armored units across the border into an area of northern Jordan that had already been taken over by the Palestinians. His move was tentative, but it aroused the most extreme reaction in Washington. Despite the fact that the Russians were urging restraint on all sides—including their supposed Syrian lackeys—the Nixon-Kissinger team was quick to conclude that this represented a power play by Moscow. The Soviets, according to Kissinger, were "playing" the crisis in Jordan.[11] He accordingly indulged himself in some "muscle flexing," putting the 82nd Airborne Division at Fort Bragg on full alert as well as deploying the Sixth Fleet closer to the action. Hussein may or may not have thought the whole business was sponsored by the Soviets, but he was extremely worried by the Syrian incursion and urgently requested American air strikes to drive them out.

Since in those days the direct intervention of American forces in the Middle East was judged too politically explosive, Kissinger reached for the Israelis. Prime Minister Golda Meir, who had succeeded Eshkol the previous year, was on a fund-raising trip to New York, in the company of Ambassador Rabin. Kissinger reached Rabin at a United Jewish Appeal dinner on the night of September 20 and, amending Hussein's request for U.S. help, announced that "King Hussein has approached us, describing the situation of his forces, and asked us to transmit his request that your air force attack the Syrians in northern Jordan. I need an immediate reply."

Rabin, somewhat rudely, retorted that he was "surprised to hear the United States passing on messages like some sort of mailman." He refused to give any kind of assurances until Israel was given an absolutely clear green light from Nixon.

(It has been suggested that Mossad was the source of alarmist reports reaching the White House from the CIA about the Syrian encroachment, which would indicate that the Israelis were determining American policy in the region. That is indignantly denied by the CIA officers directly concerned with the crisis, who today refer nostalgically to the "very, very good sources" they had inside Jordan. Since the king had been on the payroll for years and was for most of the period of the civil war "holding hands in the palace" with O'Connell, the station chief, it looks as if the CIA was well equipped to produce its own reports on the fighting. "The Israelis had some pretty crappy sources in Jordan," recalls one former official. "They never really had much idea what was going on. We did.")

Later that night, still talking from the UJA dinner, Rabin agreed that the Israelis would mobilize forces along their border with Syria and would send a reconnaissance flight to survey the Syrian invasion. In return, the Israeli government demanded a cast-iron commitment from the United States that it would intervene to protect Israel if either the Egyptians or the Soviets backed Syria up with force. Rabin also demanded that the U.S. guarantee an accelerated supply of arms to Israel.

These dramatics were not, as it turned out, really necessary to stop a Syrian/Soviet march into Jordan. Asad appears to have had no real desire to get embroiled in a war with Jordan, still less Israel. A tank brigade dispatched by Hussein to the north inflicted severe damage on the Syrian units, who turned around and rumbled back home.

The Israelis, therefore, did not have to invoke an American "umbrella," as requested, but they certainly got their reward. In a famous passage in his memoirs, Rabin recounts how Kissinger called him a few days after the crisis had passed with a message from Nixon for Golda Meir: "The president will never forget Israel's role in preventing the deterioration in Jordan and in blocking the attempt to overturn the regime there. He said that the United States is fortunate in having an ally like Israel in the Middle East. These events will be taken into account in all future developments."

For the Israelis, this was an epochal moment. Gone were the days when the only security relationship they could hope for was the employment of Communist Bloc Jews in the service of the "connection" with the CIA, the covert errand running of KK Mountain, or the tense finessing before the Six Day War. Now a modest deployment of

Israeli military strength had brought a fulsome message from the president of the United States, acknowledging Israel as a key ally. As Rabin was moved to observe in his memoirs, "I had never heard anything like it."[12]

In any event, Nixon and Kissinger were not slow to hand out rewards to Israel. Despite the release of expensive weapons such as the Phantoms for sale following the 1967 war, American financial assistance to help pay for these purchases had remained slim. Military aid, in the form of loans, approved in 1969 for 1970 amounted to only $30 million, together with a further $60 million in the form of economic loans. But the days of such parsimony were about to be left behind forever.

On September 17, as the plan to crush the Palestinians went into operation in Jordan and before the Syrians intervened, Nixon had agreed to increase military aid by $500 million, as well as to accelerate delivery of more Phantoms. In the next three years the Americans lavished more money on Israel—$1,608 million—than the total amount that had been dispatched—$1,581 million—since the founding of the state.

There was no going back. In future years the aid steadily increased, both in overall dollar figures and in the indulgence with which loans from the U.S. Treasury to Israel were forgiven. The money not only enabled Israeli governments to offer the voters something akin to a First World standard of living, it also ensured that the Israeli economy would be inextricably linked to the U.S. military-industrial economy.

The huge infusions of American cash allowed Israel to spend a disproportionate share of its gross national product on defense—20 percent in 1971. When the U.S. sent economic as well as military funds, the "economic" dollars could be and were used to simply free up Israeli government expenditure for defense or, more directly, for payment of interest on the unforgiven part of military loans.

The aid did not come merely in the form of cash, but also in the form of direct assistance to Israel's economically vital defense industry complex. In December 1970, the U.S. and Israel signed a Master Defense Development Data Exchange Agreement. Israel was to be given the technical information from which it could manufacture, or in some cases maintain, military technology developed in the U.S. The following year a further agreement permitted Israel to build U.S.-designed military equipment. Israeli air force fighters were soon carrying a locally produced heat-seeking air-to-air missile: the Shafrir, "developed" at the government-owned Raphael Armament Development Authority. It was identical in almost all respects to the classic U.S. air-to-air Sidewinder missile. Most importantly, the U.S. granted permission for Israel to manufacture the American J-79 engine for use in the Kfir, the frontline fighter the Israelis had developed from the French Mirage 5.[13]

(The domestic military products developed by the Israeli defense industry have enjoyed a high reputation, which is not necessarily deserved. For example, since the J-79 was more powerful than the original French engine in the Mirage, this should have resulted in a "hotter" fighter. Tellingly, this was not what happened. U.S. Navy pilots who later flew the Kfir reported that they found it "sluggish" compared to the Mirage, and although it could make one very fast turn, useful in fighter combat, it then "lost energy" and had to dive out of the fight. It seems that Israel Aircraft Industries had managed to botch the simple task of mating an existing airframe design to an existing engine, an interesting reflection on the capabilities of Israel's best-funded industry.)

With American military aid pouring in during the early 1970s, unaccompanied by any serious American demand for Israeli concessions on local territorial issues, the little country was in a self-confident mood. Most confident of all were the leaders of the IDF. "I'm worried about our generals," remarked the aging Ben-Gurion after the 1967 war. "They're starting to act like *generals*."

Both Washington and Israel agreed that there was little reason to fear the Arabs. This was not a conclusion based on careful intelligence, however. Archie Roosevelt, a CIA official who spent most of his career in the Middle East, remarked in his memoirs that he found the Israelis quite deficient in their intelligence on the Arabs because they view Arabs as "alien, threatening, hateful, and inferior . . . a people with whom they have nothing in common. Hence their intelligence failures."[14] Therefore, while the IDF and its partners in the defense complex continued to increase their size and budgets—draft service was increased by six months *after* the 1967 war—there was little feeling that the beaten enemy could rise again.

In July 1973 Defense Minister Moshe Dayan told *Time* magazine that there was unlikely to be a war in the Middle East for another ten years. Israeli politicians, including Dayan, were gearing up for elections at the end of October. The ruling Labor Alignment was campaigning on a platform of peace and security, rendered possible, as Dayan put it, by "the superiority of our forces over our enemies" and "the jurisdiction of the Israeli government from the Jordan to the Suez."[15]

This complacency was shared by U.S. intelligence. A handbook circulated to CIA analysts in 1971 reported that the Arab fighting man "lacks the necessary physical and cultural qualities for performing effective military services."[16]

This nonsense was being propagated even as President Sadat, the apparent nonentity who succeeded the long-feared Nasser in 1970, repeatedly threatened that the lack of any American or Israeli interest in peace would lead to war.

Early in 1971 a CIA analyst named Fred Fear, perusing intelligence data on arms shipments, noted that the Egyptians seemed to be acquiring a great deal of military bridging equipment. Since bridgeable bodies of water in Egypt amount to two, the Nile and the Suez Canal, Fear concluded that the Egyptians were serious about crossing the canal and attacking the Israelis. Accordingly, he wrote up a report for his superiors replete with calculations about the number of bridges the Egyptians would put across the canal, predictions of how many troops would be able to cross in the first twenty-four hours, and even a map showing where the crossings would most likely occur. His superiors in the Intelligence Directorate looked at this amazingly prescient report and then filed it away without taking any further action. These higher-level bureaucrats might have paid closer attention, if only for the fact that Fear had been on the team that had forecast that the Israelis would win the 1967 war in six days.[17]

Anwar Sadat later claimed that he felt insulted at this lack of attention. For example, the first obstacle facing the Egyptians after crossing the canal was the fortified "Bar Lev line" constructed by Ariel Sharon. Part of this consisted of a sand wall some sixty feet high. The Egyptians found that the only viable method of clearing a breach in the wall was to use high-pressure water pumps. After the war Sadat recounted to UN Deputy Under Secretary-General Brian Urquhart how production of the pumps, on order from a West German firm, had been held up by a strike. When the strike ended the Egyptian high command felt it was too late to have the pumps delivered by ship, so they ordered a rush airlift. Consequently, Frankfurt Airport filled up with Egyptair transports frantically loading water pumps. Frankfurt is not exactly out of the way so far as U.S. intelligence is concerned, and yet no one took note of this curious activity or asked why the Egyptians suddenly needed so many pumps. "It was at that moment," declared Sadat dramatically, "that I realized that no one took us seriously and we would have to go to war."[18]

As usual with intelligence surprises, it subsequently turned out that there had been an abundance of warning of the Egyptian-Syrian attack on October 6, 1973. The National Security Agency and the CIA picked up clear signs that the two Arab nations were preparing for a major offensive. The Israelis, for their part, blithely disregarded similar warnings. After the war, the major part of the blame fell on Eli Zeira, chief of Military Intelligence. (Many of his military colleagues felt he owed his position to his role as a toady of Defense Minister Moshe Dayan.) However, a senior Israeli intelligence official who made it his business to conduct an extensive study of the classified archives concluded that the blame lay "51 percent with Mossad, 49 percent with Military Intelligence."[19]

More significantly, Henry Kissinger himself had been directly informed, both by King Hussein and by emissaries of Sadat, that unless there was some sign of diplomatic movement the Arabs would attack. From early in 1973 he was in back-channel communication with Hafez Ismail, Sadat's national security adviser.[20]

To understand Kissinger's actions, or lack of them, it is worth bearing in mind the central aim of his Middle Eastern policy, which was to exclude the Soviets from all possible avenues of influence in the area. Egypt's ongoing dispute with America's ally Israel (which still occupied all of the Sinai Peninsula) clearly ensured that the Egyptians would remain within Moscow's orbit, if only because of their need for arms. But if Kissinger could so maneuver matters that he was in a position to broker an Israeli-Egyptian accord, then the Soviets would have no further role in Egypt.

The problem for Kissinger was that if he accepted the possibility of a serious Arab offensive, as predicted by Hussein and others, he would be duty-bound to pass this information on to his Israeli allies. The Israelis would then almost certainly mount a preemptive attack against their enemies, to which the U.S. would be obliged to lend support, making it impossible for Kissinger to broker any kind of settlement between Egypt and Israel. Indeed, Kissinger repeated his injunction against Israel firing the first shot—at the last minute, Mossad did accept a clear warning from an agent of what was about to happen—even as the Egyptians were preparing to open fire. Golda Meir accordingly rejected appeals from her chief of staff that Israel get in the first blow. "She was well aware of the meaning of this refusal, but had no choice," noted the faithful staff officer Israel Lior, whom Meir had inherited from Eshkol. "It was important to her to enlist the support of the United States and perhaps that of other countries as well." Later on there were indeed suspicions in Israel that Kissinger had been less than dismayed at the opportunity the Yom Kippur War gave him to display his negotiating talents.[21]

On October 6, when confused reports of the attack and the Egyptian canal crossing reached Washington, someone at the CIA remembered Fred Fear's years-old report on the bridging equipment. It was speedily extracted from the files and the map showing crossing points and troop deployments (which had been written purely as a speculative prediction) was rushed to the White House as a current intelligence report on what was actually happening on the ground.

What was happening in the first few days of the war was, of course, a shattering Israeli tactical defeat. Dayan, who a few months before had claimed that Israel was "on the threshold of the crowning era of the return to Zion," now had a near breakdown and talked about the "destruction of the Third Temple," as Israelis in apocalyptic moods sometimes term the modern state of Israel. After visiting the fighting fronts in the north and south on the second day of the war, October 7, he communicated his sense of panic both to Prime Minister Golda Meir and to the White House.

The Americans grew even more alarmed when intelligence reported that the Israelis could be reaching for their ultimate weapon. Deep in the Negev Desert the Israelis had their force of nuclear-tipped Jericho missiles, the weapon developed and tested with the French. On the night of October 7, 1973, a select group of high-level U.S. national security officials were informed that the Jerichos had been armed and were ready for firing. It may be recalled that in the past the Israelis had been sent conventional weapons partly in an effort to dissuade them from going nuclear. Now the awful moment had arrived. For the first time since 1956, Israel might be about to make a momentous military move without U.S. authorization.[22]

Nuclear explosions in the Sinai (on the presumption that the invading Egyptian forces would be the target) were definitely not on Washington's agenda. We do not know precisely what measures Henry Kissinger and Richard Nixon took to keep the Jerichos in their silos. It is a matter of record that within a day of the outbreak of war, the Pentagon had agreed to an emergency airlift of conventional weapons and ammunition, much of it taken out of war stocks held by U.S. forces in Germany and flown straight to a forward Israeli base in the Sinai.

Unlike 1967, there was a large and visible American presence in this particular conflict. For almost the entire period of the fighting, according to Israeli and U.S. defense officials, there was an actual Israeli command post inside the Pentagon itself, buried deep in the bowels of the cavernous building. From there IDF officers worked round the clock to coordinate the American supply shipments, which became both massive and highly publicized a week after the fighting began.

From October 13 until three weeks after the fighting officially ended, the skies between the United States and Israel were dark with the huge C-5 and C-141 transports of the U.S. Air Force Military Airlift Command. By the time of the first cease-fire, this vastly expensive shuttle had flown in 22,497 tons of equipment. Twenty-six thousand military and civilian personnel were involved in what was, until the great 1990 Persian Gulf buildup, the largest airlift in history.

The Pentagon made the most of this achievement, coming as it did at a time when the military had just relinquished its activities in Southeast Asia. An internal report from the Defense Intelligence Agency claimed, "There have been many examples of the international significance of military airlift since World War II. The Berlin airlift saved a city; in South Vietnam there were many examples where timely airlift of men and supplies turned the tide; and now, in the Middle East it saved Israel and supports the cease-fire."

This was basically nonsense. Very little of the heavy equipment flown in after October 13 reached the battlefields before the shooting actually stopped on October 24. Fortunately for the Israelis, this did not matter much. According to one Pentagon official intimately involved in the American contribution to the war, "The Israelis didn't need the airlift of arms—it was a psychological and morale booster." William Quandt, who was a member of the high-level "Washington Special Action Group" on the crisis, has written, "From interviews with top Israeli officials I have concluded that the impact of the airlift on strategic decisions was minimal."[23]

However, while the airlift may have made little difference to Israel in its hour of need, it did a great deal for the U.S. Air Force. The air force had a particular interest in highlighting the performance of the C-5, since the development of this enormous transport had been marked by scandal, cost overruns, and technical deficiencies. Among the requirements cited by the air force for developing the huge plane had been a perceived need to fly tanks overseas. The General Accounting Office investigators who probed the actual record of the airlift discovered that the total number of tanks delivered to Israel amounted to four. Perhaps embarrassed by the seeming irrelevance of the enormous effort to the outcome of the war, the investigators stated that nevertheless, the sight of all those big planes flying into Lod Airport outside Tel Aviv had "an incalculable effect" on the morale of the Israeli population.[24]

Such quibbles were not allowed to get in the way of the Airlift Command claiming that it had "saved" Israel. The fact that the entire tonnage delivered amounted to no more than the equivalent of one shipload went unpublicized. Big money continued to flow to the aerospace industry for military air transports. This was only one example of a little-understood but crucial aspect of the liaison between the military systems of the U.S. and Israel that emerged after 1967: the advantages derived by the American military-industrial complex from the relationship.

UP UNTIL the 1967 war Israel's most important security link with the U.S. was through the CIA. The Pentagon had been unenthusiastic about the Zionist state in its early years. Isser Harel still grumbles at the memory of General Arthur Trudeau, chief of army intelligence in the early 1950s, whom he considered "totally anti-Israel." (Trudeau visited Israel in 1954 and expressed his firm opposition to supplying Israel with arms in the event of a world war.) Despite the shipments of Hawks, which were followed in 1964 by an agreement to deliver A-4 Skyhawk attack planes, Israel was not an important market for U.S. defense products. Nor were the performance and tactics of the Israeli military of any great interest to the American military-industrial complex. That changed on the morning of June 5, 1967, when the Israeli air force eliminated its Egyptian counterpart in two hours.

It may be recalled that the Americans had embarked on the military campaign in Vietnam with high expectations that heavy use of air power would soon bring the Vietnamese to their knees. Unfortunately, despite a lavish deployment of high-technology ordnance, well publicized in Pentagon briefings at the time, "Operation Rolling Thunder" was not performing as advertised. Notwithstanding massive strikes by B-52 and other bombers, the North Vietnamese retained the will and capability to fight. The spectacle of the Israeli air force delivering what appeared to have been a decisive, war-winning blow had, therefore, a highly bracing effect on air-power partisans in the U.S. Here at last was striking proof that the best way to combat communism was from the air. As the editor of the influential trade journal *Aviation Week & Space Technology* put it immediately after the war: "The major political lesson which seems to have escaped many people in Washington is that the Soviet leaders' policy is as ferociously anti-American as ever and they will go to almost any lengths short of a direct nuclear war to implement their implacable hatred of the West . . . They fanned every spark of Arab hatred into a conflagration they hoped would sear Western Europe, consume Israel, and open a second front for the U.S., already heavily committed in Vietnam. Without the brilliant performance of the Israeli air force they might indeed have achieved these goals."[25]

While historians may have tempered *Aviation Week*'s dramatic ascriptions regarding the Soviet master plan in 1967, the notion that the Israeli air force won that war in a matter of hours has remained firmly embedded in the record. That the passage of twenty-four years had not dimmed that perception was apparent in the reporting on the American surprise air attack on Iraq on the night of January 16, 1991. A primary target of that assault was the Iraqi air force, which the Americans assumed could be destroyed on the ground as easily as the Egyptian planes had been in 1967. Two days after the unleashing of "Desert Storm," CBS News was hailing the "remarkable parallel" with the famous Israeli attack. But, as the Americans soon discovered, the Iraqis had learned from the Egyptians' mishap and had taken the precaution of putting their aircraft in well-protected shelters that had to be intensively bombed for weeks afterwards.

The presumption that the Israeli air force won the war in two hours in 1967 assumes that if it had not been so speedily destroyed, the Egyptian air force would have been able to impede the Israeli armored advance across the Sinai to the Suez Canal. This seems such an eminently logical conclusion that it is not even discussed in the numerous histories of the June War. There is, however, a secret Pentagon report, compiled almost a quarter of a century ago, that shows it to be completely untrue.

The report was the work of a lieutenant colonel of the United States Marines named Russ Stolfi. When the war ended Stolfi conceived a singular ambition: to know more than anyone else about what had actually happened on the desert battlefields. Accordingly, he set out for the Middle East under the aegis of an obscure branch of the Pentagon bureaucracy known as the Joint Technical Coordinating Group/Munitions Effects. Stolfi may or may not have learned more than anyone else about everything that had happened in the fighting, but he did make himself the preeminent pathologist of tanks, and what had killed them. With a beguiling lack of consciousness of the bizarre nature of his calling, this somewhat intellectual soldier reminisces happily on the hundreds of dead tanks he investigated, frequently with the corpses of the crew still decomposing inside—"The smell could be pretty bad at times."

What he discovered was that the most effective antitank weapons were other tanks, followed by artillery. Recoilless rifles, used to good effect by the Israelis, had also done good execution. But, more significantly, he found that none of the tanks he examined had been knocked out from the air. Not one.

Following the 1973 war Stolfi set out again to tour the battlefields. This time he looked at even more tanks, but the result was the same: none had been destroyed from the air. His overall conclusion—that air power had had in fact very little bearing on the outcome of either war—had the most terrible implications for both the Israeli and U.S. air forces. Stolfi's autopsy reports on the tanks of the Sinai and Golan remain both little known and classified to this day.[26]

Stolfi's researches were of immense benefit to the U.S. forces during the war with Iraq. A group of Pentagon officials privy to his researches took them to heart and promoted development of the A-10 "Warthog" antitank plane. On the basis of a German experiment on the Eastern front during World War II, they concluded that a high-velocity, rapid-firing heavy cannon mounted on a plane would be highly effective against tanks. They therefore designed the "Warthog" to carry such a gun. The plane is slow and relatively cheap. The U.S. Air Force hated it and tried to avoid sending it to Saudi Arabia. The

U.S. Army insisted on its deployment, and the A-10 proved highly effective in its role. (The U.S. air force commander admitted afterwards, "The A-10 Warthog saved my ass.")

Touting the supposed achievements of Israeli air power was one way in which interested lobbies within the U.S. military-industrial complex could extract useful service from America's strategic asset in the Middle East. By 1973, however, the Israelis were being required to provide endorsements for specific American weapons.

The Maverick air-to-ground antitank missile, supplied to the Israelis in the much-heralded airlift, was one such item that emerged from the Yom Kippur War with an enhanced reputation. William Quandt, a National Security Council staffer in 1973 and a thoughtful and scholarly historian of these events, describes it as "being used to good effect in the last days of the fighting and may have raised the prospect of a full defeat of the [Egyptian] Third Army Corps." From this "fact" Quandt draws this elegant conclusion: "Ironically, the United States resupply put Israel in a position to do something that Kissinger was determined to prevent [the destruction of the corps]."

The Maverick had first been tested in combat in Vietnam in 1972, where it had shown itself to be a dud. But the Maverick's Vietnam experience has been consigned by its sponsors to a decent obscurity, while its supposedly triumphant performance in the Sinai a year later has become a matter of record.[27]

Yet the indefatigable Lieutenant Colonel Stolfi was on hand to record the truth. Whatever had killed the eleven hundred tanks lost by the Egyptians and the twelve hundred lost by the Syrians, it had not been Mavericks.

Nevertheless, the U.S. Air Force was determined that the Maverick should emerge from the fighting with an unblemished record. The category of targets against which the Israelis were to employ the missile was broadened from tanks to include "command centers," and here the Maverick was recorded as scoring a number of hits. There was, however, less to these scores than it might appear. A former U.S. Air Force officer who paid close attention to this affair recalls: "In the Sinai you'd have these Egyptian divisional or brigade headquarters that were really just a few tents with sandbags and then quite a distant perimeter of piled-up sand around the whole thing—about as big as a football field. The air force view was that anything inside that perimeter counted as the command headquarters. So the Israelis went out in

F-4s that we sent them and fired off the Maverick and if one of them landed inside the perimeter, why, they recorded a hit. Of course, the explosion just kicked up some sand and didn't do much to the Egyptians, but it sure made the air staff happy back home."[28]

Thus the Israelis, in the midst of a desperate war, carried out field tests for promotional purposes of an essentially useless American weapon. On the other hand, since the weapons arrived as part of a $2.2 billion package financed by a loan from the U.S. Treasury ($1.5 billion of which was forgiven soon after), it may have seemed a small price to pay.[29]

The Maverick was not the only weapon for which an Israeli seal of approval was solicited. The U.S. Air Force and Navy had long dreamed of fighter planes that could shoot an enemy down "beyond visual range," i.e., that the pilot could not see except on a radar screen. To this end both services had introduced the Sparrow missile. Costly and complex, it could at least in theory perform the task. However, the "BVR" (beyond visual range) missile faced one insuperable problem, which was (and is) that radar cannot identify the target as friend or foe. Since there are almost never clearly defined front lines in aerial warfare, the identification problem has made it almost impossible to use the Sparrow's vaunted properties. In fact, of the more than two thousand BVR missiles fired in combat from the time they were first introduced in 1958 to the beginning of the Gulf War, there were only four recorded instances of "kills" out of sight of the attacking pilot. Two were in Vietnam, a record marred by the fact that one of those downed turned out to be a U.S. plane, not a Mig.

Since this was not a particularly distinguished record for a multibillion dollar weapon program, the air force was keen to use the 1973 war to up the score. "The Israelis," according to former USAF Col. James Burton, who made it his business to find out what really happened, "did their best to placate the U.S. Air Force." What they did, according to Burton, was to issue a special order one night during the war that their entire air fleet be on the ground, save for a single fighter. That one plane carried a Sparrow missile. The pilot, assured that anything he saw on his radar screen was an enemy, loosed off at one of the blips and shot down a Syrian Mig. It was, as Burton puts it, "an exercise in public relations on behalf of the U.S. Air Force."

Not long after the war, Motti Hod, the former commander of the Israeli air force, came to Washington. While visiting old U.S. Air Force friends at the Pentagon, he was shown a highly classified multivolume report on the recent conflict. The burly airman sat down and carefully read through the whole impressively detailed and footnoted study. Then he turned to his expectant hosts. "That," he said, "is a very interesting war. But it's not the war we fought."

The report had been prepared by a Pentagon team known as the Weapons Systems Evaluation Group, a high-level panel that had the blessing of the secretary of defense and the Joint Chiefs of Staff. Hod's reaction was provoked by the sweeping claims made for the vital role played by U.S.-supplied high-technology weapons in the fighting. The WESEG study, for example, had cited not only the lone beyond-visual-range Sparrow kill, but eleven other successful firings against enemy planes. However, Hod, who is sometimes inclined to forget the necessity of shading the truth in the interests of diplomacy, happily acknowledged to interested professionals in the U.S. that the Sparrow had been pretty much of a flop in the war, scoring, at the most, two hits.

Motti Hod, hailed around the world for the exploits of his pilots in the 1967 war, could get away with committing awkward truths like these. His successors soon learned to be more politic. Colonel Burton, whose career in the USAF suffered from his interest in the real performance of weapons in combat, spent a lot of time in Israel trying to discover the genuine combat record of various weapons systems. He was therefore in a good position to watch the Israelis learn to play U.S. Air Force politics. "You could never really trust the data they gave you," he remembers, "because they were playing to different communities within our air force, telling them what they wanted to hear."

In the early 1980s, for example, the upper ranks of the USAF were thronged with partisans of the F-15 McDonnell Douglas fighter. These were powerful generals and they were anxious for their favorite plane to be seen to give a good account of itself, especially in comparison with the cheaper F-16 fighter, which the air force had been forced to buy on orders from its civilian overseers at the Pentagon. During the 1982 war in Lebanon, therefore, the Israeli air force commander, a polished military diplomat named David Ivri, did his best to arrange matters so that the F-15 would emerge from the war with a better combat record than the F-16. The F-15 was given the bulk of the "air-to-air" missions, the ones that would bring it into contact with Syrian Migs, while the F-16 was left with the more prosaic task of "air to ground"—bombing. (Most of the targets were civilian, and thousands of civilians were indeed killed both in Southern Lebanon and in Beirut itself, but no one on the Air Staff at the Pentagon seems to have been unduly worried about that.) On some days F-16 squadrons were kept on the ground in order that its rival should reap greater glory in the attaché reports flowing back to the Pentagon.

It may seem a strange way for the IDF to deploy its forces in war, but as Motti Hod likes to say, "This is a no-alternative situation." This point has not always been perfectly understood by Israeli combat fliers. During the 1982 war a flight of F-15s was "jumped" by some Syrian Migs and had to fight hard to escape unscathed. The Israelis returned to base in an angry mood. They had thought that a U.S.-supplied IDF Hawkeye radar command and control plane that was cruising in the neighborhood would warn them if the enemy approached. Their irate complaints were rapidly subdued, however, when General Ivri himself arrived posthaste at their base and warned them to shut up, as one observer recalled, because "the Americans wouldn't supply any more equipment if we bad-mouthed their technology."

As well as sweeping such unpleasantness under the carpet, the Israelis did their American patrons the favor of presenting them with the fourth-ever beyond-visual-range "kill." According to Burton, who made a careful review of the data, this was another exercise in placating the Americans. "There was a high-altitude Mig 25 reconnaissance plane going over at the same time on a daily run. So they sent up an F-15. Easy to track, nothing else at that altitude. The F-15 fired the Sparrow, and it was heading straight for the target, but before it got there someone else fired an I Hawk (a high-altitude antiaircraft missile) which hit the Mig 25. As the wreckage tumbled down, spinning and smoking, the Sparrow finally arrived and hit it." Since the Sparrow lobby is infinitely stronger than the Hawk lobby, it was agreed by all (except, presumably, by the Israelis who fired the Hawk and spoiled the show) that the Sparrow should get the credit.[30]

Such assiduous attention to the Byzantine politics of the American military-aerospace complex may have been galling to Israelis who cherished their independence, but it helped furnish rich dividends for the local defense economy.

After the 1973 war, the Egyptians effectively gave up any idea of settling matters with Israel by force, choosing to rely instead on imaginative diplomacy and intercession by their new patrons in Washington. Kissinger's strategy had worked. Despite the fact that Israel had lost a major military threat, the U.S. continued to pump money into Israeli defense, and in ever-increasing amounts.

The year before the war military aid had amounted to just over $300 million. Then it soared to $2.5 billion, promised in the course of the fighting. One and a half billion dollars of this amount was ultimately classified as an outright grant, rather than a loan, the first time this favor had been granted to Israel. (It had been previously reserved for the dependencies in Southeast Asia: South Vietnam, Cambodia, and Laos.) From now on, half of all military loans for Israel were to be automatically written off.

Given the importance of the bounty flowing into the Israeli defense system, it was only fitting that Israel, with the help of a cunningly executed covert operation in the United States, was able to come to the aid of the U.S. military-industrial complex in its hour of need.

DESPITE THE FERVENT LOYALTY of many American Jews to Israel throughout its brief history, it is a fact that a large proportion failed for a long time to realize how closely official American support for the state was linked to the Cold War in general. In fact, until the 1970s, the American Jewish community was largely liberal in its response to non-Middle Eastern foreign policy questions.

Lyndon Johnson, for example, found it irksome that after all he had done for Israel, American Jews still refused to back his own war. "A bunch of rabbis came to see me in 1967 to tell me I ought not to send a single screwdriver to Vietnam," he once complained to Abba Eban, "but, on the other hand, should push all our aircraft carriers through the Straits of Tiran to help Israel."[31]

Whatever its feelings about the desirability of aid to Israel, the Jewish community by and large remained antipathetic to the war in Vietnam, as did an increasing proportion of the American people. This public outrage eventually impelled the withdrawal of U.S. forces from the fighting, but the war left a residue of general distrust and disenchantment with the defense establishment, coupled with support for arms control and detente with the Russians. By early 1973, only 8 percent of the population favored increased defense spending.[32]

Warmer U.S.-Soviet relations were not necessarily viewed with favor in Israel. Its newly enhanced status as a strategic asset, after all, very much depended on the Cold War. A telling remark by Yitzhak Rabin after the 1973 war gives a good illustration of where some Israeli leaders thought their interests lay. Rabin argued against any moves toward a political settlement with Egypt and Syria, on the grounds that Israel should "gain time" in the hopes that "we will later find ourselves in a better situation: the U.S. may adopt more aggressive positions vis-à-vis the USSR."[33]

Hopes of more aggressive American attitudes toward the USSR were not confined to Israel. The defense lobby in the United States was alarmed by the dovish attitude of the times, an atmosphere that it perceived to be infecting the Congress. Fortunately, the lobby had powerful and experienced champions on Capitol Hill to defend its interests. One of these was Henry Jackson, senator for the State of Washington since 1948.

Jackson carried impeccable credentials as a Cold War Democrat. In 1960, for example, he had been influential in persuading John Kennedy to make the wholly fraudulent "missile gap" a central issue in his presidential campaign. In 1972, however, the Democratic Party had rejected Jackson and his militant ideology and instead opted for the dovish George McGovern as its presidential candidate.

Undeterred by this defeat, Jackson began looking ahead to the next presidential election in 1976, by which time, he thought, the Cold War would have come back into fashion. In August 1972, he denounced the recently signed Strategic Arms Limitation Treaty as a "bum deal" and introduced legislation to make any future arms agreement contingent on there being "equality" in superpower weapons levels.

On its own this initiative did not strike any widespread political chord, but Jackson soon found a related issue that did. In October 1972, he launched a proposal to link trade concessions to the Soviets (a key plank in Kissinger's detente policy) to increased levels of emigration for Soviet Jews. This initiative, crafted by a young staffer of Jackson's named Richard Perle, attracted much more support than the senator's sniping at SALT. No fewer than seventy-two senators quickly signed up in support of Jackson's position. Before the end of the year, as McGovern crashed to defeat in the election, Jackson was riding the emigration issue hard. Among other gestures, he went to New York to be a keynote speaker at a public meeting to protest the oppressive circumstances of the Jews in Russia.[34]

Sharing the platform on that occasion was a man for whose work on behalf of the "brethren" in Russia Jackson expressed the greatest admiration: Rabbi Meir Kahane, the leader of the militant and violent Jewish Defense League.

To understand what the senator and the rabbi were doing on the same platform, it is necessary to appreciate what the 1967 war had meant for the Jews of Russia. The war had caused the Soviet Union to break off diplomatic relations with Jerusalem. At the same time, the Soviets stopped the emigration of its Jewish citizens to Israel, which had been running at an unprecedentedly high level for the first six months of 1967. The emigration program had been kept secret by the two governments, but now that the Soviets had clamped down, the Israeli government burnt the bridge by publicly announcing what had been going on.

Two years later Golda Meir told the Knesset that government policy from now on would be to make an international issue out of Soviet Jewish emigration to Israel. "Israel," she said, "will no longer rely on quiet diplomacy."

Up until that point Meir Kahane and the Jewish Defense League he had founded in 1968 had been best known for their militant confrontations with black organizations in New York. Kahane himself, the product of an Orthodox family in Brooklyn, had a somewhat seamy past as a government informant on the antiwar movement. He had also lobbied in favor of Jewish support for the Vietnam War at the behest and with the financial support, so he later claimed, of the CIA.[35]

In December 1969, however, a messenger from Israel arrived to tell Kahane to cease squabbling with American blacks and to direct the JDL's violent energies at a more important target: the Soviet Union. The messenger was Geula Cohen, a denizen of the fanatical Israeli right wing, best known for her role in setting up the Gush Emunim settlers' movement. (Cohen had once withdrawn her support for Menachem Begin in his urban guerrilla days because she found his policies "too mild.") Her message for Kahane was that the plight of Jews in the Soviet Union was the most pressing issue facing world Jewry, since the Soviets were planning to "liquidate our people," and that the JDL should do something about it.

This was not Cohen's own scheme. She was apparently speaking for a group of wealthy Israeli and American businessmen, former IDF officers ready to give military training to JDL recruits in Israel, and most significantly, senior serving officers of Mossad. The executive director for the operation was Cohen's old commander in Lehi: Yitzhak Shamir.

Shamir, like many other veterans of the more militant terrorist groups that had fought against the British, had been absorbed into the intelligence establishment after independence. After serving as Mossad station chief in Paris, he had formally retired in 1965. As he later recalled, his years in Mossad were "among the happiest in my life." After leaving the underground world in which he had spent most of his adult years, this fierce ideologue tried his hand at business, unsuccessfully, before going into politics. Even after leaving Mossad, according to several Israeli sources, he stayed in close touch with his old colleagues.

Kahane was quick to follow Geula Cohen's directions. Less than a month after the meeting, the JDL took over the New York offices of Tass, Aeroflot, Intourist, and a Soviet airliner at Kennedy Airport, spraying nationalist slogans in Hebrew on the walls. After a JDL riot in front of the Soviet UN mission, Kahane announced, "Our attacks upon the institutions of Soviet tyranny in America represent the first step in our campaign to bring the issue of oppressed Soviet Jews and other religious groups to the attention of an apathetic public and indifferent news media . . ."[36]

Publicly, Golda Meir disassociated herself from Kahane's activities, on the grounds that they imperiled the people he purported to help. "I make decisions that can send thousands of Israeli soldiers to their death," she is said to have explained, "but I have no right to do that to Soviet Jews."[37]

Commendable though that attitude might have been, there is evidence to suggest that Meir's Labor government may not have been as aloof from the Kahane operation as it pretended.

Golda Meir, as prime minister, had direct responsibility for Mossad. According to Kahane's biographer, Robert Friedman, no fewer than three senior active-duty Mossad officers were involved in the group superintending the JDL's violent campaign. It is extraordinarily unlikely that such a high-profile operation would have been carried out by serving officers without their chief being informed or passing on the news to his superior, the prime minister. The head of Mossad at the time, Zvi Zamir, who was extremely close to Meir, later remarked, "Of all the operations and activities that I was responsible for, the strongest and most exciting experiences were saving our Jewish brethren from countries of oppression and bringing them over here."[38]

One Israeli scientist who had occasion to visit the United States in the early 1970s recalls a more direct link between the Israeli government and Kahane's young bombers. "Israelis are nuts about security, so that when one of us had to give a public lecture there would be protection arranged through the local consulate. I remember that at that time there would be someone from the JDL given this job. Since there was actually nothing for them to do, it was a neat way of putting these people on the payroll."

That Jewish emigration from the Soviet Union should become a major issue in U.S.-Soviet relations was very much in the interests of the Israeli government. The idea that Soviet Jewry, which equaled in number the entire Jewish population of Israel, might one day move to Israel had long been a fundamental policy objective for all Israeli leaders. In the early 1950s, the men who were launching the new state were ever conscious of the possibility that the Soviet leaders might one day relent and let the people go. In the wake of the 1967 war, it no longer seemed possible that diplomacy could do the trick. Eshkol's revelation of the secret emigration channel, together with Meir's later statement that Israel was going to make a public issue out of emigration, suggest that the decision had been made to try a new tack.

The use of violence against Soviet targets in the U.S. and Europe certainly succeeded in putting Soviet Jews on the front page, as well as galvanizing the American Jewish community into taking an active interest in the fate of its Soviet brethren. The Kremlin bitterly protested the attacks and declared that it was holding the Nixon administration directly responsible for Kahane's activities, which in 1971 included four bombing attacks in New York City alone. Soviet Jewish emigration had become a hot international issue.

The Russians, meanwhile, did their best to defuse the matter by vastly increasing the number of people allowed to leave. Emigration began to soar in 1971, when fifteen thousand Russian Jews left. Two years later no fewer than thirty-five thousand poured out.[39] So anxious indeed was the Brezhnev regime to satisfy the Americans that in a few cases Jews who had applied to emigrate and had then changed their minds were summarily told by the KGB to pack their bags and get going. The Soviet authorities tried, in a ham-handed fashion, to keep people with national security secrets from leaving. Cases of such "refuseniks" brought their own share of invidious publicity, but by no means prevented emigrés from passing useful intelligence to the CIA and Mossad. By the early 1970s there was a joint debriefing operation, including CIA personnel, operating under the auspices of the Mossad Tevel—liaison unit—in Tel Aviv. In addition, according to U.S. intelligence sources, the increased flow of emigration gave the CIA the chance to extract from the USSR interesting people who were not Jewish but who could be equipped with false documentation and spirited out of the country in the general flood of emigrants.[40]

Soviet charges that Soviet Jews posed an espionage threat were derided as propaganda in the U.S. Standing up to the Communist menace, the traditional preserve of the military and the right wing, was becoming a respectable cause for honest liberals dedicated to human rights and free emigration.

Having helped to set the ball rolling, Meir Kahane moved to Israel and started a far-right political movement there—to the irritation of his erstwhile backers, who did not appreciate his poaching on their political turf and who also wondered what he had done with the large sums of money they had given him to finance the anti-Soviet campaign. Henry Jackson, however, continued to raise the emigration issue until the final passage of the Jackson-Vanik amendment, which legally bound emigration and trade concessions together and effectively killed that phase of detente. (Passage of the amendment also killed off emigration for a period. The Soviets, feeling there was no further point in trying to appease American public opinion, sharply curtailed the supply of exit visas.)

As noted, the American Jewish community had in the past been dovish on issues of U.S. foreign policy that did not concern its particular cause. The furor over the fate of Jews in the Soviet Union had brought about a change. (The Israeli government was concerned that the human rights question not get out of hand. Nahum Goldmann, an eminent Zionist leader, suggested in 1971 that rather than stressing the emigration issue, the Zionist movement should concentrate on securing human rights for Jews remaining inside the USSR. His invitation to address the World Zionist Congress was promptly withdrawn.)[41]

The widely advertised role of U.S. military assistance in saving

Israel from destruction during the Yom Kippur War gave further ammunition to those who wished to fuse the issues of support for Israel and the Pentagon budget. The former chief of naval operations, Elmo Zumwalt, launched a short-lived political career in 1974 with a stump speech to Jewish groups around the U.S. that stressed one recurring theme: a dollar for defense meant twenty-five cents for Israel. Zumwalt was neither the first nor the only politician who sought to defend the Pentagon budget on the grounds that it was good for Israel. A detailed memo on White House strategy for the 1972 election, coauthored by Pat Buchanan, suggested that Defense Secretary Melvin Laird should speak out on what effect cuts in the navy's budget proposed by George McGovern would have on Israel, "with the conclusion, not unjustified, that the future of Israel, the survival of Israel—with McGovern's naval cuts—would be the decision of the Soviet Politburo. Again, the lead should be that . . . without building the F-14 and F-15 to combat the Mig 23, 'U.S. Navy could not intervene to save Israel.' "[42]

One instructive example of what this line of reasoning meant for many Jewish doves can be found in the career path of New York journalist Norman Podhoretz. Podhoretz had been active in agitating against the Vietnam War during the 1960s, but by the mid-1970s, his politics had undergone a drastic change. In 1976 he was a key adviser for the former college professor and Nixon administration staffer Daniel Patrick Moynihan in the latter's bid for the U.S. Senate. Moynihan, though running in a traditionally liberal state, ran on a pro-defense platform. As Podhoretz later explained, "The inextricable connection between the survival of Israel and American military strength was an idea I would soon also have the opportunity to lend support to during Pat Moynihan's race . . . for the Democratic nomination in New York. . . . The ideological defense of Zionism was . . . dictated not only by moral considerations but by the American national interest." Moynihan was duly elected and reelected without causing any undue discomfort to the defenders of Zionism, or American military strength.[43]

Podhoretz was a prominent example of a group that became known as the neoconservatives. The increasingly powerful "neocons" gave loyal support to American military spending on the basis of a reciprocal level of military assistance to Israel. A sign of their influence on the lobbying activities of the military-industrial complex was their heavy representation on a group formed specifically to bolster Pentagon spending in the mid-1970s: the Committee on the Present Danger.

The committee was the brainchild of Paul Nitze and Eugene Rostow. Nitze was a veteran of many campaigns to boost defense spending, but unlike Rostow, a former under secretary of state, he had not previously been noted as a friend of Israel. Standing alongside Nitze, the veteran hawk, and Rostow, the friend of Israel, in the founding triumvirate of the Committee on the Present Danger was Charls Walker. Walker, a former secretary of the treasury, was the most powerful corporate lobbyist of his day. There were many major defense contractors among his clients. "Walker got us the money; that was his job," recalls W. Scott Thompson, at that time Nitze's son-in-law and privy to the committee's operations.[44]

Other prominent figures who were soon recruited for the group included many who later surfaced as senior national security officials in the Reagan administration, such as Reagan himself; Richard V. Allen, Reagan's first national security adviser; William Casey; and Richard Perle. There were, however, less well-publicized individuals who were very much in evidence in the early days. Thompson, who was not only active on the committee but also a close aide to Secretaries of Defense James Schlesinger and Donald Rumsfeld, recalls that "Israelis were very much part of the discussions. They were in and out of the building [Pentagon] all the time at the beginning, until Paul took a decision that there was to be no overt foreign involvement. On the other hand, everyone was conscious of Jewish voters." Thompson remembers Nitze as having no particular affection for Israel but nonetheless expressing the opinion that "when it comes to ball-splitting time in the Middle East, the Israelis will fight." The committee, in Thompson's opinion, "was probably the most successful lobby of modern times" in terms of gaining public acceptance for increased defense spending.

In 1977 the politically astute Congressman Les Aspin informed a convention of defense contractors in Philadelphia, "The Israeli lobby in Congress is no longer in favor of cutting the defense budget."[45]

Just how far pro-Israeli sentiment toward the Pentagon had shifted can be gauged from a remarkable book published by the Anti-Defamation League of B'nai B'rith, in 1982. In *The Real Anti-Semitism in America*, Nathan Perlmutter, the national director of the ADL, asserted that discrimination against Jews was a thing of the past in the

U.S. Contemporary anti-Semitism, according to Perlmutter, lay in the actions of "peacemakers of Vietnam vintage, transmuters of swords into plowshares, championing the terrorist PLO . . ." and "nowadays war is getting a bad name and peace too favorable a press" from a left that is "sniping at American defense budgets."[46]

If the leader of a respectable and powerful organization lobbying for Israel could equate a lack of support for the Pentagon's budget with anti-Semitism, the U.S. defense lobby had found itself a loyal ally indeed. On the other hand, it was soon to become clear that the Kahane campaign was not the only covert operation being run by the Israelis in the United States.

8. Betrayal

ZVI REUTER'S day-to-day activities supervising all arms exports for the state of Israel normally involved his keeping out of the public eye as much as possible. In October 1988, however, he gave a party. Neatly accoutered in a smart suit and tie (for daily business in Israeli arms-dealing circles, a tie is considered optional), the burly military intelligence official greeted his distinguished guests at the Dan Accadia Hotel in Herzliya.

Pretty girls in combat fatigues from the IDF public relations branch handed out roses, while high-ranking generals, also in combat fatigues, patrolled the room. Amos Yaron, who had been appointed military attaché in Washington after the Canadians had refused to accept him because of his role in the massacre at the Sabra and Shatila Palestinian refugee camps in Beirut, stood in the corner, a shy smile creasing his somewhat fearsome features. Yitzhak Rabin, then minister of defense, held court in the center, a drink firmly clenched in one hand and a cigarette in the other.

Not far away the Intifada was raging at full strength, giving Israel its most disobliging reviews in the international press ever, but for Reuter and the other high officials gathered in the modern hotel just off the beach, the issues under discussion at the gathering rivaled the Palestinian question in importance.

The occasion was the U.S. Israeli Defense Industry Cooperation Conference, and the guests of honor were a group of executives from major American defense corporations. The object of the conference was to get American defense corporations and the Pentagon to increase their stake in the Israeli defense complex and to buy more of its wares. The Israeli civilians in the room, senior executives of companies such as Israel Aircraft Industries, Israel Military Industries, Rafael, Tadiran, and other defense enterprises, were collectively responsible for the employment of 130,000 people in Israel. The economy of Israel depended on the prosperity of their industry, and that depended on a relationship with the American military-industrial complex.

One aspect of this relationship was evident from the respectful way in which these powerful satraps of the Israeli security system treated their American visitors. It was clear that they were anxious to be on their best behavior, and to make sure that their powerful American counterparts went away with a good impression. The Israelis knew who had the whip hand in this particular aspect of the relationship. It had not been long, after all, since the Pentagon had abruptly cut off aid for Israel's effort to build the Lavi fighter. This vastly expensive high-tech project, billed as "Israel's Apollo Moon Program," had not been popular with the U.S. aerospace industry. The American contractors had seen no reason why aid should be given to assist a potential competitor in the world market, and so it had died. Israel could not always depend on U.S. indulgence to get what it needed. That was why, while we watched Zvi Reuter smile ingratiatingly at the man from McDonnell Douglas Helicopters, the CIA's report on Israel's intelligence priorities came strongly to mind.

The agency's helpful little booklet on Israeli intelligence, as released to the world by the Iranian students who occupied the U.S. Embassy in Tehran in 1979, lists the objectives of Israeli intelligence in order of importance. First comes the requirement to gather intelligence on the military capabilities of the Arab states; then "collection of information on secret U.S. policy or decisions, if any, concerning Israel . . ." Third on the list, ahead even of intelligence on the USSR, comes "collection of scientific intelligence in the U.S. and other developed countries."[1]

The high order of priority given to this last task reflects the intense effort invested from the earliest days of the state to make Israel a technologically advanced industrial country. As we have seen, this ambition was most successfully realized in the area of defense.

Much of this development had been accomplished with the open cooperation of Israel's allies. The French had given the Israelis the technological know-how to build jet planes and nuclear missiles. The Jericho missile, still the basis for all Israeli long-range rockets, was developed in conjunction with Dassault. When the military relationship shifted from France to the United States, the Americans had been most obliging in furnishing "technical data packages," the fruits of American research and development, which were vital for Israel's production of advanced weaponry.

The only problem with this technical largesse was that, in handing it over to the Israelis, the U.S. retained some control over its use. This flew in contradiction to the official reason for investing so heavily in defense production in the first place: securing for Israel the means to defend itself without dependence on foreign suppliers. As the U.S. General Accounting Office noted in 1983, "Most [Israeli] exports [contain] an import component of about 36 percent" and "almost every Israeli production effort includes a U.S. input . . ."

For example, President Nixon had allowed the Israelis to manufacture the American J-79 engine under license. The Israelis wanted this engine to power the Kfir, which is essentially the airframe of the French Mirage fighter, but with a different and more powerful engine. Israel, for its part, had given assurances that it had no intention of exporting this plane. Nevertheless, Israel Aircraft Industries and the Israeli government were deeply gratified when Ecuador ordered Kfirs in 1976 and highly indignant when President Carter killed the deal (by banning the export of the U.S.-licensed engine) soon after he took office. (The president was persuaded that Latin America did not need more jet fighters.) IAI workers demonstrated in front of the U.S. Embassy in Tel Aviv (carrying placards reading "Bread and Work") amid dire predictions from the government that the ban would result in massive unemployment. Al Schwimmer, the veteran arms smuggler, turned up in Washington to get the ban lifted, and Yitzhak Rabin, who succeeded Golda Meir as prime minister in 1974, declared, "It is not that we seek to become a merchant of arms; we need military exports for our defense capability." The ban stayed, though Carter gave the Israelis an extra $285 million in economic aid as compensation.

Nevertheless, the Israelis did sell jet fighters to Ecuador, by means that illustrate neatly what Israel is prepared to do to get around restrictions from foreign suppliers.

Originally, Israel had had an agreement with the Dassault Corporation to build Mirage jets. Then, after the 1967 war, de Gaulle had embargoed further military supplies, which included the engines for the Israeli Mirages. Israeli intelligence then stole the blueprints for the French engine from Switzerland, where it was being built under license. Using the blueprints, the Israelis then built a copy of the engine, and the resulting aircraft was called the Nesher. It was this plane, untrammeled by foreign connections, that was sold to the Ecuadorans after Carter enjoined the sale of the Kfir. Finally, the Reagan administration, which had less problems with the sale of jet fighters to Latin America, gave the go-ahead for Ecuador to get the American-engined Kfirs after all, so the whole affair turned out well for Israel.[2]

Israel has, of course, no control over exports of American weapons that contain components made in Israel, even when these weapons go to countries officially classified as enemies of Israel. This does not appear to cause the Israeli industry undue concern, as can be seen from the story of the F-15 fuel tanks.

In February 1978 President Carter informed Congress that he proposed to sell fifty F-15 fighter planes to Saudi Arabia. The announcement quickly ignited a storm of outrage among Israel's friends in the U.S. The Israeli lobby mobilized to protest the sale. Angry rhetoric filled the opinion columns on the potential threat posed by these aircraft to the security of Israel. Demonstrators picketed Carter with professionally lettered signs proclaiming, "Hell No to the PLO!" and "Aid to Israel! Best Investment for America." The White House liaison to the Jewish community resigned in protest.

Carter ultimately got his arms deal approved, though only after agreeing to compensate Israel with further military aid for the threat now posed by the Saudi F-15s. In addition, it was agreed that the Saudis would be denied conformal fuel tanks normally fitted on the aircraft. Without these tanks the planes would not have the range to attack Israel.

Three years after the sale, the ban on Saudi acquisition of the conformal fuel tanks was quietly dropped. Such a surrender to the Saudis might have been expected to spark outrage from Israelis, now within range of enemy bombs. That, however, was not the way that Marvin Klemow, Washington representative of Israel Aircraft Industries, saw the issue. In the fall of 1981, chatting about business in his office close by the Pentagon, the plainspoken Klemow could not contain his glee at the humor of the situation. "Remember those fuel tanks that the Saudis weren't supposed to get, and remember that the ban got dropped?" he asked puckishly. "Well, where is the one place in the world that those tanks get made?" He laughed happily, as did the arms dealers and other regulars at the Olympia restaurant in Tel Aviv, who all considered it a great joke that the infamous fuel tanks were being made by IAI at its plant outside Tel Aviv. None of them seemed to think that longer-ranged Saudi F-15s posed much of a threat or had anything to do with the PLO. On the other hand, they were very pleased that Israel should get the subcontract from McDonnell Douglas, makers of the F-15.[3]

While the Reagan administration may have been generous in meeting the needs of Israel's defense industry, there was still a great deal of technical information that Israel could not obtain even from the most friendly of regimes in Washington, which was why the "collection of scientific intelligence in the U.S." was a job for Israeli intelligence.

The most important scientific intelligence mission of all for the Israelis had almost certainly been the NUMEC operation discussed earlier. As the secret FBI memos on the case make clear, the U.S. government believed that the affair involved the acquisition of technical information as well as enriched uranium for the Israeli bomb. Despite the fact that the famous CIA handbook found in Tehran did not mention LAKAM, former intelligence officials attest that they were well aware, at least by the mid-1970s, that the Israelis had a special scientific intelligence unit.

LAKAM had been founded for the specific purpose of both obtaining and protecting Israeli nuclear secrets and had flourished under the personal and jealous protection of Shimon Peres. The first director, Binyamin Blumberg, proved adept at bureaucratic self-protection and managed to make himself and his highly secret agency autonomous within the Israeli intelligence community. By the late 1960s, when LAKAM paid a Swiss engineer named Alfred Frauenknecht $200,000 to steal the blueprints for the French engine that powered Israel's Mirage jets, Blumberg's agents were stealing a lot more than nuclear secrets. Interestingly enough, according to one former Defense Intelligence Agency official, Shimon Peres was particularly active in developing a "technology penetration and acquisition network" to help the industry he had done so much to father.

While the network—with LAKAM at its heart—operated all over

the world, the United States was the main target. The reasons were obvious: the U.S. was (and remains) far ahead of the rest of the world in technological research and development, and at the same time was on the best of terms with Israel. While a retired KGB official would not have been allowed to take a tour around the Lawrence Livermore Laboratory south of San Francisco, Yuval Ne'eman, a veteran of Military Intelligence, was. At the time of his tour around the secret research center, Ne'eman was supposedly no more than a disinterested academic. When the FBI attempted to get him to register as an agent of the Israeli government, the CIA intervened to get the demand quashed.[4]

While LAKAM functioned as one direct instrument of the Ministry of Defense in the United States, the Military Purchasing Mission in New York serves as another. The Mission is the direct institutional descendant of the old covert arms-smuggling office run by Teddy Kollek above the Copacabana nightclub on East 60th Street. These days it functions in a rather less exotic setting: the sixth floor of a nondescript office building on Third Avenue. Whereas in the early days Shimon Peres would have to go to rich Jews like the Bronfmans to ask for money for arms, and be told to go and change his socks, the Mission now has at least $1.4 billion a year to dispose of, courtesy of the U.S. taxpayer. As its name suggests, the Mission does the shopping for the IDF in the United States, spending the military aid money that arrives promptly every October, the beginning of the financial year. Until irritated Pentagon officials made the fact public, the actual operating expenses of the Mission, $2.8 million a year, were themselves charged to U.S. military aid.

It is fair to say that the Purchasing Mission has not made itself entirely popular with some sections of U.S. law enforcement. The following examples may help explain why.

Making modern tank guns is a complex affair. The barrel of the 120-mm smooth-bore gun, for example, must be chrome-plated to very specific thicknesses throughout its length, which is difficult, because it is seventeen feet long, has seven different diameters, and must be able to withstand the shock of multiple explosions. In 1981 the U.S. Army's Watervliet Arsenal in Albany, New York, invented a new chrome-plating process that was easier to carry out and made for a longer-lasting gun. The secret of this process was considered government property.

In 1984 Israel Military Industries, which had come a long way from the days when Uzi Gal first submitted the design for his gun, decided to go ahead with building its own 120-mm tank cannon, but kept the project secret from the U.S. IMI had heard about the new chrome-plating process, but could not legally get hold of the relevant technology. However, it did find a Connecticut company in the chrome-plating business, called Napco, which claimed to have been working on the new secret process at Albany. This was not true; Napco had been working at the arsenal, but not in the section that interested the Israelis. IMI gave Napco a contract to build a chrome-plating plant in Israel for $1.9 million, but told the Americans that they were not to mention the fact that it would be used for chrome-plating 120-mm tank cannons. They were to refer to the cannons only as "hydraulic cylinders."

Napco had promised the Israelis that it could deliver the equipment necessary to carry out the secret process, which it now had to steal from the arsenal. This was accomplished, and the plant in Israel was duly built—the $1.9 million coming out of U.S. aid. Thus, despite a ban on its export, the Israelis had gotten hold of the new chrome-plating process for free. Napco not only lost money on the contract, but was eventually raided by the Customs Service, pled guilty to exporting military commodities to Israel without a license, and paid a $750,000 fine.[5] Although the secret was already lost by the time of the raid, the Customs agents took along a network news crew to publicize the affair, an initiative that the Israeli Ministry of Defense considered outrageous when it heard about it.

Among similar cases that surfaced in the 1980s was the attempt to obtain up-to-date machinery for making cluster bombs; the deal for cluster-grenade technology that went awry when someone left a sample grenade in a Los Angeles restaurant; the California businessman who fled the country after being indicted for illegally exporting 810 electronic triggering devices sometimes used for detonating nuclear weapons; and many others. Sometimes the Americans holding the technology desired by Israel were witting, sometimes they were not. Recon-Optical, a medium-sized defense contractor based in Barrington, Illinois, belonged in the second category.

Recon's claim to fame is that it is the world's leading manufacturer of aerial reconnaissance systems, or cameras, for the military. One such system is called LOROP, which stands for "long-range oblique photography." This enables an aircraft to fly high and fast and yet manage to take usable pictures of something on the ground as much as a hundred miles away and transmit the picture almost instantaneously to a ground station, which can then relay it to interested military command posts.

In 1984 Recon won a contract to supply one of these systems to the Israeli air force for $40 million, the money coming out of American aid to Israel. The contract was to be managed through the Military Purchasing Mission in New York. Under one of the more generous provisions of U.S. military aid to Israel, the Israelis were allowed to demand that 40 percent of the work be "offset." In other words, the U.S. was giving the Israeli Ministry of Defense $40 million to buy an American product, but Recon in turn had to spend $16 million of that money with firms in Israel.

The Israelis had specified that they did not simply want an off-the-shelf LOROP, but one tailored to their own requirements. Recon set to work, and three Israeli air force officers dispatched by the Mission moved into offices at the company's plant in Barrington. Two of them, Baruch Moran and T. K. Harkabi, the son of Yehoshua Harkabi, a former head of Israeli Military Intelligence who is now a noted dove, were well versed in the technology involved, but the Americans wondered about the third, Udi Gal, who was "young and smart" but appeared to be entirely ignorant of the software technology on which he was supposedly working.

All might have been well, save for the fact that the Recon executives began to get restless at the scale and cost of the special Israeli requirements. Since the price of $40 million was firm, the extra development costs had to be borne by the American company, and its officials could see their profit, and more besides, going up in smoke. Bitter quarrels ensued, in the course of which Avraham Ben Joseph, the head of the Mission, threatened to get the Recon officials fired by their parent company, a large California contractor called Bourns Inc. Israelis like to use such rough tactics in bargaining, but they were surprised when the polite midwesterners at Recon finally turned around in May 1986 and announced that they were suspending work on the contract, pending arbitration.

At the same time as it stopped work, the company told the Israelis to leave without taking any technical information with them. Thus, the Recon management was more than irritated to find that the Israelis were, when intercepted, carting away ten boxes of detailed drawings and thousands of pages of notes in Hebrew. The notes turned out to be the trade secrets of Recon's camera which, so further translation revealed, were being turned over to an Israeli company called El-Op. In an operation so straightforward it could hardly be called espionage, Harkabi and Moran were laying their hands on as much of Recon's proprietary information as possible and passing it on to a former air force colleague who had gone to work for El-Op. So closely were they working with the Israeli company that they had even smuggled their contact into the Recon plant as part of an Israeli air force delegation.

An outraged Larry Larsen, chief executive of Recon, flew to Washington to complain. His first stop was the office of Illinois Senator Alan Dixon whence he was dispatched to tell his woes to the deputy undersecretary of defense for trade security policy, Stephen Bryen. Stopping the leakage of military technological secrets was Bryen's job, but some might have thought him the wrong person for Mr. Larsen to complain to.

While working for the Foreign Relations Committee eight years before, Bryen had had the bad luck to be overheard discussing what sounded like U.S. military secrets with a group of Israeli officials. The man who'd overheard him, a former director of the National Association of Arab Americans, had gone straight to the FBI. The FBI, after due investigation, had concluded that it had enough evidence of espionage activities by Bryen to take to a grand jury. But higher authority had intervened, the case was quashed, and Mr. Bryen had gone on to obtain his senior Pentagon post as a guardian of secrets.

Someone at Senator Dixon's office certainly seems to have belatedly decided that perhaps Bryen was the wrong man to deal with Larsen's woes. As the team of Recon executives waited for an audience, Larsen got an urgent phone call from one of Dixon's staffers urging him in the strongest terms to get out of Bryen's office without talking. With instinctive but perhaps misguided politeness, the midwesterners felt that since Mr. Bryen was ready to receive them they had to go ahead. The meeting passed pleasantly if inconclusively, although at one point Bryen insisted on retaining a document that Larsen showed him. Larsen thought it curious that the first news about the dispute surfaced in *Davar*, an Israeli newspaper, shortly afterwards and that the article, which was highly critical of Recon, seemed to be based in part on the document he had given Bryen.

The *Davar* coverage was in line with the standard Israeli approach to such imbroglios, which is to deny everything. El-Op, like almost all Israeli defense corporations, is headed by a retired general. Nathan Sharoni, known to one and all as Natti, certainly does not have the manner of a man who would intrigue against America. Nevertheless, he dismissed the embarrassing tale of the fifty thousand documents as "corridor gossip" and suggested, in the course of a somewhat emotional discussion, that complaints about this sort of carry-on might help "some American industries lobby in order to avoid work [being] taken out of the country, no matter to what extent [meaning the vexed issue of offsets]."

As evidence that nothing very serious had been going on, he cited the fact that "if it had been a real issue, the Pentagon reaction to it would have been completely different." Considering Mr. Larsen's experience when he took his complaint to the Pentagon, this raises an interesting point, on which, unfortunately, the general was loath to follow up. Like most Israelis, he is adept at raising the rhetorical temperature of any argument whenever the moment seems opportune. However, it became clear in the course of his indignant peroration that the penetration of the American defense contractor had been a policy ordained from above and one with which Sharoni did not necessarily agree.[6]

General Sharoni was presiding over El-Op and the Recon scandal because of his bitter relations with Arik Sharon. Sharoni had enjoyed a flourishing military career and had been spoken of as a future chief of staff, until Sharon became minister of defense in 1981. The two had been at odds since the 1973 war, and when Minister Sharon revealed to the higher command his plans to invade Lebanon, Sharoni had vigorously opposed the idea and resigned in protest. This lends an ironic twist to the Recon affair, since Sharon had a lot to do with the "collection of scientific intelligence in the U.S." that caused General Sharoni so much trouble.

While Sharoni departed for El-Op, Sharon not only pursued his plans for the conquest of Lebanon, he also took care to get firm control of the "technology penetration and acquisition network" crafted over the years by Peres and others.

This was a move of some political significance, and important in understanding why Israeli intelligence officials are prepared to betray their U.S. ally by stealing defense secrets.

Power over the technology penetration network in Israel means power to dispense enormous patronage in the form of "imported" technology to favored recipients inside the Israeli defense industry. Central to this network are Sibat, the arms export agency, the Purchasing Mission in New York, and LAKAM, the secret scientific intelligence unit. Sibat at that time was run by the saturnine Shapik Shapiro, the man with the expensive dark glasses and silk shirts. Shapiro, who had made his career in the days when the Labor Party reigned supreme over all aspects of the Israeli state, was not destined to get on well with Sharon. More specifically, he was alarmed at the way Sharon talked about the Americans and how careless he seemed about offending them. So Shapiro, whom an American arms trafficker who dealt with him describes affectionately as a "snake-oil salesman," was replaced by the less lissome figure of Zvi Reuter, while another of Sharon's allies, Avraham Ben Josef, was posted to Third Avenue. That left LAKAM, for which Sharon had just the right man in mind.

However big a legend Rafael Eitan had built for himself in the Mossad, thanks to exploits such as the Eichmann kidnapping and the NUMEC operation, in 1972 "Stinking Rafi" seemed to have reached the end of the road. Partially blind, stone deaf, and addicted to vitamin pills, he had been passed over for the top job in Mossad in part because of his close friendship with Arik Sharon. He had therefore retired and gone into the tropical fish business, together with an old colleague from Shin Beth.

As so often happens to graduates of the Israeli security establishment, his business profited from official favor; Tropi Fish got the concession for the highly lucrative Red Sea tropical fish business. Even so, the business failed, so when Sharon began to build his political career in the mid-1970s, Eitan followed in his wake. When Sharon got a job as security adviser to the prime minister, Eitan came along as his assistant. When Sharon launched the short-lived Shlomzion party, Eitan found a berth there, too. (Shlomzion is a good illustration of how Sharon will follow any route to power. The party was financed by contributions from the clannish and wealthy worldwide network of Jews originating in the Syrian town of Aleppo. Sharon sought a new political direction by trying to meet with Yasser Arafat in 1977. With characteristic ineptitude, the PLO leader turned down the overture. After the 1977 election, the little party merged with Menachem Begin's Likud.)

To his disappointment, Sharon failed to get the defense ministry in Begin's 1977 government. Instead he accepted the agriculture post, which he used to bolster his right-wing credentials by promoting the growth of settlements on the West Bank. Stinking Rafi was not forgotten, however. Begin had invented the job of antiterrorism adviser to the prime minister as a sinecure for an old comrade in arms from the Irgun. When that individual was killed in a car crash in 1978, Sharon got Eitan the post. Finally, after Begin won the 1981 general election and formed a new government, Sharon became minister of defense, the job he had wanted for a long time. Hardly had he moved into the Kirya when he dismissed Blumberg and appointed Eitan as head of LAKAM.[7]

It was an auspicious time to be taking over an espionage agency specializing in defense technology. The recently installed Reagan administration was engaged in bolstering the Pentagon budget to undreamt-of heights; money was pouring into military research and development. Friends of Israel, such as Stephen Bryen, were well represented in senior positions. Richard Perle, Bryen's boss, had actually been lobbying for an Israeli defense corporation when he moved into the Pentagon. Formal recognition of the enhanced defense relationship between the two countries came with the Memorandum of Understanding on military cooperation signed in October 1981.

Under Reagan, the U.S. military-industrial complex entered into a golden age. Defense had priority over all other claims on the budget; the "threat" was magnified through the prism of ever more alarmist intelligence; intelligence itself accumulated unprecedented institutional power. In other words, the U.S. was becoming more like Israel.

Among signs that Washington was beginning to see things the Israeli way was the attention given to "terrorism" as a phenomenon in itself and divorced from any political context. (Groups whose modus operandi appeared to resemble terrorism, such as the Nicaraguan contras, but whose objectives were supported by the U.S. could be given the alternate classification of "freedom fighters.") The actions of the pre-independence Stern Gang, Irgun, and Haganah had served Israel well in driving out both the British and a large proportion of the Palestinian population, but Menachem Begin, for example, grew extremely indignant whenever someone described him as a former terrorist. For Israelis, "terrorism" meant any military action by Palestinians and their supporters. They had little trouble in persuading the men and women who took power in Washington in 1981 to accept this world view. Upon becoming secretary of state, Alexander Haig announced that terrorism (which he chose to believe was masterminded by Moscow) would henceforth replace human rights as a prime concern of U.S. foreign policy. The myriad offices of America's far-flung intelligence system were directed to concern themselves with the topic.

So far as naval intelligence was concerned, this preoccupation found institutional expression in the formation of an Anti-Terrorism Alert Center (ATAC) of the Naval Investigative Service's Threat Analysis Division. Since this organization was new, its staff was made up of people transferred from other naval intelligence offices. One of those so assigned, in June 1984, was a plump, bespectacled, 30-year-old civilian analyst named Jonathan Jay Pollard.

Like Rafi Eitan, Pollard had been fascinated by intelligence from an early age. By all accounts a morose and somewhat neurotic individual, Pollard had found solace, as an American Jew, in identifying with the state of Israel. While an undergraduate at Stanford he had boasted to fellow students of being in Mossad, and when he went to study at the Fletcher School of Law and Diplomacy at Tufts University he indulged the fantasy by informing on fellow students to the CIA. Despite such efforts, however, the CIA refused to hire him, so he sought and obtained a less prestigious berth at naval intelligence.

Pollard's vocal and aggressive Zionist sympathies did not preclude his employment in secret work, although his unofficial liaison with South African intelligence in 1981 caused his superiors to lift his security clearance. Even this setback was only temporary, and the following year he was back at work and, according to his own subsequent admission, slipping classified information to a visiting Israeli delegation. At the same time, he also began passing classified information to friends in the investment business, in the hopes of subsequent reward.

The Anti-Terrorism Alert Center was staffed by assignees from other offices of naval intelligence. Given the nature of bureaucracies everywhere, it is likely that the people posted there were the ones their bosses wanted to get rid of. The fuss over his dealings with the South Africans might well have put Pollard in that category, but he had no reason to feel slighted. He was inaugurating a potentially flourishing career spying for LAKAM.[8]

Arik Sharon was driven from the Ministry of Defense in the wake of his disastrous invasion of Lebanon and the public massacre of Palestinians that followed. Rafi Eitan, however, survived the downfall of his patron, and in fact was helpful in providing interesting details about Sharon to his new boss, Moshe Arens. Business for LAKAM was still brisk, so when an ambitious air force colonel named Aviem Sella on a study assignment in the U.S. came across a promising intelligence possibility, he knew where to take it.

Sella was a member of the elite of the elite. Ezer Weizman, who had done so much to create it, had said "the best to the air force," and Israeli society has always agreed. The service enjoys a fatter budget, proportionately, than the army, and a style of life to go with it. As one Israeli journalist has described its situation: "A regular air force base has a high standard of living, including sports installations, saunas, swimming pools, clubs, waiters, etc. On the other hand, an armor base could exist nearby with no hot water and if anyone complained no one [in authority] cared . . . the chief of staff [of the IDF] has very little influence on what happens in the air force between wars and even less during a war." By careful design, air force officers are encouraged to think and behave like a privileged tribe.

As a combat pilot Sella was therefore in a very favored position within Israeli society, but even within this group he was considered a "first," one who is destined for the very top. "Firsts" are distinguished not just by the number of enemy planes they shoot down but by additional virtuosity in the air and in successful command assignments. Nothing is considered too good for such men. Another legendary "first," sent to study at Harvard, had his term papers prepared for him in Israel and flown out in the diplomatic pouch.[9]

Sella had sealed his status by commanding the raid that demolished the Iraqi Osirak nuclear reactor in June 1981. It was a stellar performance and did no harm at all to the election campaign of Prime Minister Begin. Tipped as a future air force commander, he was sent to round off his resume by getting a Ph.D. in computer sciences in New York. Notwithstanding his academic labors, he was ready to serve Israel while abroad, which was why early in 1984 he lectured a group of Jewish stockbrokers and investment advisers on the Iraqi raid. The aim of the gathering was to inspire the Wall Streeters to show a more loyal interest in Israel Bonds than they had in the past. Whether more bonds got sold as a result is not known, but the host of the gathering happened to tell his cousin, Jonathan Pollard, about the dynamic Sella. Pollard immediately asked for an introduction.

Intelligence ranks below combat flying in the Israeli air force order of things, but Sella apparently knew enough to consult with Yosef Yagur, the attaché for scientific affairs at the Israeli Consulate in New York. These scientific attachés were the LAKAM station chiefs in various parts of the U.S., as interested members of the U.S. intelligence community well knew. The most important of these is the science attaché in Los Angeles, a useful spot from which to survey the Southern Californian aerospace industry.

Sella wanted to know if he should indeed meet with the Jewish naval intelligence analyst who, as his cousin would certainly have known, was already supportive of Israel to the point of fanaticism. Yagur in turn checked with headquarters. Rafi Eitan was keen that Pollard's approach be followed up, as was the military high command. Sella reportedly received direct authorization from Air Force Chief Amos Lapidot and IDF Chief of Staff Moshe Levi—in writing—to go ahead. [10]

Sella accordingly flew to Washington and met with Pollard. They agreed that Pollard would supply as much classified material requested by the Israelis as he could, a service for which he was offered and accepted rich cash rewards. The operation was under way.

Pollard's employment with LAKAM coincided with his move to the antiterrorism intelligence office. It is ironic that the obsession with terrorism in the U.S., which the Israelis had done so much to foster, facilitated the work of the Israelis' spy. The Israelis had convinced many in U.S. intelligence that they were uniquely skilled in dealing with the problem. In 1981 Theodore Shackley, formerly deputy director of operations at the CIA, and the man who had dismissed all suggestions that there had been a diversion from NUMEC, wrote that the "countering of the Palestinian threat [by Israel] . . . is a textbook example of how a . . . nation should fashion its own secret services." Since terrorism could supposedly strike from anywhere, anytime, intelligence analysts on the alert for it had to be able to draw on an enormous range of information sources. Thus workers at ATAC, including Pollard, were cleared for access to areas of classified information normally denied to low-level analysts on a "need to know" basis. [11]

Pollard began work in June 1984 and was arrested in November

1985. Though he always maintained that he was motivated purely by devotion to Israel, he was well paid for his services. Much of his ill-gotten gains served to support a Washingtonian's notion of high living. When Sella came down for a meeting not long before the operation came to an end, he was amazed to notice how fat both Pollard and his wife had become on their diet of expensive restaurant fare.

During those sixteen months of working for the state he revered, when he was not on vacations lavishly financed by his paymasters, Pollard removed on the order of 800,000 pages of documents for perusal and copying by the Israeli backup team in Washington. Defense Secretary Caspar Weinberger later suggested in a graphic image that all the stolen material put together would make a pile six feet by six feet by ten feet.

The modus operandi developed by the LAKAM operatives was that Pollard would take the documents home to await collection by Irit Erb from the embassy, who would remove them for copying in an apartment specially set up for the purpose and then bring them back.

Judging by the quantity of paper she had to lug back and forth, Ms. Erb must be a strong woman. In accounts of the affair she has commonly been described as a secretary to the science attaché—i.e., the LAKAM station chief—in the Washington embassy. This sounds reasonable, in view of her lowly if necessary role as a porter. However, former inmates of the Defense Attaché's Office at the U.S. Embassy in Tel Aviv recall Irit as something more than just a secretary. Prior to coming to Washington she had had the important job of liaison between the Defense Ministry and the Attaché Office. "She was definitely no secretary," says one staffer.

The question of Irit Erb's true status is only one of many indications that the official history of the Pollard affair does not quite fit the facts. The Israelis, naturally, were anxious that the whole business be "put behind us" as fast as possible and were less than forthcoming to American investigators. The government in Jerusalem was particularly anxious to stress the unique nature of the case. There was much breast-beating, particularly among American supporters of Israel, over the fact that an American Jew had been enlisted to spy in America for Israel.

The recruitment of Pollard supposedly violated the firm injunctions within Israeli intelligence against recruiting a Jew to spy in the country of which he or she is a citizen. The claim of such injunctions was treated with a certain amount of scepticism in the U.S. press, as well it might have been.

The press considered the possibility that there might be a "Mr. X," a high-ranking Israeli spy inside U.S. intelligence who had pointed the Israelis to useful material for Pollard to steal. The Colonel, the American intelligence agent in Tel Aviv, considered this debate amusing. He had repeatedly found instances in which even the most highly classified messages from officials in the American Embassy direct to the White House were known to the Israelis within hours. His conclusion was that there was at least one high-level Israeli agent operating at the upper reaches of the Defense Intelligence Agency. An agent working at that level would be more important to Israel, and damaging to U.S. security, than Mr. Pollard.

Other equally pertinent questions were left unresolved. What was it, for example, that Pollard actually stole? The Israelis' fallback position, once their hands were actually spotlit in the till, was that even this admitted crime had its justifications. Zvi Rafiah, who advises Israeli companies on doing business with the Pentagon from an office on the fourth floor of Shaul Eisenberg's Asia House building in Tel Aviv, articulated it this way:

"If the United States government and people were offended that one had to resort to spying on the United States, that was . . . that was *bad*. I mean, we didn't like it. It's not just being caught, it's the fact that among very good friends, close allies, etc., one had to resort to such a means to get something. Although on the other hand one can say, and I don't mean to justify what took place, but I can only say that if one had to resort to such a case, maybe one didn't get what he thought he should get from an ally and a friend." In other words, the Americans drove the Israelis to it.

Rafiah was referring to the defense advanced by Pollard himself, which was that the bulk of what he handed over consisted of intelligence data on weapons systems supplied by the Soviet Union to Israel's Arab enemies but which the U.S. was cruelly withholding from its friends. Of course, this excuse rather contradicts a boast, frequently advanced by the Israelis, that they are a major source for the U.S. of information on Soviet weapons systems that are used by the Arabs.

It has been reported that Pollard was able to hand over highly secret information on U.S. code-breaking techniques, thus greatly assisting Israel's own communications intelligence efforts. Also widely reported as part of the Pollard "take" was intelligence crucial to the Israeli bombing raid on PLO headquarters in Tunis in October 1985.

Conveying such intelligence, reprehensible though it may have been, would hardly justify Weinberger's heated observation to a caller who interceded on the convicted agent's behalf: "Pollard should have been shot." The remark makes more sense, however, in light of a bitter observation by a former American intelligence officer who served in Israel that Pollard had betrayed U.S. agents operating there: "He took all of our reports and fed them right back to Tel Aviv."

What may have incensed Weinberger even more was the possibility that at least some of Pollard's stolen secrets may have ended up in Moscow. The Pollard case, it should be recalled, occurred in the days before the crumbling of the Berlin Wall and the vaporizing of the Cold War. Israel had painstakingly constructed its status as a strategic asset of the U.S. on the back of superpower confrontation. On the other hand, as Zvi Rafiah might say, Israel had a perennial interest in good relations with the Soviets because of its interest in securing the emigration of Soviet Jews, the only possible means—since American Jews seemed unlikely to emigrate—of bolstering its non-Arab population. That is why information gleaned from Pollard's illicit researches was almost certainly passed to the Russians.

Astounding as this aspect of the story is, it has been confirmed directly and unequivocally by two very well-placed U.S. sources with a direct interest in the Pollard case and, in a backhanded fashion, by a former Israeli intelligence officer who answered a question on this topic by saying, "The Russians didn't get anything that was really important." The quid pro quo, reportedly, was a speedier supply of Soviet Jewish emigrants for Israel. (UPI also relayed the story of a Soviet connection, in a 12/13/87 dispatch, quoting a Justice Department source. Our sources for the story were obtained independently.)

Surprisingly, Pollard's contribution to the basic mission of LAKAM—"collection of scientific intelligence in the U.S. and other countries"—has also gone unremarked. A source very much concerned with the damage wrought by Pollard asserts that in fact the bulk of the material demanded of and furnished by the spy consisted of very highly classified technological data that the U.S. had previously managed to withhold from Israel. Included in this was data vital to the development of Israel's reconnaissance satellite, which went into orbit during the second year of Pollard's life sentence in maximum security.

Soon after its launch, the suggestion was mooted in Israel that the satellite should in fact be named "Pollard."

The irreverent Israeli press had some fun at the expense of the problems that Pollard caused for the blindly loyal lobby in America. Remarking on a visit by American Jewish leaders, one article reported that one leader said, " 'Yitzhak Shamir appeared before us and said that he cannot tell us all the truth, but that all that he will tell us is true. We wrote this down. Shimon Peres appeared and said that he cannot tell us all the truth, but that all that he will tell us is true. We wrote this down. Then Teddy Kollek came and told us that they are both liars. What can we do?' One of the Israelis [listening to the leader's story] said 'Kollek is senile.' The American looked at him in despair. This is not a claim he can write down in his copybook."[12]

The underlying significance of the Pollard affair was best captured by an Israeli journalist who pointed out that the various cases of Israeli technical espionage in the United States and the Pollard affair were connected. "The string linking all [these events] lies right under our nose, but it is a kind of 'sacred cow' that must not be touched. This 'cow' provides today a living, according to statistics, for a hundred and thirty thousand families in Israel. This sacred cow fills the state treasury with a third of its foreign currency and has gradually become Israel's number one export business."

The sacred cow described here is what Israelis call the "security system," the system that runs Israel's defense affairs and its defense business. At the top of this system, according to the journalist, stand the " 'good fellows' . . . sons of the Palmach generation. Others have been promoted from the corridors of the Ministry of Defense. Most know each other, either from a background of joint comradeship in one of the political camps, or from joint military service and security activities (i.e., the intelligence agencies). Most of them still believe that they take part in a very important Zionistic endeavor, the security of Israel, which immunizes them against afterthoughts resulting from a bad conscience that sometimes goes with their occupation.

"The sacred cow," the journalist continued, "is the giant industry that includes the system of security production and exports . . . To maintain this big organization of the security industries, it is necessary to feed it all the time with up-to-date information on current developments in this area throughout the world . . . A respectable enterprise must spend each year at least 10 percent of its budget on [research and] development. The average in Israel ranges from 3 to 8 percent. Against this background the need for importing technologies becomes increasingly vital . . ."

Almost as vital, it might be said, as maintaining the U.S. aid that had nourished the sacred cow so well. Fortunately for Israel, not only has the U.S., wittingly or otherwise, fed it the technology, it has also found reasons to help its defense industry's export drive.

9. The Intangibles

On a warm Halloween day in 1988, a small convoy left the low apartment blocks of Tel Aviv and turned north along the Mediterranean coast. A battered Renault van loaded with a chain saw and odds and ends for chopping wood led the way. Behind came a red dune buggy. Its occupants, casually dressed in jeans and matching navy T-shirts, might have been heading for the beach. Nothing gave away the profession of this as-yet-obscure party of Israelis except their excellent physical condition and very exotic conversation.

The driver of the modest van passed the time by reminiscing about his last visit to Puerto Boyaca, a small and dangerous city with the highest murder rate in Colombia. The lush Colombian countryside, the rare and beautiful birds, compared well, he thought, with arid Israel. At home, on his own small farm in the foothills west of Jerusalem, he was experimenting successfully with organic tomatoes and "clean" potatoes grown in straw. But Israel's conservation policy was a shambles; Israelis did not take care of the land as God had instructed in the Bible. In Colombia, there were possibilities. The rich farmland of the vast Magdalena Medio region was like a dream. The people, too, were charming, "always laughing," not at all like the sullen Bolivians next door, at least in his experience.

It was not until nearly a year later, in August of 1989, that this congenial Israeli's image would be captured in a revealing home movie, seized by Colombian security forces from one of Colombia's most prominent drug lords.

Lt. Col. Amatzia Shuali, like the others in the convoy that Halloween, was an exceptionally well-trained killer. The driver of the dune buggy, Col. Yair Klein, would later be singled out by the Colombian internal security chief, Gen. Miguel Maza Marquez, as the man most responsible for the training and equipping of the death squads known as "sicarios" who had ravaged Colombia on behalf of the Medellin cartel. Klein was impressive, a solidly built and balding reserve colonel in the Paratroops and Commando Corps. He had studied military history at Tel Aviv University and was a graduate of the Israel Defense Forces' Command and Staff School. He had parlayed his military experience and his defense connections into a commercial venture called Spearhead Ltd., which offered "instruction and training" for "antiterror combat units," according to a handsome promotional brochure.

Klein and his men were careful to point out that Spearhead was authorized by the Israeli Ministry of Defense and required permits from the ministry for each "project" the company undertook, including those in Colombia. Spearhead received a glossy full page in the official Ministry of Defense publication, the Israel Defense Sales Directory.[1]

The cars pulled up to a dusty, isolated spot where "live" gunfire in the canyon below would not disturb neighbors or invite unwelcome attention. The Partridge Club was a convenient place to train clients who chose to do their course, whether it be "antiterror combat," "VIP security," or "presidential guard force" training, in Israel. For intensive short-term instruction, Klein offered the attractive package of a "survival" course combined with "a tour of the holy land." It was a thoughtful mix of "submachine gun training," parachute drops, "helicopter sliding to a point target," "contact combat," and sightseeing. Even the tours promised to be "unconventional." Colonel Klein's entrepreneurial flair seemed without limits; there were even plans for a restaurant on the banks of the Jordan River, where busloads of fundamentalist Christians could relax and enjoy simple Israeli fare after baptism.

As Klein and Shuali made their way to the one-room clubhouse to collect a variety of Uzis and Berettas, they were joined by Spearhead "marketing manager" Dror Eyal, who had picked up his excellent

English "here and there." Avraham Tzedaka, another Spearhead "team" member on hand that day, listed his credentials as "commander of IDF's antiterror unit and head of the IDF antiterror department." The group was greeted warmly by the Partridge Club's honorary chairman, Colonel Maxim Kahan, a South African by birth who had served with the Jewish Brigade of the British army in World War II. Colonel Kahan had been given the land for the club by the Rothschild family, in gratitude for Kahan's supervision of the return and burial of the bodies of Edmond de Rothschild and his wife, who had paid for much of the early settlement of Israel.

Klein and his colleagues loaded the back of the dune buggy with weapons and ammunition clips and drove down the dusty track to the shooting ranges. The canyon was already echoing with rapid gunfire, from a crowd of seasoned gunmen in the midst of assault training. When asked who they were, a self-appointed spokesman claimed they were "bus drivers." A photograph was out of the question.

Spreading out the assorted weapons on a picnic table, the men from Spearhead volunteered Amatzia Shuali, the organic farmer who was their chief instructor for special combat units, to demonstrate his peculiar skills. Shuali was an instructor at the Israeli Security Forces School and at the police antiterror unit. He had also trained nearly everyone above the rank of captain in the Guatemalan army. Well regarded and much in demand in Latin-American military circles, he had served time with the Nicaraguan contras in Honduras, not to mention sharing his expertise with the cartel hit men in Colombia.

The reserve lieutenant colonel was exceptionally lean and graceful, with pale blue eyes that no doubt impressed his students in the Guatemalan jungles and in the camps along the Rio Coco. He assembled the arms on the picnic table with the intense concentration of a watchmaker. When he drew a gun, his feline movements were so quick and fluid, his body appeared to be an extension of the weapon. Shuali started off his trainees with a small elegant Beretta. The classic Uzi was, in his view, far too easy to handle and shoot to be useful in improving technique or reforming bad habits. Once a pupil could speedily draw the Beretta from behind the hip, drop to a crouch, and fire repeatedly into the center of the target with just one hand, Shuali was pleased with his morning's work. As he circled each bullet hole in the target, the trainer's words of praise and encouragement were in Spanish rather than Hebrew.

What Lieutenant Colonel Shuali found satisfying about training the armies of Latin America was their "motivation and willingness to learn."[2] "If people have got motivation," he explained, "you can give them everything." It was essential that the training ground should be as realistic as possible, that trainees should feel the tension of being "under pressure." When Shuali had visited the FBI Academy in the United States, he was impressed with the shooting techniques taught there but disappointed at the lack of "pressure." One could see the point when watching the Medellin cartel home movie of the Spearhead trainees. The recruits shimmied breathlessly along ropes strung across ravines; they tore across open village streets and hugged the whitewashed walls before blasting holes in the sleeping quarters and parlors of mock village homes. They shouted "Communist guerrillas, we want to drink your blood." It all looked very real. "Motivation" was unquestionably high.

By the fall of 1988, Shuali had done four tours in Guatemala, one or more tours in Honduras, and had plied his trade twice in Colombia. He had been hired in each case by Israeli middlemen in the region, for, as he put it, "they know my reputation." In at least one instance he was offered as a sweetener to facilitate an arms deal. "I was a gift," he said. Like the Uzis, the Galils, and the Arava transport planes that flooded into the region from Israel, Shuali was a defense export. As Dror Eyal, marketing manager of Spearhead, said of the men that day at the range, "All of them were commanders of antiterror units [in Israel] and they mainly deal with instruction of those combat units . . . all of our instructors have this operational experience."[3]

Spearhead, Eyal emphasized, was selective about its client list. "We always prefer to work for governments or for official organizations. In some cases we would work for private or semiprivate semigovernmental organizations, but in that case, of course, it would be under the complete approval and authorization of our Ministry of Defense . . . if the authorities object, then we would not do it."

To demonstrate some of the skills they successfully marketed abroad, the men from Spearhead loaded their Uzis into a white four-door sedan on the canyon floor. Once several trainers had leapt in and rolled down the windows, the car moved rapidly into a figure-eight maneuver. As it roared past the fixed target, Shuali, Klein, and their colleagues popped out of the windows and shot dozens of rounds into the mock-up victim. As the sedan swung around, they fired again and again. It was chilling to see that exercise repeated in the video footage of the Medellin cartel death squad—recorded, in fact, as a training aid and promotional gimmick for Spearhead.

Marketing manager Eyal believed Spearhead's operations in Colombia and elsewhere quietly contributed to the ongoing war against the guerrilla threat that polite governments could not openly wage. "Fighting terrorism, especially in that part of the world, is fighting against leftist guerrilla groups. This is the terrorism today in Latin America." The subtle distinctions between Colombian "ranchers" like drug lord Gonzalo Rodriguez Gacha, who required his army to be trained to eradicate such undesirables as union-organizing banana pickers, and clients such as the Guatemalan army and the contras, who targeted the same leftist "threat," were lost on Spearhead. It was all of a piece, dovetailing neatly, believed Eyal and Klein, with the interests of the United States. "We are positive that what we are doing is within the interests of the Americans, and so far it was always like that." They would have heard about it, said Klein, if it was not.

No one had interfered with Spearhead's Colombian mission, even though in July of 1988, an internal report of DAS (the Colombian equivalent of the FBI) had alerted U.S. agencies to the presence of Israelis in cartel training camps. One reason for the American silence may be that DAS had also detected the presence of Americans there.[4] The Colombian army, according to the secret police reports, were partners in the cartel's death squad activities. As "collaborators," DAS named the commander and subcommander of the military base at Puerto Calderon. The report also named the police chief of La Dorada, as well as the police commander of the town that Shuali remembered so fondly, Puerto Boyaca. Drug boss Rodriguez Gacha was on the best of terms with the army. He had, after all, bought an entire brigade, the 13th, as detailed later in bank records seized from the Gacha ranch. Since Israel did considerable legitimate business with the Colombian military, the presence of the men from Spearhead in paramilitary camps with strong regular-army endorsement seemed natural in the complicated world of Colombia. Colombians called it "the Labyrinth," and until their Hebrew commands were recorded on tape, the men from Spearhead had navigated it well.

In order to understand why these accomplished Israeli military advisers were much in demand thousands of miles from home in the jungles of Latin America, one has to go back over fifty years to a relationship that first began with the Somoza family of Nicaragua. Nine years before the founding of the state of Israel, the Jewish underground forces needed covert supplies of weapons to fight both the British, who controlled Palestine, and the Palestinians, who lived there. The Haganah turned to the founder of the Somoza dynasty, Gen. Anastasio Somoza Garcia, who had been installed first as commander of the American-inspired National Guard and then as head of state by the United States. General Somoza obligingly went along with the deception that a batch of weapons secretly shipped to Palestine had been destined for and had landed in Nicaragua. Thus the man whose savage methods on behalf of U.S. interests in Central America caused President Franklin Roosevelt to label him "our son of a bitch" began a warm friendship with Israel. What began in 1939 flowered in 1948, when General Somoza issued Nicaraguan passports for Haganah agents and lent his services to smuggle arms for the War of Independence. The general's largesse was often cited as the excuse for large quantities of Israeli arms being shipped to his son in the late 1970s after Somoza Jr.'s appalling record of indiscriminate bombing, torture, and execution forced the Carter administration to abandon him. But the generosity of 1948 came at a price, since the elder Somoza charged $200,000 for his friendship. The cash was paid into Somoza's private account in the Bank of London and South America in New York City. That deposit plus additional gifts, including a large diamond, bought both a conduit for arms and an immaculate record of votes in the United Nations supporting Israeli statehood and Israel's admission to the UN.[5]

Another staunch ally in the region was Guatemala. It was thanks to a Guatemalan diplomat at the UN, Jorge Garcia Granados, that the key UN Committee on Palestine recommended that the British Mandate should give way to partition. Granados hailed from one of the last progressive governments in Guatemala and believed that the socialism displayed on the kibbutz was an excellent model for Third World countries like his own. Later, a U.S.-engineered coup put an end to such thinking in Guatemala, but Israel continued steadfastly to support its old ally, even in the face of the cruel and systematic destruction of the Indian population there.

Such early relationships, germinated at the UN, matured into technical assistance offered by Israel in the 1960s. Advisers roamed Central and South America fighting cotton pests in El Salvador and opening vegetable cooperatives in Guatemala. "Mobile teams" created "model settlements" in the region, while experts were dispatched from the Israeli Ministry of Defense to train paramilitary youth groups along the lines of similar organizations in Israel. By 1964, Latin Americans were accepting invitations from the Israeli Ministry of Defense to see firsthand the successes of the Israeli "Nahal concept" of agricultural cum military settlements. It was no coincidence that this spate of activity occurred during the Kennedy administration's "Alliance for Progress." As Israeli analyst Benjamin Beit Hallahmi put it, "Israel's activities in Latin America—even at an early stage, and even when these activities were mostly civilian—were part of an American strategy to counter radicalism in the area." Washington was busy setting up the secret police in countries like El Salvador while the Israeli Histadrut labor federation was reportedly working with the foreign branch of the AFL-CIO (AIFLD), which itself cooperated closely with the CIA, "to organize a tame network of rural cooperatives" in that country. (In El Salvador, the Kennedy administration was also engaged in funding and training what are now called "death squads." General Medrano, recognized as the father of death squad activity in modern El Salvador, proudly showed a visiting journalist a handsome medal he had received from Lyndon Johnson for his efforts in fighting communism.)

With visions of Castro's influence poisoning the Central American well, the Kennedy administration asked Israel to step in with "civic action" programs as an antidote to Cuban-style revolution. Thus the ostensibly humanitarian task of organizing poor farmers was an integral part of U.S. policy, using methods that would later be refined into "pacification" programs. The "image" of the military was, as it remains today, of particular concern. The Israeli concept, as articulated by the Ministry of Defense, was to "turn the army into a constructive force which, though capable of combat operation, would in times of peace be interwoven within the national creativity."[6] Although the lessons of "creativity" were somewhat lost on the Latin-American generals, from Israel's point of view, the American A.I.D. (Agency for International Development) money spent on such Israeli projects was worth the investment.

Israel, through its instruction of high-ranking officers from twelve Latin-American countries, made exceedingly valuable contacts for future business. It was a "creative" use of U.S. funds to lay the groundwork for sizable arms sales and military cooperation. Latin generals poured into Israeli military bases on at least 160 visits between 1964 and 1971. Some of those generals later graduated to chief of state. Alfredo Ovando Candia of Bolivia, Kjell Laugerud Garcia of Guatemala, and João Baptista Figueirdo of Brazil had all made a pilgrimage to Israel while in uniform. Naturally, Israeli military men took the time to make return trips to Latin America. The exchange, subsidized by the U.S. Treasury, was fruitful. What had begun as the responsibility of a small unit inside the Israeli Defense Ministry called the Department for Cooperation and Foreign Liaison became the major part of the business of the Defense Ministry Sales Office (Sibat) as Latin America ripened into the prime market for Israeli weapons.

This lucrative dividend of the alliance of convenience with the United States came with the tacit understanding by all parties that Israel could do what the United States could not. As Dror Eyal of Spearhead put it, "The Americans have the problem of international public opinion, international image . . . we don't have this problem." Israeli Knesset member Gen. Matityahu Peled put it more bluntly. "In Central America, Israel is the 'dirty work' contractor for the U.S. administration. Israel is acting as an accomplice and arm of the United States." For example, when Secretary of State Alexander Haig made a direct request for Israel to assist the unappealing Guatemalan regime in 1981 (Congress was blocking the Reagan administration from doing so), Israel happily consented to reap credit in Washington for supplying what was already one of its best customers. The Guatemalans, for their part, were delighted with the Israelis. "The Israelis do not let this human rights thing get in the way of business," one prominent politician said. "You pay, they deliver. No questions asked, unlike the gringos."[7]

Israel also enabled Guatemala to sidestep criticism from liberals in the U.S. Congress who might raise a fuss about the Guatemalan government's gross abuses against its citizens, which filled endless volumes of human rights reports. One former senior Reagan administration official recounted how a delegation of Democrats had come to him to ensure that Israel was getting enough military contracts from Guatemala. The U.S., they thought, should guarantee that Israel had a monopoly on the business.

Israel had already been the Guatemalan military's largest supplier of arms since 1977. Embarrassed about arming such a bloodthirsty crew, the Carter administration had cut military aid, allowing Israel to take over the market. Israeli shipments of Arava planes, artillery, and light weapons were followed by fifty thousand Galil rifles, one thousand machine guns, and five helicopters. Uzis, grenade launchers, armored cars, and patrol boats flooded into the Guatemalan inventory. As the Israeli daily *Ha'aretz* reported:

> The Uzi submachine gun is the preferred personal weapon of the liquidation units operating in the early hours against dissidents, Indians and non-Indians, or against the "Campesinos," the poor farmers, whenever they dare take the initiative to organize agricultural cooperatives or attempt to find out the fate of disappeared relatives. Israelis who visit Guatemala are shocked to see the Special Army units wearing Israeli uniforms and armed with Israeli weapons. . . .

The Israeli firm Tadiran (at the time partly U.S.-owned) supplied the Guatemalan military with a computerized intelligence system to track potential subversives, thus improving the efficiency of the counterinsurgency offensive. Those on the computer list had an excellent chance of being "disappeared." "They had printout lists at the border crossings and at the airport," said one American priest who himself was singled out for execution. "Once you get on that—then it's like bounty hunters." The computer had been installed in an annex of the National Palace, where Guatemalan military intelligence officers met regularly to select targets. One army officer described this macabre annex as containing "an archive and computer file on journalists, students, leaders, people of the left, politicians, and so on." The Israeli computer system facilitated sorting through dossiers and making up death lists.[8]

Then there were the advisers, like Spearhead's talented Amatzia Shuali. In 1982, Israeli advisers were prominent participants in "Plan Victoria," a scorched-earth campaign (ostensibly launched to deny sanctuary to guerrillas) in the Guatemalan highlands ordered by born-again Christian leader Gen. Ephrain Rios Montt. (Rios Montt was an elder of the Arcata, California "Church of the Word.") As the Guatemalan Embassy in Washington delicately put it, "Personnel sent by the Israeli government were participating in the repopulation and readjustment programs for those displaced as entire villages vanished." The operations were assigned such slogans as *Techo, tortilla, y trabajo* (shelter, food, and work) and *Fusiles y frijoles* (bullets and beans). The Roman Catholic Conference of Bishops called the policy "genocide." Guatemalan leader Rios Montt explained his antiguerrilla strategy: "We declared a state of siege so we could kill legally."

The "model villages" (strategic hamlets) thrown up for the hundreds of thousands of Guatemalans whose villages had been bombed or burned were reminiscent of Khmer Rouge-controlled communities in Cambodia, in which military "commissioners . . . control everything from latrine installation to food distribution." The food grown was strictly for export, just as the Khmer Rouge shipped rice to China. The Guatemalan military leaders dictated who would receive seeds, fertilizer, and credit. They assigned village inmates to work projects, such as cutting roads through the highlands, to simplify the task of routing guerrillas. Lucky villagers were subjected to two to six months in political reeducation camps. The unlucky ones, branded as "subversives," were tortured and executed. Those coerced into civilian "self-defense patrols" were required to turn in a quota of "subversives." Failure to do so prompted sadistic punishment. "They will be forced to denounce their own neighbors and to execute them with clubs and fists in the village plaza."[9]

When Lt. Col. Amatzia Shuali was training every officer above the rank of captain in the Guatemalan army, he received $5,000 for each six-week contract. It was a long time to be away from his farm and his unit of the Israeli Border Guards, but he says he found the work fascinating and the company congenial. Shuali was also commandeered to train the bodyguards of Gen. Rios Montt and his successor, Oscar Mejía Víctores. The opulent presidential farm was the setting. "It was very nice," recalled Shuali. "At night I used to have a good time with the army officers in the bars in the neighborhood. Afterwards I used to carry them on my back to the army base. These people don't know the limit of drinking."

Shuali had been hired by perhaps the most prominent Israeli in Guatemala, Pesakh Ben Or. Ben Or, whose passion was thoroughbred horses, had risen from a humble driver at Israel Aircraft Industries to chauffeur of fellow arms merchant David Marcus Katz. Katz, who controlled much of Israel's arms dealings in Central America from his Mexico City base, had nurtured Ben Or in the business and had introduced him to the right people in Guatemala City. Displaying a remarkable aptitude for the arms business, Ben Or captured the

Guatemala market soon after 1977, shuttling between his base there and a suite of offices in Miami. Ben Or, according to Shuali, had a genius for "throwing gifts"—that is, bribery. It was the attention to detail, such as the four-liter bottles of whiskey for second lieutenants and above for the holidays, that was effective. "Afterwards, every officer remembers Señor Ben Or very well."

The "gifts" for the little-known bureaucrats paid off. "Pesakh is clever," said Shuali. "He knows that it's no use to pay the big shots there, because they rise and fall all the time. But the officials of the presidency remain, and they take care of the contracts. If one of them opens the envelope and sees that Pesakh's bid is high, he calls him and tells him to reduce the price." For the "big shots," Ben Or did favors, such as training their bodyguards at his own expense.

Ben Or's enthusiasm for sales caused him to saturate the market with Israeli arms, until there was nothing left for the Guatemalans to buy. As Shuali remembered, Ben Or "sold them all possible weapons, and until the equipment becomes outdated they won't buy more arms." Ben Or's affiliation with the Israeli government was perfectly clear to Shuali. "He was an agent of Ta'as"—that is, Israel Military Industries, the huge state-owned arms corporation. Ben Or confirmed that he was also the agent for Tadiran (the computers of which kept the list makers in the National Palace busy) and was a partner in a modest seaside hotel.[10]

The dashing young Ben Or mingled in Guatemalan society and could be found at all of the best horse auctions. He managed to separate himself from the sordid end use of his product. Shuali saw the arms merchant as "not interested in meddling in politics. He was only interested in money." Ben Or kept a villa near Ramlah in Israel, complete with Guatemalan servants, pool, and stabling for seven race-horses. As Ben Or did much of his business in Miami, it was the logical place to keep the yacht.

Shuali himself was equally shy of politics. The affable gunman was only interested in his craft. What the Guatemalan army would do with its newfound skills and knowledge imparted by the Israelis was of little consequence. Shuali put his lack of moral concern in a cold light when speaking with a fellow Israeli: "I don't care what the Gentiles do with the arms. The main thing is that the Jews profit." (Shuali was too polite to make such a remark to a non-Israeli.) It was a crude way of saying that the business of arms sales kept Israel solvent and any unpleasantness in far-off Central America that might result paled beside that central fact.

Ben Or's impressive offices in Guatemala City occupied a well-guarded floor of the Cortijo Reforma Hotel. This was the regional headquarters of a company variously known as Eagle Israeli Armaments & Desert Eagle, Eagle International, and Eagle Military Gear Overseas. His company in Miami went under yet another name, Shiran. Eagle in Tel Aviv occupied a floor of the fashionable and equally well-guarded IBM Building across from the Kirya, the Ministry of Defense. The chief executive of Eagle was the very cosmopolitan Shapik Shapiro, who had served in the 1950s in the Israeli Purchasing Mission in New York, purchasing arms.

Since that time, Shapiro had nurtured his American connections and had been present at some of the most important events in the history of U.S.-Israeli military cooperation. He had signed the deal for the purchase of the Phantom fighter in 1968 with "a 25-cent pen." His Eagle company had a subsidiary in Tennessee. "We bought them out" in order to sell equipment to the U.S. Army. On the wall of his office there was a plaque from the Tennessee Manufacturers Association, amidst the displays of helmets and bullet-proof vests. A particularly fine poster to advertise Eagle's wares showed a sultry Israeli model wearing that bullet-proof vest and little else.

Shapiro, from behind a pungent cloud of cigar smoke, described the importance of such brokers as Pesakh Ben Or to the relations between the U.S. and Israel with one word—"intangibles." It embraced the activities of men who preferred to remain hidden in the covert demimonde of Third World capitals but who could be called upon for the special services required by Washington. Ben Or had been well placed to sell Israeli-owned weapons of Eastern Bloc origin to the contras, for example, when the need arose. He rented the services of a high-ranking Honduran military officer (Colonel Julio Perez, chief of logistics) to expedite the fake end-user certificate required to smooth the transactions. These were chores that required seasoned operators without American passports and with plenty of credit. There were others like Ben Or.

Emil Sa'ada, for example, arrived in Honduras at an auspicious moment. It was 1981, two years after the Sandinista revolution in neighboring Nicaragua had forced Israel's old friend Anastasio Somoza into exile in Paraguay. The remnants of Somoza's forces, particularly his infamous National Guard, had migrated to Honduras and were being courted assiduously by the newly elected Reagan administration. The "contras" had dropped their old name, the "15th of September Legion," which had come to be associated with bank robberies and general thuggery in the region. The U.S. Defense Intelligence Agency had issued a secret report labeling them a "terrorist group." Reborn as the Nicaraguan Democratic Force (FDN), the exiles were placed under CIA management with a first presidential "finding" (which legitimizes covert action) six weeks after Ronald Reagan took the oath of office. Nineteen million dollars was released for the group, which would be molded, at least for public relations purposes, into "the moral equal of our Founding Fathers." By November 1981, a National Security Decision Directive laid out the plan. The U.S. would "support the opposition front through formation and training of action teams to collect intelligence and engage in paramilitary and political operations in Nicaragua and elsewhere. Work primarily through non-Americans to achieve the foregoing, but in some circumstances CIA might (possibly using U.S. personnel) take unilateral paramilitary action."[11]

"Non-Americans" was the operative word, for it afforded the CIA "deniability" and opened the door to such helpful allies as Argentina (which could offer then-idle veterans of its own "dirty war" as trainers, an arrangement worked out between CIA chief William Casey and Argentine Chief of Staff Leopoldo Galtieri) and Israel. As one Israeli observer put it, "When the contras were being created by the CIA, the United States turned to Israel, because Israel could offer expertise and weapons and do it without any hesitations and without any political problems. When the administration is blocked from offering direct aid, by political pressure or by act of Congress, Israel can step in very easily."

Emil Sa'ada, like Pesakh Ben Or, was one of those who stepped in. Sa'ada was a former Israeli army officer who arrived in the capital of Honduras as a bodyguard. Tegucigalpa was Emil Sa'ada's kind of town. "Where else," he asked, "could I live two hours by plane from Miami and still live the life of a 17th-century adventurer?" The romantic image was somewhat tempered by his trade. When a guest at a dinner Sa'ada was attending in Marblehead, Massachusetts, asked in polite conversation what the Israeli did for a living, he answered, "I kill people." (Sa'ada had followed his girlfriend, a Honduran beauty from a wealthy family, to Massachusetts. She was on the run from her volatile husband, a prominent cocaine trafficker, who subsequently came to a violent end.)[12]

Sa'ada made his debut in Honduras as part of the entourage of former IDF Col. Leo Gleser. A flamboyant veteran of the 1976 Entebbe rescue mission in Uganda, Gleser had founded a company called International Security and Defense Systems based in Rehovot, outside Tel Aviv. Like Spearhead, ISDS was displayed prominently in the Israel Defense Sales Directory published by the Ministry of Defense. Among the specialties offered was "the training and setting up of antiterror units." In bold print in the directory entry for the Gleser security firm it states, "Following an approach by a potential client the company will carry out a risk-factor survey. The results thereof will indicate methods of application and recommendations for a proposed security structure as well as economic analysis of cost."

The Honduran "approach" came from Gerard Latchinian, at the time the most successful arms dealer in the country. The intense, chain-smoking Latchinian sat at the right hand of Honduran Gen. Gustavo Alvarez Martinez, commander in chief of the armed forces and the CIA's favorite general north of Panama. Alvarez was the pillar of the contra operation in Honduras, providing bases, training facilities, and a conduit for arms. He gave the CIA carte blanche and was well paid for his trouble. (Alvarez later retired to Miami as a born-again Christian. He was subsequently murdered by persons unknown.)

The general's arms supplier, Latchinian, chose to import Israelis to train his personal bodyguards and those of the general. The initial $9,000-a-month contract, paid by Latchinian, was just the entree. Entebbe veteran Gleser and such talented trainers as Emil Sa'ada and even Amatzia Shuali had so much to offer. Gleser made a strong impression. As Latchinian recalled, "He's six-foot-four, blond, well-built; he runs somersaults in the air, pulls his two .45's, and hits two bull's-eyes at a hundred meters! Two bull's-eyes!"

The Armenian Latchinian, who now languishes in a Dickensian high-security prison in Terre Haute, Indiana, was, by contrast, small, dark, and nervous, drawing deeply on his cigarettes. He spoke in a rapid staccato not unlike machine gun fire. (He was incarcerated for allegedly plotting a coup against the president of Honduras, Roberto Suazo Cordova.) The arms dealer found Amatzia Shuali to be thoroughly professional. "Amatzia came to do training in Honduras. There were three courses for [General] Alvarez bodyguards, two courses for [President] Suazo bodyguards, and they were looking into how to train the contras. Once the White House got the no-no from Congress, the Israelis got the job. The Hondurans could not afford this. The Americans paid. The books had to be adjusted. It was very easy—contra training cost a couple of million a year."

Latchinian had also employed the man who would take charge of the White House contra resupply line from the operation's major base in the region, Illopango. Felix Rodriguez had once worked for Latchinian in his firm Giro Aviation in Miami. Latchinian described the former CIA man (whose clout in the contra-supply set derived from his close ties and repeated meetings with the office of Vice President Bush) as a "faithful Doberman." One Israeli trainer described the "outstanding" relationship between the trainers and their contra charges. "You feel after a day," he said, "like you've known them for years."

In addition to training contra troops, the Israelis were given another highly secret mission—to train a Honduran death squad. As the base of the burgeoning contra war, Honduras was rapidly corrupted by a huge influx of dollars and arms. Bribery and black marketeering were pervasive. Honduran military intelligence officers were, according to U.S. officials, on double salary from the CIA and the Colombian cartels, who saw the advantage of using Honduran airstrips for transiting cocaine under cover of the war effort. The Senate Foreign Relations Committee revealed that the most prosperous cocaine trafficker in Honduras, Ramon Matta Ballesteros, was also a State Department contractor in good standing, for his services in ferrying "humanitarian" aid to the contras. In this louche atmosphere lubricated by American covert funding, the CIA was concerned that what had been a negligible leftist opposition in Honduras could grow and interfere with American operations. The ever-cooperative General Alvarez therefore hired Leo Gleser and his Israeli team to train "Battalion 316" to do the dirty work of silencing dissent. Back at Gleser's corporate headquarters outside Tel Aviv, a photograph of his company's Honduran graduates included Captain Alexander Hernandez, who became infamous as the commander of Battalion 316. By 1984, over two hundred and fifty people had been "disappeared" in Honduras, thanks to the deadly efficiency of Hernandez and his men.

In March 1984, when General Alvarez Martinez was toppled in a coup by slightly more moderate officers, his successor was Gen. Walter Lopez. Lopez sported Ray-Bans and was consumed with fear that the CIA would one day kill him. He was alarmed at the Israeli penetration of the Honduran armed forces and severed the ties with Gleser's company, ISDS. "We had Israeli advisers in the Honduran special forces," Lopez said. "They were seconded [transferred] to our special forces by the Israeli Ministry of Defense, although they came officially as 'nongovernmental.' Their front was that they were training special security groups for the president and military chiefs, but behind that was everything else: special operations courses, courses on how to take over buildings, planes, hostages . . . and the contras were also taking the courses. There was coordination between them and the CIA. So I didn't renew their contract."[13] According to Latchinian, the Israelis' contra business nevertheless continued to thrive. General Lopez watched their progress.

Contra training, said General Lopez, took place at a Honduran special forces base called Tamara outside Tegucigalpa. Lopez believed the Israelis, along with the CIA, were engaged in the rather more sinister activity of running a contra death squad, trained to "execute subversives from Nicaragua or El Salvador that were on Honduran soil." According to a contra defector, debriefed by Lopez, the commander of the forty-five-man squad was Ricardo Lau. "Chino" Lau, as he was known, was in fact the contras' chief of intelligence. According to former Salvadoran intelligence chief Col. Roberto Santivanez, Lau had "received payment of $120,000" for organizing the murder of Archbishop Romero of El Salvador in 1980. Administration officials later conceded that Lau was still entrusted with contra intelligence as late as June 1985, long after he had been reportedly forced out because of his excessive contempt for human rights. General Lopez said that he had unsuccessfully raided the camps of Lau and his "death squad." He recalled, "They got away from us. We deduced that the CIA and the Israelis had trained them."

General Lopez, who as Honduran chief of staff was in a position to know, stated unequivocally that the "advisers" from the security firm were working directly under the Israeli Ministry of Defense. Gerard Latchinian had the opportunity to travel to Israel to meet their overseer.

Zvi Reuter was unquestionably one of Israel's most powerful men. As the director of Sibat, the export arm of the Defense Ministry, he commanded respect from defense ministers, generals, and intelligence chiefs. The men from Spearhead, who could decapitate a target with Uzis in record time, feared only one man, and that was Reuter. Latchinian called Reuter "the brains behind everyone."

When Latchinian was ushered into his presence in January 1984, Reuter was pleased with the treatment Israeli arms dealers and advisers had received in Honduras. As Latchinian remembered, Reuter said, "I appreciate what you are doing for my boys." When the subject turned from men to equipment, Reuter was anxious to enlist Latchinian in expanding the Honduran trade. "He wanted me to push Israeli goods. I said, why? You have your boys all over the world. But, you see, I was so close to these people [the Honduran military]. I was part of their decision making." Reuter gave Latchinian his private number and, according to his visitor, offered to pay the bill for his exorbitantly expensive suite at the Hilton. "It was $1,500 a day. He made a fuss and said it should only be $250 a day at the Hilton. A terrible place. He wanted the bill."

While in Tel Aviv, Latchinian conferred with his old friend Leo Gleser and another familiar figure in the Israeli Central America fraternity, Pesakh Ben Or. Latchinian thought Ben Or had risen a bit too fast in the arms trade. "I knew Pesakh when he was a messenger boy, a page for Marc Katz."

At one meeting at the Hilton poolside terrace, recalled Latchinian, "Pesakh wore gold chains. He was eating with his mouth open. You can't inject class into people. He wanted to pay for the food. I said, I won't only throw you in the pool, I'll drown you in the pool. Gleser didn't like Pesakh either."

Ben Or kept tabs on Latchinian's business activities in Israel. "I would go to a little factory in the country and when I arrived, there would be a message from Pesakh," according to Latchinian. Although it would seem that Ben Or was harassing a competitor, one Israeli report later linked them, citing Miami sources, as business associates. Both had close ties to an interesting American corporation called Sherwood International.

Sherwood was a well-established American-Israeli firm with branch offices in Washington, Miami, and the West Coast. Its business was the sale of surplus arms no longer needed in the inventories of the Israeli Defense Forces. There was, over the years, some particularly marketable Soviet equipment brokered by Sherwood that had been captured in Israel's various wars. Two Israeli executives of the company were close friends of Ben Or. Pinhas Dagan, who once represented IAI (Israel Aircraft Industries) in Central America and Colombia, lived for a time at Ben Or's comfortable house in Miami. Amos Gil'ad, who had served as a transport officer in the Israeli army and had done business in Honduras, introduced Ben Or to Gerard Latchinian. Since Ben Or told one Israeli journalist that Latchinian did business with Sherwood, this was a reasonably close crowd. According to a former U.S. diplomat, Sherwood International was used as a front by the CIA to purchase Eastern Bloc arms from Israel for the contras.[14]

The significance of the CIA's relationship with such Israeli agents became clear from declassified memos introduced in court during the trial of former White House aide Oliver North. For during the early 1980s, the CIA began transshipping large quantities of Soviet Bloc arms captured by Israel in the 1982 invasion of Lebanon. The destination of these Israeli arms was Honduras, where they were handed over to the contras. Operation "Tipped Kettle" began in 1983, and was ordered personally by William Casey, then director of the CIA. In a memo to National Security Adviser Robert McFarlane on March 27, 1984, Casey said that with regard to "Supplemental Assistance to Nicaragua Program," a joint CIA and Defense Department survey team had acquired "some $10 million worth" of arms, including machine guns and ammunition, from the Israelis. A second trip to Israel was planned for April 1984, "to inspect captured PLO ordnance" and "to determine current Israeli inventories and to negotiate thereafter to receive appropriate weapons free or at low cost. Of course, the cost of packing and delivery will have to be factored in."

Also submitted at the North trial was a U.S. government "stipulation," an admission that certain facts are true. The document filled in more details of Operation Tipped Kettle. According to the stipulation, "In 1983, DCI [Director of Central Intelligence] Casey asked Secretary of Defense Weinberger if the Department of Defense [DoD] could obtain infantry weapons that Israel had confiscated from PLO forces. Following discussions between Major General Meron of Israel and Retired Major General Richard Secord of the United States Government [USG], Israel secretly provided several hundred tons of weapons to the DoD on a grant basis in May 1983." The 1984 negotiations yielded more weapons. "The DoD then transferred the weapons to the CIA. Although CIA advised Congress that the weapons would

be used for various purposes, in fact many of them were provided to
the Nicaraguan Resistance as appropriated funds ran out." The document made clear that Israel could expect a quid pro quo for the gift of
arms. "DoD assured Israel that, in exchange for the weapons, the U.S.
government would be as flexible as possible in its approach to Israeli
military and economic needs, and that it would find a way to compensate Israel for its assistance within the restraints of the law and U.S.
policy."

One American military attaché based in Israel at the time had been
able to inspect and photograph the stockpiled arms in northern Israel.
In vast warehouses, "the stuff was stacked all the way to the ceiling.
There were millions and millions of dollars' worth of weapons."[15]

In April of 1984, the White House needed Israel more than ever as a
"cut-out" for contra supply. The CIA had run into trouble with its
"hands-on" management of the Nicaraguan war. For the three preceding months the agency had been busy laying mines in the harbors of
Porto Corinto, Porto Sandino, and El Bluff. The contras were only
alerted after the fact. One contra leader was dragged from his bed at
two in the morning and handed a press release by a CIA liaison who
ordered him to broadcast it over the contra radio before the Sandinistas could break the news. Both the international community, and
more importantly Senator Barry Goldwater, chairman of the Senate
Intelligence Committee, were furious. Goldwater sent a pithy note to
CIA Director William Casey:

Dear Bill,

All this past weekend, I've been trying to figure out how I can most
easily tell you my feelings about the discovery of the President having
approved mining some of the harbors of Central America. It gets down to
one little simple phrase. I'm pissed off . . . . This is an act violating
international law. It is an act of war. For the life of me I don't see how we
are going to explain it.

Within five months, Congress would ratify the Boland Amendment,
which was designed to take the U.S. government out of the contra war
for at least twelve months. The amendment stated, "No appropriations
or funds made available to the Central Intelligence Agency, the Department of Defense or any other agency or entity of the United States
involved in intelligence activities may be obligated or expended for the

purpose or which would have the effect of supporting, directly or indirectly, military or paramilitary operations in Nicaragua by any nation, group, organization, movement, or individual." In anticipation of the squeeze, the White House turned to Israel. In April, National Security Adviser Robert McFarlane delegated Howard Teicher "to discuss aid to the Resistance with David Kimche of the Israeli government." The mild-mannered former deputy Director of Mossad, a past master of covert operations, served as the Israeli liaison to the White House on the delicate matter of the contras. Now director general of the Israeli Foreign Ministry, Kimche was told that "Israeli aid to the resistance should be arranged through Honduras; [and] that the USG [U.S. government] would furnish a point of contact."

As it was (and as the White House well knew), Israel had a sufficient number of seasoned operators in place to carry out whatever was needed to sustain the war effort. Accounts that had been opened in Geneva by the White House that year ensured that the cash required would wend its way to Tegucigalpa. Additional funds, as well as large quantities of equipment, were, according to U.S. officials in the region, diverted from U.S. aid earmarked for Guatemala, El Salvador, and Honduras. American covert operators were recruited to take care of the bulk of the operation headquartered at bases like Illopango in El Salvador. But the Israelis were very useful in Honduras and, the Reagan administration believed, in Washington.

Following Kimche's talks with the White House, the *Jerusalem Post* reported that Israel was expected to lobby, to "encourage its own supporters in the Congress, the Jewish community, and elsewhere to become more assertive in backing the contras." President Reagan endeavored to frame the Central American situation as just one part of the greater Arab-Israeli conflict. By fighting the Nicaraguan Sandinistas, supporters of Israel could strike a blow against the PLO, who, after all, had an office in Managua. The guerrillas in El Salvador and Guatemala could also be swept into the same net. As Reagan put it, "It is no secret that the same forces which are destabilizing the Middle East—the Soviet Union, Libya, the PLO—are also working hand-in-glove with Cuba to destabilize Central America."[16] The rhetoric gave a palatable context to the unpleasant realities on the ground.

Israeli adviser Emil Sa'ada, the man who described his livelihood with the words "I kill people," had settled into a ground-floor office at the Maya Hotel in Tegucigalpa, the social and business headquarters of the contra war. American special forces officers sunbathed by the strangely green pool. CIA operatives, black marketeers, currency traders, and the contra high command haunted the casino and bar. Contra representative "fat" Frank Arana held court in the lobby, flanked by potted palms.

Arms dealers did brisk business there. (There were reports at the time in Honduras that the contras sold off some of their weapons cache to the Salvadoran guerrillas, while one American contra adviser saw their food stocks siphoned off for sale on the local market.) Emil Sa'ada also used the Maya Hotel as the headquarters for his "melon" business. Five thousand Honduran peasants, he said, tended the melons for this Israeli agribusiness concern, Shemesh Agrotech International S.A.

According to a senior Israeli Foreign Ministry official, ISDS (the Gleser corporation for which Sa'ada worked while the firm trained presidential bodyguards, contras, and members of a Honduran death squad) was a "branch" of the melon firm. An American adviser in Central America called the "melon" business the Israeli "front."

Shemesh chose extremely convenient locations to conduct its agribusiness. Comayagua was the site of a major American military base in Honduras. Choluteca was in the Nicaraguan border region, an area of significant contra activity. Sa'ada was named repeatedly by Honduran military sources as a conduit of Israeli arms destined for the contras. Even contra recruits had heard of him.

One contra, Horacio Arce, whose nom de guerre was "Mercenario," spoke to the Mexican daily *El Día* after his return to Nicaragua. Arce remembered the Israelis:

> Regarding the arms shipments, everyone knows the sellers were Israelis and that they had grabbed the arms from the Palestinians in Lebanon. I have no doubt—many people told me so—that people involved with the CIA were sent to Israel to deal with the shipments. It is also said— I can't vouch for this myself, but they say—that the guy who grows melons in Honduras for export to the United States, Emil Sa'ada, is one of them.

Contra commander Enrique Bermudez confirmed in April 1984 that his troops had received Israeli weapons captured from the "PLO in Lebanon."

Edgar Chamorro, an urbane former Jesuit who had served on the contra Directorate (selected for the post and paid by the CIA), remembered an Israeli shipment of "two thousand assorted weapons" at the end of 1983. "When I was in the FDN [contras], the CIA station chief, the deputy [station chief], and Duane Clarridge," who was running the war for the agency, "all told me that the weapons [they were giving us] were the ones the Israelis had captured in Beirut . . ." Among Chamorro's duties during his tenure on the Directorate was stopping in to see the Israeli consul in Honduras to be debriefed. He remembered several such visits in 1983, "to inform him of our operations."

The Israelis were not the soldiers' favorite suppliers, however. Contra commanders, said Chamorro, complained to the CIA that the condition of the Israeli arms was poor. The CIA's response was that the defective weapons had come from PLO stocks and that the commanders had best keep quiet about bad shipments because the "route" that the arms had traveled was very secret.

Chamorro had been told while serving with the FDN that the trainers who appeared to instruct the contras on the use of SA-7 antiaircraft missiles were Israelis. He understood that they were the same team who had coached the UNITA fighters in Angola, financed by the United States. In 1985, contra leader Adolfo Calero (bankrolled at the time by the secret White House accounts in Geneva) was flown to Jamba, Angola, for a "contra summit" arranged by billionaire and Reagan fund-raiser Lewis Lehrman. There Calero joined UNITA leader Jonas Savimbi, also drawing a salary from the U.S. In Jamba, Calero clarified the relationship between the U.S. and Israel with regard to such wholly owned rebel groups. He said, "The foundations were set for an international network [of U.S.-backed anti-Communist guerrilla forces] with Israeli advisers."[17]

That global approach was manifested in a little arms company called Geomiltech, headquartered in Washington and Tel Aviv. GMT, which also stood, according to participants, for "God's Mighty Team," was designed as a vehicle to arm "freedom fighters" on three continents with the help of Israel, the White House, and the CIA. The beneficiaries were outlined to CIA Director Casey in one memo as guerrillas in "Nicaragua, Angola, Afghanistan, and Cambodia" (where the U.S. was nurturing a non-Communist wing of the "resistance coalition" very much dominated by the bloodstained Khmer Rouge). Much of the energies of the Geomiltech "team" were devoted to arming the contras.

The chief executive officer of the American-Israeli company, at least on paper, was a former Miami talk show hostess and beauty queen named Barbara Studley. Although it would seem from congressional testimony that Ms. Studley had more experience gluing on fake fingernails than selling arms, she surrounded herself with seasoned generals who had plied the rough trade of special operations from the OSS to Vietnam. General John Singlaub was Studley's mentor and the guiding hand of Geomiltech. Singlaub, who called himself the "lightning rod" of the White House covert efforts in Central America, aggressively sought publicity as an organizer of the "private aid" network that the White House encouraged as a front for its own activities. Singlaub had a long and distinguished career in covert operations, parachuting behind enemy lines for the OSS and working with the French Resistance against the Nazis and the Chinese Resistance against the Japanese. He served a tour with the CIA in the Korean War and headed the joint conventional task force, or MAC SOG, in Vietnam. One of his admirers in Saigon was fellow General Robert Schweitzer who recalled, "I met him in Vietnam when he worked on special operations . . . and heard his appeal that we be alert and resourceful and do something to stem the tide, the war that we were losing to communism. There is a subversive war being fought in many countries and the free world is losing that war—that's essentially his message— because we are not doing the right things."

By 1981, General Schweitzer was in a position to do "the right things." As the general described his post, he was the "senior military officer on active duty serving the president of the United States in the White House system. I was director of the Defense Group . . . In that context, I had responsibility for all of the Department of Defense programs, all of arms control, all of the veterans programs, the entire defense budget, and, of course, the area—the interface with all the area problems. The Middle East, the Far East, Latin America were included in those." At the White House, General Schweitzer had the chance to sit down with General Singlaub to discuss those "area problems." Latin America, they agreed, needed a "strategy." Singlaub, said the White House military man, was "really a Homeric figure in the sense of all this counterinsurgency stuff."[18]

Together with Barbara Studley, the general surveyed the battlefields of Central America, touring El Salvador, Honduras, and Costa Rica. General Schweitzer also rallied to the beauty queen's side.

When he retired from his last Pentagon posting as head of the General Defense Board in 1986, Schweitzer became executive vice president of Geomiltech, and later described for congressional investigators the origins of Studley's international arms business:

Q. She formed GMT herself; is that correct?
A. Yes. She had a vision to form it.

Q. When you say a vision, what do you mean?
A. Sir, I leave that to you.

In Washington, Geomiltech maintained an office with a prestigious Pennsylvania Avenue address, steps away from the White House. In Tel Aviv, the GMT office was equally well situated, a block from the imposing tower of the Ministry of Defense and surrounded by neighbors like Shaul Eisenberg and Zvi Rafiah. General Singlaub, as the company's very active consultant, traveled to Israel in April 1985 and was warmly received by Zvi Reuter, the ubiquitous chief of Sibat. When Reuter organized a tour of Israel's defense industries for Singlaub, it was not just a courtesy visit. Singlaub, who also met with the minister of defense, was shopping for Israeli weapons systems to sell abroad. Geomiltech had become the exclusive representative for the Israeli government for "a variety of weapons systems," as Singlaub put it.

It was a busy season for Geomiltech, for while the company was snapping up Israeli weapons to market, General Singlaub arranged a shipment of $5.3 million worth of arms to the contras. Fresh from his visit with Reuter, Singlaub convened a meeting at the Sheraton Carlton Hotel, just down from the White House. In attendance were Studley, the contras' titular leader Adolfo Calero, and a CIA-approved arms dealer who specialized in Soviet weaponry. There was a great deal of discussion about prices for Soviet-made AK-47s, a discussion that continued in the White House office of Oliver North, who was kept fully abreast of Singlaub's operations. "We agreed," as Singlaub recalled the North discussions, "we would use non-U.S. carriers, no U.S. bank transactions, so that it appeared to be completely legal." The former talk show hostess had set up two Swiss bank accounts to accommodate the need to remain offshore. The arms, shipped in July 1985, ended up on the Central American end in an "Arms Supermarket" controlled by Miami arms dealer Ron Martin and his Honduras-based partner, Mario Dellamico. This was the same "Supermarket" that Oliver North dutifully noted in his diary as being heavily financed with drug money.

In his frequent visits with CIA Director Casey (both were old OSS hands), General Singlaub took the trouble to praise Barbara Studley's efficient management of the $5 million shipment, with the result that in September 1985, with further recommendations from a former deputy director of the CIA, the talk show hostess was ushered into the director's office at Langley. What was discussed, as Singlaub describes it, was a proposal that Geomiltech, already the exclusive representative for the Israeli government for various weapons, should become a vendor to the CIA.

An ingenious three-country trade was proposed that would allow the CIA to arm "counterinsurgencies" without causing undue suspicion in Congress. As the Geomiltech documents outlined the plan, the three countries involved were the United States, Israel, and China. The objective was "to create a conduit for maintaining a continuous flow of Soviet weapons and technology, to be utilized by the United States in its support of Freedom Fighters . . ." The "problem" this was designed to overcome was a Congress "increasingly unpredictable and uncooperative regarding the President's desire to support the cause of the Freedom Fighters."[19]

The elaborate shell game began with Washington giving Israel "credit towards the purchase of High Technology from the U.S." Israel, which already had a booming covert trade in arms with China (thanks to the energetic sales force of Shaul Eisenberg), would "deliver military equipment" to Beijing. China would then supply Soviet-compatible arms to a "trading company," which would be the clearing house for "arms to be disbursed as per U.S. instructions" to "Afghanistan, Angola, Nicaragua, and Cambodia." All traces of U.S. involvement would be erased. Thus, when guerrillas in Cambodia, for example, received large quantities of Chinese arms, a U.S. provenance could not be proved. (Interestingly enough, in the summer of 1990, CIA officials admitted to angry members of the Senate Intelligence Committee that arms supplied by the United States were ending up in the hands of the Khmer Rouge.)

The Israelis, according to the Geomiltech memo for CIA Director Casey, were pleased with the plan. "We have received confirmation from Israel and China that they are most interested in pursuing their role in this trade arrangement. Upon your encouragement and belief that the United States could perform its role, we will proceed with China and Israel defining their respective roles and the equipment they are willing to trade. As for the benefits to Israel, "There are many avenues available regarding the forms of credit which could be extended to Israel."

Studley's Tel Aviv office was well staffed, with a retired Israeli air force officer as the local vice president. Ron Harrell was named in the German press as an energetic participant in the sale of arms to Iran during his tenure at Geomiltech. Studley's close acquaintance with Israeli "heads of state, ministers of defense," as General Schweitzer put it, kept her in the company of men who had shipped vast quantities of arms to the Ayatollah. Yet, congressional investigators were told, the arms proprietress was "shocked and dismayed" when she heard that her Israeli vice president had been "moonlighting" in the Iran trade.

It is not clear to what extent Geomiltech was able to fulfill its role as the provider for freedom fighters on three continents, but the company did use its involvement with Israel to great advantage while supplying the contras. Documents provided by Israel covered the tracks of purchases of Soviet-made arms from Eastern Europe. When Geomiltech acquired thousands of weapons from the government of Poland, the official destination was Tel Aviv. But the arms were shipped from Gdansk to Portugal and on to Honduras, with bills of lading listing their origin as Israel. The Israeli Ministry of Defense, with the approval of Zvi Reuter, authorized the transaction, knowing full well that the Polish shipment was bound for Honduras. Not only was Israel fully complicit in this subterfuge, but it called into question whether the seemingly inexhaustible inventory of arms captured in Lebanon included other arms simply purchased by Israel from the Communist government of Poland. In the Geomiltech case, Poland was spared the embarrassment of selling arms to the CIA, instead selling them, on paper at least, to Israel. Geomiltech was paid with the millions of dollars parked in Switzerland by North and company for the contras. The operation was coordinated by the White House, blessed by Casey, and carried out by an American company, which thanks to Zvi Reuter, was a representative of the government of Israel.[20] It was an excellent example of how the CIA, the White House, and Israel could work together through a cut-out to circumvent Congress.

Meanwhile, the spores of the military "branch" of the Israeli melon business were spreading across Central America. ISDS, whose trainers, according to the Honduran chief of staff, had been "seconded to our special forces by the Israeli Ministry of Defense," opened a suite of offices at the Sheraton Hotel in San Salvador. Their mission was to provide "military training services to official Salvadoran bodies." This was convenient for the U.S. administration, which was funding the Salvadoran military's war against the guerrilla insurgency. Although Congress was free with taxpayers' money, spending roughly $2 million a week on the war, the vexed question of U.S. advisers caused enough soul-searching on the Hill that the authorized number of advisers was limited to fifty-five. In the Reagan years, the U.S. military regularly violated the restrictions by bringing in advisers for the day from Honduras, and of course, could always count on the Israelis, whose permanent presence in the Salvadoran capital never upset the congressmen.

For its part, the Salvadoran government was keenly aware of the benefits of graciously accepting Israeli assistance. In 1983, there were "hopes in the Salvadoran government that the influential pro-Israel lobby in the United States [would] lend a discreet hand in congressional debates over the wisdom of administration policy on Central America."

Israel had been shipping a steady flow of weapons and advisers to the Salvadoran military since 1973. The first jet fighters in Central America, eighteen French Ouragans, were sold by Israel, along with jet trainers and Arava transports. Uzis, 80-mm rocket launchers, tons of ammunition, and quantities of napalm poured into the Salvadoran arsenal. In 1977, when the Carter administration cut off military aid on account of the country's grisly human rights record, Israel stepped into the breach, becoming El Salvador's primary supplier. When the Reagan administration resumed sales in 1980, Israel settled into second place. Between 1979 and 1983, there were upwards of forty thousand civilian deaths in El Salvador. Up until at least 1984, the Salvadoran air force was dropping Israeli napalm on supposed guerrilla strongholds, much as the U.S. had (in vastly larger quantities) in Vietnam. The use of napalm sold by Israel was confirmed by Salvadoran Air Force Col. Rafael Bustillo, as well as by officials in the Reagan administration, including U.S. Ambassador Thomas Pickering. American medical workers, among them Harvard University burn specialist Dr. John Constable, also found that napalm had been dropped on the civilian population.[21]

Israeli advisers, meanwhile, set to work training such government organizations as ANSESAL, the Salvadoran secret police, which had been created at the urging of the Kennedy administration. Former Salvadoran Army Colonel and Undersecretary of the Interior Rene Francisco Guerra y Guerra saw the training firsthand in the 1970s and recalled that one of the young pupils, who would go on to gain somewhat dubious political prominence, was Roberto D'Aubisson. Founder of the extreme right-wing ARENA party, D'Aubisson studied under the Israelis as a junior ANSESAL officer. Known as "Major Blowtorch," he became the inspirational leader of cadres of hired killers and was widely credited with planning the death-squad murder of Archbishop Romero of San Salvador (with the help of contra "Chino" Lau, whom Honduran Chief of Staff Lopez named as another Israeli trainee) as punishment for the archbishop's inconvenient concern for the plight of San Salvador's poor. Another alumnus of Israeli training was Colonel Sigifredo Ochoa, who completed his course in Israel. Ochoa was deemed responsible for a massacre of civilians in 1981. Massacres had become common.

In a dispatch for the *Sunday Times* of London on February 22, 1981, David Blundy described a very ugly scene at the time in the Salvadoran countryside. The massacre he chronicled took place at Las Aradas, a settlement of about fifteen hundred peasants on the Salvadoran side of the Sumpul River, which marked the frontier with Honduras. The inhabitants had fled to this remote riverbank to escape the war. Most had no shelter other than plastic sheets spread under trees. "There was no electricity, no clean water, no medicine, barely enough food and no road," Blundy wrote. Three hundred new refugees arrived that morning, mostly exhausted women and children who had trekked for three days through the Salvadoran mountains. As they sat eating tortillas, hundreds of Salvadoran soldiers took up positions behind the hills, two of their helicopter gunships loaded with machine guns and bombs. On the other bank of the Sumpul, a hundred and fifty Honduran soldiers waited behind a stone wall.

According to the dispatch, this was a joint "*operacíon de limpieza*," a "cleaning" operation, to wipe out guerrillas who maintained camps along the border. There were no guerrillas at Las Aradas that morning, but the peasants were regarded as a "fair military target," for peasants sometimes provided food and shelter to the enemy, not that there was much of either here. The gunfire lasted for six hours.

The "cleaning" began at about ten A.M. . . . Genaro Guardado heard the thud of bombs falling outside his hut. With his 17-year-old daughter, Ernestina, he grabbed five children all under 12 who were standing outside and ran. Rosabel Sibrian, a 22-year-old, saw the helicopter gunships buzzing low over the trees and heard the rattle of their machineguns . . .

The peasants "ran to the river in flocks," said Genaro. It was the beginning of the rainy season and the river was flowing deep and fast. Margarita ran into the water and found it came up to her neck: "Children were drowning. The Salvadoran soldiers stood on the bank and fired at us. . . ."

The Honduran troops on the far side of the river very deliberately forced those who had reached their territory back into the river, and thus back into the nightmare.

The Salvadoran army, it appeared, was not acting alone in this endeavor. Soldiers worked side by side with "members of Orden, a paramilitary right-wing group, distinctive in their black shirts with skull-and-crossbones insignia." Genaro Guardado's wife, Lolita, had managed to escape with three of her eight children and her brother-in-law. They made their way upstream, hiding in the bushes, approximately a mile up the Sumpul River. Just as she started to cross the river at about four P.M., she was hit by fifteen bullets "in an arc from her thigh across the small of her back."

Two of her children lay dying in the water beside her. One died quickly—a bullet had passed through his armpit into his chest; the other, shot in the testicles, did not. "He lasted half an hour," said Lolita. "I couldn't move. I couldn't comfort him." . . . [her third child lay wounded in her arms]

That night she felt an object bump against her in the river. Then it floated off downstream. It was, she says, the head of a child. The next morning a Honduran fisherman pulled in his nets. They contained the bodies of three dismembered children.

At noon the day after the massacre, a Roman Catholic priest from the Capuchin order walked over the hills towards the Sumpul. He noticed that the river banks looked strangely black. When he got closer he saw why. They were covered in a thick carpet of buzzards.

(David Blundy, who filed the dispatch, was killed by sniper fire in San Salvador in 1989.)[22]

The powers that be in El Salvador were decidedly out of control.

But neither of their chief suppliers demanded that they stop, not the United States nor Israel. On December 22, 1981, the Tel Aviv paper *Davar* carried a letter to the editor signed by 144 high school students protesting Israeli arms sales to El Salvador. But this sort of protest was rare. The Salvadoran military was full of praise for the Israeli trainers, as expressed by a Salvadoran colonel in charge of counterinsurgency operations in the north: "The Americans know nothing. Don't forget they lost in Vietnam. The Israelis do know." It was, in fact, the sales pitch that one could hear while training with the men from Spearhead in the canyon of the Partridge Club.

In 1988, former Mossad official and Foreign Ministry Director David Kimche, who had been Israel's point man for Central America during the Reagan years, was still painting a benign picture of Israeli involvement in El Salvador. As he sat in his study, surrounded by the souvenirs from a lifetime of covert operations, Kimche said: "We have good technical cooperation with certain countries in agricultural things, mainly in agricultural things, and this has been very much encouraged by the United States—things like how to grow crops more efficiently and in a better way. Our experts are quite happy to go in completely out-of-the-way places where you don't find many other non-Latin-American people, and they do very good work, if I may say so. Now, this has happened in countries like Salvador, and that's been our only presence in Salvador, contrary to what some people have said about all sorts of military advisers. We haven't had any, but we have had agricultural advisers, that's true. I would say that's our main help in Central America."

Israeli military trainers—like the acrobatic Col. Leo Gleser, who could hit two bull's-eyes at a hundred meters, who could recount tales of the Entebbe raid, and whose security firm, prominently displayed in the catalogue of the Ministry of Defense, had a permanent suite of offices at the San Salvador Sheraton—were somehow overlooked. When pressed, the caveat "official" military advisers crept into Kimche's conversation, although the obvious follow-up question of "How about unofficial?" received the same firm denials.

Kimche maintained that the host of Israeli military advisers and arms dealers in the sensitive region were all somehow free-lance. "Look," said Kimche, "we are a free country, we're a democratic country. If somebody leaves the army and becomes a private citizen and what he knows is military stuff and he is contacted or he contacts some guy outside and goes and works for that guy, providing he's not selling military secrets, Israeli military secrets, we've got no possibility whatsoever to prevent him"—presumably even if the "guy" was the president or chief of staff of Guatemala or Honduras.[23]

When asked whether "all the reports of an arms conduit with strong Israeli support and involvement starting in 1983" for the contras, at the behest of the CIA, were false, he answered, "To the very best of my knowledge, yes." The definitive U.S. government documents confirming without question that Operation Tipped Kettle had accomplished just that had not yet been released. As for "private citizens" roaming the jungles of Central America, Kimche had somehow forgotten that every project of every Israeli involved in military activities abroad had to be approved and supervised by the formidable Zvi Reuter, director of Sibat at the Ministry of Defense.

Even the doyen of the Israeli arms trade in Central America, David Marcus Katz, had to seek the approval of Reuter. Katz was the man whose former chauffeur was now buying racehorses with the proceeds of the Guatemalan counterinsurgency. Katz ran his operations from a discreet distance, either from his base in Mexico City or from his sumptuous suite overlooking Central Park at the Essex House in New York City. Being somewhat shy and retiring, Katz listed Suite 2901 as the property of Brookdale Holdings Ltd., of Brickle Avenue, Miami. (When the Essex House was gutted for renovations, Katz removed himself to Trump Tower.)

Katz had influential friends in high places in Washington and Jerusalem. In 1988, when he threw a lavish sixtieth birthday party at the Pierre Hotel in New York, celebrities and power brokers rolled up to pay their respects. As fellow veteran arms dealer Shapik Shapiro remembered, "It was a big event. There were lots of people from the administration there." For Shapiro, the Katz story was simple: "He made millions and got respectability." When asked who this Israeli expatriate was before he left Tel Aviv, Shapiro gave a laconic reply, "Who knows? Who knew?" It is doubtful that the guests at the glittering affair at the Pierre knew that when Katz landed in Mexico nearly forty years ago, he tried his hand at being a Hebrew school teacher and kosher-wine importer before settling on the lucrative career in weapons. As well as becoming very rich, he had become a political force, both in Central America and at home in Israel.

When Israeli Defense Minister Arik Sharon wanted to visit Honduras in 1982, he flew in on the Westwing jet belonging to Marcus Katz. When Prime Minister Yitzhak Shamir turned up in Honduras in 1987 to push the sale of Israel's Kfir fighter plane, Katz was by his side. It was Marcus Katz who attempted to rescue the sagging dictatorship of Anastasio Somoza with airlifts of Israeli arms.

After the Carter administration could no longer stomach shipping arms to Somoza, the Nicaraguan dictator received $250 million worth of arms (98 percent of his supplies in the final months) from Israel. A U.S. Embassy cable, now declassified, stated, "Israel has supplied significant quantities and types of military equipment, arms, and munitions to Nicaragua, especially in recent months and [deleted] more is probably on the way in the near future." Civilian cargo planes were used. Said the embassy, "These were El Al planes . . . they landed after dark and then immediately departed." This was at a time when Somoza's National Guard (many of whom later became contra commanders) were engaged in an orgy of killing, and felt free to execute an ABC News correspondent, Bill Stewart, in cold blood as he knelt before them in the dirt.

Katz represented an estimated seventeen Israeli arms firms for sales in the region, including Israel Aircraft Industries. The arms merchant had built up an impressive client list over time. According to fellow arms dealer Gerard Latchinian, Katz was a popular representative because of his extremely close financial ties with Israel's religious right. "Katz is big because of the exclusivity he has. He was their [the religious right's] income. He would give one-half of his take to the Religious Party. They would push for Katz to be the exclusive agent." High fees charged by Katz reportedly cost Israel some major contracts that otherwise would have gone through. When Ezer Weizman ascended to the post of defense minister, he made an attempt to rein in Katz. But the arms dealer's Jerusalem allies, whose party had a monetary stake in his success, put a stop to it. Deputy Foreign Minister Yehuda Ben Meir and Education Minister Zeveloon Hammer, both of the National Religious Party, pressured Weizman. According to the Israeli paper *Davar*, Katz "had the backing of political circles, including those close to the prime minister." The paper also reported that Marcus Katz gave substantial sums to the extremely right-wing settlers' movement on the West Bank, Gush Emunim. Gush Emunim believed that the correct "solution" for the Palestinian problem was to "transfer" nearly two million inhabitants of the occupied territories to some other country.[24]

Marcus Katz's host country, Mexico, may have briefly considered transferring him when his activities became the center of a political storm, reflected in the headline, "Mexico: A Trampoline, Reinforcer of Dictatorships." The Katz office, tucked away in a leafy residential district, was staffed and guarded by Israelis and was distinctive because of its thick electronic doors and closed-circuit television. The "IAI Mission," said the Mexicans, was arming Latin America's dictatorships and was therefore a political embarrassment to the Mexican government. The Israeli Embassy initially denied knowledge of its existence. The Katz office, as configured, quietly disappeared. Katz, however, remained.

The former kosher-wine importer reportedly went on to broker at least one load of contra arms in 1985, thus supplying the men who had loyally served his longtime friend Somoza, by then murdered in Paraguay. Swiss bankers named one "Marcus Kritz" as an intermediary for arms funded out of one of the many Swiss accounts, some of which were controlled by Israelis rather than Oliver North. (Al Schwimmer was also named.)

As Katz remembered, it was Al Schwimmer who initiated him into the world of "the aircraft business." (Katz is loath to identify himself by the title "arms dealer.") "In the late 1960s Al Schwimmer came down from New York," Katz explained. "He was president of IAI. That guy knew more about airplanes than anyone in the world." Schwimmer and "two guys from New York" were in Mexico to select a suitable representative for Israel Aircraft Industries. "They were interviewing a few people to represent the Westwing [jet] and the Arava [transport plane]. So they picked me," said Katz, "maybe because I speak Hebrew. Maybe because, you know, some people say I'm a nice guy."

When asked what his principal occupation was when he was tapped for this plum job in the defense business, Katz replied, "Plastics." In fact, this man—credited with being a titan of the Latin American arms market—said that his first loyalty was always "plastics." "I've been in plastics for thirty years," Katz elaborated, "making containers for cosmetics companies. You know, bottles for shampoo, things like that. My clients are companies like Avon, Colgate, Johnson & Johnson, Kimberly-Clark."

When asked why Gen. Ariel Sharon chose to fly on the Katz West-wing (during the Israeli defense minister's selling mission to Honduras) and keep Katz by his side, the "plastics" magnate answered, "I speak Spanish." As well as this facility for language, shared by the thriving local Israeli community in Honduras, Katz had other essential skills. "I took care of the social side of things. The dinners."

Katz thought it perfectly reasonable that Israeli arms merchant Pesakh Ben Or should leave the Katz establishment to grab the lucrative Guatemalan weapons market. "I guess," offered Katz, "he didn't want to be a driver anymore." Katz had only offered Ben Or the chauffeur position in the first place to please the young Israeli's father. "Ben Or worked as a driver at IAI. His father worked at IAI, in security. He was an acquaintance of mine. One day Pesakh appeared in Mexico. His father asked me to take care of him."

As for taking care of the National Religious Party, Katz contradicted all accounts of his financial largesse. "I only give money to charity," he insisted. "I have a lot of friends in the Religious Party. I have known some of them since I was a boy. I give money to Yeshiva University."[25]

In October 1990, Katz was commuting regularly between Mexico and New York, with side trips to Washington. His "aircraft business" had expanded into spare parts, French as well as Israeli contracts, and an airline. He was powerful enough to intimidate the smaller fish in the region like Emil Sa'ada and to command grudging respect from others, like Gerard Latchinian, who had watched Katz operate with great skill and financial acumen in the rough arena of the Latin arms trade.

But among the handsomely rewarded middlemen for arms in Central America, there was one who in the course of the 1980s would eclipse all of the others. This quintessential operator, who was forced to gracefully sever "official" ties with the Israeli intelligence agency Mossad because he had murdered a Moroccan waiter whom he mistook for a Palestinian terrorist, sat at the right hand of Central America's most celebrated general. The general was Panama's Manuel ("Tony") Noriega. His closest friend and business associate was Israeli Mike Harari. Together they would do a great many favors for the men in the White House.

10. The Man Behind the General

In the spring of 1984, an honor guard assembled at the Kirya, the compound of the Israeli Ministry of Defense. They had gathered to greet a foreign general, a small, squat figure known to his detractors as "pineapple face," thanks to his unfortunate skin. The general looked resplendent in full dress uniform, with his Israeli paratrooper wings pinned just above his left breast pocket. Manuel Antonio Noriega, "Tony" to his friends, had flown thousands of miles from his home in Panama for the occasion. Flanked by Moshe Levi, commander in chief of the Israeli Defense Forces, and other top IDF commanders, Noriega had come to receive a decoration, reportedly for services performed providing fraudulent "end user" certificates for Israeli weapons secretly destined for Iran. For such requirements, Panama was a country of easy virtue and its commander in chief was ever available. As one of Noriega's American political consultants put it, "Noriega was a lovely hooker." The CIA thought the general lovely enough to keep on a retainer of up to $200,000 per year, the same salary as the president of the United States.

In a much-published photograph of General Noriega standing at the salute on the Kirya steps in Tel Aviv, his companions are all in uniform, all saluting while the anthems of Israel and Panama fill the air—with the exception of one man. A lean, dark figure standing in the shadow of the Panamanian dictator, he wears a simple, expensive black suit and a carefully knotted silk tie. His black hair is slicked back and large sunglasses obscure his features. Michael Harari had once been chief of clandestine operations for Mossad. He was now inseparable from Manuel Noriega and had earned the reputation as the "brains" behind the General. The aging spy, known to Panamanians as "Mad Mike," had carved out a powerful and lucrative niche for himself as General Noriega's best friend, business associate, and as the general once said, his "mentor."

It was Harari who had arranged all of the trappings for Noriega's trip to Israel: the meetings with top government officials, the VIP tour of IDF bases, and a crack Mossad team to rescue the general from would-be assassins supposedly dispatched to Paris (where Noriega stopped on his way home) by the Medellin cartel. Before setting out for Israel, Noriega had alarmed cartel executives, who paid him a handsome percentage for the privilege of operating in Panama (their accountant put the figure at $10 million per month), by raiding one of their labs. Harari received intelligence, or so he said, that a "hit" had been planned, though one of Noriega's advisers later observed, "I always thought it was Mike who set that whole thing up." In fact, after the Darien raid, Noriega was receiving frantic scrambled messages in Israel from aides in Panama City that "El Padrino"—drug lord Pablo Escobar—wanted a "business meeting." As the telephone scrambler was made in Israel, it is doubtful these were private conversations. "El Padrino" and 120 cartel friends were residing in Panama at the time, in former U.S. officer housing at Fort Amador and in the very best suites at the Caesar Park Marriot Hotel. Good relations with the gentlemen from Medellin were eventually restored, but in the meantime Mike Harari took credit for saving Noriega's life.

The Mossad veteran was modest about his exploits and his status in Panama City. When he first met, in 1983, with Roberto Eisenmann, publisher of Panama's *La Prensa* newspaper, Harari delivered a brief and succinct introduction. "I'm Mike Harari. I am a member of Israeli intelligence and a good friend of Manuel Noriega." His official ties to Mossad had supposedly been severed three years earlier, when Harari briefly became chief executive officer of Israel's Migdal Insurance Company. But from the time Harari flew into Panama in 1982 to his departure in the dead of night in December 1989, "the friend," as he was known at the Israeli Embassy in Panama, was accorded every privilege of a top Israeli official. As one former embassy employee observed, "This tale that Mike Harari operates in Panama as a private party has no basis in reality. Mike Harari enters the embassy in Panama not like a household member, but like an owner. I know this from close acquaintance, and I can say that Mike Harari enjoys all possible services in the Israeli Embassy in Panama. He uses the diplomatic mail, and in fact, he knows everything that occurs in the embassy, including secret cables."[1]

Harari had spent the better part of his life in the intelligence business. Born into a well-known Sephardic family in Tel Aviv in 1927, Harari joined the Palmach at the age of eighteen and graduated to the Gid'onim, the secret communications unit of the Jewish underground's illegal immigration operation. After World War II, Harari was posted to Rome, where he prospered and became commander of the Italian branch. His career there was immortalized in at least one Israeli novel (*The Gid'onim* by Shabtai Teveth), in which Harari is given yet another name, Alex. Following the War of Independence, Harari served briefly as a security officer in the Foreign Ministry, after which he joined the young Mossad. His reputation inside the spy agency was as someone infinitely forgettable; "an introverted, grey man." As one former colleague put it, "He was not groomed for the top."

Despite this inauspicious beginning, Harari surfaced in the early 1970s as the man in charge of Mossad assassination squads then combing Europe for Palestinian targets. Harari owed his promotions to his protector and mentor Zvi Zamir, who rose to chief of Mossad under Prime Minister Golda Meir. "Zvi Zamir raised him," said one former colleague. Harari, unfortunately, did not distinguish himself in his role as European hit-squad coordinator, with the result that his patron the spy chief was dismissed.

Harari's path to exile in the Americas started in Munich, with the bloody events of the 1972 Olympics. Just before dawn on September 5, eight men armed with Kalashnikov machine pistols and hand grenades walked through an unlocked door into the Israeli Pavilion of the Olympic Village. The men shot a weight lifter from the Israeli team and a security guard and proceeded to tie up nine more athletes. At five A.M., the gunmen threw a note out the window demanding that two hundred Palestinians be released from Israeli jails within four hours. The men also wanted safe passage out of Germany. Otherwise they would kill the better part of Israel's Olympic team.

In the course of the exceedingly tense hours that followed, it became clear that the men in ski masks peering over the balcony were members of Black September, a radical Palestinian faction born from the lingering bitterness over the brutal force employed by King Hussein to crush the Palestinian guerrillas in Jordan. The "Black September" of 1970 had left thousands of casualties, and the group that took its name had launched a terror campaign to avenge the crackdown. Their operations produced a trail of murdered Jordanians, bombings, oil-pipeline sabotage, and a failed hijacking. They told the head of the Egyptian Olympic team, who tried to negotiate the freedom of the Israelis: "Money means nothing to us; our lives mean nothing to us."[2]

By the time the episode ended in gunfire and grenade explosions at Fürstenfeldbruck Military Airport outside Munich, seventeen people, including all the hostages, were dead.

At the heavily attended funeral for eleven Israelis, there were promises that there would be payment for this tragedy "in blood." Israel chose to fight terror with terror. On September 8, three days after Munich, Israeli jets bombed both guerrilla and refugee camps in Syria and Lebanon, killing upwards of three hundred Palestinians, including women and children who had never heard of Black September. Guerrilla enclaves were attacked by Israeli ground forces. One Lebanese taxi was flattened, along with its seven passengers, by an Israeli Centurion tank.

Golda Meir set up a secret committee, which she chaired, known as Committee X. Its mission was to extract further revenge by tracking down and eliminating anyone whom committee members deemed were involved with the Munich massacre. Mike Harari was put in charge of the operation. Posing now as a French businessman, he gathered a team and set to work. Harari's commandos managed to shoot or bomb twelve people on the target list. But the man regarded as the prize catch eluded them. He was Ali Hassan Salameh, identified by Mossad as the operations officer for Black September in Europe. Code named "The Red Prince," Salameh was spotted by Mossad agents in northern Norway. The Harari gang descended on the unsuspecting residents of Lillehammer to track down the Red Prince, reportedly in their midst. Locating a man who fit the profile, the Mossad agents tailed him for several hours to make sure they had identified him correctly, before shooting him in cold blood. The trouble was, Harari and friends killed the wrong man. Ahmad Bouchiki's only crime was being a Moroccan waiter. His pregnant Norwegian wife watched him die.

After this mishap, the Harari team displayed remarkable ineptitude in covering its tracks. Six Mossad operatives were rounded up by the Norwegian police with little effort. Two were arrested as they turned in their rental car, hired in their own names, at Oslo Airport. They readily confessed to working for Israel and helpfully supplied safehouse addresses. Another just happened to have the key to a Paris apartment, where French authorities gathered up other keys to other apartments, unraveling the entire operation. The Mossad operative Dan Aerbel had only to be ushered into a small, dark room before he cracked. Aerbel, the Norwegians were astonished to discover, suffered from acute claustrophobia. In exchange for less confining quarters, Aerbel obliged them by giving all of the details of Lillehammer the authorities needed to know. He threw in an added fillip of details of a secret shipment of stolen uranium diverted to Israel on a ship called the Sheersburg A in 1968. The botched operation was reduced to farce when one of the Mossad operatives fell in love with and married her Norwegian lawyer. Harari, along with his girlfriend and fellow agent Tamar, escaped, leaving the wreckage scattered across Europe.

Harari's punishment for the disaster was a gentle change of scene. He was exiled to the comfortable and influential post of station chief in Mexico City. The genuine Red Prince, meanwhile, survived for five more years before being vaporized in a bomb attack by another Mossad team in Lebanon. This apparently annoyed the CIA, which had used the dead man as a liaison with the Palestinian guerrillas.[3]

From Mexico, Harari moved throughout Latin America, attending to Mossad chores and promoting Israeli arms. It was then that he became acquainted with a fast-rising intelligence chief in Panama, Col. "Tony" Noriega. At the time, Noriega divided his loyalty between Panamanian leader Gen. Omar Torrijos and the CIA, which bribed him generously. Noriega also had discovered the benefits of being friendly with everyone else, including the Cubans, and began running a lucrative trade in intelligence information. This was, of course, useful for a Mossad station chief like Harari. More importantly, "General Mike," as Noriega liked to refer to Harari, saw the simple elegance of using Panama as an entrepot for Israeli arms destined for regimes

throughout Central and South America. He and Noriega refined an
end-user racket that would eventually attract the admiration and patronage of the Reagan White House.

Like Nicaragua under the first General Somoza, Panama had been
used to smuggle arms to the Haganah before the founding of the state
of Israel. The ubiquitous arms dealer Al Schwimmer had smuggled
World War II surplus arms from the United States via Panama to
Palestine. The underground set up a Panamanian aviation company to
facilitate the transfers. At times, when Israel's excellent relations with
Noriega came under attack, the alliance could be justified as a repayment of debts from 1948.

With a guiding hand from Mike Harari, Israel did a brisk business
with Panama, shipping $500 million worth of arms during the 1980s.
At least $100 million worth of rifles, machine guns, explosives, and
advanced communications equipment was dispatched *after* Noriega
had been exposed by the Senate Foreign Relations Committee in early
1988 as being heavily involved in narcotics trafficking. Harari's orders
for Panama were filled without protest. As one Israeli commentator
put it, the Ministry of Defense in Tel Aviv "routinely approves all arms
and equipment sales requested by Harari." Harari was influential
enough in Jerusalem and Panama City to fire both Panama's ambassador to Israel and Israel's ambassador to Panama. He was sensitive to
the extensive security needs of a man like General Noriega, who was
adept at collecting enemies. Harari "provided Noriega with sophisticated Israeli-made eavesdropping and security equipment—installed
by Israeli experts—which allows Noriega to spy on political opponents." Along with the equipment came advisers. Israeli military advisers, recruited by Harari to serve as Noriega's elite bodyguards,
supervised the crackdown on political opponents. Harari even
equipped Noriega's bunker, where the general had reportedly hung
portraits of Adolf Hitler and Moshe Dayan. (Harari is credited with
counseling Noriega that the Hitler portrait was in bad taste and should
be removed.) Along with the arms, advisers, and listening devices,
Harari extended his services to financial planning. "Israeli and Panamanian financial sources" told Israeli journalist Uri Dan that "Harari
provided the means for laundering Noriega's profits in Swiss and other
foreign banks and has used the money for arms purchases."

Home for Harari was a plush oceanfront apartment in the Mirador
del Pacifico complex in Panama City. He was easily recognized driving

around town in his signature blue Toyota Land Cruiser. "Mad Mike" never traveled without his driver and bodyguard, who kept the Uzi submachine gun in a discreet black leather attaché case. According to General Noriega's telephone logs, Harari called every day. There was a great deal of business to discuss, for not only had Harari secured through Noriega such deals as a $20 million contract to supply equipment for the Panamanian Civil Aeronautics Agency, but as Israeli merchants complained, Harari charged a 60 percent commission for the privilege of doing business in Panama. "Mr. 60 Percent" split the profits with the general.

In spite of the stiff commissions, the roughly five hundred members of the emigrant Israeli community made substantial fortunes under the Noriega regime. The Jewish community as a whole, many of whose ancestors had arrived as Syrian traders at the turn of the century, was exceedingly rich. A spiritual leader of the community, Rabbi Zion Levy, warned them on more than one occasion at the Jewish Club in Panama City that their excesses could endanger their interests. (After Noriega was ousted, many of their businesses were sacked.) For one extravagant wedding, for which the price tag was around a million dollars, the band was imported from Damascus. For fashionable bar mitzvah gatherings, Godiva chocolates were flown in from Belgium and the halkum and peanuts arrived from Syria. For another memorable party, guests received boarding cards as invitations and were ushered into a life-size model airplane by waitresses dressed as stewardesses. When the popular Israeli singer Hayim Moshe performed, he was, as reported in the Israeli press, "literally drowned in dollars. Some of the guests refused to dance, as the dance floor was covered with a layer of banknotes."[4]

The six-thousand-strong Jewish community owned the largest businesses in the Avanida Center, Via España, and Sona Libre. They lived in the expensive neighborhoods of Punta Paitia and San Francisco. As *Yediot Aharanot* in Tel Aviv reported, "From time to time, Noriega used to hold an exclusive dinner for the big Jewish traders. 'I am strong, you have nothing to worry about, I shall not break,' he told them at a meeting after American sanctions against trading with the Noriega government were declared. 'We have to go with the strongman,' said a merchant who asked, of course, to remain anonymous. 'Maybe it is not nice to say but our situation with Noriega was wonderful.'"

The source of a significant portion of Harari's fortune, and what made him particularly attractive to the covert operations men in Washington, was a neat arrangement the Mossad veteran had with the Panama Defense Forces. PDF aircraft naturally required parts and maintenance, and Harari had the concession. According to Maj. Augusto Villalaz, who took over Panama's air force after the U.S. invasion of Panama, Harari "made millions" out of this business. His company, Shellydor Amlat, ordered the parts from Commodore Aviation, a Miami subsidiary of the government-owned Israel Aircraft Industries. As an expedient, Harari simply opened an office of the Panama Defense Forces at IAI's Commodore facility at Miami International Airport. According to Jessie Quiroga, a pilot and Miami businessman who had once supplied parts and advised the Panamanian air force, "Harari became head of the air force. Not a screw was turned without Harari knowing about it."

With such control, the possibilities were endless. Floyd Carlton, who served as Noriega's top pilot before being jailed in Miami on drug charges (and becoming a chief U.S. government witness against General Noriega), told Senate investigators that boxes leaving Miami destined for the Panama Defense Forces were sometimes stuffed with cash rather than parts. The pilot said laundered drug money was shipped via this route with no questions asked by authorities on either end. "Very often boxes go to the air force as if they were spare parts for their airplanes," Carlton testified under oath, "but they actually have money there."[5] Thus Harari, business partner of the general, whose country would later be invaded in order to drag him to Miami for trial on drug charges, controlled a safe conduit for money and arms between the U.S. and Panama. Because the Miami company with which he did business and where he set up an office was owned by the Israeli government, it begged the question of who in Israeli officialdom knew about his activities. But as Harari also appears to have worked assiduously on behalf of the U.S. government to facilitate the passage of arms to the contras, he was, according to former Panamanian officials, too important to touch.

When José Blandon, General Noriega's former chief of political intelligence, defected from his post as Panamanian consul general in New York, Harari's key covert role in the service of the White House was exposed. In early 1988, Blandon walked out of the consulate and into the protection of federal marshals. He became a chief U.S. government witness against Noriega, testifying in great detail about the general's narcotics trafficking organization, an organization that Blandon said had utterly corrupted his country. The former intimate of the general went on to explain Noriega's close relationship with CIA Director William Casey and the general's substantial contribution to the contra war. Noriega, he said, supplied pilots, planes, a top-secret training base, and arms. The arms were the department of General Noriega's "friend" Mike Harari.

To meet José Blandon in the days after his defection required waiting for an escort of large federal marshals who said little as they led visitors to ever-changing locations, usually in the Virginia countryside. Blandon moved constantly. With Noriega still in power, the high-level defector was terrified that his life expectancy might be short, and he had formidable enemies not only in Panama but also in the CIA. A lot of people would have been delighted to hear that he was dead. This diminutive, middle-aged man with white hair and glasses possessed damaging secrets. His knowledge of the inner workings of what he called Harari's "network" was among them.

Blandon had been intimately involved with the Panamanian end of the contra war. He had been present, for example, at two secret meetings in 1985 between General Noriega and White House aide Col. Oliver North. The first meeting, held in June 1985, took place on board a sleek yacht moored on the Pacific side of Panama Bay. The nautical setting included the requisite blond in the bikini, though she slipped away when the discussion turned to the serious matter of perpetuating the war. As Blandon remembered, they covered "training the contras in Panama, on Panamanian bases, and also the supply of arms to the contras." Noriega was a man the White House could depend on. "Noriega played a key role in the supply of arms to the contras, because he had in Panama a complete enterprise, the infrastructure, planes, and networks."

Before North came on the Central American scene, Noriega had provided invaluable assistance to his good friend and employer, CIA Director William Casey. As Blandon recalled, "Noriega was a very close friend of Casey's. This was a very special relationship. Noriega had at least three meetings and always received support from Casey. Casey knew about Noriega" and his unsavory activities, "but Noriega was such an important piece. When anyone tried to investigate Noriega, Casey stopped it and said "Look, he's a very important piece in this war." Noriega and friends were in a position to take advantage of the Reagan administration's fixation with Nicaragua. "For the White House," said Blandon, "for the Reagan administration, Nicaragua was so important, and the focus of the foreign policy of the United States in Central America was Nicaragua and the fight against the Communists, so for them, drugs took second place. If Noriega could help support the contras, for the administration, that was enough." This relaxed attitude extended to Noriega's business partner.

Blandon first met Mike Harari in 1975, when the Mossad station chief came to assist Gen. Omar Torrijos during Panama's negotiations with the United States over the canal treaty. Harari "established good relations with Torrijos first and then Noriega." The Noriega friendship, Blandon said, blossomed in 1982. "They started in business together, especially in arms traffic." This matured the following year into a pipeline to the contras. "In 1983, a Harari network started to supply the contras with arms they bought in Yugoslavia and other countries." In his capacity of arms supplier, Harari, said Blandon, worked both with Noriega and the Israeli government.

"Harari was part of a powerful network, a more complete network— the Israelis. The most important country to supply arms to Central America between 1980 and 1983, especially in Guatemala and El Salvador, was Israel. From 1983 to 1985, the most important network to supply arms to the contras was this network." The Israeli arms conduit preceded the host of U.S. operatives who later flooded the region, airlifting arms until one of their planes was shot down over Nicaragua in October 1986, thus exposing the operation. But there was reluctance on Capitol Hill to go into precisely what Israel had contributed. With literally hundreds of tons of captured weapons from PLO stocks shipped at the request of Casey, with seasoned Israeli military trainers like Emil Sa'ada and Amatzia Shuali in the field, and with the Panamanian operation run by Mike Harari, the contribution was substantial.

There was, however, a rather delicate problem with the Harari arrangement: his reported involvement in the cocaine trade. According to Blandon, "Harari was part of the Noriega business. They moved the cocaine from Colombia to Panama." From there, the former intelligence adviser explained, the product was transshipped to "airstrips in Costa Rica or Honduras and on to the United States. Since the beginning of the supply of arms to the contras, the same infrastructure that was used for arms was used for drugs. The same pilots, the same planes, the same airstrips, the same people." As the former Panamanian consul general saw it, the cartel used Noriega's involvement with the contras to gain access to the facilities of the covert war while "Noriega used the connections that Harari had in Israel and they put together a complete business."[6]

When asked whether the CIA knew of the dark side of Harari's business dealings, Blandon stated that the agency had known of Noriega's involvement with the Colombian cartels since 1980 and that "since 1980, Israel has supplied arms in Central America . . . and the relationship between Israel and the United States in terms of these things is so close that I don't believe the United States didn't know about that." The United States certainly did know that some of the arms destined for the contras were purchased with drug money. That was made very clear in the diaries of Oliver North.

The overworked National Security Council aide kept copious notes of his daily business dealings with the insalubrious world of arms traders that he had tapped in the interest of "national security." There were frequent references to an enterprise appropriately called the "Arms Supermarket." The Supermarket was a series of nondescript warehouses nestled in a side street of the Honduran city San Pedro Sula. There, Eastern Bloc weapons destined for the contras were stacked to the ceiling (including some of those gathered by former talk show hostess Barbara Studley). By the spring of 1988, after the revelations about the covert White House operation had shut much of it down, there were still millions of dollars' worth of weapons sealed in their crates. Three years earlier, on July 12, 1985, North had written about the Supermarket, "[Deleted] plans to seize all . . . when Supermarket comes to a bad end. $14 M[illion] to finance came from drugs." A year later, in June 1986, North noted that he still needed to "pay off" arms dealers involved in the Supermarket operation. *Newsweek* reported the Supermarket's partnership as a collection of "longtime CIA arms merchants, agents of the Israeli Mossad secret service, and the intelligence arm of the Honduran military." For "unnamed" Reagan administration officials, as *Newsweek* put it, "it was natural to turn to Israel, which had been helping to arm Guatemala after human-rights abuses made that government ineligible for direct U.S. aid. The Israelis agreed to be middlemen if someone else would put up the money."[7]

William Casey, of course, had turned directly to Israel for arms, but according to a senior Panamanian official, as well as José Blandon, Mike Harari had other influential contacts in the Reagan administration. He had met with both the flamboyant CIA Latin Directorate chief Duane ("Dewey") Clarridge and Vice President Bush's national security adviser, Donald Gregg, on the matter of contra support. Former CIA man Gregg denies having ever met with Mossad veteran Harari. But then Gregg consistently denied having any knowledge of contra operations at all, even though a North notebook entry for September 10, 1985, records a meeting with Gregg and the chief of the U.S. Military Advisory Group in El Salvador, Col. James Steele, to discuss "log[istic] support" for the contras. Support, according to the notes, included arms from Mario Dellamico, a Cuban exile who was intimately involved, according to numerous reports, with the Supermarket. Delamico was a friend and business associate of Pesakh Ben Or, who had captured the Guatemalan market for Israel. The major arms merchants in Central America made up a very small club.

"A senior source" in Sibat, the arms-dealing branch of Israel's Ministry of Defense run by Zvi Reuter, told the Tel Aviv paper *Hadashot* that Israeli dealers had marketed $40 million worth of arms to the contras. "These were also financed by interests related to the drug cartel." The Sibat official said that the U.S. and Israeli governments were well aware of the sales and that the Ministry of Defense tacitly authorized them.

Mike Harari boasted that he had excellent relations with the CIA. On the receiving end of Harari's Eastern Bloc arms was Felix Rodriguez, a longtime CIA veteran. As José Blandon remembered, "Felix Rodriguez was working in Salvador. Since 1983, he traveled frequently to Salvador. General Gorman [head of the U.S. Southern Command in Panama] wrote a letter to Ambassador Pickering in El Salvador saying how important Felix was to the contras. He was the manager at the Illopango Airport, the Salvador airport used to supply Costa Rica and Honduras with arms. Part of those arms that came from Yugoslavia to Panama were sent to Illopango base, and Felix Rodriguez was in charge of that." The memo from Gorman to Pickering noted in fact that Rodriguez's ties "to the VP were very real." The VP was Vice President Bush. Felix Rodriguez was in constant phone contact with Bush adviser Donald Gregg and had met with the vice president personally. Naturally enough, although the Salvadoran counterinsurgency was a topic of discussion with Bush, no one acknowledged ever bringing up the contras. It was very difficult to explain why two memos prepared by Bush staffer Colonel Samuel Watson stated that at a meeting with Bush and Gregg in May 1986, Rodriguez would brief the vice president on "the status of the war in El Salvador and resupply of the contras." Although the memos were initialed by Donald Gregg, the obvious references to the contras were dismissed publicly as a secretarial error.[8]

Although Rodriguez was most certainly involved with the Supermarket group (on the payroll, according to his colleagues in the White House operation, of one of its principals), the former CIA agent cloaked his work in patriotism and denied any wrongdoing. Blandon, who watched from his high-level post in Panama, did not regard it as particularly patriotic. "First of all, it was a dirty business. His relationship with the Harari network is not something a patriot is supposed to do. Harari was involved with drugs and Harari was working with him. Are drugs patriotic work?"

As for financing arms purchases (aside from the $14 million in drug money cited by North), ABC News said the Harari operation was "launched in spring of 1983 at Washington's request with at least $20 million of Israeli government money, later reimbursed . . . from U.S. covert operations funds. The Israelis purchased the weapons from Poland and Czechoslovakia and began shipping them secretly from Yugoslavia to Bolivia and then to Panama." From there, the ABC report said, the arms were transferred on DC-6s and C-123s to Costa Rica and El Salvador, bound for the contras.

For well over a year after he was indicted in the Southern District of Florida on drug charges in 1988, partly on the strength of the testimony of Blandon, Noriega kept his talons firmly embedded in Panamanian soil, until the U.S. Army invaded. Part of the delay was caused by tension inside various agencies in Washington over what to do with this ally who knew so much about U.S. covert operations and the men who ran them. Blandon had a succinct analysis of this very sensitive problem. "Noriega is blackmailing some important officials in the U.S. . . . Noriega is a specialist in using information against people . . . there are important key members of the government who are so afraid that Noriega will say something against them that now there is panic."

When Blandon testified before the Senate Foreign Relations Committee, he read a letter from Noriega that openly threatened the powers that be in Washington. A portion of the text read:

> I do have evidence, proof, that the politicians of the United States of America have been supporting lawyers and politicians in Panama involved in drug trafficking, . . . I do have proof of the political manipulation of the Government of the United States regarding drugs, regarding the laundering of money, [and] arms traffic which goes to the Latin American countries . . .
>
> I do have proof that the lying policy against drugs of the United States has not protected our Honduran brothers from the invasion of cocaine, which is brought from Honduras to the United States, leaving ports which are just a few kilometers from the U.S. military bases which are located in Honduras . . .[9]

It is interesting to note that after the U.S. invasion of Panama in December 1989, the U.S. official in charge of the disposition of sensitive documents seized from General Noriega was Col. James Steele, who had played an intimate part in the covert operation to support the contras.

As for the equally sensitive question of the involvement of Israel, there was little said in open hearings, partly because Blandon requested that he discuss the matter in closed session. But for the open record for all to see, he stated that the Harari network "was established with Israeli citizens, Panamanians, and United States citizens for arms-supply purposes" and that its planes, ferrying arms to the contras, also carried cocaine.

One would have thought that Noriega's partner in crime, who was arguably the second most powerful man in Panama, would have been a target for U.S. forces when they rounded up Noriega's friends after the predawn invasion of December 20, 1989. But Mike Harari escaped to Israel, at a time when the U.S. military had complete control of the roads throughout the Panamanian capital, as well as the airports and Panamanian airspace. Harari left his apartment at the Mirador del Pacifico at three-fifteen A.M. and vanished with his driver and bodyguard in the blue Toyota Land Cruiser. Three days later, when U.S. troops began blowing down other doors at the Mirador, they ignored Harari's apartment until a retired U.S. Army officer who lived next door suggested that perhaps it should be searched. The U.S. Embassy team that did the job left Harari's eight-hundred-pound safe untouched. The safe disappeared.

On December 28, the deputy chief at the U.S. Mission in Panama, John Bushnell, announced that Harari was "a prisoner of war." At that moment, Harari was in fact sitting comfortably in Tel Aviv. Two days later, Bushnell retracted his statement, explaining that the U.S. Army had made an error. "On further checking, either they didn't have him—most probably—or he convinced them he was someone else." When questioned about Harari, the newly appointed chief of the Panamanian armed forces was reluctant to talk. Col. Eduardo Herrera told the *Wall Street Journal* that he had been "advised" by U.S. officials to forget Mr. Harari. Herrera added, "I'm an unimportant soldier and this is a matter with international implications." But the unimportant defense forces chief was bitter about "Mad Mike," saying, "He is corrupt, a thief and an assassin. He did plenty of damage to Panama."[10]

In the months before Harari's flight from Panama City, he had begun building an impressive house in a posh enclave outside Tel Aviv. It was a joint project with his sister-in-law, Dorith Beinish, then Israel's attorney general. Outside his other house in Tel Aviv, there was a new Audi in evidence, along with an expensive Volvo, equipped with diplomatic plates, thanks to Harari's status as Panama's honorary consul in Israel. His neighbors were retired military and intelligence officials, many of whom had been given directorships of companies, one of the perquisites of long years of government service. There was no name or number outside the Harari house. Visitors admired the extensive collection of artifacts from Asia and Africa, as well as from Central America. Among Harari's mementos of a long and varied career were letters of appreciation for his efforts to forge closer ties between Israel and Panama, signed by Shimon Peres and Prime Minister Yitzhak Shamir.

Three weeks after the invasion of Panama, Mike Harari appeared on Israeli television to say that he had been the victim of a disinformation campaign. "It was alleged that I am Noriega's adviser," said Harari, warming to the theme. "I am not Noriega's adviser, nor was I in the past. I am neither number one, nor number two. Noriega is not my partner. I did not run his affairs, nor manage nor train his forces, nor organize his personal security. I am simply a private person engaged in business." When asked to say a few words to describe Noriega's character, Harari replied, "I knew Noriega as a wise man, energetic, patriotic, cunning, and with extraordinary survivability. It was easy for him to find ways to the hearts of the people surrounding him."

There were reports that an Israeli C-130 cargo plane appeared in Panama several days before the invasion and departed, loaded with documents and files, just six hours before the paratroopers landed. (Spiriting away incriminating records to Israel had been done before, when an Argentine air force cargo plane, loaded with the secrets of the discredited military regime, took off from Buenos Aires in 1983. The Argentine generals had been excellent customers for Israeli arms.)

The Panamanian newspaper *La Prensa* tried to offer some explanation of why a man as notorious as Mike Harari would be given safe passage to Israel by the American authorities.

Did Harari secretly collaborate with the gringos in ousting Noriega? Immoral individuals such as Harari are only loyal to themselves . . . It is very possible that months ago he reached the conclusion that his buddy was lost and he ran to offer his services to those who were going to give Noriega the coup de grace. Likewise, it is also very probable that Mad Mike bought his freedom by providing information, or that he made his way to Israel through blackmail. A high-ranking official . . . says that Mike bought his freedom with Xerox copies of all the secret Mossad files in Panama. In this case, I predict a rapid and violent end to his criminal career, because an intelligence investigator (if there is such a bird) could use some of these documents to reconstruct the Mossad-Noriega-Medellin tripartite relationship. [11]

The awkward fact of the Medellin "relationship" was to surface again in one of the more embarrassing scandals of the decade. That relationship stretched far beyond Mike Harari into the military camps of Colombia's Magdalena Medio region and the upper reaches of the Colombian government. The shock waves of its exposure would put Israelis on Colombia's most-wanted list, implicate at least one Caribbean government, and leave a dead body in the trunk of a car in Miami. The scandal would single out the Israeli military trainers from Spearhead, who had served faithfully in Guatemala and with the contras. These were men who had talked passionately of "fighting terrorism" while displaying their prowess in the canyon of the Partridge Club in Israel, but who found it difficult to explain that their motives were the same while training the death squads of the Medellin cartel.

Who it was that placed these foot soldiers of the Israeli legions in

Latin America with the cocaine cartel in the first place was not clear. According to Colombian government documents, an Israeli called "Mike" who fit the description of Mike Harari had been sighted at one paramilitary training course for cartel hitmen in Puerto Boyaca in March 1989. Spokesmen for DAS, the Colombian internal security service, named Harari as involved with training the army of Gonzalo Rodriguez Gacha, then a top executive of the Medellin cartel. Interpol had received information that Harari was training "ultrarightist paramilitary groups in Colombia."

Initial contact with the Colombians may have come through Pesakh Ben Or, who had acted as the trainers' agent in the past for Guatemala. But there were other Israelis actively involved with the Colombian military. Even Rafi Eitan, the ubiquitous chief of LAKAM, who had run Jonathan Pollard as a spy and paid a visit to the NUMEC plant in Apollo, Pennsylvania, had surfaced once again in Colombia, running a counterinsurgency course at the Colombian Ministry of Defense. Eitan had been extremely active in Colombia, where he was (correctly) regarded as a protégé of Ariel Sharon. The veteran spy was asked by the Colombian president to advise him on state-of-the-art home security systems for his residence in Bogota and his family ranch.

When Yair Klein and the men from Spearhead first arrived at the Cosmos Hotel in Bogota in 1988, Colombia was buying substantial quantities of arms from the government of Israel. In fact, that year, Colombia accounted for one-third of all Israeli arms exports—$500 million worth. The Colombian arsenal boasted twenty-five thousand Galils, twelve Kfir fighters, and sophisticated Israeli-made electronics. Israel was purchasing Colombia's coal. The counterinsurgency campaigns of the Colombian armed forces against the four active guerrilla groups in the country presented excellent opportunities for advisers and trainers with the right connections.

Colombia's much-hailed democracy had been on a precarious footing for forty years, ever since the "Violencia," a "low-intensity" civil war that left two hundred thousand dead. Colombia was in fact constantly under a state of siege, by which the constitution was suspended. It was the one country in the world that boasted an academic discipline called "violentology." Violence was as much a part of the landscape as the emerald mines, the oil wells, the vast stretches of Amazon jungle, and the magnificent ornaments of pounded gold stolen by the Spanish conquistadors that filled the darkened rooms of the Museo de Oro in Bogota. In 1988 there were eighty-two massacres (as the Colombians describe the killing of five or more people in the same place at the same time) in Colombia. Skulls and rib cages, along with bits of rotted clothing and old shoes, could be found at the bottom of deep pits, a silent testimony to the savage methods used in Colombia to settle political scores.

The volume of violent death had risen sharply since the surge in the cocaine market during the 1980s. The drug was a product so cheap to produce and so profitable to market that those who entered the trade became rich beyond the dreams of avarice, provided they stayed alive. A new class emerged with wealth that far exceeded that of the coffee and sugar barons of the old oligarchy. "The new millionaires," as one of their ranks called them, built fabulous haciendas with gold taps, jukeboxes, classic cars, and racing stables. One Medellin cartel chief, Pablo Escobar, placed his first drug plane astride the arch leading to his estate and stocked his private zoo with exotic wildlife. (The wild-animal dung judiciously sprinkled in drug shipments put off the dogs.)

Along with the conspicuous consumption came political ambition and an insatiable appetite for land. Cartel executives bought up vast stretches of the Magdalena Medio, the region in the heart of the country, with Colombia's richest farmland. They purchased millions of acres with drug cash, and the price was cheap. Guerrillas from both the Revolutionary Armed Forces of Colombia (FARC) and the ELN were active in the area and commonly extracted protection money or "vacuna," from local cattle ranchers. The cartel men chose to fight this extortion with armed force. They hired killers, known as sicarios, to ensure the peace. The hit squads matured into trained armies, licensed by the Colombian Ministry of Defense. As former Minister of Government Carlos Lemos Simmons put it, these "self-defense groups" were legal because the drug lords "were protecting their land and property against the threat of the guerrillas."[12]

Thus, in the context of Colombia, cartel death squads were a legitimate means to protect property. (Finally, as 1989 wore on and the excessive zeal with which the sicarios carried out their mandate littered the countryside with unspeakable carnage, the law was quietly changed.) As ranchers, cartel executives shared the interests of the other conservative landowners in the Magdalena Medio, as well as those of local military commanders. Confidential documents from DAS, the Colombian internal security service, spelled out the alliance and even named some of those from the army and police who were actively involved in paramilitary groups funded by the cartel. The human rights organization Americas Watch explained that cartel ranchers "coordinate their activities with long-established land-owners, form alliances with local and regional political leaders, and count on the complicity of local, and at times, regional police or military authorities. Ideological alliances with officials intent on defeating the left at any cost, the corruption of other officials, and intimidation of the rest help to insure that their crimes go unpunished." As former Medellin cartel trafficker Carlos Lehder put it, "In Colombia, because of all this war going on, people have the tendency to use self-defense teams or hit squads or hitmen because it's a matter of survival. It's a very dirty cold war going on there."

Carlos Lehder was the flamboyant trafficker credited with devising a splendidly efficient system of transportation by air for cocaine traveling to the United States. In April 1990, Lehder was languishing in a six-foot-by-six-foot cell at the maximum-security prison in Marion, Illinois, not far from the cell of convicted spy Jonathan Pollard. Three years before his colleagues in the business sacrificed him, according to cartel sources, when pressure mounted to turn over a relatively large fish to U.S. law enforcement.

Lehder's sentence was life without parole, plus 135 years. As he talked, there was a rhythmic clicking from his handcuffs. He occasionally looked down at his sneakers below his shackled ankles. Divorcing himself from present circumstances, Lehder's mind wandered with pleasure back to the heady days when he had his own political party and a life-size statue of John Lennon in his garden. His Latin National Movement had once issued a manifesto calling the drug trade "a revolutionary weapon against North American imperialism." But Lehder was hardly a leftist. Like Noriega, he was an admirer of Adolf Hitler. When told that he was accused of being a Nazi, Lehder replied, "Is that a crime?" He paused, then added revealingly, "Not in Colombia."

Although his colleagues from the Medellin cartel were somewhat less extreme in their views, together they wrote checks for millions of dollars to fund political candidates. Lehder described one fund-raising event in 1982 for presidential candidate Alfonso Lopez Michelson at the Intercontinental Hotel in Medellin. "Most of these people that were there were not only wanted by American justice, they were very famous people . . . either mafia or smugglers, drug smugglers . . . and we raised about ten million for Lopez Michelson. That same day we gave him half a million dollars . . . in checks." As happens with big donors everywhere, Lehder felt that he and the others did not get their money's worth. "These politicians were just ripping us off." Although Lopez Michelson would certainly deny Lehder's account, the fact was, a great many Colombian politicians were receiving "narco-dollars"—which meant that not only were cartel members in league with some of the traditional oligarchs and regional military men in their paramilitary efforts, but they had considerable clout in the halls of government.

Carlos Lehder had been a founding father of the Medellin cartel's first paramilitary death squad. In 1980, there was a rash of kidnappings orchestrated by M-19, an ambitious local guerrilla group whose most spectacular act was the takeover of the Colombian Palace of Justice (the military's response was to drive a tank into the building and shoot everything that moved, including most of the justices). When M-19 began kidnapping family members of cartel dons, this was regarded as a declaration of war. After a series of high-level meetings among cartel bosses from both Medellin and Cali, MAS (in English, "Death to Kidnappers") was born. MAS quickly and effectively slaughtered most of M-19. As Lehder, who was himself kidnapped by the guerrillas, remembered: "We fought back and, assisted by the military, assisted by the police, we fought back for about six months. Most of them [M-19] ended up overseas . . . I mean the ones that didn't die." One Cuban-American counselor to the cartel said he had advised that MAS murders should be as public as possible to maximize fear. Corpses were hung like Christmas ornaments from trees.

Carlos Lehder credited Israeli advisers with molding the old death squads into "very sophisticated machines of murder."[13] Though Lehder's observations on Israeli influence had to be regarded as the observations of a virtual Nazi, it was his old friend and colleague Gonzalo Rodriguez Gacha who had paid the reported sum of $800,000 for the services of Yair Klein from Spearhead. (Klein disputed the sum, saying the fee paid by "local farmers" was $38,000 per three-week course.) Klein's contribution to the sophistication of death-squad activity was substantial, according to General Maza Marquez, chief of DAS. "He taught them," said General Maza, "how to make bombs."

In December 1989, General Maza received visitors in his modest office at the internal security headquarters in Bogota. The office had become a good deal more modest a few days earlier, when a powerful bomb explosion had ripped off the front of the concrete, multistory building. Top-secret documents blew wildly in the fresh breeze, through offices that no longer had walls. The busy thoroughfare outside had become a deep, ugly trench. The dynamite, packed into a bus, had exploded at morning rush hour, leaving sixty-three people dead.

The man responsible was Gonzalo Rodriguez Gacha, and his target had been General Maza. "I was working as usual," said Maza, "when I felt the effects, you could say, of a mini-atomic bomb. In my office, the glass pane, which was bullet-proof, was pulled out of its frame. It landed here on my desk. Had it been hurled at the chair where I work, it would have crushed me." Maza was still shaken by the narrowness of his escape. "At the same time I heard voices calling for help, people crying, that's when I realized one of my secretaries was dead. We realized the extent of the damage, the loss of life . . . It had no doubt been the most horrifying attack we Colombians had ever suffered."

It was the second serious attempt on the general's life. This crusader against the most violent traffickers was, to anyone's knowledge, not for sale and therefore a dangerous adversary. Maza was sanguine about the death warrant he faced every morning as he left for work. "I go out very little, and now have a social life which, I would say, has been reduced approximately 90 percent." The man who had ordered the bombing of the DAS building had been irritated by General Maza's relentless probing of the massacres in the Magdalena Medio around the murder capital of the region, Puerto Boyaca. It was the town that Spearhead's best combat trainer, Amatzia Shuali, had remembered so fondly back in Israel. It seemed peculiar, sitting in the bombed-out offices of General Maza, to think that Shuali's colleague Yair Klein, the man Maza called responsible for training the cartel in bomb techniques, had once approached General Maza for a job. "Mr. Klein, when he arrived in Colombia, was in these offices, offering his services as an expert in security."[14]

Klein had moved into a discreet little hotel in Bogota called the Residencia 85. The large, balding colonel spoke little Spanish and preferred the company of other Israelis. He struck up a friendship with an old Colombia hand, Lt. Colonel Yitzhak Shoshani, who had run the Bogota branch of Israx, a subsidiary of the Israeli Clal concern in the early eighties. Shoshani had the connections and political savvy that Klein lacked. Clal still had about $250 million worth of Colombian contracts, including military equipment, radar systems, and improvements for armored vehicles and tanks. The new friend also had a fondness for snakes. Israelis remember Shoshani turning up at parties with a little snake tucked in his pocket. Klein also met Arik Afek during his stay at the Residencia. Afek was something of a Renaissance man: flower merchant, travel agent, and arms dealer. Based in Miami, he imported Colombian flowers and ran his company, Ultimate Travel, when he was not selling weapons.

Klein had fallen into capable hands. Colonel Shoshani, according to Israeli reports, brokered the contract for training one hundred and fifty soldiers of the Medellin cartel. It was presented to Klein as an opportunity to train "ranchers" in the Magdalena Medio, a deal set up by middle-ranking officers of the Colombian army. Klein met with a Colombian captain and major and, apparently, the directors of two major Colombian banks, the Banco de Granaderos and the Colombian National Bank. The Israeli then set out for the Magdalena to negotiate terms: three courses, each lasting three weeks, with fifty trainees in each. The price of the package was said to be $800,000 plus expenses, with arrangements for the cash to be paid in Miami. The students were to supply their own weapons but would be given Israeli-made combat vests and, apparently, Israeli telescopic sights for their guns. Klein would round up four other Israelis to conduct the courses, which is just what he did. Confidential Colombian security documents named Klein and his Spearhead trainers, along with Shoshani and Afek, as all being intimately involved with training the sicarios.[15]

The training camp was conveniently close to a regular army base. Colombian soldiers regularly visited and held friendly competitions with the cartel hit men. The training provided by the men from Spearhead was impressive. Conscious that good marketing was the key to success, they chose to record the wide variety of jungle and urban guerrilla training on videotape. The footage of the tough troops in their fatigues with their up-to-date equipment (and their battle cry of "Communist guerrillas, we want to drink your blood") was practically indistinguishable from training films made with the Guatemalans or the better units of the contras.

Everyone in the region knew who was financing these sicarios. Klein and the others did not hide their affiliation. They even appeared at parties in Puerto Boyaca. Colombian military men had served as middlemen in the deal and the Colombian military had exceedingly close relations with the governments of both Israel and the United States. All of them shared the same goal—effective counterinsurgency.

A chilling insight into what was entailed in this effort is conveyed by a statement given in August 1989 to the attorney general in Bogota by an eleven-year veteran of the Colombian security services. Ricardo Gamez Mazuera had served in a hitherto secret army brigade called Charry Solano, responsible for both intelligence and counterintelligence. Charry Solano specialized in torture, murder, and espionage, as laid out in staggering detail by Gamez. The brigade was, from an army perspective, on the front line of counterinsurgency. Among its exploits was a gruesome operation carried out after the seizure of the Palace of Justice in Bogota by M-19 guerrillas in 1985. After the army recaptured the building, having machine-gunned most of the occupants, some of the wounded were taken to Simon Bolivar Hospital. Among them was a secretary of one of the justices. Ruth Zuluaga de Correa was dragged from her hospital bed and taken by the army to the Escuela de Caballeria. There the innocent secretary was tortured to death. Another victim of Charry Solano interrogators was the manager of the Palace of Justice cafeteria, Carlos Rodriguez Vera. He lasted four days. The cafeteria manager and the secretary had nothing to confess.

After listing the abuses of the brigade, Gamez stated that the counterintelligence officers had received courses in espionage and pursuing suspects from two security officers at the Israeli Embassy. He named "Señor Yossia" as training Charry Solano. Yossi Biran was the chief security officer attached to Israel's embassy in Bogota. When the Gamez testimony was picked up by Amnesty International, there were strong denials from the Israeli Ministry of Foreign Affairs that Biran had ever been "involved in activities of this kind." The spokesman compared the Gamez revelation with the "Protocols of the Elders of Zion." Interestingly enough, Amnesty had not mentioned the fact that Gamez had named Yossi Biran. According to sources in Israel, the security officer had been keeping tabs on the progress of Yair Klein.

There is little doubt that some officials at the American Embassy were also aware of Yair Klein. At least one DAS document, which, according to DAS chief Maza Marquez was distributed as a matter of routine to American DEA (Drug Enforcement Administration) and

CIA men, stated that the death squad responsible for a massacre of banana workers in the province of Uraba had been trained by Israelis in Puerto Boyaca. That document was dated July 20, 1988, a full year before the scandal broke. It detailed the "collaboration" between local police and military commanders (by name) with the cartel-financed hit squads, and even gave the precise locations of the training schools where the Israelis were working. [16]

The U.S. government was therefore fully aware of the strong links between the Colombian military and the drug cartels. U.S. officials also knew that millions of dollars of U.S. aid money, earmarked for the war on drugs, was being used instead to fight leftist guerrillas and their supporters.

When cartel-financed paramilitary forces entered the town of Segovia in November 1988, the military stood by and watched. As Colombian Professor Alejandro Reyes remembered, "They killed forty-three people, just at the center of town. Anybody who was close to that place was shot. They were defenseless people, common people of the town." After the massacre, there was a river of blood running down the main street. Footage showed children jumping over that river, as though it was just part of the landscape. A spiked heel had been dyed red, soaked in blood. "In the days before the massacre," continued Reyes, "there had been threats against the whole popula- tion because the town had voted for the Union Patriotica, the leftist party. So it was a kind of sanction against the whole town for their political vote . . ." Forty-three people had been killed for voting the wrong way. The State Department knew about Segovia. Michael Skol, the deputy assistant secretary for Latin America, had served in the Bogota embassy before assuming responsibility for the entire region from his office in Washington. When asked specifically about the documented links between the military and the "narco-traffickers," men in the Segovia case, he said, "Well, we know such things are going on. The government of Colombia knows that such things are going on. We discuss this on a constant basis . . . we are insistent in our conver- sations with foreign governments that human rights is a basic tenet of U.S. foreign policy, and obviously is a basic condition for the use of U.S. funding . . ."

In 1989, in the midst of the so-called War on Drugs (before the Gulf crisis caused this temporary obsession to vanish almost without trace), the U.S. shipped $65 million worth of military equipment to Colombia. The Colombian chief of police politely pointed out that the items received were totally unsuitable for a war against the traffickers. They were, however, suitable for counterinsurgency. U.S. military equipment turned up in the region of Puerto Boyaca, where Klein and company were training. U.S. helicopters were used in antiguerrilla bombing campaigns, where, unfortunately, many of the victims were civilians. The State Department knew that, too.

In a squalid refugee camp in the very dangerous area of Barranca Barmeja, not far from Puerto Boyaca, a Colombian priest was assisting refugees from the bombing. Father Flores Miro managed to maintain his beatific smile as he talked about what was happening to the villagers. "They feel fear and anger when they see these helicopters, because they know they come to attack, the artillery helicopters come to attack, and the sound itself is terrible for anybody, especially a peasant. They flee when they hear the helicopters." The destitute refugees were confused. "Everybody says that the army's supposedly going after the drug traffickers, but I don't understand this because here, in these areas, there's not any marijuana or any coke," said one. "They say they're going after the drug traffickers and they're really going after the civilian population. We're the ones that are being bombarded, not the drug traffickers."[17]

When asked about the refugees displaced because of aerial bombardments from Hueys, Blackhawks, and A-37 aircraft, Skol, the senior State Department official for Latin America, replied, "I can't give you a percentage figure, but we are satisfied, [and] the Colombian government is satisfied, that the mix is the correct one, that it's primarily being used for antinarcotics purposes, but if you expand that just a little bit further, if you have a government with very limited resources, as we have in the Colombian government, it has to fight not only the narcotics cartels—Medellin, Cali, et cetera—but it has to fight guerrillas. If we provide assistance to the Colombian government which relieves it of resource pressures, no matter how the government uses that equipment or funding, it is relieving it of resource pressures which it can then ship to other areas." In other words, the Colombian military could do what it liked.

Given that the Colombian military had discretionary use of millions of dollars in U.S. aid money, it should have been cause for concern that a significant proportion of the military had another benefactor—the cartels. Gonzalo Rodriguez Gacha had, after all, bought the Colombian army's Thirteenth Brigade with its thousands of men. Bank records showed that he had contributed millions of dollars to their coffers, and it was not a charitable contribution. In spite of a great deal of antidrug rhetoric from Washington and Bogota, this state of affairs continued until Rodriguez Gacha launched his bombing campaign, blowing up, among other things, an Avianca airliner. One hundred and seventeen bodies lay scattered across the Colombian countryside. It spelled the end of a long and profitable career. Rodriguez Gacha was hunted down and shot. The intelligence for this operation came not from the army, but from his deadly rivals in the Cali cartel. For two days after his death, the equally rich Cali cartel executives celebrated their victory. Through an intermediary in Bogota, the Cali men had passed along their excellent intelligence to Gen. Miguel Maza Marquez at DAS. (The day Gacha died, leaflets fluttered in the streets of Cali, bearing a warning from Medellin. They read, simply, "All Colombia will mourn the death of Cali.")

General Maza put Yair Klein and his colleagues from Spearhead on the most-wanted list. Klein, said Maza, had not only taught Rodriguez Gacha's men how to make bombs (including the one exploded on board the commuter flight), he had also trained the killers of Luis Carlos Galan, a presidential candidate in 1989 who was often compared to John F. Kennedy and who almost certainly would have moved into the Presidential Palace. General Maza also accused Klein of importing quantities of Israeli arms for the Medellin cartel.

The weapons in question were Israeli Defense Force surplus, a variety pack of mortars, mines, and explosives, infrared equipment for night fighting, machine guns, medical supplies, and plentiful ammunition. Five hundred assault rifles and two hundred thousand rounds of ammunition came via an Israeli "melon" farmer, this time on the Caribbean island of Antigua.[18]

After the corpse of Rodriguez Gacha had been lined up alongside the bodies of his son and lieutenants in December 1989, Colombian authorities found a cache of 178 Galil assault rifles, shipped to the drug lord from Israel through Antigua. Colombian intelligence files concluded that from the start, the arms were destined for Rodriguez Gacha and the Israeli government had to know. As one high-ranking Colombian official put it, "All the information obtained . . . permits one to declare unequivocally that officials of the Israeli government knew and consented to the sale of the arms shipment to Colombia, up to the point of expediting a vessel to complete the first step of the route."

In January 1989, Rodriguez Gacha had arranged to have a ship "pick up an arms shipment destined for Colombia via Panama," said Colombian intelligence documents. "The shipment would have no difficulty because everything had been arranged with certain Israeli authorities." One of the government reports said that Yair Klein and his associate Arik Afek, the flower merchant/arms dealer who owned Ultimate Travel, discovered a hitch. "Noriega planned to intercept the arms shipment and appropriate the arms for his own purposes." The entrepot was switched to the island of Antigua, where a pliant high-ranking official was willing to assist, said the intelligence reports, for "a payoff of $125,000."

After the arms arrived in Antigua, a second ship would collect them and transfer the containers to a boat belonging to Rodriguez Gacha in Colombian coastal waters between Cordoba and Sucre. The assault rifles were then off loaded at a ranch belonging to the mayor of Monteria, Jesus Maria Lopez Gomez, and picked up by a Gacha associate known as the "Samurai."

Meanwhile, back at the training camp, the men from Spearhead were running one of their three-week death squad courses. Klein had scurried off to Antigua, said Colombian intelligence, to "coordinate the arms deal and installation of the new training school in Antigua," a campus for the Medellin cartel. Just to make sure the arms came through, the pragmatic Gacha decided to hold Spearhead adviser Teddy Melnik and a sixtyish Polish Israeli called "Mike" as guests until delivery.

The story of how the arms made their way from Israel Military Industries to the jungle camp outside Puerto Boyaca is very interesting indeed, for it involved men and institutions that were a good deal more powerful than Colonel Yair Klein. The obligatory melon farmer was Maurice Sarfati, whose Antigua melon plot was on land owned by the Swiss American Bank. Swiss American operated out of an even smaller Caribbean island called Anguilla, but was owned by a Geneva-based shipping magnate, Bruce Rappaport. Rappaport was an Israeli expatriate who counted Israeli prime ministers among his closest friends. Shimon Peres, according to friends, regarded Bruce Rappaport's home as his Swiss address. Rappaport was also a good friend of CIA Director William Casey, which is why it was hardly surprising that there were reports that $10 million may have landed in Rappaport's Swiss account in the course of the Iran-Contra deal.

Rappaport's Antigua tenant, Mr. Sarfati (last seen in Geneva), regarded himself as a diplomat as well as a melon farmer. The Antiguan cabinet had appointed him to negotiate on its behalf for a desalinization plant that never materialized. It was Sarfati who reportedly called Tel Aviv to say that the nearly nonexistent Antigua defense force needed the five hundred assault rifles and two hundred thousand rounds. The men at IMI did little to check out this buyer or the state of the island's ninety-man force. The Antiguan end-user certificate faxed to IMI headquarters in Israel bore the signature of the island's "Minister of National Security." It did not faze the Israeli government that there was no such post. The "Minister" was meant to be the prime minister's son, Vere Bird Jr., who had served as minister of public works and communications. Bird later swore to investigators that he did not have "any knowledge whatever" of the arms ordered in his name. In any case, the end-user certificate had been faxed from Miami.

The Miami front company used to expedite the arms transfer was a fly-by-night outfit called Nova International. Nova's partners included Pesakh Ben Or, the racehorse enthusiast who had last teamed up with Spearhead trainers to polish the skills of the Guatemalan officer corps. Nova had another notable partner with the right credentials—Reserve Brig. Gen. Pinchas Shachar, named as both an agent for Mossad and an "undercover representative" for Israel Military Industries. Spearhead trainer Amatzia Shuali had also named Ben Or, who paid his fees in Guatemala, as an agent of IMI. Thus, these IMI men smoothed the flow of arms and ammunition from Israel to the cartel, funneling the $2 million used to pay for them through General Shachar's Miami bank account. [19]

A spokesman for the Ministry of Defense in Tel Aviv later said that the transaction was carried out "under all the usual procedures at the Defense Department," despite the fact that Israel Military Industries shipped the weapons in a sealed container under an export license identifying them as "machine parts." This sort of subterfuge may be normal for covert shipments, but not for a straightforward government-to-government deal to arm the Antiguan military. Someone at the state-owned IMI obviously had doubts about the arms staying in Antigua.

The shipping records for the Danish ship Else TH, hired to ferry the arms from Haifa to Antigua, show that an Israeli Defense Ministry official was on board. Somehow the vessel failed to report to Lloyds of London, as is customary, that it was calling in at Haifa. Thus, the arms for the Medellin cartel were treated as part of a covert operation from the time they left the government-owned arms company IMI to the time they reached Colombian waters. One of the Galils from that shipment would later fire the fatal shot that killed the front-runner for the Colombian presidency, Luis Carlos Galan.

Sarfati, the melon farmer, had apparently been another keen enthusiast for the notion of an island training school, according to Vere Bird. The island's army commander, Col. Clyde Walker, said Yair Klein had expressed the need for arms if the school received approval. Antigua turned it down. Klein later explained that the school was not at all for cartel hit men, as claimed by Colombian intelligence, but for Panamanian dissidents bent on toppling Gen. Manuel Noriega. Their leader, he said, was Eduardo Herrera, now chief of Panama's armed forces. Herrera said this was complete nonsense and added, "Mike Harari is behind all of this."

The mysterious "Mike" and the Spearhead trainers did manage to eventually leave Colombia after the arms were safely in the hands of their cartel patron. Yair Klein said that he was assisted by the Israeli security officer Yossi Biran, who had been named as an instructor of the Charry Solano Brigade. Biran, said Klein, facilitated his escape in exchange for cash. Biran called this "slander."

When General Maza shut down the burgeoning cartel training industry in Puerto Boyaca, Yair Klein, reasonably enough, was confused. As he later claimed, it was the local army commander who arrived to deliver the warning "that the Colombian security agency would arrive at the base and arrest us." Klein could not understand the friction between the branches of the military, or so he said. Maza's campaign against military collaboration with the cartels had been in full swing for over a year. (The campaign was in part a personal vendetta. When the Medellin cartel had nearly succeeded in killing General Maza in his car, the vital intelligence for the "hit" had come from the army.)

Klein was indignant. "It's impossible. I'm supposed to work with the army, yet the secret police is after me. Then I discovered that in Colombia, there is a conflict of interest among the secret service, the police, and the army. The situation was so ridiculous that the Colombian secret police accused the Colombian minister of defense of being my business partner." In fact, that is just what he was. The Atlas company that contracted Spearhead to train in the Magdalena Medio had a rather important local shareholder, in the person of the minister of defense.

It had seemed clear to Yair Klein that he was serving both the needs of Colombian security and the policy of the United States. "The big problem," he said, "was the guerrillas, not drugs. The guerrillas were in charge of big parts of Colombia. The guerrillas took over the parliament. It took Colombia apart." Although guerrillas never "took over the parliament," from the vantage point of the extreme right (to which Klein by his own admission belonged) the threat required vigilance, and that meant "top fighting units" to do what the army could not legally do. Klein was acutely aware that in Colombia, he was working within the American sphere of influence, as his men had in Guatemala and Honduras. "The Americans first had their interest to curtail the Communists in Colombia. Then it became drugs and all of that. First I was serving American interests, and now they want to lynch me."[20]

The Israeli trainer had a point. "The Americans have dominated every aspect of Colombian life," he said with some bitterness, "and when things don't go well for them there, they have to blame it on somebody . . . they are a bunch of cowards, because they don't know how to deal with the truth." The truth was, as Michael Skol at the State Department had made clear, the guerrilla war was at the top of the agenda, so much so that equipment earmarked for the drug war could be transferred to the guerrilla front without so much as a murmur from Washington. When asked what the U.S. was doing to combat drugs in his region, Gen. Jose Manuel Bonnett, military commander of a vast region surrounding Cali, home of the prosperous Cali cartel, seemed puzzled. After a long pause the general replied simply, "I don't know."

Klein felt betrayed by Washington. "It's so hypocritical. Spearhead was the only organization that served American interests, because it was fighting the Communist guerrillas, which were such a threat to the interests of the Americans. Now they turn around and say that cocaine is the biggest threat, so they turned against Spearhead. It just shows that we no longer served American interests and as a result, we were thrown to the side and persecuted."

When Klein returned to Tel Aviv he led a quiet life until the release of Spearhead's promotional videotape of death-squad training brought him the sort of fame he never wanted. The Israeli attorney general announced a police investigation of Klein and his Spearhead colleagues. The attorney general was still putting the finishing touches on the splendid house she would share with her brother-in-law, Mike Harari. The police duly inspected the documents and licenses from the Ministry of Defense. Among them was a document signed by Defense Minister Yitzhak Rabin. Dated March 31, 1986, the letter gave Spearhead permission for "the export of military know-how and defense equipment," with the usual stipulation that the company would require authorization for each contract. Now that Spearhead's activities were such an embarrassment to both the Ministry of Defense and the Prime Minister's Office, no one came forth to say that Klein had asked for or received permission to train in Puerto Boyaca. Klein himself said that he had not required approval for training civilians employed by "ranchers." But in October 1988, as he and the other trainers talked about their work in the canyon of the Partridge Club, they made it absolutely clear that Zvi Reuter, chief of Sibat at the Ministry of Defense, was duly informed of every move they made. At that time, they had already served in Colombia and would do so again.

After his exposure, Klein reiterated the point that the Israeli Ministry of Defense was far from ignorant. "Before I left Israel, I reported I was going to train the farmers . . . I was only told to take good care of myself. And so, the government knew where I was."

When Klein first came under attack he declared, "I claim that we committed no crime. And if I broke the law, so did others." Presumably he was pondering the responsibility of the men at Israel Military Industries who sealed the crates full of assault weapons and labeled them "machine parts." He also no doubt thought of Mike Harari, business partner of one of the world's most notorious drug profiteers. Klein was faced with stinging public criticism from Prime Minister Shamir, who said, "It is hard for me to believe that officers would engage in such a loathsome thing. Yes, one must check and investigate, but instinctively I do not believe it." Perhaps Shamir did not believe that Noriega was very rich thanks to the drug trade when the Israeli leader wrote to Harari, commending him for his service in bringing Israel closer to Panama.

Defense Minister Rabin called the Spearhead men "mercenaries."[21] He had never complained about their trainers' sterling work with the contras or the Guatemalan military. Interestingly enough, the chronology put out by the defense minister was selective. He stated, "The initial information about possible violation of the law was obtained in April '89." This was nine months after the Colombian internal security service DAS had stated unequivocally that the Israelis were training cartel death squads in the Magdalena Medio. It was seven months after that document had been leaked in Bogota. Rabin was suggesting that Israel had the world's most incompetent intelligence service.

Israeli politicians did not believe it. Ya'ir Tzaban of Mapam demanded that Shamir answer questions: "Do not certain official parties have a direct or indirect share in this? Didn't our secret services know about these activities?" When the Security and Foreign Affairs Committee chose to take the matter into closed session, leftist Knesset member Yossi Sarid commented, "One gets the impression that maybe the government itself has something to fear, that they want to cover up for someone, for high-ranking officers and parliament members. Eight hundred Israelis walk around in every corrupt and rotten place on earth, and in their pockets they have official Defense Ministry licenses."

Yair Klein became, for a time, the Oliver North of Israel. The men from Sibat, at the Ministry of Defense, from IMI, and the Israeli Embassy in Bogota laid low while the nation debated the culpability of Klein. Israeli journalist Nahum Barnea of *Yediot Aharanot* observed that what Klein did in Colombia was no worse than what the Israeli army had done in Lebanon. "The truth is that Yair Klein and myself have already gone to war in the service of the drug cartel once. It happened seven years ago in the Lebanon war. I know that there is a legal difference between what Ariel Sharon did in '82 and the allegations against the Spearhead men. But what is the moral difference?" The Christian Phalangists, Sharon's allies in Lebanon, were, according to numerous reports, active participants in the flourishing Lebanese drug trade.

The bitter members of the Spearhead team confided in one Israeli journalist that the man they held responsible for their involvement in the whole sordid affair was Arik Afek, the flower merchant and proprietor of Ultimate Travel, whom Colombian intelligence documents placed with the trainers in the camps of Puerto Boyaca. One Spearhead man remarked, "I hope that Arieh Afek is now stuck in Colombia in one of the secret service's interrogation cellars." A few months later the stench of Afek's corpse would lead Miami police to the trunk of his Buick Regal. The thirty-nine-year-old Israeli arms dealer, known to friends and enemies alike as the "flower man," in honor of his more polite business, had been executed in a very professional "gangland" hit. He was left riddled with bullets, in a city full of professionals.

Afek, it appears, had ties to both Israeli intelligence and U.S. government agencies, including the CIA. He confided in one of his partners in First Paragon Inc., the flower business, that he worked for Israeli military intelligence. The Israeli press identified him as a former intelligence officer, by one account active during the invasion of Lebanon. He had reportedly been cooperating with both the CIA and the U.S. Secret Service, traveling to Colombia, according to one U.S. government source, on a diplomatic passport, issued under a sealed federal court order signed in Miami. Israeli television reported that the CIA had issued the U.S. passport in exchange for information on Israeli activity in Colombia. Two weeks before he was murdered, Afek told the Israeli paper *Yediot Aharanot* that the Agency was by then offering him citizenship as a quid pro quo.

At the time Afek's body was stuffed in the Buick trunk in the Miami International Airport parking garage, President George Bush was finalizing his arrangements for the Cartagena drug summit on February 15. The drug summit was seen as a major public relations event for the president, willing to face any threat the henchmen of the cartels could pose on their own dangerous turf. As it turned out, the Colombian resort of Cartagena (a good distance from any cartel chiefs) was practically hermetically sealed for the event. The forward planning on the part of the Secret Service required great effort and ingenuity, including a presidential look-alike who walked down the steps first, in case of a sudden burst of bullets. The Secret Service also called Arik Afek.

Before his death, Afek told friends that he was in daily contact with Secret Service agents in Miami and had traveled with them four times in recent weeks to Colombia, to assist with presidential security. There was concern that the Medellin cartel could employ surface-to-air missiles to shoot down the president's plane. Afek called Yair Klein to check whether the cartel had received such weapons. Klein used the call as evidence that his Colombian camp mate was "unstable, confusing fantasy with reality." The Secret Service admitted conferring with Afek about the cartel's military strength. But an agency spokesman said he was not aware of "further assistance. That is probably not something that we would give out anyway."[22]

In the midst of this flurry of activity to protect George Bush from the cartel armed by Israel, Afek was also calling Israelis and Colombians. He spoke with the Israeli National Police Office at the Israeli Consulate in New York nearly every day. The busy "flower man" was also in touch with the Israeli consul in Miami and placed frequent calls to an unidentified woman at the Colombian Embassy in Washington. This was all monitored, curiously enough, by the Immigration and Naturalization Service, which was investigating Afek for entering the U.S. illegally as a "special agricultural worker," a category designed for seasonal migrant farm laborers.

The Miami DEA was also interested in Afek. The local DEA office was just over a mile from the flower-import business. When Interpol alerted the DEA to Colombia's arrest warrant for the Israeli, special agent Tom Cash assigned a man to the Afek case. Cash informed headquarters in Washington about his neighbor the flower merchant. No orders came back to pursue this man whose intimate knowledge of the Medellin cartel was a very rare find. "We had to forget about it," said Cash. It was a common phrase uttered by local Miami agencies, whose targets had other associations farther up the line, either too sensitive or too useful to investigate. The day Afek disappeared, he told his daughter he had an appointment to meet some friends. After the body, still in shorts, was removed from the Regal trunk, official interest quietly died. An Israeli police spokesman said, "Our representative in the United States is examining the case"—no doubt the same office Afek called nearly every day before his death. A spokesman for the Secret Service folded that agency's hands by saying, "It's just another homicide in Miami."

If the CIA had indeed used the dead man to gather information about Israeli activity in Colombia, and Afek, as Spearhead trainers claimed, had been in part responsible for their death-squad contract, it put the CIA in the awkward position of condoning extreme violence in the name of intelligence. One wealthy Colombian trafficker, serving time across the prison courtyard from Manuel Noriega in Miami, had said in 1989 that Klein and company were passing information back from Puerto Boyaca to the agency. Afek would have been the messenger. Klein believed that Afek's relationship with the Americans was a very dangerous liaison. "They thought that Arik could be their friend, like he was to me . . . they killed my best witness and a great friend."

Gen. Miguel Maza, chief of Colombia's DAS, told one confidant that he believed the CIA and DEA had "different policies" in Colombia. The CIA, he believed, had ties to Medellin. Certainly the drug-financed Arms Supermarket in San Pedro Sula and the nature of Mike Harari's arms "network" for the contras suggested a familiarity with Medellin that the agency was not anxious to advertise. In context, it seemed less strange that an Israeli Defense Ministry-approved company like Spearhead would end up in the pay of such notorious "ranchers" as Gonzalo Rodriguez Gacha. Interestingly enough, after Klein was implicated in the cartel scandal, he said that he had received approval to run a "survivalist" school in Antigua from the CIA.

At the end of the Colombia affair, the Israeli government announced that Klein would be tried for "having planned to run an insurgency school" and "exporting equipment and defense know-how to Antigua" without required permits. The maximum sentence was three years, and the veteran army man received a one-year sentence, which he appealed. The Spearhead corporation was still receiving desirable government contracts. Colombia, like Panama, had been an episode everyone wanted to forget.

One retired U.S. military intelligence officer, who had worked closely with Israel in the past, said that probing this murky business, particularly the official Israeli government sale of arms to Antigua destined for the Medellin cartel, was "supersensitive." "He said that the 'special relationship' between Israel and the United States adds to the sensitivity, because most Israeli arms merchants are 'past and present members of the Israeli military and intelligence communities,' including some who have assisted the United States in the past in covert operations."[23]

Such covert operations had been thick on the ground in the 1980s. The sensitivity was such that history had been carefully adjusted, by both Congress and the White House, to protect the "special relationship."

11. A Marriage of Convenience

ON A GRAY MORNING in March 1990, the Israeli ambassador to Washington made his way to what promised to be an acrimonious meeting on Capitol Hill. Moshe Arad faced the unpleasant task of defending Israel's unwillingness to terminate its extensive military and intelligence cooperation with South Africa. His critical audience in the closed-door session included both Israel's most loyal advocates in Congress and members of the Congressional Black Caucus, who regarded Israel's sustained support of the South African government as unconscionable and possible grounds to cut U.S. aid. The irritated congressmen, some of whom had fought hard to enforce antiapartheid legislation and others who scented danger for Israel's most-favored status in Washington, warned the ambassador that the delicate problem of South Africa was "the most troubling issue in U.S.-Israel relations."

In this charged atmosphere, the ambassador did his best to defuse the main point of contention, that it had been three years since Israel had promised to forswear military contracts with the South African government and to permit existing contracts to expire. Just when they would expire had been left deliberately vague, and congressional demands for a concrete timetable had been ignored. Moshe Arad assured his audience that a schedule would be "forthcoming" and that Israel was "phasing out" this embarrassing military alliance. The congressmen had received the same soothing reassurances from Prime Minister Yitzhak Shamir four months before. Even when the lawmakers offered to compensate Israel for the $400 to $800 million it was earning annually from its lethal South Africa trade by boosting U.S. aid, the response was tepid. The meeting ended, as had all the others, with no guarantees.

Randall Robinson, director of TransAfrica and one of the chief lobbyists in the fight against apartheid, had expressed the frustration of the caucus three years before when he said, "Can you imagine providing weapons to one of the most vicious regimes on earth and saying, 'We will stop selling arms once we terminate the contracts'?"

When congressmen, including Israel's strongest supporters, came out of a briefing by U.S. intelligence agencies in November 1989, they were impressed by the sheer size of Israel's South Africa trade. Congressman Stephen Solarz observed, "Israel's military relations with South Africa, regarding financial value, volume, length of time, and content, are very important, especially in comparison with other countries . . . they are much larger than has been rumored or suggested." Another lawmaker commented anonymously, "The impression the Israelis leave is that these are minor contracts which will soon expire. Our impression is that these contracts involve extensive cooperation and will last until the end of the century, if not beyond."[1]

Soon after the congressmen were briefed, Israeli Defense Minister Yitzhak Rabin told his parliament's Foreign Affairs and Defense Committee that the country's defense industry was in a slump thanks to the spate of settlements of the small wars Israel depends on for foreign exchange. He was not inclined to damage the industry further by pulling out of South Africa. "Rabin's comments to the Knesset panel," reported the *Jerusalem Post*, "were seen in some circles as a signal that he would not be willing to cancel existing contracts with the apartheid state."

Thus Israel's arsenal, financed largely by the United States, remained available to the South African military, supposedly prohibited by law from acquiring U.S. technology. The easy flow of patents and weapons from the Pentagon to the Kirya in Tel Aviv was matched only by the easy flow of weapons and know-how from Tel Aviv to ARMSCOR, the state-owned arms industry in South Africa. Although everyone along the trail claimed there was never any transfer of U.S. technology to Johannesburg, the claim was false. Because such sanctions-busting was punishable by law, it was only in the closed world of secret cables and classified memos that it could be discussed.

The U.S. military attaché in Harare, Zimbabwe sent such a cable on February 12, 1989. He alerted the Defense Intelligence Agency in Washington that American aircraft engines, made under license in Israel, were wending their way to the South African air force. It was forbidden for Israel to export the engine without U.S. approval. Sales to Ecuador of Israel's Kfir fighter plane, which was fitted with the General Electric J79 engine, had been stopped by the Carter administration on the grounds that the White House did not want to upset the military balance in Latin America. Washington had had the final say. In 1989 the military attaché in Zimbabwe wrote: "The SADF [South African Defense Forces]/ARMSCOR has recently taken delivery of an unknown number of Israeli-manufactured J79 engines. It is assumed that the engines will be employed in some kind of upgrade program for the Cheetah [fighter aircraft]." Judging from the heavily censored cable, there had been other shipments of the engine in the past. "The SADF through ARMSCOR had [deleted] taken delivery of several J79 engines."

While congressmen were berating the Israeli ambassador for failing to implement the promises made in 1987 to scale down sales dramatically, intelligence sources were leaking assessments that the Israel-South Africa trade had actually increased. Joint projects such as the Jericho medium-range missile, the Shavit rocket, the Ofek spy satellites, and the airborne early-warning system were shamelessly moving ahead without a word of protest from the White House. At the same time they were developing myriad conventional arms, the military partners were also forging ahead with their long-term efforts to develop efficient tactical nuclear weapons.

For much of the summer and fall of 1989, the villagers in Arniston, South Africa were forbidden to fish along their coast. They lived next door to the Arniston missile test range, where on July 5 of that year, South Africa launched what it mendaciously called a "booster rocket." According to observers from American intelligence agencies, the weapon was in fact a medium-range missile that could carry a nuclear warhead. It was the sister missile of Israel's Jericho IIB. The billowing plume tracked by American satellites was virtually the same as the

Jericho's, not surprising since Israel had shared its design. The Arniston, as the South African variant was designated by the CIA, flew
nine hundred miles across the Indian Ocean to the Prince Edward
Islands, halfway to Antarctica. The test was part of what U.S. intelligence officials called Jerusalem's "full-blown partnership" with Pretoria to perfect the technology for small, sophisticated hydrogen
bombs, as well as the latest ballistic missile designs to carry them.[2]

Preparations for that particular test had been monitored by the CIA
for two years. The excuse leaked to explain the agency's curious paral-
ysis in the face of this stunning development and its inability to
recommend strong sanctions was that the CIA did not want to "complicate" the "delicate peace negotiations" in southern Africa. Nor did the
CIA wish to upset the "peace process" in Israel. The delicate negotiations in southern Africa had little to do with peace and a great deal to
do with the CIA, which was taking over the guerrilla war in Angola
from South Africa. As for Israel's "peace process," the process seemed
permanently on hold. In any case, the PLO and the rest of Israel's Arab
neighbors were acutely aware of Israel's nuclear weapons program. To
the extent that leaders such as Saddam Hussein harbored nuclear
ambitions (though his facilities in Baghdad were inspected regularly,
unlike Israel's), they viewed the "Arab bomb" as a potential deterrent
against an already well-advanced Israeli arsenal in the same way that
Pakistan nervously eyed the Indian nuclear "threat."

Israel's joint development with South Africa of advanced delivery
systems for low-yield nuclear warheads was quietly allowed to proceed, while President Bush and the State Department declined comment on such "intelligence matters." Facing reporters during a visit to
San Jose, Costa Rica in 1989, Bush said of the missile cooperation,
"The transfer of forbidden technology is taboo. We're not going to
have that. And we will find ways to assert that with any country that
abuses the system." It was the sort of comment that had emanated
from the White House for a decade.

In 1979, it was the Carter administration that energetically covered
up the joint Israeli-South African nuclear weapons program. On September 22 of that year at 0100 GMT a double flash of light was picked
up over the Indian Ocean by the optical sensors of a Vela reconaissance
satellite. The twelve Velas orbiting the earth were expressly designed
to detect nuclear explosions. The twin flashes monitored at the U.S.
Air Force Nuclear Detection Agency in Florida were the signature of a

nuclear detonation. The location was the Prince Edward Islands, where the medium-range missile modeled on Israel's Jericho would land ten years later.

It was Saturday night Washington time when the Carter White House received word of the nuclear test. The president met with both Defense Secretary Harold Brown and National Security Adviser Zbigniew Brzezinski. The following morning, they convened a crisis committee that included the National Security Council's senior Africa specialist, Gerald Funk. As Funk remembered, "I was told by Zbig to get my toucus into work, that we had a little bit of a problem . . . that satellite had never failed to react positively, and had never given a false signal." If, as some believed in the Situation Room that Sunday, Israel was involved, the immediate problem was the Symington Amendment. By law, Israeli participation would trigger the cutoff of all U.S. military and economic aid, a disastrous political move for the Carter camp in the early stages of the 1980 presidential campaign. (The Foreign Assistance Act of 1961, amended by the International Security Assistance Act of 1977, required the cutoff of U.S. military and economic assistance or grant, military education or training to any country that manufactures, transfers, receives, or detonates "a nuclear explosive device.")

In the days immediately following the test, the crisis managers maintained that there was no conclusive evidence, no extraordinary levels of background radiation at the site, that would prove beyond doubt that a test had occurred. It was a curious assessment, for no one had bothered to check. U.S. Air Force high-altitude reconnaissance aircraft did not "sweep" the test site to collect air samples until three weeks after the event. There was one other minor scientific fact about the test site that was surely not lost on the South Africans or the Israelis. The ionospheric cap was thinner there than anywhere else on earth, with the result that background radiation was exceedingly high. It was the perfect place to hide a test.

In mid-October, a "blue-ribbon" panel of eminent scientists was convened by the White House to review the evidence coming in from various quarters that a nuclear explosion had indeed taken place. The scientists found fault with every piece of data. The U.S. Air Force Technical Applications Center offered "acoustic evidence from listening posts in widely separated parts of the world that seems to confirm an explosion." The Naval Research Laboratory submitted a three-hundred-page report concluding that a small nuclear device had been exploded. The navy had detected two hydro-acoustic pulses generated by the test and added that mathematic computations pinpointed the "pulse" as matching the location of the Vela "flash."

The navy also concluded that the test had occurred precisely ten minutes before sunrise, the optimum moment for measuring radiation in the dark and observing blast effects at dawn. The director of the Naval Research Lab, Alan Berman, pointed out, "The computation is sufficiently complicated that it would be an amusing coincidence if that were entirely accidental." The White House "panel" was unimpressed. Further evidence from the Arecibo radio observatory in Puerto Rico of a "traveling ionospheric disturbance" was dismissed as "a very weak data base" that could have been a storm. The U.S. Air Force early-warning-net signal picked up on September 22 was discounted as too ambiguous.

While the select group of scientists was busy trying to find some natural phenomenon (such as a meteorite) that might explain away all of the signals, the CIA was briefing Congress with some hard facts on the South African navy. The navy had been exercising precisely where the "flash" had occurred, and the exercises had been conducted under extraordinary security precautions. The CIA told a subcommittee of the House of Representatives that the exercises seemed to involve standard nuclear test monitoring procedures. While the scientists gathered their thoughts to release a very inconclusive public study, the CIA was preparing its own report, also commissioned by the White House, that would remain secret. It was not until the summer of 1990 that the document, heavily "sanitized," was released.

The Interagency Intelligence Memorandum, titled "The 22 September 1979 Event," was dated December 1979 and contained a good deal of information that the White House neglected to pass along to the blue-ribbon panel. The report stated: "Technical information and analysis suggest that:—An explosion was produced by a nuclear device detonated in the atmosphere near the earth's surface.—It had a yield equivalent to less than three kilotons.—It took place within a broad area, primarily oceans, that was generally cloudy." The report detailed events in South Africa at the time that strongly suggested preparations for a nuclear test.

In September 1979 some special security measures were put into effect which indicate that certain elements of the South African Navy were exercising or on alert on 22 September. The harbor and naval base at Simonstown were declared, in a public announcement on 23 August, to be off limits for the period 17–23 September. The US defense attache gathered from several reliable sources that harbor defense exercises took place there during this period. Although such a closure might not be required for a nuclear test at sea, it could have screened sensitive loading or unloading operations as well as ship movements. Also, the Saldanha naval facility, which includes a naval search-and-rescue unit, was suddenly placed on alert for the period 21–23 September.

The CIA, as well as the Defense Intelligence Agency, also knew that South Africa's military attaché in Washington had requested information on nuclear test detection systems in the U.S. and elsewhere. Immediately after the test, South Africa's Prime Minister Botha could not resist, according to the CIA classified report, expressing quiet pride at its success. As the CIA noted, "Three days after the nuclear event he told a provincial congress of the ruling National Party that 'South Africa's enemies might find out we have military weapons they do not know about.'" The prime minister's remarks grew less enigmatic the following month. The CIA went on to say:

On 24 October—before the US disclosures of the technical indications of a test—the Prime Minister addressing an anniversary dinner attended by past and present members of the AEB (Atomic Energy Board) as well as members of the local diplomatic corps, reportedly paid tribute to the South African nuclear scientists who had been engaged in secret work of a strategic nature. He reportedly said that, for security reasons, their names could not be mentioned and that they would never gain the recognition in South Africa or abroad that they deserved.[3]

They certainly deserved recognition in the view of the top men at CIA headquarters in Langley, Virginia. In early 1988, nine years after the test, a former senior CIA official confided that the test, conducted by both South Africa and Israel, was much more than just an explosion of a small atomic device. At a Cantonese restaurant in Bethesda, the CIA man revealed that the two countries had been testing the fission trigger known as "the pit" for a hydrogen bomb. The dramatic assessment that both Israel and South Africa were building H-bombs was classified top secret. "That," said the senior CIA official, "is what [CIA Director] Stan Turner signed off on" and reported to Jimmy Carter's White House. It was thus the official CIA view, which the White House conveniently suppressed.

In an election year, when the tone of published reports left readers with the impression that the facts of the "mysterious flash" would never be established, the White House was spared the pain of confronting the political consequences of this rather significant nuclear event. Relations between the Carter White House and the Begin government in Jerusalem had already deteriorated considerably since the heady days of Camp David. Thanks to a series of unpleasant rows, such as Carter's threat to cut off aid if Begin did not withdraw forces from Southern Lebanon in 1978, and petty personal slights, as when Begin refused to kiss young Amy Carter good night on her first visit to Jerusalem, the alliance was on the verge of divorce. Carter also had the Iranian hostage crisis to contend with and was loath to generate more political fallout. The deliberate obfuscation made the White House very much a party to the South African and Israeli deception over the "event."

The White House blue-ribbon findings, released six months after the CIA completed the secret internal report, reflected none of the intelligence available to the agency. With much fanfare, the "panel" claimed to have reviewed "all available data" before reaching its verdict that nothing much had happened in the Indian Ocean the previous September. CIA Director Stansfield Turner later pointed out that no one from the White House panel had ever requested information from Langley about what the CIA knew. Without that intelligence, he said, the panel's conclusions were "absurd."

It was not until 1986 that the possibility of Israeli thermonuclear weapons, or H-bombs, was raised in public. Mordechai Vanunu, the Israeli nuclear technician who defected that year from Dimona, said Israel was producing such weapons and he had photographs to support it. After the London *Sunday Times* showed the photos to a number of nuclear physicists, there was agreement that the secret Machon II facility had the necessary ingredients. "Unit 93 on Level Four produces tritium. This is of immense significance," said the *Sunday Times*, "for it means Israel has the potential to produce thermonuclear weapons far more powerful than ordinary atomic bombs." The photos also revealed a lithium deuteride hemisphere, used for H-bomb construction. "In the chilling jargon of the nuclear bomb makers," the report continued, "Israel has moved beyond the ability to produce small 'suburb-busting' nuclear bombs to 'city-busters.'"

Vanunu also talked of South African nuclear technicians being a common sight at the Israel reactor in the Negev. But at the time of Vanunu's stunning revelations, no high-level CIA source had as yet linked those facts with the nuclear "event" of September 1979.

When, ten years after the event, George Bush assured reporters that "the transfer of forbidden technology is taboo" and "we're not going to have that," his top intelligence man on the National Security Council staff was Robert Gates (who owed his brief moment of fame, during the Iran-Contra hearings, to his post as CIA Director William Casey's right-hand man). Gates served as the intelligence aide to Zbigniew Brzezinski during and after the 1979 test. Therefore he should have known a great deal about the transfer of hidden technology, and must have been aware that the White House had been willing to break the "taboo" for a decade. The CIA assessment of December 1979, which was available to Gates, spent two full pages examining probable Israeli participation. The document noted that Israel "might have considered desirable a small tactical nuclear warhead for Israel's short-range Lance surface-to-surface missiles," American-made missiles deployed by the Pentagon at the time for U.S. forces in the "nuclear battlefield" of central Europe. The CIA report went on to say, "Israeli strategists might even have been interested in developing the fission trigger for a thermonuclear weapon." This last is precisely what the CIA eventually determined with confidence. The memorandum goes on to make clear that Washington was apprised of the Israeli-South African cooperation on nuclear and other military matters.

> Israelis have not only participated in certain South African nuclear research activities over the last few years, but they have also offered and transferred various sorts of advanced nonnuclear weapons technology to South Africa. So clandestine arrangements between South Africa and Israel for joint testing operations might have been negotiable.[4]

The Bush White House, with a former CIA director in the Oval Office, seemed to have little appreciation for history, as detailed in the agency's own files. While the president made his false assurances, calling the overwhelming evidence of Israeli collaboration "a hypothesis that I'm not accepting," Pentagon officials were leaking the fact that Israel's "partnership" with South Africa meant a transfer of "advanced nuclear weapons designs."

The reaction on Capitol Hill seemed tailored to project vigilance while quietly ensuring minimum consequences. Congressman Howard Wolpe, as chairman of the House Subcommittee on Africa, promised to "get to the bottom of this." Four years before, Wolpe had been instrumental in blunting fellow Congressman John Conyers's amendment to cut off aid to countries supplying South Africa with nuclear weapons technology. Wolpe made promises then as well to hold hearings on the issue. Unfortunately, his enthusiasm for such hearings flagged indefinitely. Later in 1987, Wolpe helped persuade the Black Caucus not to do anything rash about Israel's ongoing contracts with South Africa. The caucus was appeased with yet more promises that no new contracts would be signed. Three years later, when the contracts seemed infinitely renewable, the caucus felt used. The missile developments aggravated matters.

According to the CIA, the new medium-range missile, copied from Israel's advanced Jericho, was built by ARMSCOR. "The front company transferring the military technology" was identified as the Israeli firm Urdan Industries Ltd., which also had contracts with the U.S. Army to supply suspension parts for tanks. Urdan was a member of the Clal group, which was also doing brisk business in Colombia. A major shareholder in Clal was Shaul Eisenberg, the very rich and secretive arms dealer who counted such old Africa hands as former Mossad official David Kimche among his employees. Urdan denied the CIA assertion that the company was the vehicle for the transfer of tactical nuclear missile technology, just as David Kimche denied Israel's ongoing military relationship with South Africa.

While the two countries were gearing up for the missile test, Kimche was coy about the alliance. "The policy of the state of Israel," he said judiciously, "has been to go along with other democratic countries regarding the policy towards South Africa. We have acted in accordance with what the other democratic countries have been doing regarding South Africa." When asked whether he implied that the United States was happy with Israel's close relationship with South Africa, Kimche demurred. "I didn't say that. I didn't say that at all. I said that at one time or other they were selling arms—at one time or other. I'm not saying they're doing it today. I'm not saying that we're doing it today. I'm saying that at one time or another that had been the situation and then it was"—he paused for a moment—"cut out."

The obviously delicate question of U.S. reaction to Israeli transfers of arms and technology and complicity in the trade was not one that Kimche, who had worked so closely with the White House in the Reagan years, cared to answer. When confronted with the fact that Israeli shipments had not been "cut out," Kimche replied disingenuously, "I don't know." Gen. Mordechai Hod, then chairman of Israel Aircraft Industries, was more candid. When asked whether it bothered him that the U.S. had veto power over some Israeli sales overseas, he smiled and said, "Yes, it does. So what?" In the case of Israeli sales to South Africa, he continued, "We have to cooperate, because it is a 'no alternative' situation. We know that we have to coordinate it with the U.S. authorities and we know that if we want to continue to enjoy the $1.8 billion a year of military aid, and the outcome of it is military products, and we want to sell them outside of Israel, we have to coordinate it with the U.S. government. It's not a question of liking it or not liking it; those are facts."[5]

As General Hod went on to clarify, most Israeli weapons systems represented not only substantial U.S. investment, but had U.S.-made components or parts manufactured under license. "Most of it has U.S. components, and the Israeli government is a responsible government." The vast government-owned IAI, General Hod explained, "has four hundred products. IAI gets its permission from our Ministry of Defense. The political relations are done between the two governments, between our MOD and U.S. defense authorities. So for us, if we get permission from our MOD that means all the rest was done and we have permission for them. That means there is U.S. permission to export to that country."

A number of IAI weapons, some with U.S. parts and others built in Israel with U.S. financing, had turned up in South Africa. IAI refueling tankers, adapted from Boeing aircraft, enabled the South African air force to dramatically increase range for bombing raids. The Israeli Kfir 2 jet fighter, powered by the American J79 engine, had metamorphosed into the Cheetah, the Kfir's South African twin. The Cheetahs, some of which carried identical American engines (built under license in Israel), could, when refueled by the modified Boeing tankers, hit targets 2,000 miles from South Africa. The tankers also served as electronic warfare platforms. The South African air force had neatly skirted the restraints of U.S. sanctions.

The United States invested heavily in the South African air force by financing its latest generation of fighter aircraft, to the tune of $1.5 billion in research and development costs. The money was approved by Congress to underwrite the expenses of Israel Aircraft Industries' development of the Lavi fighter plane. As far as IAI was concerned, the Lavi project, mired in cost overruns, was killed in 1987. But months before the cancellation, the Italian paper *Il Giornale*, followed by the Israeli daily *Yediot Aharanot*, reported a secret agreement between Israel and South Africa to produce a South African version called the Simba ("Lion" in Swahili). Israeli Lavi technicians flocked to South Africa, and as the aviation editor of *Jane's Defense Weekly* observed, the Israelis "obviously brought their skills to bear in South Africa . . . maybe we will see another Lavi, or a Lavi look-alike." He estimated that the Simba would be in the air in eight to ten years.

When members of the Congressional Black Caucus challenged Prime Minister Yitzhak Shamir on this unauthorized use of U.S. aid money, they were stonewalled. Congressman George Crockett said of the March 1988 meeting, "In his response to the questions put to him Shamir indicated no willingness to change his government's policy in any way." The Black Caucus had presented Shamir with a letter condemning the transfer of Lavi technology.

> The United States provided Israel with nearly $1.5 billion in assistance in developing the Lavi fighter aircraft. We have since learned that following the cancellation of the project by your government, the Israeli engineers who worked on the Lavi project are taking the benefits of U.S. foreign assistance to South Africa. We consider this an unconscionable use of our aid.[6]

Outside the caucus, the "unconscionable use" was simply ignored. The laid-off Lavi technicians also reportedly did yeoman work developing an upgraded Cheetah, unveiled as the Cheetah-E in August 1988. The new fighter was advertised as having a "modernized and integrated navigation and weapons system" and the ability to take on Angola's Russian Mig 23s. Even before celebrating the debut of the Cheetah-E, however, the chief of the South African air force announced that a "top priority" of the military was to forge ahead with the new Simba, the Phoenix of the Lavi program. IAI in Tel Aviv then declared that the government-owned firm would "continue the development and production of the B-3 avionic Lavi prototype with independent financing." Like the United States, South Africa, though to a lesser extent, had long financed Israeli research and development in the arms field. While shifting both its talent and U.S.-funded prototypes to South Africa, Israel also sold the aircraft's avionics (aircraft electronics systems) to Communist China.

An authorized biography of Israeli Labor Party leader Shimon Peres claims that the blatant flow-through of U.S. (and U.S.-funded) technology to South Africa was deliberate on the part of Israel and its partner, the United States. The biography contends, "Israel's main role in the partnership was as a go-between. There were countries such as . . . South Africa, that the United States wanted to assist. It was very convenient in cases such as this to give the aid via Israel, or to encourage Israel to step up its exports to these countries."[7]

This convenient use of a "go-between" was consistent with IAI Chairman Motti Hod's contention that the Israeli Ministry of Defense received permission for those South Africa sales. In light of the cooperative spirit amongst the players in this exercise to evade sanctions, it is useful to remember that South Africa had, in a crisis, acted at the behest of the United States to resupply Israel. In the dark days of the '73 war, the U.S. requested South Africa to supply Centurion tanks to shore up Israeli tank forces. The South Africans were amenable, so long as their stocks could be replenished without delay. The U.S. then called on Canada to make up for the South African Centurions lost to the war effort. Canada obliged.

It would appear that tacit approval by a series of Democratic and Republican administrations for Israeli arms sales to South Africa has resembled the duplicitous policy on arms sales to Iran: public sanctions together with covert sales. Although certain members of Congress have balked at the flow of arms and blueprints to the apartheid regime, U.S. defense and intelligence agencies, as well as inhabitants of the Oval Office, have at times had classified agendas which have undermined the good intentions of the guardians of sanctions. This was in part because Cold War strategic thinking placed South Africa firmly in the Western camp, while neighbors such as Angola and Mozambique were regarded as Soviet surrogates.

When asked whether the Bush administration had acted on reports that Israel and South Africa were cooperating in designing and building nuclear weapons, the State Department demurred. Assistant Secretary of State for African Affairs Herman Cohen responded, "Israel is a sovereign state. We have advised them to honor UN sanctions. The rest is up to them." It was a terse justification of U.S. inaction. None of the levers of power available to every administration since the advent of sanctions against South Africa had ever been pulled. Israel's defense relationship with Pretoria ran very deep, going back thirty-five years to when the first shipment of Uzis landed in South Africa.

There had been strong support for the young Israeli state among South Africa's Nationalist leaders since the latter came to power in 1948, the year of Israel's War of Independence. Nationalists had appalling records as Nazi sympathizers. Much of the leadership had been jailed by the British for energetic activities on behalf of the Third Reich. Thus, when the Nationalist Party emerged victorious in postwar South Africa, with apartheid as a pillar of its extreme racist platform, its warm embrace of Israel was not an expression of particularly honorable sentiments. The Afrikaner newspaper *Transvaaler* ran a telling editorial in 1946 stating that it "grants the Jew his ideals in Palestine but, at the same time, desires an increasing exodus of Jews thither and not their increase here."

Yet a stream of Israeli leaders, including Moshe Dayan, made the pilgrimage to Pretoria and Johannesburg in the fifties to curry favor with the former Nazi collaborators. By the early 1960s, the friendship had become a marriage of convenience, based on the exchange of arms for cash and shipments of uranium. In 1962, Israel sold the apartheid regime thirty-two Centurion tanks. That same year, South Africa shipped ten tons of uranium to fuel Israel's Dimona reactor. The first UN resolution to embargo arms to South Africa passed by the Security Council in August 1963 had no effect on such business, although Israel had publicly "slapped South Africa in the face" by assuming a UN posture condemning apartheid. Israeli leaders were mindful of their relations with black African states, at a time when Mossad was receiving heavy subsidies to carry out its intelligence-gathering mission there for the CIA.

However, the vicissitudes of UN politics were outweighed by the needs of two military establishments that shared a similar view of their countries' isolation amidst hostile neighbors and fickle allies. After

1967, when the French embargo against Israel depleted supplies of spare parts for Israel's Mirage aircraft, South Africa made up the shortfall. During the '67 war, South African observers flew to the battlefield to study tactics. The lessons learned were incorporated into the curricula of South Africa's maneuver schools. General Hod, then chief of staff of the Israeli air force, lectured the South African military on strategy. In 1976, Israeli Prime Minister Yitzhak Rabin summed up where Israel and South Africa's interests converged: "Our countries have in common the problem of initiating dialogue, coexistence, and stability in our respective parts of the world, in the face of foreign-inspired instability and recklessness." It was the same language employed by apartheid leaders to justify their draconian security measures. In 1974, Moshe Dayan said that a "great civilization" was being created in South Africa, at a time when savage measures of repression were employed in the townships and the homelands. Former Chief of Staff of the Israel Defense Force Rafael Eitan told a group of Israeli professionals at Tel Aviv University that the South African Bantustan policy, that of isolating people of "color" on reservations, was a possible solution to the "Palestinian problem."[8]

Among the many twinned cities in Israel and South Africa, there are the capital of the Ciskei Bantustan and the West Bank settlement of Ariel. When the Ciskei parliament opened in 1985, five members of the Knesset were present. Israeli Liberal Party member Yehezkel Flumin praised the Bantustan system, while General Efraim Poran said, "As of today, in Ciskei people have houses to live in, employment and education for their children, and there is no apartheid." The Tamuz Corporation, which earned its international reputation by supplying security services to Philippine dictator Ferdinand Marcos, also took care of security for Ciskei's local despot, President Sebe.

It should be said that the views of Israeli military men did not necessarily match those of the large Jewish community in South Africa, many of whom had fought courageously against the cruel application of pass laws, detentions without trial, and enforced destitution in the "homelands." But much of the high-level cooperation between the South African and Israeli military establishments was shrouded in secrecy and immune from lobbying efforts, just as contacts between the Pentagon and South African military intelligence was not a subject of public debate in the United States.

During the Reagan years, while sanctions were fully in place, there was widespread cooperation between American and South African intelligence agencies. There was a brief chill in the otherwise convivial atmosphere of this secret society when a U.S. air force intelligence officer refused to play his part. John Boyell had been dispatched from Washington on a fact-finding tour of the "frontline" African states. When he dropped in on the U.S. military attaché in Pretoria at the end of the tour, Boyell was invited along to what he believed would be a briefing from South African military intelligence. Boyell was alarmed to discover that he was the briefer, expected to update the South Africans with his observations of their enemies. When the American officer declined, saying he had no such orders, the South Africans were both irritated and amused by his reticence. They directed him to a nearby military airfield, where a U.S. air force reconnaissance aircraft was parked on the strip. The vivid message was that in view of such obvious U.S. support, the intelligence officer's coy behavior was out of line. The U.S. military attaché was so enraged by his colleague's discretion that he threatened to fire off a disobliging memo to the Pentagon recommending Boyell's dismissal. The story leaked, with the result that Boyell's career was saved, but his refusal to assist the South African military was very much the exception to the rule.

Israeli intelligence cooperated closely with the South African National Intelligence Service, formerly known as BOSS, the Orwellian Bureau of State Security. Interestingly enough, the Israeli internal security service SHABAK maintained a permanent mission abroad in South Africa. SHABAK's talents at home ranged from cultivating informants in the occupied territories to running death squads, a fact revealed at the height of the Intifada uprising in 1988. (SHABAK agents sometimes carried out their unpleasant work disguised as foreign television crews, which put genuine crews at risk.) In South Africa, SHABAK liaised with security forces charged with similar missions in the black townships.

South African security forces, including hundreds of police officers, received training in Israel. Even the man known as the Beast of Soweto was an honored guest in Jerusalem. Brigadier "Rooi Rus" Swanepoel earned the title for his ruthless treatment of black rioters in 1976. The "Beast" had also acted as chief interrogator in the 1964 Rivonia trial, which put African National Congress leader Nelson Mandela in prison. The ANC experienced Mossad expertise in an operation reportedly designed to eliminate leaders in exile in the early

1980s. Mossad agents allegedly helped coordinate a campaign of parcel and letter bombs, the equipment for which was shipped from the United States via Israel.

In 1988, after a number of carefully planned bombings by South African agents, a spokesman for the ANC in Lusaka said, "We know the South Africans, working hand in hand with the Israelis, are exchanging opinions and ideas on how to eliminate our leadership." There was speculation on whether the name of one South African hit team, the "Z Squad," was inspired by the "Z Team" dispatched to kidnap Adolf Eichmann.

Elite special forces units, part of whose mission was to carry out assassinations, trained in Israel. In 1989, Mervyn Malan, from one of South Africa's most notable families, sought asylum in the Netherlands. He was a cousin of South Africa's defense minister, Magnus Malan. The defector had served with Special Forces Recce 5.3 in both Angola and Namibia. Malan said his unit made a practice of dressing up as members of SWAPO, the South West African People's Organization, in order to identify and eliminate SWAPO sympathizers. Recce 5.3 used phosphorus bombs, he said, on civilian villagers. Phosphorus, as Beirut doctors discovered in the 1982 invasion of Lebanon, was an insidious agent that smoldered in the skin, burning slowly through the bodies even after its victims were dead. The Israelis had used U.S.-manufactured phosphorus bombs, and Recce 5.3 may have as well. Malan said his unit's relations with Israel were very close. "From our side," Malan explained, "people went to Israel for advanced training."[9]

Such cooperation was cloaked in the rhetoric of antiterrorism. Israeli technicians built an "electrified wall" along South Africa's borders and laid a "carpet of electronic sensors." The electronic fences, radar, and mine fields looked much like those found along Israel's border with Lebanon. It is no wonder that Ariel Sharon felt very much at home there. At a cocktail party for a Texas congressman in Tel Aviv in late 1981, the then defense minister reminisced about his trip to the Angolan front with the South African army, some of whom were receiving counterinsurgency training from Israelis. Sharon was proud to have advised his South African counterparts on battlefield strategy, and had ambitious plans for increasing Israeli influence in that part of the world.

Uri Dan, one of Sharon's advisers who had also traveled to Angola, later wrote, "When I look at the South African officers, when they speak Afrikaans or English, and during operations, I imagine that soon they will be giving orders in Hebrew. Their physical appearance, their freshness and openness, their battlefield behavior, all remind me of IDF [Israel Defense Force] officers. And I never said that about the U.S. and South Vietnamese officers I met eleven years ago in Vietnam, during the war." Dan added an observation from the South African side. " 'Don't play down the effect of the IDF as an example to us as a fighting body,' said a high-ranking officer in Pretoria."

The man who had first urged the Israelis to play such an active role in South Africa's war was Henry Kissinger. After CIA covert operations in Angola were publicly exposed in 1975, Kissinger turned to Israel, requesting arms, advisers, and even troops. The troops stayed at home, but the rest was forthcoming, a "green light" from the White House smoothing the passage. Kissinger's dispassionate view of South Africa—what some might call cold-blooded—concentrated on that country as a strategic asset rather than as a society racked by racial torment. In 1969, he issued a National Security Study Memorandum ("39") ordering a National Security Council study of policy options for the region. In it, he and his staff outlined U.S. interests with regard to defense:

> Southern Africa is geographically important for the U.S. and its allies, particularly with the closing of the Suez Canal and the increased Soviet activity in the Indian Ocean. The U.S. uses overflight and landing facilities for military aircraft in . . . South Africa. There are major ship repair and logistic facilities in South Africa with a level of technical competence which cannot be duplicated elsewhere on the African continent . . . The DOD has a missile tracking station in South Africa under a classified agreement and some of the military aircraft traffic involves support of this station.

NASA also had a space-tracking facility "of major importance in South Africa." Five policy options were discussed, and the choice of Kissinger and Nixon was "option two." The premise was as follows:

> The whites are here to stay and the only way that constructive change can come about is through them. There is no hope for the blacks to gain the political rights they seek through violence, which will only lead to chaos and increased opportunities for the communists. We can, by

selective relaxation of our stance toward the white regimes, encourage some modification of their current racial and colonial policies . . . Our tangible interests form a basis for our contacts in the region, and these can be maintained at an acceptable political cost . . . We would maintain public opposition to racial repression but relax political isolation and economic restrictions on the white states . . .[10]

With regard to military considerations, "option two" recommended: "Enforce arms embargo against South Africa but with liberal treatment of equipment which could serve either military or civilian purposes." It was a generous loophole. Kissinger was more than willing to ship arms and fuel to the South African Defense Forces (through a $14 million CIA program) to carry out the invasion of Angola.

The same year that Kissinger turned to Israel to discreetly assist South Africa, the Pretoria government turned to Israel to facilitate covert operations in the United States. In June 1975, South African Interior Minister Connie Mulder secretly flew to Israel. With him were the two top officials of the Information Ministry, Eshel Rhoodie and Les de Villiers. The three senior officials met with Prime Minister Yitzhak Rabin, Defense Minister Shimon Peres, and six other cabinet ministers. The visitors from South Africa received silver statuettes of David and Goliath in battle, which moved the interior minister to remark, "This I will always treasure, because it symbolizes not only Israel's struggle for survival but our own fight against the world."

The fight at that moment required putting a multimillion dollar South African slush fund to good use in what Eshel Rhoodie called a "psychological war." The men from Pretoria needed Israeli advice on the sensitive matter of selecting a very capable lobbyist in the United States. At the high-level meeting, the Israelis recommended a New York public relations man called Sydney Baron. Baron was adept at pressing the causes of difficult clients such as Taiwan and accepted South Africa as a client for $500,000 per year. Baron's skills included funneling foreign money into American political campaigns, which is precisely what he did for the South Africans. Baron laundered a $200,000 contribution from the South African government into the 1976 Senate race of S.I. Hayakawa, a California Republican running against a particularly vocal critic of apartheid, Democrat John Tunney. Tunney had blocked covert funds from continuing to reach South Africa for the Angola campaign. Baron put his skills to work again in a key 1978 race in Iowa, where Sen. Dick Clark was running for reelection. Clark had given his name to the amendment barring the CIA from operating in Angola. Clark's victorious opponent, Republican Roger Jepsen, was the beneficiary of $250,000 of South African government money. By 1980, the South Africans had enhanced their lobbying power by hiring John Sears, former campaign manager for Ronald Reagan. Connie Mulder had met the new president while Reagan was governor of California, and according to Mulder associate Les de Villiers, Reagan "showed great understanding for the need to have closer relations between South Africa and the United States."[11]

As well as recommending Sydney Baron as the right "lobbyist" for South Africa, the Rabin government recruited an Israeli arms dealer, Arnon Milchan, to launder cash. This money was used to "lobby" in Europe, as well as to purchase influential publications such as *West Africa* magazine in London. Milchan admitted his laundering activities, including one occasion when he deposited sixty-six thousand pounds in a Swiss bank. The ensuing "Muldergate" scandal in South Africa resulted in charges of financial irregularities to the tune of $100 million. (Nearly $4 million had poured into Gerald Ford's campaign in 1976.) But while the lobbying operation was still under wraps, known only to a select group of South Africans, Israelis, and their agents, the Rabin government extended a coveted invitation to visit Israel to a very controversial guest, South African Prime Minister John Vorster.

When Vorster laid a wreath at Yad Vashem, Israel's memorial to the Holocaust, it made some observers exceptionally queasy. Vorster had served nearly two years in jail during World War II for his Nazi collaboration. This leader of an extreme racist regime had never acknowledged that the Nazi doctrine was in any way distasteful. He had recently been warmly received by Paraguay's president, Gen. Alfredo Stroessner, a notorious admirer of the Nazis. At a state banquet in Vorster's honor, Prime Minister Rabin said, "We here follow with sympathy your own historic efforts to achieve detente on your continent, to build bridges for a secure and better future, to create coexistence that will guarantee a prosperous atmosphere of cooperation for all the African peoples, without outside interference and threat."

Vorster assiduously built bridges during his four-day tour, visiting military installations and arms manufacturers such as Israel Aircraft Industries. The old Nazi sympathizer came away with bilateral agreements for commercial, military, and nuclear cooperation that would become the basis for future relations between the two countries. There was talk of a joint cabinet-level group and a steering group to oversee the trade. Thus, when the United Nations made mandatory the resolution that all states should cease shipments of military goods to South Africa in 1977, Israeli Foreign Minister Moshe Dayan could state with confidence that Israel intended to ignore the resolution. The Israeli Ministry of Defense ignored it with a vengeance.

When questions were raised in the Israeli parliament in 1976 about "hundreds" of Israelis from the IDF participating in joint training with the South African military, Defense Minister Peres denied the charge. *The Economist* later estimated that as of 1981, there were two hundred Israeli military advisers in South Africa. The elite South African Reconnaissance Commandos owed a great deal to their Israeli trainers. The Israeli Labor Party daily reported, "It is a clear and open secret known to everybody that in [South African] army camps one can find Israeli officers in not insignificant numbers who are busy teaching white soldiers to fight black terrorists with methods imported from Israel."[12]

Israeli hardware and components arrived in plentiful supply. Gabriel sea-to-sea missiles, Reshef class boats, coastal radar stations, night vision and communications equipment poured in. Joint projects ranged from the Barak naval missile to nuclear submarines. The Israeli Galil, manufactured under license, became the standard weapon of South Africa's ground forces in 1981. American technology and components were in evidence among the plethora of arms. IAI reconnaissance drones, discovered when one of the pilotless craft (complete with IAI identification number) was shot down over Mozambique, had been copied from American blueprints. The research and development costs and the costs of the components were paid for by the United States. American-manufactured equipment, including four hundred M-113A1 armored personnel carriers and 106-mm recoilless rifles, landed in South Africa via Israel. Anyone who believed that Washington was enforcing military sanctions against South Africa failed to appreciate the energetic role of Israel as entrepot. With such dealings in mind, the comment on Israel's South African alliance by President Chaim Herzog in 1988 was particularly resonant: "Israel need not apologize for its relations with South Africa," he said, "any more than the U.S. should feel compelled to do so for its ties with Israel."

The CIA's concern that South Africa should not suffer from any crippling deficiencies in its arsenal on account of the arms embargo was amply demonstrated in the case of a talented and eccentric weapons designer named Jerry Bull. This Canadian-American's engineering genius so impressed the Israelis and South Africans that he was drawn into the center of their secret trade, with the blessings and encouragement of the CIA. Bull had designed a superb piece of artillery, a 155-mm howitzer, which could deliver a shell farther than the Soviet-made Katyusha rockets that paralyzed South African forces for three weeks during the Angola War. Israel had tested the weapon on the Syrian front during the Yom Kippur War and found its fifty-kilometer range gave it a tremendous advantage on the Golan Heights. Bull came to the attention of the Israelis in 1972, when Yitzhak Rabin, then Israeli ambassador in Washington, went to Kissinger with a request for a superior 155-mm shell. Kissinger reportedly recommended Bull's company, the Space Research Corporation, and the sale of several thousand shells was arranged between the U.S. and Israeli governments.

At the time, Bull was an affable forty-four-year-old maverick, obsessed with "aeroballistics" and the possibility of building a "space gun" that could launch satellites or "hit Mexico" from the little kingdom he had purchased on the Vermont-Canadian border. He ate too much ice cream and was ever in debt. As one financial associate and close friend described him, "Jerry was a great engineer. He didn't understand a thing about politics."[13] But his peculiar talents so excited the Israelis that the ubiquitous Shaul Eisenberg befriended Bull, with a view to purchasing the Bull operation. Bull was a frequent guest at Eisenberg's sumptuous residence in Tel Aviv. Eisenberg saw the possibilities of marketing Dr. Bull, even if the Uzi of the howitzer world would not sell his firm. The Israeli arms dealer saw to it that the South Africans were invited to Israel to witness this splendid artillery that had helped win the '73 war. After an impressive display in the Negev Desert, the gentlemen from ARMSCOR wanted Bull howitzers of their own.

As Space Research was a U.S. firm, the South Africans turned to their friends at the CIA station in Pretoria. Both the CIA and the South African Bureau of State Security were preoccupied with events in Angola, and their relationship was exceedingly close. As the CIA's former chief of the Angola task force noted, "CIA officers liked the South Africans, who tended to be bluff, aggressive men without guile.

They admired South African efficiency." Together, as CIA man John Stockwell recalled, they ran operations. On one occasion, "Two South African C-130 airplanes, similar to those used by the Israelis in their raid on Entebbe, feathered into Ndjili Airport [Angola] at night to meet a CIA C-141 flight and whisk its load of arms down to Silva Porto. CIA officers and BOSS representatives met the plane at Ndjili and jointly supervised the transloading . . . CIA officers clamored for permission to visit South African bases in South West Africa [Namibia]. On two occasions the BOSS director visited Washington and held secret meetings with [CIA Africa Division Chief] Jim Potts. On another he met with the CIA station chief in Paris . . . The CIA has traditionally sympathized with South Africa and enjoyed its close liaison with BOSS."

The liaison was forged, as the CIA's former Angola task force chief saw it, by "a violent antipathy toward communism." The CIA and BOSS had shared memories of the Congo rebellion, when they worked hand in hand to build a mercenary force (including Miami Cubans) to suppress the rebels and install a friendly dictator. The agency's Africa Division chief "viewed South Africa pragmatically, as a friend of the CIA and a potential ally of the United States . . ." There were no qualms about apartheid. "Eventually Potts concluded," said Stockwell, "that blacks were 'irrational' on the subject of South Africa. This term caught on. It even crept into the cable traffic . . ." As the CIA and South African intelligence were so compatible, it is not surprising that the CIA station chief's reaction to the South African request for the sophisticated extended-range howitzer shells produced by Jerry Bull was to do everything in his power to expedite it. When the request reached Washington in October 1975, the Africa Division chief was equally enthusiastic. The CIA was having logistical problems sending shiploads of arms through congested African ports to Angola and was longing to use South African facilities at Walvis Bay in what is now Namibia. An exchange of shells and a transshipment base suited the CIA very well. But when the illegal shipment of arms to South Africa was proposed at a high-level interagency working group meeting, one opposing voice spoiled the plan. The deputy assistant secretary of state for African affairs, Ed Mulcahy, threatened to resign over such a shipment. It was clear to those present that he would not hesitate to air his views in public, which would have jeopardized the entire covert war.

The CIA's reaction to Ambassador Mulcahy was instructive. Potts of the Africa Division sent an aide to the CIA library to peruse the sanctions law. In triumph, Potts returned to the next working group meeting with the text and announced that it really was not binding. As Angola Task Force Chief John Stockwell recalled, Potts announced, "You see, gentlemen, it isn't a law. It's a policy decision made under the Kennedy administration. Times have now changed and, given our present problems, we should have no difficulty modifying this policy." Mulcahy sucked his pipe and held firm. The CIA men, however, were unbowed. They would simply enlist the Israelis, who had hoped to market the artillery to South Africa in the first place.

At a Space Research corporate gathering in Rio de Janeiro, Gerald Bull assured his colleagues that the CIA fully approved of South Africa's ARMSCOR acquiring the company howitzer, even though a raft of laws, including U.S. and UN embargoes and the Arms Export Control Act, would be broken. The agency, he said, would smooth the way, should there be any difficulties in Washington. That evening the group was entertained by a Brazilian prostitute whose name, Elana, was adopted for the operation. The plan, as mapped out in Rio and at a later meeting with South African officials in Vermont, was that fifty thousand artillery shell forgings would be shipped to Israel and unspecified NATO countries. Space Research, acting as "agent" for its clients, would receive permission to manufacture the shells at the U.S. Army Ammunition Plant in Scranton, Pennsylvania. This in itself was against the law, as laid down by the Army Material Command. Private contractors were barred from using this U.S. government facility. In this case, however, the U.S. Army Armament Command approved the request the same day, and final authorization from the Pentagon came four days later. The man credited with this miracle of bureaucratic efficiency was General Howard Fish, who had sat quietly in the high-level working group meeting while the CIA's Africa Division chief had argued so passionately for the right to ship arms to South Africa.

In the contract with the Chamberlaine Manufacturing Corporation, running the Army's Scranton plant, Israel was listed as "assignee," meaning it would honor the contract if Bull's firm for some reason defaulted. Israel Military Industries was subcontracted to supply South Africa's ARMSCOR with the propellants for the shells, which were to be shipped to Tel Aviv before following the well-worn trail to South Africa. IMI supplied three hundred propellants before the newly arrived Carter administration, still intoxicated with campaign promises about human rights, informed the Israeli government that its brisk trade with South Africa might endanger passage of Israel's U.S. aid package. The Rabin government was already in serious trouble, with revelations of bribery, corruption, the suicide of a cabinet member, and the little matter of Mrs. Rabin's illegal U.S. bank account. Meanwhile, Bull's first batch of seven hundred and fifty shells was waiting to be shipped from Canada to Israel, and the engineer expressed his frustration in a memo to his partners: "Israel is without an effective government . . . it is clear that political chaos and turmoil have spread from Washington. While the Israelis hesitate, the shells continue to await shipment from Canada." The besieged Israeli cabinet told IMI that Israeli ships could not be used to move the goods. The venue had to be changed.

The ever-pliant island of Antigua filled the bill, just as it would serve so well over a decade later as the transit point for Israeli arms shipped from IMI to the Medellin cartel. When Gerald Bull approached the Bird family (this time Prime Minister V.C. Bird), he offered to create an army for the island in exchange for a suitable test site. This was the same "army" that IMI claimed to be equipping years later at the request of the nonexistent defense minister. As far as Bull was concerned, the army was his personal security force to guard his compound at Crab's Point, a setting that could have inspired an Ian Fleming novel. In 1977, both Israeli and South African military men converged at the isolated spot for an operational test of the newly manufactured artillery shells. That May, a German-registered ship, owned by a New York company called South African Marine and controlled by the government in Pretoria, sailed from New York to Antigua and on to South Africa. The Tugelaland was carrying thirty-six containers of Jerry Bull's shells, forged by the U.S. Army.

To go with the extended-range shells, the South Africans needed a properly bored gun barrel. The problem was easily solved when Jerry Bull borrowed one from the U.S. Army's Aberdeen Proving Grounds in Maryland. Space Research trucks arrived, loaded the cannon, and drove it to the Canadian side of Bull's Vermont statelet, where it was promptly packed and shipped to Antigua so as not to miss the Tugelaland. The army had authorized the loan, and when in 1980 it was told that the artillery piece was "in possession of the Antigua Government Defense Forces"—a rather grand title for the country's ninety-man force—paperwork meandered through the Pentagon until the case was closed in 1981 because "the property in Antigua is obviously not available for disposal at this time." As the "property" had been in South Africa for four years, it obviously was not "available" ever.

All in all, according to a Senate report in March 1982, Space Research had shifted "approximately 60,000 155-mm extended range artillery shells, at least four 155-mm guns including three advanced prototypes, technology and technical assistance to establish its [South Africa's] own 155-mm gun and ammunition manufacturing and testing capability, and other military equipment. Almost all of the equipment sent to South Africa was acquired in the US, mainly from US Army plants and supply stocks." This, protested the Senate subcommittee, "made major contributions" to South Africa's "regional military capabilities." The investigators recommended that "the House and Senate Intelligence Committees should investigate the possible roles of employees, agents and contacts of the CIA in efforts to evade the US arms embargo against South Africa during the Angola conflict, and in the development of the SRC (Space Research)/South Africa relationship." There was no investigation.

The Justice Department did bring a criminal case against Bull in 1980–81. But as the Senate report noted, "Of particular concern to government lawyers in a potential trial was the appearance of possible US government authorization of SRC shipments to South Africa. The upshot was Justice's acceptance of a plea bargain in which only the two top officers of SRC paid a price—four and four-and-a-half months at a minimum security prison—for a $19 million illegal arms deal . . . At the CIA, a preoccupation with the immediate bureaucratic need to move arms efficiently into Angola through South Africa appeared to supersede the larger US policy of enforcing the arms embargo against South Africa."

Jerry Bull survived the brief flurry of concern over his business and continued working on innovative weapons systems until finally his close relationship with Israel soured. Bull had been flirting with the military command in Baghdad, who were naturally anxious to add the Bull capability to their arsenal. Bull intended to sell the Iraqi regime the gun of his dreams, far more powerful than the howitzer that had enabled the Israelis to shell Damascus in 1973. The Bull "space gun" would finally have a client in Baghdad and, to the horror of Israel's Ministry of Defense, could target Tel Aviv. According to one of Bull's closest friends, the Israelis contacted the ambitious engineer and made their position absolutely clear: if he chose to go through with the Iraq sale, they would kill him. "He was warned orally by a representative of the Israeli government," said the friend. "He was warned by Israel in writing, as well as on the phone." Bull's gun was not just another piece of hardware for Saddam Hussein's arsenal. "What Jerry Bull was playing with," said his former associate, "was a change in the balance of power in the Middle East. He was playing, literally, with dynamite."[14]

Preoccupied with realizing his life's ambition, Jerry Bull made the fatal error of ignoring Israel's threats. "It was sheer arrogance," observed Bull's friend. "He only cared about one thing—being right about that gun. The buyer could have been the Nazis or Martians and he would have sold it to them. Jerry was a jerk with a mission. He was the Einstein of his field and he just wanted to be proved right." In the fall of 1990, as he walked to the door of his home in Brussels, Jerry Bull was murdered with a burst of bullets fired into his back and head.

At the same time that the Justice Department was struggling with the complications of CIA involvement in the Bull case, some Israeli officials were strident in expressing a vision of Israel as surrogate for the United States in the transfer of arms. Yaakov Meridor, minister of economic coordination in the Begin government, made his views plain at a time when the Reagan administration was just coming to appreciate the value of its ally. As the minister put it, "We are going to ask you, the United States government . . . Don't compete with us in South Africa . . . Let us do it. I even use the expression, 'You sell the ammunition and equipment by proxy.' Israel will be your proxy."

There was the occasional irritant in an otherwise amicable relationship. Among thousands of documents passed to Israel by LAKAM spy Jonathan Pollard were classified U.S. intelligence reports detailing American covert operations in South Africa, which the CIA had neglected to coordinate with South African intelligence. In the past, the agency had much preferred to spy with, rather than on, South Africa, but in 1974, the station in Pretoria had been expanded to accommodate personnel spying on the South African nuclear program. When BOSS discovered the deceit, the CIA agents involved were expelled, while the old hands settled comfortably back into the cozy relationship with BOSS they had always enjoyed.

Pollard opened an old wound when he handed over raw reports to

Tel Aviv that gave the South African government the means to identify agents and operatives, therefore endangering their lives. The CIA believed that "much of what reached Jerusalem was promptly handed over to Pretoria." One statement that profoundly influenced the court to mete out a life sentence to Mr. Pollard was Defense Secretary Caspar Weinberger's contention that Pollard had severely damaged U.S. intelligence. One of the egregious examples of this was, according to Weinberger's affidavit, the exposure of CIA men in South Africa. Regardless of how close the American and Israeli intelligence agencies were, each ran its own spies: the CIA and DIA (Defense Intelligence Agency) men based at the American Embassy in Israel were offset by Mossad's "Al" network, spying in Washington, and LAKAM's U.S. government operatives like Mr. Pollard.[15]

If Pollard's betrayal caused some enmity among the intelligence agencies, there were also the occasional bad feelings generated in the arms community when their activities were exposed. U.S. Customs, following the letter of the law on sanctions, stepped into the fray. (Customs also stepped into the Iran trade, even though the White House was breaking its own arms embargo.) In 1988, Customs ran a sting operation to catch arms merchants in the act of shipping gyroscopes for missile guidance systems to South Africa. Operation "Exodus" implicated two South Africans, one American arms dealer (and former Navy SEAL), and Israel Aircraft Industries. It was a revealing example of the mechanics of using Israel as a go-between.

Seymour Behrmann was a South African lawyer who, when he was not shipping gyroscopes, traded diamonds in Canada. According to a Customs affidavit, Behrmann flew to Israel to establish a front company that would purchase the missile guidance system components from the United States. Kivun Communications and Guidance Systems Ltd. was also set up to serve as the means to transfer South African funds. To save time and trouble, Behrmann told the Customs agents (posing as American arms dealers) that he hoped the goods could "just be delivered directly to the South African Embassy in Tel Aviv." The purchase order specified that Kivun would receive thirty-five gyroscopes from the Northrop Corporation at a total cost of $293,720. Behrmann sent the Customs agents in disguise a fake end-user certificate, promising that Kivun's order was intended only for use in Israel. According to the Customs document, Behrmann stated that in August 1988 he met with officials from IAI who "would help

South Africa obtain the gyroscopes," adding that "the price would be very high." IAI later contacted Northrop directly for gyroscopes which matched the South African specifications. Northrop informed Customs.

Although the independent agents in the ring were indicted, IAI was well beyond the reach of a federal grand jury. The sting recalls the time independent agents, including a retired Israeli general and a former Israeli military intelligence agent, were rounded up for attempting to ship arms to Tehran, at a time when the U.S. government and the Israeli government were both deeply involved in shipping arms themselves. The explanation for this kind of confusion may be either that Customs was simply doing its job without knowledge of what other agencies (or indeed the Israeli government) were involved in, or that the presence of independent dealers in the field, potential "loose cannons," was interfering with the orderly conduct of covert business.

Israeli corporations that serviced the South African military were also engaged in the defense business in the United States. This generally went unnoticed, until the defense electronics firm Tadiran decided to settle in Tallahassee, Florida. The City Commission was delighted that the Israeli company, in partnership with General Dynamics, would choose Tallahassee as the place to manufacture military radios for the U.S. Army. Tadiran was swayed by the fact that moving into the industrial park there gave the firm $4 million in tax subsidies. The problem was that Tallahassee had passed an ordinance making it illegal for the city to put money into a company doing business with South Africa. Local antiapartheid sentiments were strong, and Tadiran was forced into the awkward position of denying any dealings with Pretoria. Antiapartheid groups doggedly pursued the matter, until the Commission was obliged to say that if Tadiran had lied, the spanking-new building in the industrial park and the $4 million subsidy would no longer be available.

The Tallahassee city auditor, Ricardo Fernandez, began patiently dialing the number listed for Tadiran in Johannesburg. In his report to the city he noted, "Tadiran Electronics in Johannesburg has refused to furnish any information on their company" either to Mr. Fernandez or "to the Foreign Commercial Service of the United States Department of Commerce, who made such inquiries at our request." When a Foreign Commercial Service official paid a call on Tadiran at its Morkel Road address in Johannesburg, he found a large fenced villa and an unfriendly German shepherd. Tadiran officials gave the city auditor a host of different dates on which the company supposedly cut its South Africa ties, ranging from 1982 to 1987. They compromised with 1986. The Tadiran spokesman in Jerusalem, David Yechieli, said in the spring of 1989 that the subsidiary had been closed down seven or eight years before. When the *Jerusalem Post* queried him on the name of the subsidiary, Yechieli said, "Funny, I can't remember, and I was chairman of the board."

When front-page reports in Jerusalem said that the Tallahassee investigation put Tadiran's (and General Dynamics') multibillion dollar contract with the U.S. Army in jeopardy, Defense Minister Rabin thought it significant enough to raise with Pentagon officials, who were anxious that the deal should go through. Florida investigators had found that Tadiran's parent company, Koor Industries Ltd., had received substantial loans from South African banks. Koor was owned by the Histadrut, the Israeli labor federation, and had at least one subsidiary, Iskoor, with a 49 percent South African government share. The South African component began going through a curious metamorphosis in 1988. Iskoor, the South African government Iron and Steel Corporation, turned over its 49 percent share to Asoma, based in Switzerland and the Netherlands as well as in South Africa. Asoma then emerged as an American multinational based in the U.S. The shell game continued when the Israeli-South African company Iskoor became Iskoor/Helfur Ltd., "jointly owned by Koor and the multinational American company Asoma Ltd. which imports some 35% of the 700 tons of steel Israel exports annually." At the end of the day, an American company was shipping South African steel to Israel. Board meetings were still held in South Africa, but on paper the South African government ownership had been erased.

Meanwhile, Congressman Ron Dellums put the matter to Secretary of Defense Dick Cheney, citing the history of South African connections of Tadiran and its parent company Koor. He asked if it was "appropriate for the DOD to be awarding contracts to a company which was instrumental in developing South Africa's sophisticated military surveillance capability." Dellums, on the House Armed Services Committee, went on to say, "Koor's heavy involvement with the South African arms industry, and its apparent continued dealings with the South African military, raises ethical questions about dealing with a Koor subsidiary."

In Tallahassee, Tadiran hired the son of Senator (now Gov.) Lawton Chiles to lobby on its behalf. The industrial park lease and the $4 million subsidy were subsequently approved by the City Commission by a vote of 3–2. The lease now carried the clause that Tadiran should comply with the city's antiapartheid policy. As of the summer of 1989, the matter was closed.

Congressman Dellums was one of the House members who would later ask more questions about the cooperation between Israel and South Africa to develop medium-range nuclear weapons. But there always seemed to be political considerations that somehow were more pressing than the exposure of the hard facts of this military alliance, which by law endangered Israel's aid package. It was thought, as 1989 drew to a close, that open hearings on the missiles might upset relations between Washington and Jerusalem. As one pro-Israel lobbyist told *Washington Jewish Week*, "They don't want to beat up on Israel right now. It's a delicate state of the peace negotiations between [Secretary of State] Baker and Shamir."

Likewise, the apparent sweeping changes in South Africa the following year, with the legalization of the African National Congress and the easing of apartheid regulations, took precedence over the secret dealings of the South African military. But factional fighting inside the ANC and dramatic political violence in the black townships (which claimed seven hundred and fifty lives in just two months) left the situation inside South Africa tense and unstable. ANC leader Nelson Mandela blamed the epidemic of murder in the townships in part on elements of the South African security services who wished to sabotage the efforts of South African President Frederik de Klerk to make constitutional changes and negotiate with the ANC.

In September 1990, a massacre on a commuter train traveling from Johannesburg to Soweto forced de Klerk to admit that a "third force" seemed to be orchestrating some of the violence.[16] Six black men ran through the train hacking their victims with machetes and throwing commuters out of the moving train. The attackers, who killed twenty-six innocent civilians and wounded a hundred more, never said a word. Mandela suggested that the men may have been imported from neighboring Mozambique, where the lingua franca is Portuguese. He believed the tactics were reminiscent of those used by rebels from the Mozambique National Resistance, or Renamo, which had been backed by the South African government in its efforts to destabilize Mozambique. That country's president, Joaquim Chissano, said that some Mozambicans had been employed in the past by the South African Defense Forces. "There were brigades, special brigades [training] there for the destabilization purpose, and these people were not thrown out [of South Africa]."

Even if the tensions diminished and there were to be a smooth transition from apartheid to majority rule, with Nelson Mandela as South Africa's new president, there would still be the delicate question of the nuclear arsenal. Perhaps the white regime would gracefully hand over control of South Africa's H-bomb to Mandela. Perhaps not. It was a question that someone inside the South African Defense Forces was no doubt pondering as the politicians talked of dramatic change.

As for the Israeli military alliance with South Africa, it had thrived with blessings from Washington because of the overriding obsession with an East-West balance in the Cold War. By 1990, the "Soviet threat" was no longer an issue, in southern Africa or anywhere else. The excuse of arming South Africa to do battle with Soviet surrogates had vanished from the lexicon. Israel's preeminent role in the military trade had also been a function of South Africa's pariah status over three decades. Relaxation of apartheid made it likely that American sanctions would be gradually dismantled and that direct trade would resume. It was during the time when no one could or would be seen doing business with South Africa that Israel had been such a convenient way station.

With the focus of U.S. foreign policy shifting dramatically to the Middle East, as four hundred thousand U.S. troops took up positions in the Saudi desert, both Israel and the United States grew utterly preoccupied with the "post-Cold War" threat—Iraqi President Saddam Hussein. In order to understand the effect on the U.S.-Israeli alliance of Iraqi tanks steaming into Kuwait City, one has to go back a decade to the twilight of the Carter years. It was Iran then that cast a dark shadow over the Middle East and prompted the rash of yellow ribbons and late-night sessions at the White House. Iraq was the enemy of our enemy, and thus, a convenient friend. When Saddam Hussein launched his forces against the Ayatollah in 1980, no one at the White House lifted a finger to stop him. Our allies, Saudi Arabia and Kuwait, were ready and willing to bankroll the Iraqi adventure, and U.S. intelligence happily passed along satellite photos and reports on the Iranians' order of battle.

Israel, meanwhile, was arming Iran, while American hostages were still under the boot of the Ayatollah's revolutionary guards. It was an awkward moment in U.S.-Israeli relations. But then, Jimmy Carter had his ups and downs with Jerusalem.

12. Proxy Wars

"IF I GET BACK IN," said President Carter in the spring of 1980, "I'm going to fuck the Jews."

The occasion was a meeting in the upstairs family quarters of the White House between the president and some of his senior political advisers to discuss his reelection efforts. Unusually for a sitting president, Carter was facing the rough-and-tumble of a serious challenge for the Democratic nomination from Sen. Edward Kennedy. The going was especially bitter in New York, where the president had to deal not only with the senator, but also with the abrasive mayor, Ed Koch. Koch spoke for the electorally vital Jewish voting bloc in New York, which had come to regard the administration as treacherously disposed in favor of the Palestinians. The year before, for example, news of a meeting between UN Ambassador Andrew Young and the PLO representative at the world body had sparked outrage among Israel's friends in the U.S., as Mossad had intended. The Israeli intelligence agency had learned through a phone tap that the meeting was planned. Rather than immediately protesting to Washington, which would have undoubtedly resulted in the meeting's cancellation, the Israelis let it go ahead, bugged the proceedings, and then leaked the news to the press. Young, a friend and long-standing supporter of the president, had to resign.

Now, in March 1980, Carter had discovered that the Israelis were once again covertly intervening in the U.S. The National Security

Agency had intercepted conversations between Koch and Menachem Begin's office in Jerusalem. The Israeli prime minister was advising the American mayor on the best means of defeating the president of the United States. Given this intelligence, it was hardly surprising that Carter bitterly vowed revenge.

Israeli hostility to Carter went back to the early days of his administration, when he had given indications that he might actually be serious about pressuring Israel to make concessions to the Palestinians living under its occupation, and had even made reference to a Palestinian "homeland."

The Israelis were kept well informed of such threatening initiatives from their own highly placed sources. In March 1977, for example, Henry Kissinger invited the Israeli ambassador, Simcha Dinitz, to dinner. According to an Israeli report of the conversation, Kissinger took his guest aside and stated that as a Jew he could not go on if he did not share certain information. Carter, he said, had told President Sadat of Egypt that the U.S. would get Israel to retreat to the 1967 borders and to agree to the establishment of a Palestinian state. Dinitz asked Kissinger what he thought Israel should do to counter this threat. "Organize forces in the U.S. and Israel," counseled the man who had been secretary of state less than two months before. "Don't appear too hawkish, but be determined. The trick is to fight Carter's plans in a resolute manner."[1]

In October of that same year, the administration displayed a foolhardy insensitivity to Israeli concerns by issuing a joint statement with the Soviet Union on the Middle East. Clearly, it was taking the former governor of Georgia a little time to understand some of the fundamentals of the U.S.-Israeli relationship. Moshe Dayan, who had deserted his Labor colleagues to become foreign minister in Menachem Begin's Likud government, was quick to enlighten the American president. A few days after the U.S.-Soviet announcement, the one-eyed ex-general demanded that Carter state publicly that he stood by all secret agreements reached with Israel by previous administrations. If this was not done, said Dayan, Israel would consider making them public, which would certainly have been embarrassing all around. Carter's naive notions about a comprehensive Middle East settlement swiftly fell apart and Begin's initial judgment on the president—"cream puff"—seemed vindicated.

On the other hand, the following year Carter had an opportunity to remind the Israelis in his turn of some other realities of the relationship, such as the fact that Israeli wars require U.S. endorsement. In March 1978, in response to a Palestinian attack inside Israel that killed thirty-seven civilians, the IDF lunged into southern Lebanon in what the Israelis called "Operation Litani." An estimated two thousand people were killed, most of them civilians.

Carter insisted that the Israelis obey a United Nations resolution calling on them to withdraw. Though they eventually agreed to do so, the IDF continued to dally in its new holdings south of the Litani River in Lebanon. The U.S. government reiterated its demand. Finally, the Israelis reported that all their forces and equipment were back across the border. Carter knew from satellite photographs that they were lying, and sent Begin a letter stating that unless Israel did what it had promised within twenty-four hours, he would move to cut off all aid.

Richard Viets, the deputy chief of mission at the U.S. Embassy in Tel Aviv, had the task of delivering the letter directly to Begin. He found the premier at home. "As he read the letter, very slowly, he went white," recalls Viets. "Then he went over to the sideboard and poured two large whiskeys. He took a gulp and then said, 'Mr. Viets, you win.'"

Begin had been uncomfortably reminded for a moment that Carter could be tough when he wanted. Despite his carefully burnished historical image as a paragon of human rights, the Georgian developed quite a taste for gritty realpolitik while in office. His was the White House that supported the rearming of the genocidal Khmer Rouge following their ejection from Cambodia by the Vietnamese; Ferdinand Marcos found him as understanding as any other president. In other words, it was business as usual in the Third World, which meant plenty of business for Israel.

As we have seen, when the Congress cut off military aid to Guatemala in 1977 and to the tottering dictatorship of Anastasio Somoza in 1979, Israel was on hand to take up the slack. Joint operations in Uganda and Angola continued as before, and Israel's South African trade was in no way incommoded.

There is an instructive parallel to the state of relations under Carter in the history of the Eisenhower administration. Eisenhower, like Carter, was perceived as unfriendly by the Israeli leaders in his policies toward them. Like Carter, he forced them to withdraw from a country they had invaded and occupied. Yet, under both administrations, the covert intelligence connection was carried on more or less independently of public diplomatic contretemps. This is not to say that either side took the public differences lightly, and in Carter's case, at least, the Israelis came to feel that his Middle Eastern policies were positively dangerous.

Israeli enmity toward Carter was not assuaged by the Camp David agreement of 1978, his one foreign policy triumph. It was hardly a bad deal for Israel, which was happy to have peace with Egypt, thereby splitting the Egyptians off from the rest of the Arab world, even at the price of giving back the Sinai Desert. On the other hand, the Israelis had no intention of giving up the West Bank. They got their way at Camp David, because the agreement (amply lubricated by promises of aid) separated the question of a deal for the Palestinian inhabitants of the West Bank from the issue of peace between Egypt and Israel. The cost of Carter's heroic but expensive exercise in peacemaking was mordantly summarized by former Undersecretary of State George Ball: "We bought the sands of the Sinai for an exorbitant price from Israel [$3.2 billion in U.S. aid], then paid Egypt a large price [$1.8 billion in U.S. aid] to take them back."[2]

Unfortunately for Carter, the triumph of Camp David was soon followed by the debacle of Iran. The reinstallation of the Shah by the CIA in 1953 and his loyal adherence to U.S. interests over the following quarter of a century had blinded the Americans to any bad news about their protege. The Israelis, who had reaped great rewards from their quasi-covert friendship with the last of the Pahlevis, were hardly more perceptive. It is true that Uri Lubrani, the Israeli representative in Tehran from 1976 to 1978, who had previously cast a long shadow over Ethiopia and Uganda, had forecast a year before the fall that the Shah was in deep trouble. Nevertheless, when the final collapse came the Israeli Mission in Tehran found itself stranded and had to evacuate through the good offices of the Americans.

The triumph of the Ayatollah Khomeini over the Shah, and, by extension, the Americans, was not the only reason that Jimmy Carter was not reelected in 1980. Nevertheless, the public humiliation for the United States in having its diplomats held hostage after the storming of its Tehran embassy in October 1979 powerfully reinforced a feeling in the American public that the country was going soft under a soft leader. Despite the fact that Carter had continually raised the defense budget, he was accused of allowing America's defenses to decay (the

Committee on the Present Danger, which had done so much to bring the Israeli and U.S. defense lobbies together, was especially active in this campaign). He was taunted with having allowed the CIA's covert action capabilities to wither away, and with having fired no fewer than eight hundred agency personnel. This accusation was also unfair; the total number of employees dismissed from the CIA during the Carter regime came to precisely eighteen.

Carter's most dramatic attempt to extricate himself from the Tehran hostage nightmare certainly showed that he was prepared to go to considerable lengths to shake off the "wimp" image. The hostage rescue mission of April 24–25, 1980, was to have been Entebbe on a grand scale. Indeed, the chairman of the U.S. Joint Chiefs of Staff went to consult with the Israeli chief of staff beforehand, but despite such expert advice the mission was an abysmal failure.

While overt diplomatic efforts to free the captives continued, the administration had not given up on clandestine maneuvers, which was why the White House became involved in a process that was to cost a million lives and draw the U.S.-Israeli covert relationship into new and dangerous paths in the Middle East.

One of the Iranians' many gripes against the U.S. was that arms ordered and paid for under the Shah were being withheld, pending the resolution of claims by American companies against Tehran. Given that the Shah's extravagance had created a military machine heavily dependent on American spare parts and ammunition, the cutoff of such supplies obviously placed Iran in an extremely vulnerable position. A serious military threat from outside would in all likelihood make Iran's leaders anxious to improve relations with its former arms supplier. The thought was not lost on the administration.

On September 22, 1980, Saddam Hussein launched his army across the border into Iran. Saddam was under the illusion that, thanks to the revolution, Iranian defenses were in sufficient chaos for him to be able to conquer territory in a quick and painless victory. It was one of his grosser miscalculations, but it was not one that he had arrived at unaided.

The Iraqi leader had not kept his plans to himself. At a meeting in Baghdad four months before he attacked, Saddam told King Hussein of Jordan and the Crown Prince of Kuwait what he had in mind. Given their nightmare that Khomeini might export his revolutionary fundamentalism across the Arab world, the two leaders were enthusiastic about the scheme. In August, Saddam went to Riyadh to meet with King Khalid of Saudi Arabi to secure Saudi endorsement and commitments of financial support for the war. Khalid, according to one Saudi source, gave Saddam three kisses on departure. One was to signify his personal regard for the Iraqi leader (already renowned for his brutality and ruthlessness); the second was to denote the Saudi monarch's brotherly love for Iraq; and the third was in honor of the forthcoming campaign against the hated Khomeini.

The Saudis were cautious enough not to have backed the coming crusade without first checking with Washington. Saudi reports suggest that Washington, in the form of National Security Adviser Zbigniew Brzezinski, was enthusiastic. At the same time Ardeshir Zahedi, the Shah's former ambassador in Washington, was also in close touch with the Iraqis (there were several prominent officials from the old regime in Baghdad at the time). As Brzezinski's deputy for Iranian matters, Gary Sick, later recalled, Brzezinski thought that "Iran should be punished from all sides. He made public statements to the effect that he would not mind an Iraqi move against Iran." But the U.S. did more than simply encourage Saddam to start his war. According to Saudi and United Nations sources, the Iraqis received U.S. intelligence data transmitted by way of the Saudis about the wretched state of Iran's defenses. According to Aboulhassan Bani Sadr, president of Iran at the time, the Israelis were also part of the planning. He later claimed that in the summer of 1980 he had received intelligence reports that Israeli and U.S. military experts had been meeting in Paris with Iranian exiles and Iraqi officials for secret talks on the coming war.[3]

Once the fighting had begun, the Carter administration moved to reap the benefits by publicly denouncing the invasion it had so recently encouraged and privately suggesting to the Iranians that the U.S. would ship them desperately needed supplies in exchange for the hostages.

Carter's strategy depended on depriving Iran of arms, particularly spare parts for American-made weapons, until the Iranians had delivered the hostages—before, he hoped, America went to the polls in November. Hence the fury in the Carter White House when it emerged that the Israelis were already trading with Tehran. At least one shipment of spare tires for the Iranian air force's F-4 Phantoms was dispatched in October. Carter issued an outraged complaint to Begin, who promised that the shipments would not recur.

The intrigues, including the encouragement to Saddam Hussein, were all in vain. Ronald Reagan swept the polls.

For cold warriors everywhere, the new president was a congenial champion. He pledged to take a militant stand against the Soviet Union, to increase the defense budget, and to restore the CIA to its rightful place in the frontline trenches of the struggle against communism.

These were sufficient reasons for the Israelis to react warmly to the new administration (whether or not they had been informed of Carter's promise of what he would do to "the Jews" if he got back in). David Kimche speaks warmly of how, under Reagan, U.S. policy was "much more focused on the need to maintain a strong alliance with similar-minded countries (i.e., Israel) . . . From every point of view the United States saw in Israel a partner, a partner to share its opinions, its views, and even . . . to get help from in one or two things." What Kimche explicitly declines to discuss is the fact that one reflection of the newly strengthened partnership was that Israel could now sell arms to Iran without complaints from Washington.

The scale of Israeli military shipments to Iran in the early 1980s, well before the U.S.-Israeli intrigue known as "Iran-Contra" got under way, was very large. In March 1982 the *New York Times* cited documents suggesting that Israel had supplied half or more of Iran's arms supplies since the war had started, amounting to at least $100 million in sales. Other experts on the international arms market put the figure much higher, at $500 million a year in sales. When an Iranian F-4 Phantom pilot defected to Saudi Arabia in 1984 (evading, to the irritation of the Saudis, the billion dollar Awacs flying radar system they had bought from the Americans), his plane was found to contain parts that had originally been shipped to Israel by the U.S.

Israeli assistance to the Iranian war effort was not necessarily confined to high-technology weapons and munitions. The Iranians took to sending lightly armed but enthusiastic teenage recruits in human-wave assaults to clear enemy mine fields with their feet. These "martyrs" carried keys to facilitate their anticipated entry into paradise. The keys, made of plastic, were manufactured on an Israeli kibbutz.

So far as the Israelis were concerned, there were excellent reasons, both strategic and commercial, to sustain the Iranians, even though the Khomeini regime publicly abhorred the Zionist state and called for the liberation of Jerusalem. Ever since the inauguration of the "peripheral" strategy, Israel had seen Iran as an indispensable counter-weight to Iraq. As Defense Minister Arik Sharon said in May 1982, "Iraq is Israel's enemy, and we hope that diplomatic relations between us and Iran will be renewed, as in the past."

Good strategy was also good business. In fact, Israel's most authoritative military commentator, Ze'ev Schiff of the newspaper *Ha'aretz*, has stated that the strategy has served mainly as an excuse for the business. Israel's policy on Iran, he wrote in 1986, has been "guided by a ravenous hunger for profit rather than by strategic considerations." The fall of the free-spending Shah had led to unemployment in some parts of the Israeli defense industry. Yacov Nimrodi, who had made millions as the chief Israeli arms salesman in prerevolutionary Tehran, later said that when he discussed sales to Khomeini with senior Israeli officials, "People's eyes lit up here. They have been laying off people in the defense industry, and this meant jobs." With the Iranians desperate to buy, and the Israelis happy to sell, all that was required was an indulgent attitude from the U.S. government.[4]

Officially, the U.S. policy on arming Iran did not change after the departure of Carter. All shipments were embargoed, and in 1983 the government instituted "Operation Staunch," directed at cutting off international military supplies to the Iranians. Officials associated with Staunch later claimed that as a result of their efforts South Korea, Italy, Portugal, Spain, and Argentina all canceled plans to sell weapons to Iran. They made no mention of any such commitment from the Israelis, who may have appreciated the discouragement of competition.

Senior Israelis, in fact, made explicit reference, on occasion, to the fact that they were selling arms to Iran, but with U.S. permission. Ariel Sharon said so in May 1982, though his assertion was promptly denied by the State Department. The Israeli ambassador to the U.S., Moshe Arens, repeated the claim the following October.

Nowadays, the matter of Israeli supplies to Iran during the war is an unfashionable topic in Israel. Officials with firsthand knowledge of what happened, and why, are reluctant to discuss the topic. But one Israeli with privileged insight into these events is Maj. Gen. Avraham Tamir, a man well acquainted with the world of arms dealing and covert operations. Beginning with youthful forays with the Haganah, Tamir's career has been spent in the heart of Israel's national security apparatus. When General Lior was touring Israel's African outposts in 1965, "Abrasha" Tamir was at his side. News photographs of the Israeli-

Egyptian peace negotiations through Camp David and beyond, as well
as many other important meetings, frequently feature the square
face and stocky frame of General Tamir standing just behind the
principals—Carter, Begin, Sadat, Sharon—an intimate and trusted
member of the inner circle. For his masters he has been the ultimate
staff man or, as Shapik Shapiro puts it less kindly, "the ultimate survivor" and, more ominously, "Sharon's one-man think tank" who provided the ambitious general with "the rationale for Lebanon."

In 1981, Tamir was ensconced as national security adviser to the
minister of defense. Nine years later, sitting in an outdoor cafe next to
the National Theater in Tel Aviv, his rasping voice punctuated by
periodic grunts from an old war wound, he talked about the way
hardheaded people like himself, the men he served, and the Americans saw the world. As might have been expected, the dominant issue
for the U.S. was the Soviet threat to the Persian Gulf.

"The United States was always thinking about the Soviet Union. We
didn't worry about them, but the Americans thought they were going
to intervene with troops. That began with Carter; he started to build
the infrastructure for intervention in the Gulf. He had the Rapid
Deployment Force, with bases on Diego Garcia, in Oman, in Egypt,
in Kenya," Tamir recalled.

"After the revolution the Americans thought they had to save Iran
from the Soviets. They had all these scenarios. If the Soviets intervened in Iran the Americans were going to seize ports in the Gulf, then
invade Iran themselves, then partition Iran. They were worrying
about Saudi Arabia, about the Soviets intervening in Saudi Arabia
from Afghanistan. They saw the Soviets all over the Middle East, in
Turkey, in Lebanon. There were arrows all over the maps." He
scrawled arrows on the notebook across the table with a scornful
gesture. "Academic people like to draw arrows on maps."

Tamir's cynical depiction of American strategic concerns over Cold
War setbacks in the Middle East from the late 1970s on was reflected at
the time in the proclamation of the "Carter Doctrine," which asserted
American vital interests in the Persian Gulf. This policy was reaffirmed
by the Reaganites who came into office in 1981. As in the days of the
Eisenhower Doctrine, the supremely vital interests of Saudi Arabia
and the oil fields were deemed to be menaced by the Soviets and, as in
the days of Eisenhower, there was a role for the Israelis in U.S.
strategy.

At the end of 1981 the U.S. and Israel agreed to a Memorandum of Strategic Understanding, which read in part, "U.S.-Israeli strategic cooperation is designed against the threat to the peace and security of the region caused by the Soviet Union or Soviet-controlled forces from outside the region introduced into the region." The agreement, which provided for the pre-positioning of U.S. military supplies in Israel, as well as even more technological support for the Israeli defense industry and purchases of Israeli defense products by the Pentagon, was hailed by Sharon as a triumph. Israel had taken another step toward the goal of a formal military alliance with the U.S. envisioned by Ben-Gurion so many years before. But the Americans appeared to regard the agreement as being of rather less significance than did the Israelis. Caspar Weinberger, Reagan's secretary of defense, downplayed the signing ceremony as much as protocol would allow. Tamir understood very well, even if his master did not, that the Americans had other interests in mind, and that Israel occupied a useful but limited role in the American scheme of things.

"Sharon thought he was going to be the strategic ally for the Americans in this. We had strategic dialogue talks, here and in the U.S. I was the head of the Israeli delegation, but I said to Sharon, 'The United States is not being nice to you because of your blue eyes.' Sharon didn't understand that the whole American policy was to draw the *Arabs* to the West."

There was one important area in which the U.S. did have a role for Israel. General Tamir, one of the very few men who knows what happened, spelled it out for us.

"The Americans needed us to save Iran." That meant arming the Iranians. Tamir was unequivocal on who gave the clearance: "Haig gave us permission." Tamir explained that the Americans wanted to approve the type of armaments being sent to Iran, though the "controlling system," as he called it, does not appear to have been overly intrusive: "They approved everything we sent—spare parts for airplanes, antitank missiles, and ammunition for the artillery. Israel *was* a U.S. proxy."

Former Secretary of State Alexander Haig is reticent about the prominent role in arming Iran ascribed to him by General Tamir. In public, he points the blame elsewhere, speaking of "a sneaking suspicion that somebody in the White House winked."[5]

Tamir insisted that the Israeli shipments on their own did not, in fact, save Iran. "The Soviets sold trucks; they got supplies from North Korea and China." That is indeed true, but Israel's contributions to the Iranian war effort were enormous nonetheless. One interesting reflection of the military significance of the traffic is the fact that, according to Israeli reports, Saddam Hussein offered to recognize Israel at one point during the war if it would only cease its support for Iran.

Saddam did not succeed in winning Israeli support, but he was getting help from the Americans. While supplies poured out of Israeli factories bound for Khomeini's forces, Egyptian armament plants were working overtime to produce munitions for the Iraqis—with, according to one former U.S. military official who dealt with the Egyptian arms industry, the express permission of the U.S. government. "I looked over those plants," he says. "They were producing 130-mm and other artillery based on Soviet designs. The Egyptians sold them to the Iraqis. It was one way of getting money for the Egyptians and lowering the amount it cost us to keep their economy going." Israel was not the only American proxy in the Middle East doing well out of the war.

The U.S. not only facilitated arms supplies to both sides, it also furnished intelligence to both Baghdad and, on occasion, Iran. In February 1991 a senior Jordanian official, reflecting bitterly on U.S. accusations that Jordan was an ally of the now-reviled Saddam Hussein, recalled how in happier days Jordan had been the conduit for U.S. intelligence information to Baghdad. "For the first two years of the war it was passed through us," he said. "Then they established a direct link through their embassies." In February 1986 this intelligence aid led to a military disaster for the Iraqis, who relied on incorrect American information in planning for an Iranian attack in the area around the city of Basra. "Saddam thought that the Americans had deliberately misled him," said the high-ranking Jordanian. "We just thought it was bad intelligence." Saddam may have had some justification for his suspicion, since in late January 1986 President Reagan agreed that the Iranians should be given U.S. intelligence data on Iraqi dispositions.

In this welter of covert support by the Americans and their proxies for both sides in the ongoing war, it should come as no surprise that in June 1981 the Israelis, with American assistance, intervened directly in the conflict by bombing Iraq. The target was the Osirak nuclear reactor, built by the French on the same pattern as the Dimona reactor in the Negev. It was assumed that one fine day Saddam Hussein's atom bombs would emerge and be used—in the first instance, so Israeli intelligence believed, against Iran. The raid came as no surprise to the U.S. For at least ten months, the Defense Intelligence Agency had been predicting that it would happen, as the authors can directly attest. Satellite reconnaissance photographs vital to the mission were furnished by the CIA.

Yehoshua Saguy, head of Military Intelligence at the time, remembers the assistance fondly. For him, as for the other ranking members of Israel's intelligence apparatus, the arrival of William Casey at Langley brought back memories of the good old days of James Angleton. "Bill Casey was a lot better than [CIA chief Stansfield] Turner," he recalls. "Bill gave us access to the intelligence pictures, which Turner wouldn't. With Bill the relationship went back to the kind of friendship we had had with Jim."

Along with Jim and Bill, Al Haig was rapidly establishing himself in the select pantheon of tried-and-true friends of the Israeli security system. Like the others, his affection for Israel was based on his interest in an anti-Soviet crusade. The Israelis were happy to foster such a convenient obsession, even though, as Tamir admitted with disarming frankness, they did not really share it. Nevertheless, Sharon was more than happy to subscribe to the Reaganite world view and to demonstrate that, in the forthright 1981 statement of Economics Minister Yaakov Meridor, "Israel will be your proxy."

Meridor was asking the U.S. for a free hand for Israeli arms sales in areas where "you couldn't directly do it." The Begin administration was no less interested in a war to deal with enemies on Israel's northern border—a war that could also be sold as useful service against a Soviet proxy.

When Alexander Haig visited Israel in April 1981, his hosts were delighted to hear him talk in biting tones about the Syrians being more than a Soviet client state. Reporting on his intimate talks with Haig, Begin revealingly remarked, "Ben-Gurion used to say that if you're pursuing a policy that may lead to war, it's vital to have a great power behind you."[6]

The war that Begin had in mind was in Lebanon. Israeli interest in the miserably war-torn country had not been quelled by Carter's enforced withdrawal in 1978. From the earliest days, Israeli leaders had been attracted to the notion of setting up a puppet state there.

Nine days after Ben-Gurion declared Israel's independence in 1948, he confided to his diary: "The weak link in the Arab coalition is Lebanon. Moslem rule is artificial and easy to undermine. A Christian state must be established whose southern border will be the Litani. We shall sign a treaty with it."

Other wars and interventions took precedence over the next twenty-five years, but the attractions of a client state in the north never quite went away. When Lebanon began to fall apart in 1975, the Labor leaders then in power responded by supporting the Gemayel family's Phalangist Party (founded by Pierre Gemayel after an inspirational trip to Nazi Germany in 1936) with tanks and heavy artillery. For these Lebanese Christians, an alliance with the Israelis promised a means for them to deal with the Moslem majority, the Palestinians, and the Syrians, all of whom were now fighting over the rapidly disintegrating country. The Lebanese owed the presence of the Syrian army to a Byzantine scheme of Henry Kissinger's. Alarmed that a leftist-PLO coalition might take power in Lebanon, the secretary persuaded President Hafez al-Asad of Syria to intervene on the Christian side. He simultaneously persuaded the Israelis to accept the Syrian move while encouraging the Christian leaders to look to Israel for support. This last initiative was facilitated by the fact that Bashir Gemayel had been put on the CIA payroll while working at a Washington law firm in the early 1970s.

The Phalangists themselves displayed a deft approach in enlisting Israeli sympathies and support. According to a knowledgeable Israeli source, the Phalangists set up a special intelligence department in 1975 to study the opinions and weaknesses of important Israeli political and military leaders, so that when one of them met with the Phalangists they would know precisely how to flatter him and generally make him feel comfortable. Thus they noted Sharon's appetite for good food, especially (nonkosher) shrimp, and fed him well whenever he came to visit.

Some Israelis suspect that the Phalangists received helpful advice from their friends in the Mossad on manipulating Sharon and others. Career officers in the Mossad from the late 1970s on pinned their faith on the Phalangist operation. For these intelligence officers, the alliance with the Gemayels opened the golden prospect of actually being able to have Lebanon, an Arab country, under their control. The fact that the Christian Maronites were in a minority did not faze them. In position papers for the government, they repeatedly cited the example of Syria, ruled by Hafez al-Asad despite the fact that he represented an ethnic minority accounting for 10 percent of the population.

David Kimche, who had risen to be deputy chief of the Mossad, was one who believed devoutly in the link with the Phalangists. (Rather more so than his boss, Yitzhak Hofi, who had his doubts about the Lebanese adventure.) So taken was Kimche with the cause that he even rationalized a moral imperative for supporting the Christian warlords. He felt, as did the Israelis, that they were an island of civilization and Western culture surrounded by hostile Moslems. "Bashir [Gemayel] once said to me," he explained, " 'Look, if I want to bring up my children learning physics in French and not in Arabic, it's my business, and I don't want others to dictate to me in what language they'll study physics.' " Bashir's well-chronicled record of extreme brutality, notably the massacre of a rival's family, including infant children, did not faze this Mossad intellectual, any more than he had been perturbed by the behavior of friends like the Shah or President Mobutu.

The Phalangists, of course, did not perceive the Israelis as a persecuted minority. For them, Israel was a partner—and not necessarily the junior one—of the world's strongest power. Kimche recounts, with a slightly awkward laugh, how "Pierre Gemayel once said to me: 'Some people think that Israel is a colony of the United States. It's ridiculous—how can they say that? The United States is a colony of Israel. Why don't they know that?' "

Kimche's schemes for Lebanon got the powerful support they needed when the Israeli military machine fell into the hands of Arik Sharon in July 1981. Within two months of occupying the Kirya, Sharon ordered the General Staff to draw up plans for a campaign that would not only smash the PLO in Lebanon and drive the Syrians away from Beirut but also install a friendly government that would then sign a peace treaty with Israel.

Sharon made no secret of his grand scheme. In January 1982, sitting in his office in the Knesset, he discoursed expansively on his intention of not only going into Lebanon, but into Syria as well. Later, at the end of the month, he made it clear the attack would come soon, and even issued a personal invitation to one of the authors to come along with him on the adventure: "I have some business to take care of up north;

why don't you come with me." In fact, though he did not confide the exact date, the attack was scheduled for February 6.

The Americans knew that a war was coming. Begin had told Haig that Israel planned a "substantial move" in Lebanon.[7] Bashir Gemayel was himself a CIA agent. Washington got the full picture, including the planned launch date, when a middle-ranking officer contacted an American intelligence officer in Tel Aviv at the end of January. In a midnight meeting at a construction site on the edge of the city, the officer gave a detailed exposition of the plan of attack for Operation "Big Pines." As the American later recalled, "This was a guy who hated Begin and Sharon and their plans for a war. He gave us everything. Order of battle, jumping-off times, routes of advance—the whole works. I sent it straight to my headquarters by the most secure channels. Now the Israelis knew we had the information, and they could have known it only because they had a highly placed agent either in the Defense Intelligence Agency or in the White House." As soon as the Israelis knew there had been a leak, they called off the attack.

At that point Israel had not yet completed its withdrawal from Sinai, and the U.S. did not want to risk derailing the Egyptian agreement by an Israeli lunge to the north, a point Haig made explicitly clear to Military Intelligence chief Yehoshua Saguy at a meeting in late February. In April, however, the Israelis moved out of the last of occupied Sinai.

Toward the end of May 1982, Sharon journeyed to the United States, the indispensable Tamir at his side. The ostensible purpose of the trip was to raise funds from American Jews, but the most important meeting was with Secretary Haig. Lebanon was on the agenda, but it was only one part of a wider discussion of joint U.S.-Israeli interests. Superficially, these had been marred by Begin's annexation of the Golan Heights the previous December, which had led to the U.S. abrogating a Strategic Cooperation agreement signed with Israel the month before. Relations were, however, excellent in the areas that counted: arms supplies for the first half of 1982 were running 50 percent ahead of the same period in 1981, and were ten times higher than they had been in 1980.

Tamir recalled, "We went to talk about three things—Lebanon, the Iran-Iraq war, and problems with Third World countries, especially Zaire. Mobutu had asked us to do him a favor." The favor in question was the billionaire Zairian ruler's request that the Israelis assist him in wresting economic aid from the U.S. Congress. Tamir still prides himself on the successful execution of this difficult mission.

The next issue discussed by Haig and the Israelis at the meeting, according to Tamir, was the Gulf war and Israeli supplies to Iran. Haig reiterated that it was U.S. policy to prevent either side from winning. (After the meeting Sharon went on television and indiscreetly announced that Israel was selling arms to Iran with the permission of the U.S., prompting a State Department denial that this was the case.) The discussion then turned to Lebanon.

What Haig actually told Sharon to do in Lebanon has subsequently been the subject of heated argument. The secretary later said that the charge that he had given a "green light" for the invasion was "totally untrue" and a "grotesque and outrageous proposition," but in the next breath he implicitly confirmed the allegation: "The Israelis had made it very clear that their limit of toleration had been exceeded, and at the next provocation (i.e., any Palestinian military action) they were going to react. They told us that. The president knew that."[8]

In this telling admission, Haig chose to ignore the fact that the Palestinian Liberation Organization's military forces had been observing a cease-fire, brokered by the American diplomat Philip Habib, along Lebanon's border with Israel since July 1981. Some Israeli observers later concluded that the statesmanlike behavior of the Palestinians during this period was one of the motives for the invasion. One of these critics observed that Arafat's success in maintaining the cease-fire was "a veritable catastrophe in the eyes of the Israeli government" because it showed that the PLO "might agree in the future to a more far-reaching arrangement," thus undercutting the routine Israeli explanation that it was impossible to negotiate with terrorists. Tamir agreed that in the months before the war "Sharon was doing his best to destabilize the Habib agreement," as evidenced by the bombing raids on Palestinian positions in Lebanon that he ordered early in 1982.

At the meeting Sharon told Haig that Israel was on the brink of war and might have to fight the Syrians in the course of it. The IDF, he made clear, would go as far as necessary to crush the PLO. Haig recommended a swift surgical strike, which pleased the Israelis very much. "Haig said, 'We want a minor operation,'" recalled Tamir as he smiled broadly and slowly extended his arms. "It's a big word, 'minor.' Haig understood that the key to Lebanon is Syria, so Syria would be involved in the fighting."

The Israeli military team went home in a good mood. The U.S. secretary of state had given them clearance to go ahead. All that was needed now was a justification of some sort. In the meantime Sharon and his intimates left for a trip to Rumania as guests of President Nicolae Ceaucescu, a good friend of Israel. On June 3, while they were still there, the extremist Abu Nidal group, deadly enemies of Arafat and the PLO, tried to kill the Israeli ambassador in London. Tamir heard the news on his transistor radio the day Sharon's party toured Dracula's castle. This was the longed-for provocation. The IDF had begun bombing and shelling even before a special Israeli air force jet rushed Sharon and his team back to Israel. On June 6, Israeli troops began crossing the border in force.

Ironically, the Israelis may have been acting in unwitting cooperation with Saddam Hussein. The leader of the Abu Nidal team that attacked the Israeli ambassador in London turned out to be a colonel in Iraqi intelligence. It is possible that Saddam, then anxious for a cease-fire with Iran, aimed to provoke the Israeli invasion of Lebanon in the hope that Iranians would agree to find common cause in the struggle against Israel.

In any event, it is clear that the Israelis had high-level clearance from the U.S. to invade Lebanon, just as they had had for the attack on Egypt in June 1967. On the earlier occasion, the Americans did not quite realize the scale of the war that the Israelis had in mind. This time Haig was well aware that the IDF was going all the way to Beirut, though he may not have understood that the aim was to destroy the Syrians in Lebanon first, and then the PLO.

Nor did Haig necessarily understand just who he was liaising with in Arik Sharon. But many of the defense minister's fellow countrymen did. One Israeli biographer summarizes the Sharon character as "deceitful, crafty, uncouth, egotistic, and paranoid," with "little use for democracy and its values."[9] If the Israeli people did not fully appreciate his limitless lust for power when he led them into Lebanon, the experience of the invasion and its aftermath helped to clarify their understanding.

Nevertheless, the most ominous example of Sharon's lust for power has remained a secret, closely held among a very few initiates of the "security system": In June 1982, Arik Sharon tried to get total control of Israel's nuclear arsenal.

Ultimate control of Israel's nuclear weapons is vested in a committee of three: the prime minister, the minister of defense, and the head of Mossad. No one member of this group can press the button on his own.

Outsiders assume that the Israelis will use their bomb either from aircraft or on missiles. But in reaction to the experience of the Yom Kippur War, when the Syrians very nearly broke through into northern Israel, the Golan Heights have been seeded with nuclear land mines.

According to a former high-ranking U.S. official closely involved in Israeli affairs, Sharon went to Begin on the first day of the Lebanese war and said that they were facing a difficult situation: the Syrians might come in at any moment and attack in the Golan. In a fast-changing situation it might be difficult for the minister of defense, who was in touch with events on a minute-by-minute basis, to communicate in time with Begin or with the head of Mossad (Yitzhak Hofi, who hated Sharon). So, Sharon explained, he thought it would be a good idea if Begin would invest "tactical control" of Israel's nuclear war-fighting system in him and him alone.

Despite Begin's endorsement of all Sharon's other war plans, he turned this one down.

Superficially, the advance into Lebanon appeared to repeat the standard features of previous Israeli attacks. Powerful IDF units advanced up the coastal road toward Beirut, with the aim of linking up with the Christian Lebanese Forces. To cut off the Syrians, Sharon sent other units through the mountainous Shouf area, home territory of the fierce Druze, with the aim of cutting the vital Beirut-Damascus highway.

Another Israeli force advanced in the east to drive the Syrians out of the Bekaa Valley as far as Baalbek, well north of the highway.

The clash with the Syrians was portrayed to the outside world as yet another victory for Israeli martial skills and American technology. It is true that the Israelis were able to knock out the Syrian antiaircraft missile batteries and knock down as many as eighty-five Syrian fighters without, they claimed, any loss to themselves. The U.S. Air Force was quick to grab some of the credit, briefing Pentagon correspondents: "Intelligence data about the war in Lebanon [showed] that American weapons and tactics as employed by Israel can easily overpower current Soviet jets and missiles." The Israelis, as we have seen, were anxious that their American military suppliers should be happy with the performance of their favorite weapons, such as the Sparrow missile and the F-15 fighter, and deployed their forces with this in mind.

What was less clearly understood at the time was that this was not the same Israeli army that had proved itself such a useful strategic asset in 1967. It had been intended that the Israeli forces advancing on their separate axes should reach their objectives within four days, but they failed. The Syrians ambushed and defeated an Israeli armored brigade at Sultan El Yakub, thus thwarting the drive into the northern Bekaa, while initial attempts to cut the highway were also thrown back. In the west the linkup with the Christians was delayed by fierce resistance from the Palestinians and the Shi'ite militia.

While the IDF schedule was being thrown off by these military setbacks, the Israelis were facing similarly unexpected reverses in another area where they were used to easy victories: public relations.

Following the 1978 Israeli invasion of southern Lebanon, the Israeli chief of staff had made it clear that the IDF had no qualms about striking at civilians. *Ha'aretz* summarized General Motta Gur as stating that "the Israeli army has always struck civilian populations, purposely and consciously . . . the army, he said, has never distinguished civilian [from military] targets."

The 1982 invasion marked the first time that the U.S. public had its attention drawn to this aspect of Israeli military doctrine in any forceful way. Unlike previous Israeli wars, there was a large press corps ensconced on the other side of the enemy lines, complete with open telephone and satellite television links to the outside world and free of the constraints of Israeli censorship. Thus the piles of civilian bodies generated by Israeli bombing garnered more publicity than in the past. At one point Jonathan Randal of the *Washington Post* and Robert Fisk of the London *Times* were on their way to the devastated city of Sidon when they were stopped at an Israeli roadblock and told they could go no farther.

"Randal," wrote Fisk later, "strode into the road in front of another troop carrier. Behind it was a Merkava tank, its huge barrel pointing north toward the airport. Randal walked up to it, followed by the major. 'You see that tank?' he asked. The major looked at it. 'Well I pay my damned taxes so you can have these damn toys—so you damn well let us through . . . You want to damn well order an American off this road, well I'm damn well not going to move when I have to pay my dollars to support your damn wars.' The younger officer nodded at Randal. 'You can go,' he said."

In Sidon itself, the two reporters found a school that had been bombed on the first night of the invasion because the PLO, with manic irresponsibility, had deployed an antiaircraft gun right outside. The basement was full of refugees at the time. "The bodies lay in a giant heap that had left the children on top and the women beneath them. The bomb must have somehow lifted the huddled mass of refugees and sucked the heaviest of them into its vortex. The white lime dust lay more thickly over some parts of the pile than others, leaving the children exposed, their legs splayed open, heads down."[10]

Even though the U.S. media exercised restraint in conveying the extent of such atrocities, the war played very badly in America. Within the administration, the blame fell on Alexander Haig, as though his endorsement of an Israeli military adventure was something unique in the history of the relationship, and he was summarily dismissed by President Reagan on June 23.

The departure of Israel's most visible strategic ally in Washington did not derail the Lebanese campaign. While the Syrians had not been driven out of Lebanon, it was still possible to expel the PLO and to realize the old dream of creating a Christian-ruled client government in Beirut. Through July and August the IDF besieged Beirut, bombing and shelling on what appeared to those on the receiving end as an indiscriminate basis. The PLO eventually agreed to leave under terms negotiated by Philip Habib and supervised by a hastily assembled international peacekeeping force, including American marines. The U.S. had agreed to send a military force to the Middle East for the first time (apart from the UN detachment in the Sinai) since 1958.

While the portly figure of the defense minister became the target of international and domestic recrimination, the Mossad, which had done so much to encourage the adventure, had stayed well out of the public eye. On August 23, 1982, its long-nourished dream appeared to have come true. With the help of threats, bribes, and Israeli helicopters to collect members of the Lebanese Parliament who might have forgotten their duty, Bashir Gemayel was elected president.

In the parking lot outside the hall where voting took place, six armed men waited anxiously for the result. Three were intimate henchmen of Bashir's, the others were from the Mossad. At the moment the radio announced that Bashir was officially elected, one Mossad man fired his Kalashnikov machine pistol into the air in hysterical celebration, while another fell into the arms of one of the Phalangists and danced for joy.

The honeymoon was cut short three weeks later, when a powerful bomb blew up Bashir's headquarters with the president-elect inside. Israeli military engineers who turned up to sift the rubble and look for corpses found a senior executive of Mossad "running around in a frenzy, covered with clay and his head bandaged after bumping into a wall, digging with his hands in the ruins and screaming, looking for Bashir."[11]

The murder of Bashir (on Syrian orders) led to a decision by the Israeli high command to occupy West Beirut, which, since the Americans had arranged for the departure of the PLO, was easy for them to do. The next stage was the introduction into the defenseless Palestinian Sabra and Shatila refugee camps of gunmen from the Phalangist militia, who proceeded to slaughter the hapless inhabitants. The massacre took place in full view of observation posts manned by Israeli soldiers, who thoughtfully illuminated the killing ground with flares. A day after the killing began, Chief of Staff Rafael Eitan (currently a member of Israel's cabinet) congratulated the Phalangist commanders for having "carried out good work," offered the loan of an extra bulldozer suitable for digging mass graves, and authorized the Phalangists to stay in the camp for another twelve hours.

With the massacre, it seemed that the whole grand Israeli scheme for Lebanon had totally collapsed. The world was outraged, as was a large portion of the Israeli public. The government set up a commission of enquiry that eventually went so far as to lay "indirect responsibility" on a few members of the high command, principally Sharon, who thereupon had to leave the Ministry of Defense, although not the government.

Three of the principal players who had made the invasion possible were now gone: Al Haig, Bashir Gemayel, and Arik Sharon. It did not seem to make much difference. The Lebanese adventure, born in a fateful liaison between the Israelis and Washington, had taken on a terrible momentum of its own. The Israelis continued to try and produce their tame Christian Lebanese ideal, with David Kimche, as director general of the Foreign Office, taking the lead in the negotiations and Avraham Tamir at his side. The Americans reintroduced their peacekeeping marines after the massacre, while Secretary of State George Shultz tried his hand at brokering the Israeli-Lebanese talks.

The net result of the war, which had been sold in Washington as part of the grand anti-Soviet offensive of the Reagan years, was that the Americans followed on the heels of the Israelis and became overtly and directly involved in the Lebanese civil war, with far-reaching and disastrous consequences. An early indication of this came in April 1983, when a suicide bomber demolished much of the U.S. Embassy in Beirut—wiping out a group of senior CIA Middle East operatives who had gathered there for a meeting. There were initially dark suspicions at Langley that the Israelis might have had some role in the attack, since the agency was left bereft of much of its capabilities for collecting and analyzing intelligence in the region and was thereby more dependent on the Israelis. Robert Ames, the chief Middle East analyst for the CIA, was among those eliminated in the 1983 explosion. Ames had noted the Israelis' policy of choking off all U.S. contacts and relationships in the region other than themselves. In 1979 the Mossad had dealt with a vital and independent CIA intelligence source, the senior PLO official Ali Hasan Salameh, by blowing him up with a powerful car bomb. Ames had also been an influential adviser to George Shultz, Haig's successor, who certainly appeared to be in need of wise counsel.

"Shultz never read the map of the Middle East," said Tamir scornfully (and rather ungratefully). "He thought he could isolate Syria." In May 1983, having helped the Israelis get their prized peace agreement with Amin Gemayel, who had been substituted for his late brother Bashir as president, Shultz went to Damascus to discuss the matter with Hafez al-Asad. The Syrian president indicated his contempt for the secretary's peacemaking by spending most of their three-hour meeting lecturing Shultz on the Crusades and refraining from expelling his dogs and grandchildren from the room. As Tamir noted with a certain schadenfreude, "For Shultz it was a cold shower."

American hopes of scoring a Cold War victory by expelling the Russians' Syrian ally in Lebanon were now in tatters. In September 1983 Israeli forces were pulling back from Beirut, leaving their Phalangist allies in the mountainous Shouf area to be massacred by the vengeful Druze. Established behind a new line farther south, the

Israelis soon found that their vaunted intelligence services had totally failed to predict or deal with the extremely fierce and effective Shi'ite Moslem guerrilla resistance to their occupation. The following year, in the face of mounting casualties, the Israelis pulled even farther back, to a "security zone" five miles north of their own border.

The Israeli withdrawal from the edge of Beirut left the Americans as the main token of military support for the Gemayel government. This point was not lost on the militant Moslem forces fighting Gemayel, who began to direct increasingly lethal fire at the U.S. Marine "peace-keeping" force at Beirut Airport.

As if the marines did not have enough problems, U.S. policy in the area was now under the influence of President Reagan's new senior Middle East peace negotiator, Robert C. ("Bud") McFarlane. The inhabitants of the Shouf area got a firsthand insight into McFarlane's thinking when the U.S. Sixth Fleet started shelling them—on his recommendation—on September 19, 1983.

McFarlane, a former lieutenant colonel in the marines, had had an interest in the Middle East even before the election that brought the Reaganites to power. In October 1980 he had been one of a group of Reagan campaign officials that met with an Iranian emissary to discuss the hostage question. A somewhat unstable character—he once burst into tears when presented with a congressional subpoena during the CIA investigations of the mid-70s—McFarlane was much given to windy discourses on strategy and geopolitics. As counsel to the State Department in the early 1980s, he had found a sympathetic, well-informed, but not necessarily disinterested partner for such discussions in the person of David Kimche.

Kimche nostalgically recalls how he, as director general of the Foreign Office after 1982, "maintained, I must say, a very, very intimate dialogue on various parts of the world. We used to discuss what one should do in Third World countries, in the Middle East, et cetera, [and] it was Bud McFarlane who led this dialogue." Once upon a time, such discussions had been confined to the discreet channels of intelligence agencies and officials like James Angleton. Now public officials in the U.S., among them Haig and McFarlane, were conducting dialogues with Israelis such as Kimche, a "spook" turned public official. Overt policies such as bringing peace to Lebanon were inextricably bound up with the covert agenda, such as involvement in the Iran-Iraq war.

Eventually, McFarlane involved himself in both the overt and covert worlds. As the president's Middle East negotiator, he inherited the fruits of the Sharon/Mossad initiative in Lebanon. While Kimche was still trying to persuade Amin Gemayel to stand up to the Syrians, McFarlane endeavored to send the same message via the huge cannon of the aged battleship New Jersey. Neither of the strategic thinkers had much success, but it was Americans who paid the price.

On October 23, 1983, a suicide truck bomb blew apart the lightly guarded marine barracks at Beirut Airport, killing 241 marines who died without ever really understanding why they were in Lebanon at all. According to Victor Ostrovsky, a former Mossad employee whose service memoirs the Israeli government tried to suppress, the Mossad station in Beirut had been told by an informant before the attack that militant Shi'ite Moslems were preparing a truck bomb of unusual size. The Israeli intelligence agents deduced that the marines were a likely target, but decided not to pass on the information in order to protect their source and because, in Ostrovsky's words, "The general attitude about the Americans was: 'Hey, they wanted to stick their noses into this Lebanon thing, let them pay the price.'"[12]

The American troops pulled out of Beirut in February 1984. This ignominious retreat by no means released the Reagan administration from the consequences of the joint venture it had so recklessly sponsored with the Israelis. Even before the marines "redeployed offshore," the first American in Beirut was kidnapped and held hostage. A month later William Buckley, the CIA station chief in Beirut, was taken hostage while on his imprudently regular walk to the office. Other abductions followed.

The 1980 election had given the word "hostage" a terrifying resonance in American politics. Although the Beirut hostages were not as big an issue as the Tehran internees had been, they still caused a great deal of concern at the upper levels of the administration. This interest increased after Shi'ite militants hijacked TWA Flight 847 in June 1985 and, after lengthy circuits of the Mediterranean, took it to Beirut. (The passengers later demanded and received the Frequent Flyer miles accumulated on the unscheduled portion of their journey.)

The crisis was eventually resolved with the help of Israel and Iran. The Israelis agreed to release, without publicity, Shi'ite hostages they had taken from southern Lebanon. The Iranians put pressure on their Shi'ite friends in Beirut to release their American captives. The TWA passengers, with the exception of a U.S. Navy enlisted man murdered by the hijackers, returned to an emotional welcome by the president. During the crisis Reagan met with relatives of hostages kidnapped in Beirut. The handful of diplomats imprisoned by the Iranians had become a dominant political issue in 1980; the administration was prepared to go to a great deal of trouble to prevent the Beirut internees from having the same effect.

A growing American obsession with hostages and, by extension, the terrorists who held them could not but help lubricate relations between U.S. and Israeli intelligence. During the crisis caused by the hijacking of the cruise ship *Achille Lauro* in October 1985, Lieutenant Colonel Oliver North was in constant touch with the Israelis, who prided themselves on relaying intelligence on the hijackers fully fifteen minutes before the U.S. National Security Agency delivered the same information to the White House.

Given the esteem in which Israeli antiterrorism capabilities were held, it is hardly surprising that the U.S. should have attempted to emulate the Israeli way of doing things. Elite antiterror squads proliferated in the U.S. military, while the U.S. Navy set up its Anti-Terrorism Alert Center, enabling Jonathan Pollard, as we have seen, to do much useful work on behalf of his Israeli employers.

Beirut and the American hostages concealed the fact that there was one obvious target for all this burgeoning antiterrorist capability. Covert action squads, such as the U.S. Army's Delta Force and the Navy's SEALs, flooded into the city to lay plans for a dramatic Entebbe-style rescue. To those who knew Beirut, these efforts did not inspire confidence. "They were in [Christian] East Beirut," says one Westerner who had personal acquaintance with some of the Shi'ite kidnappers. "The hostages were in the west of the city, so the Americans might as well have been operating from Wales. Their plans were absolutely lunatic." Victor Ostrovsky claims that Mossad had a good idea where the captives were being held, but chose not to pass on its best intelligence to the CIA, even when ordered to do so by Prime Minister Shimon Peres. However, since the Mossad, among other of its disasters in Lebanon, had woefully failed to produce accurate intelligence on Shi'ite resistance to the Israeli occupation, the Israeli agency's lack of cooperation may not have been such a loss after all.

Fortunately for the hostages, the planners in Washington eventually decided that rather than using force, it might be better to buy the incarcerated Americans their freedom. This attempt also required liaison with Israelis, not to mention the Iranians. The resolution of the TWA crisis—which had put the dreaded word "hostage" back in the headlines—demonstrated how useful the Iranians could be. From now on the administration was to bend its attention to influencing the Iranians to deliver the remaining captives, above all the CIA official William Buckley. (The Americans did not learn until later in the year that Buckley had almost certainly died at the beginning of June 1985.)

Up until this point the U.S. had been content to turn a blind eye to Israel's burgeoning military exports to Iran, so long as there was a "controlling mechanism," in Tamir's words, to monitor the shipments. Because the volume of trade was so great and because flocks of Iranian arms buyers roaming Tel Aviv might be overly visible, the Israelis had set up a branch office in Cyprus to deal with the Iranians. The materiel being sent included both production from Israel's own factories, such as the Soltam artillery and mortar company, and supplies from other countries that were routed through the Israelis. When, for example, the Iranians struck a very large-scale deal with the Chinese in 1985, much of the hardware was "laundered" through Israeli middlemen.

To some in Israel, the "Irangate" affair was an irritating interruption in what had been a very successful commercial operation. General Tamir, who became director general of the Prime Minister's Office in late 1984, is impatient with American notions that 1985 was a significant year for Israeli arms exports to Iran. "Nothing changed in 1985. The Israeli plan was to continue the shipments, but the U.S. wanted its hostages," he said, irritated at the naivete of the question.

When the transactions later became embarrassingly public, U.S. officials were anxious to stress that the whole idea of "arms for hostages" had been an Israeli suggestion. McFarlane stated that his strategic interlocutor, David Kimche, had raised the notion with him in July and early August 1985. Kimche was quoted by his friend as suggesting that the Iranians were especially anxious to get hold of TOW antitank missiles. As McFarlane told the board of enquiry headed by Senator John Tower (who had formerly employed him on his Senate staff): "Mr. Kimche made a special proposal that one hundred TOWs to Iran would establish good faith and result in the release of all the hostages."

For at least some in the Iranian leadership, the attractions, in 1985, of a more direct link with the Americans were considerable. The U.S. had up to that point been supporting, with the help of proxies, both sides in the war (which, of course, it had encouraged the Iraqis to start). While the Israelis had had the "Iranian account," the Egyptian factories had been turning out munitions for the Iraqis. But for the Iranians, there were worrying signs of a tilt by Washington toward Iraq. The U.S. had granted a low-interest loan to Baghdad in 1983, and diplomatic relations, broken at the time of the Six Day War, were restored in 1984.

At the same time as relations were restored, Bechtel, an American construction company, began negotiations to build a pipeline to transport Iraqi oil exports across Jordan to the Gulf of Aqaba—an outlet desperately needed by the Iraqis since Hafez al-Asad had cut the line across Syria in 1982. Bechtel had a powerful political profile at the time, since two of its former executives, George Shultz and Caspar Weinberger, had gone on, respectively, to run the State and Defense departments. The administration supported the project because it would enable Iraq to earn more hard currency with which to buy arms. The State Department official who directed "Operation Staunch," Richard Fairbanks, retired from government service in 1985 and shortly thereafter went to work as a lobbyist for Saddam Hussein.

In addition to the political attractions for Iran of an improved relationship with the U.S., they also cherished the hope of obtaining some of America's fabled "high-tech" weaponry, such as the TOW missiles mentioned by McFarlane in his report of Kimche's approach.

The motives of the Israelis may have been more complex than commonly appreciated. It may be, as suggested by Tamir, that the Americans introduced the hostage issue and disturbed an otherwise routine business relationship with Tehran. However, while the notion of selling arms to Iran was not born in 1984 or 1985, one significant event did occur in Israel late in 1984. There was a general election. The voters, recoiling from the disastrous and bloody consequences of the Lebanese adventure lately ended, had stripped the Likud of its majority in the Knesset, but had not given Labor a majority. As a result the leaders of the two parties, Yitzhak Shamir and Shimon Peres, agreed to rotate the top jobs. For two years Peres would be prime minister and Shamir foreign minister, then they would swap.

It is noteworthy that the meetings, messages, and plots that are on the official record as constituting the birth of "Irangate" occurred as the Labor Party was getting its first taste of power since 1977. The finances of Israeli political parties are no less murky than those of

American parties, and possibly even more so. However, numerous sources conversant with the subject attest that Israeli parties do expect and receive a rake-off from arms sales. It is certainly a fact that major arms dealers put a lot of money into politics and politicians. Yacov Nimrodi, the former Military Attaché and Mr. Fixit in the Shah's Tehran, is reputed to have underwritten much of the costs of Arik Sharon's expensive libel action against *Time* magazine over its report of his role in the Sabra and Shatila massacres. The Israeli press has given a lot of attention to Marcus Katz's generosity to the National Religious Party over the years.

It is therefore possible that the flurry of activity over arms sales to Iran in the year after Peres's arrival in the Prime Minister's Office had a lot to do with his desire to cash in on the business, or at least to find a role in it for old friends like Al Schwimmer. McFarlane's secretary (Fawn Hall's mother) unwittingly underlined the point when she noted on July 11, 1985 that an urgent message had arrived from Peres for McFarlane that was to be delivered by "Al Schwimmer, a Jewish-American who provides lots of money to Peres."

It is possible that the key to "Irangate" lies in the fact that Peres and his friends found themselves excluded from the profitable weapons trade with Iran, and therefore decided to develop their own business links with Tehran, using American concern for the hostages as cover.

There is support for this view from one former Israeli intelligence officer actively involved in selling arms to Iran and elsewhere. Ariel Ben Menashe is someone whom the Israelis have been anxious to disavow. In 1989 he was arrested by U.S. Customs agents for attempting to export, without a license, a military aircraft from the United States to Iran. In November 1990 a New York jury accepted his defense that he was acting on behalf of the state of Israel and acquitted him of all charges. The Ministry of Defense in Tel Aviv initially disputed his claim of having worked for Israeli Military Intelligence between 1977 and 1987. However, when Ben Menashe produced letters on Defense Ministry stationery from former superiors in court that paid fulsome tribute to his "considerable analytical and executive skills," the Ministry of Defense spokesman retreated, and asserted that while Ben Menashe indeed had been an employee, he was merely a low-level translator. When questioned about the plethora of entry and exit stamps for countries such as El Salvador, Honduras, and Guatemala on his passport, the Israelis suggested that he had visited these countries "on vacation." (While fluent in Farsi and Arabic, Ben Menashe does not speak Spanish.)

Ben Menashe states unequivocally that the reason Peres and others such as Kimche encouraged the Americans to get involved in trading arms for hostages was that Mossad refused to permit a role for the prime minister in the ongoing trade.[13]

It is certainly the case that none of the "Irangate" players from the Israeli end, or at least none whose names have surfaced, were members of the Mossad. David Kimche was a distinguished veteran of the agency, but he had left it in 1981. Amiram Nir, who became famous as Peres's intermediary in the affair, was a former TV reporter who had married into the newspaper-owning Moses family. His father-in-law was unwilling to bring him into the family business and asked Peres to give him a job, which was how he came to be appointed the prime minister's adviser on counterterrorism. (He succeeded Rafi Eitan, who had bigger fish to fry.)

The two principal Israeli foreign intelligence agencies, Mossad and Military Intelligence, had set up a joint working group to deal with Iran in 1980. In the normal course of events this group and their parent agencies would have had to have been consulted on something as important as the shipments of Hawk and TOW missiles to Iran. Yet the documentary record of the various investigations into the sales indicates that Peres and Kimche, who was the director general of the Foreign Ministry, as well as Schwimmer and Yacov Nimrodi, the private arms dealers involved in the transactions, managed to steer clear of the professionals while embarking on what was definitely a covert operation. One possible reason for their doing so was that the Mossad and Military Intelligence were refusing to allow the new prime minister and his party to become involved in the Iran arms business.

While there is much circumstantial evidence to support Ben Menashe's explanation of this very murky episode, the engaging, curly-haired arms dealer does not help his credibility by claiming rather greater involvement in affairs of state than he has in fact enjoyed. In 1990 he agreed to submit to a lie detector test commissioned by a major network news organization on specific questions regarding his claims to a relationship with Robert Gates, deputy national security adviser to President George Bush. Ben Menashe failed the test.

There is, on the other hand, no need for lie detectors to confirm the fact that Shimon Peres is prepared to do a lot to raise money. The cold print of documents that surfaced in the course of a federal criminal investigation suggest that in 1985 he was prepared to use the Israeli air force as muscle for a mafia-style protection racket in partnership with a major campaign contributor who was even richer than Al Schwimmer.

The scheme grew out of the Bechtel Corporation's plans to build Saddam Hussein his oil pipeline across Jordan. The problem with this billion dollar deal was that the Israelis could easily blow it up. Iraq wanted cast-iron assurances that there would be no such sabotage. Bechtel swiftly found just the right man to get what was needed.

R. Bruce Rappaport is a very Israeli success story. A veteran of the Haganah and the War of Independence, he parlayed a business selling frozen dinners to merchant ships into a vast oil and shipping empire. In the process he left a trail of angry governments, from Indonesia to Gabon, who accused him of sharp practices in the extraction of profits from his lucrative oil concessions. Rappaport's stellar career in the rough-and-tumble of the international oil business was built from a base in Switzerland after he had left Israel, under something of a cloud, in 1954.

By 1985 all such unpleasantness lay far in the past. Shimon Peres was a frequent guest at the Rappaport mansion in Geneva, and had gratefully received his rich friend's million dollar contribution for the previous year's election campaign. Given the relationship, Rappaport was an eminently sensible choice for Bechtel to take on as a partner in the pipeline deal.

It took the urbane billionaire only two weeks to come through with a letter signed by Peres promising that Israel would not attack Saddam Hussein's strategic asset. But this was not enough—Bechtel and the Iraqis wanted some form of insurance guarantee by which they would be reimbursed should the Israelis go back on Peres's word. To meet this demand, Rappaport and Peres—according to an "eyes only" memo addressed to Edwin Meese, then the attorney general of the United States, by his friend and attorney Bob Wallach—concocted a scheme by which the Israeli Labor Party would receive $65 million a year in return for a guarantee that the pipeline would not be attacked. This money was to come from profits from the pipeline. Although Peres and his associates later denied any plans for a protection racket, the prime minister was enthusiastic enough to offer to freeze $400 million in U.S. military aid in a bank account as "salvage" funds. U.S.

taxpayers would thus be ensuring Saddam Hussein's assets instead of financing the defense of Israel.

Of course, Peres could not apportion the aid money in this way on his own. Bechtel needed clearance from an obscure U.S. government agency, the Overseas Private Investment Corporation (OPIC), which in turn needed administration endorsement from a very high level, which was where Wallach and Meese came in.

Wallach was already deeply embroiled in the murky affairs of the Wedtech Corporation, later the subject of criminal indictments for bribery and fraud. (Wedtech was in part owned by Fred Neuberger, a graduate of Yitzhak Shamir's Stern gang.) Rappaport had hired Wallach to ease his way with the administration, which Wallach did by deputing Meese to arrange an appointment for the Israeli with National Security Adviser Robert McFarlane. McFarlane was obliging. The OPIC bureaucrats, queasy over the turn things were taking, found their objections given short shrift from McFarlane's NSC. "National security is our business," they were told on one occasion. "You mind yours."

Rappaport had other friends in high places in Washington. According to one of the Israeli's former employees, CIA Director William Casey used Rappaport's operation as a cover for undisclosed projects. Throughout this employee's service for the shadowy businessman, there was a CIA operative working out of the Geneva office. This may help explain Casey's smiling presence at a party thrown by Rappaport in the Fourways Restaurant in downtown Washington in the summer of 1985. It may also throw some light on the purging of the CIA file on Rappaport before it was sent over to OPIC.

Despite the potent interest of high-ranking national security officials, the pipeline scheme eventually ran into the sand. OPIC suspicion hardened into effective bureaucratic opposition, and when McFarlane was replaced by Admiral John Poindexter at the end of 1985, the "creative" insurance idea died.[14]

The affair provides a vivid illustration of the workings of the "security systems" of both Israel and the United States, and the degree to which the two were becoming intertwined. At exactly the same time as high U.S. officials were covertly arming Iran with the help of Israel, they were also considering paying off Israeli politicians to leave Iran's enemy unmolested. It was the logical consequence of the secret U.S. decisions that had covertly promoted the beginning of the Iran-Iraq war, the support of both sides in that war, and the invasion of Lebanon. As a former U.S. intelligence official once remarked to the authors, "The problem with covert actions is that they come back to bite you." U.S. foreign policy in the 1980s became increasingly subsumed in clandestine activities and objectives. It was only fitting that the partner in these affairs should be Israel, the long-standing covert ally.

In such a world anything was possible, which was why Robert McFarlane, Oliver North, Amiram Nir, Howard Teicher (an NSC official who later went to work for Shaul Eisenberg), and George Cave of the CIA arrived in Tehran in May 1986 bearing a chocolate cake from a Tel Aviv kosher bakery as a present for the Ayatollah.

The American participation in the Iranian arms business had not been overly blessed with good fortune. The Israeli middlemen had been unable to resist the temptation to substitute older and cheaper models of the Hawk and TOW missiles than the ones on order from Tehran. Hostage releases, with the midterm U.S. elections only six months away, had been sparse.

Nor did the trip to the Ayatollah's capital help matters much. The Revolutionary Guards at the airport ate the cake, the delegation members failed to meet the high-ranking Iranians they had expected to, and no hostages were released. On the other hand, some on the American end of the operation had taken an educated interest in the financial possibilities of the operation. The "Enterprise" run by retired General Richard Secord garnered a total of some $30 million in gross income from the Iran deals. After expenses there remained about $15 million in profits, which was variously expended on arming the contras, paying the contra leadership, and handsomely rewarding Secord and his associates.

Terry Anderson remained a hostage when the Iran-Contra affair exploded just after the fall 1986 elections and, tragically, he remains a hostage at the time of this writing. Before being snatched to pay the penalty for American involvement in Lebanon, he had formulated a succinct answer to Israeli complaints of unfair press coverage: "When you do bad things, people are going to say bad things about you."[15]

In reality, not that many bad things get said about Israel in the U.S. Israelis are rougher on themselves. In November 1986, Boaz Evron, a columnist for *Yediot Aharanot* (the largest paper in the country), reflected on the implications of the Iran arms-dealing revelations:

"Since countries want to have things done which a gentleman would not touch, they turn to one who gives services, who is prepared to serve his master and dance for him; he is not only willing to fulfill any wishes, but also enjoys the fact he is serving and is proud of it . . . He even makes an ideology out of his servitude and calls it 'realpolitik.' Moreover, as befitting a corrupt servant, he even drags his master into dirty adventures, like a pimp winking at a hesitant client in order to tempt him.

"Yes, the famous lobby will get us out of this mess as well, but we shall remain dirty. Of course, we shall be used again, but we shall find ourselves more often standing at the servants' entrance and less in the living room, and the day will come when it will be a shame to have us seen even at the servants' entrance. Then the meetings shall be held in the small hours of the night in some small pub near the port while in the nearby water the bodies of servants whose services are no longer required float by."

Official investigations of the illegal U.S. government machinations that came to be labeled "Iran-Contra" paid as little attention as possible to the part played by Israel. The majority report of the congressional committees, for example, devotes precisely 5 out of 423 paragraphs to Israel. In Oliver North's testimony before the committees, however, there was a revealing exchange with Chief Counsel Arthur Liman that serves as an apt summary of how American policymakers view their ally:

"Was one of the reasons for wanting to have Israel involved," Liman asked North, "so that we could say it was Israel that was selling, and Israel, everyone knows, sells arms?"

"Well," replied North, "Israel was already involved . . . we did not want the U.S. government's hand, or role in this activity, exposed, and thus, . . . as I said earlier, we tried to mirror the Israeli model."[16]

13. Endgame

FROM THE FIRST MINUTES of the 1991 war, Israeli bombs were falling on Iraq. The bombs, laser-guided projectiles code-named "Have Nap," were carried to their targets on B-52 bombers of the United States Air Force. They were used because the Americans considered them more reliable than the comparable weapon produced in the U.S. However, the fact that Israeli weapons were used from the outset was not publicized either in the U.S. or Israel. Nor was the fact that desert boots worn by U.S. forces on the ground bore the imprint "Made in Israel," both in English and in Hebrew.

This was a different kind of Middle East war, one in which the United States took the lead and did the fighting, while its traditional strategic ally in the region was forced to stay out of the limelight.

As in the United States, the initial attacks on Iraq generated a mood of euphoria in Israel. Shimon Peres spoke for most experts when he said that Iraq would be defeated by the American attack within "four to twenty-four hours."[1] Two days into the war, that feeling disappeared.

Saddam Hussein had been promising for some time that any attack on Iraq would be answered with an attack on Israel, and the Scud missiles that slammed into Tel Aviv on the night of January 17 showed that he was as good as his word.

The city, which had survived five wars without coming under serious attack, was seen in a state of semihysteria. By dusk each day, its broad avenues were deserted, abandoned by the edgy population. The more affluent residents, sporting their gas masks in neat cardboard containers with plastic shoulder straps, raced to their cars and joined the massive traffic jam along the Ayalon Road to Jerusalem. They assumed they would be safe there because of the Moslem shrines in the Old City. Tens of thousands of "deserters," as Tel Aviv's Mayor Shlomo Lahat derisively called them, had suddenly discovered an urgent need to visit Europe on business or to take a vacation in the distant Red Sea port of Eilat. Only El Al was flying out of Ben-Gurion Airport, and every seat was booked for weeks ahead.

The frigid January wind whipping down Dizengoff Street in the center of Tel Aviv only added to the gloom of darkened restaurants and storefront windows crisscrossed with masking tape to guard against bomb blasts. On the corner of Arlozorof Street, leading to the beach-front hotels, a vast billboard shouted "Saddam*n* 1945–1991, the Real Linkage." It was in English, for the benefit of the hundreds of foreign TV journalists crowded into the seafront hotels.

There were no tour groups and solidarity delegations deplaning at Ben-Gurion Airport. Instead, vast C-5 Galaxy transport planes un-loaded Patriot missiles hurriedly flown in, along with their U.S. Army crews, to defend Tel Aviv. Some Patriots were dispatched to an empty field along the Ayalon Road, where their crews built a tent city they called "Hotel California." More of the American antimissile missiles were deployed north of the Hilton Hotel, next to the power station farther up the coast.

On the night of January 25, the sirens wailed once again, indicating that American satellites had spotted Scud missiles lifting off from western Iraq. Less than a minute after the population of Israel had dashed to rooms sealed against gas and struggled into their gas masks, the sky above the city lit up as a Patriot missile burst into a glittering shower of white-hot metal that then plummeted down onto the city. As the roar of the explosion rolled over the rooftops, it was clear—at least to journalists who had chosen an open balcony on the fourteenth floor of the Hilton in preference to a sealed room from which to report on the attack—that the missile had self-destructed. Another Patriot streaked across the night sky, flying so low that it could easily have plowed into one of the high-rise office towers, before it slammed into the city. A third, fired at the incoming Scuds, exploded in a sudden glow of red light just beside the tower of the Kirya. A fourth shot up from the battery just north of the Hilton and then, almost immediately, doubled back along its path and crashed to earth not far from a popular restaurant named Mandy's. The soothing official pronouncement at the regular midnight military briefing in the Hilton was that seven Scuds had approached Tel Aviv and that all had been shot down.

In truth, the American Patriots had caused as much damage as Saddam Hussein's high explosives, and there was one death and seventy injuries that night. The truth, however, was censored. The Israelis had no desire to irritate their American protectors.

Along with the missile-bearing transports arriving at Ben-Gurion, there were other and even more significant arrivals. Soviet Jewish immigrants, up to four planeloads a day even after the beginning of the war, were pouring into the country.

Their first Israeli experience was to be issued gas masks and instructed in the proper procedure for injecting the nerve-gas antidote Atropine (highly dangerous if improperly applied). Their second was to be given an "absorption basket" of $10,000 to ease their entry into Israeli society. The government was making plans to absorb a million of these people over the next three years. The Russians were a momentous sign of how much the world had changed in just a few years. The Israelis had finally realized an ambition as old as the state itself: to secure the vast pool of Soviet Jews as citizens.[2]

However, the end of the forty-five-year-long contest between the United States and the Soviet Union for power and influence around the world has other, less attractive consequences for Israel. The state has, as we have seen, in great degree been molded by the Cold War. Above all, the connection with the United States that generates billions of aid dollars every year grew out of Israel's service in the struggle. Even before Israel earned its certification as a "strategic asset" for humiliating Nasser in 1967, Operation KK Mountain had helped give the state a laissez-passer, lubricated with CIA money, to make its way in the Third World. The surreptitious acquisition of the wherewithal for making nuclear weapons had been eased by the fact that Israel was a "fiercely anti-Communist nation," as James Angleton's old friend John Hadden put it, and was thereby entitled to the means to defend itself.

So it had gone on—Israel saving Jordan from the allegedly Soviet-dominated PLO and Syrians in 1970, levering the Egyptians into the U.S. sphere of influence after 1973, taking on the Syrians again in 1982, helping to "save" Iran in the 1980s. Beyond the Middle East, in

Central America, or in southern Africa, Israel had had its role to play in the bigger game.

But Mikhail Gorbachev's decision to abandon military and political confrontation with the United States and its allies had meant that Israel was no longer facing Soviet proxies in the Middle East. Egypt had opted for American client status and aid in the 1970s. Syria, the one militarily formidable frontline Arab state left, no longer received arms supplies on easy credit from the Soviets. Around the world, the hot extensions of the Cold War, whether in Central America or southern Africa, were dying down, with grave implications for Israel and its most important industry.

In 1989, at least 75 percent of Israeli defense production had gone for export, earning no less than $1.6 billion in sales. But, discussing the imminent prospect of defense budget cuts worldwide, an executive of Israel Military Industries told the newspaper *Ha'aretz* in November 1989, "The Israeli producers and exporters of weapons are very worried by this tendency. The world scenario is apocalyptic. Most of the conflicts in the world are ending now and there are no signs of any new ones on the horizon. We are faced by the threat of peace . . ."

There was just one Arab leader left who was not threatening peace. In 1988 Saddam Hussein had finally secured a narrow victory over Iran after a million casualties and eight years of war. His ill-considered and ineptly conducted struggle with Khomeini had left his unfortunate subjects burdened with war wounds and debt, but he had not forsaken his martial pretensions. The Iraqi army, which had expanded during the war to a million men (in units of varying quality), was not demobilized. Grandiose projects of dubious military utility, such as the "supergun" devised by the Canadian ballistics engineer Jerry Bull, continued to receive lavish funding.

In June 1990 the Iraqi leader was asked by a Canadian journalist whether he aspired to be "the second Nasser." "No," came the reply, "I shall be the first Saddam."[3] Saddam differed from Nasser in many ways, one of which was in his ability to enlist both superpowers as patrons, at least for a time. Although he received much assistance from the Soviet Union, his ultimate success in the war with Iran was due to the lavish support he was given by the West, particularly the United States. The intervention by the U.S. Navy against Iran in the Persian Gulf in the last year of the war, as well as the supply of intelligence to

Baghdad throughout most of the eight years of fighting, had tipped the balance for Iraq.

As Saddam Hussein celebrated his limited and bloody victory in Baghdad, Israelis in general were well aware that they faced a new force in the region. The Iraqi army was very big—three-quarters of a million men remained in uniform even after the cease-fire—and tested in battle. Saddam gave no sign of abandoning his grandiose pretensions. He continued to invest in chemical weapons, long-range rockets, and even a nuclear weapons program.

Dangerous though it seemed for a strong and well-armed Arab leader to go unchallenged, the Israelis displayed a certain ambivalence toward Saddam. A 1987 Israeli newspaper cartoon summed up Jerusalem's wavering policy. It depicted Defense Minister Yitzhak Rabin responding to the question of whether Israel supported Iran or Iraq with the response, "What day is it?" Israeli sources assert that even before the U.S. intervened decisively on Iraq's side in the conflict there had been a strong body of opinion in the upper ranks of the IDF that perhaps Israel had erred in supporting Tehran so vigorously. Saddam himself courted the Israelis, offering, as previously noted, to recognize and make peace with Israel (the two countries have been technically at war since 1948) in exchange for a cessation of help to Iran. In 1982 he had told the staunchly pro-Israeli Congressman Stephen Solarz that Iraq recognized Israel's "need for a state of security" and that "no Arab leader has now in his policies the so-called destruction of Israel or wiping it out of existence."

As late as the fall of 1989, according to Israeli reports, Defense Minister Rabin tentatively agreed to meet with Saddam Hussein. The Iraqi president apparently nominated an American oilman of Arab descent to make the contacts with the then defense minister, and the two met in secret while Rabin was on a fund-raising tour in the U.S. Dates for the meeting with the Iraqi president, to be held in Europe, were actually fixed, though later Saddam asked to shift the venue to Baghdad. (Rabin's response to this suggestion is not known.) The intermediary, meanwhile, was passing along all details of the ongoing negotiations to the White House.

Despite the interest shown on both sides, these negotiations ultimately came to nothing. Saddam had been motivated to explore the notion of talks by the fear that Israel was going to attack him. However, in February 1990 he opted for a harder line, denouncing both Israel and the United States as potential aggressors. In April he followed up with an even harsher excoriation in which he claimed that Iraq possessed advanced chemical weapons and threatened that "We will make fire eat up half of Israel if it tries anything against Iraq."

Israel had of course attacked Iraq once before, in 1981, when its air force bombed the Osirak nuclear reactor. Undeterred by that setback, Saddam had continued to try and build an arsenal of weapons of mass destruction. The Israelis were not overly concerned about the Iraqi nuclear weapons program once they had destroyed the Osirak reactor. As Shlomo Gazit, former head of Military Intelligence, said during the U.S.-Iraq war, "We did not have any expectation that he might reach a nuclear capability anytime soon." (This was not, incidentally, the public attitude of the Bush administration at the time.)[4]

Saddam's chemical weapons program was a different matter. Not only did he have chemical weapons, which he had employed in liberal quantities against both the Iranians and his disaffected Kurdish subjects, but he also claimed to be able to deliver them by missile to Israel.

Through the Gulf crisis, the Iraqi president and his associates claimed that it had been precipitated not by the occupation of Kuwait, but by a conspiracy between Israel and the U.S. to attack him. As Saddam put it on February 15, 1991, in one of his last desperate attempts to stop the American military onslaught: "Ever since the United States, Zionism, and the United States' imperialist Western allies came to realize that . . . Iraq was developing a force of its own, capable of being a counterweight to the imperialist-backed Zionism . . . the United States, Zionism, and all colonial powers set about taking measures, making decisions, and waging campaigns of falsehoods and incitement against Iraq . . ."

By the time he had made that statement, hardly anyone in the U.S., or anywhere else, was prepared to put much store by Saddam Hussein's pronouncements. His efforts to link a withdrawal from Kuwait to a settlement of the Palestinian issue had been fended off by the U.S. Claims by the Iraqi government that Israel had planned an attack on Iraq's nonconventional capabilities were, however, correct. Knowledgeable Israelis are reticent on the topic, at least on the record. Yehoshua Saguy, who had been head of Military Intelligence at the time of the raid on the Osirak reactor, talked in late January 1991 of how "there was, let's say, a little bit of discussion about it last year, before the war, before this conflict (the U.S.-Iraq war) even started."

According to reliable information from within the Israeli military, planning for an attack got well beyond a "little bit of discussion." In contrast to the reactor raid, this was to be a ground attack. A special highly trained force of commandos was to be "inserted," as the military phrase goes, inside Iraq to attack key chemical production facilities. Preparation had apparently been under way for up to four years. Originally scheduled for June, the attack never happened because, to the intense disappointment of the raiding party, the White House refused to grant permission.[5]

Once upon a time it might have been easier for the Israelis to get clearance from Washington. The Reagan administration, after all, had known all about the operation against Osirak several months before it happened, and had done nothing to stop it.

With George Bush and James Baker in charge of U.S. foreign policy, however, Israel found the atmosphere more chilly than in the palmy days of Al Haig or George Shultz. After he had become secretary of state, Baker was asked by a friend whether he had noticed that "every administration leaves office having conceived an intense dislike of the French and the Israelis." Baker laughed and replied, "What do you do about someone who comes into office feeling that way?"

The Bush-Baker team had made known its displeasure at Israel's unwillingness to undertake even the semblance of peace negotiations over the issue of the Palestinians living under military rule on the West Bank and in Gaza. Bush was reported to be particularly incensed that Yitzhak Shamir had repeatedly violated promises not to expand Jewish settlements on the West Bank. The president was also less than pleased that Israeli intelligence was acting in an independent manner. For example, in 1989 undercover Israeli units had kidnapped a Shi'ite cleric in Lebanon without U.S. intelligence being notified in advance. In addition, as Bush further complained to Shamir, Israeli intelligence had failed to pass on the news to the Americans that Lt. Colonel William Higgins, a U.S. Marine officer kidnapped by the Shi'ites in retaliation for the loss of their cleric, had been killed by his captors. There were strains in the covert relationship.

Nevertheless, even though the Cold War was winding down, and even though the U.S. administration was irritated by Prime Minister Yitzhak Shamir's obdurate intransigence on matters of peace, the two countries were about to be bound together in a Middle East crisis unlike any ever seen before.

George Bush's actual plans regarding Iraq and the Gulf in the weeks and days before Saddam made his fateful move into Kuwait remain a mystery. The transcript of U.S. Ambassador April Glaspie's last interview with the Iraqi president, on July 25, which was unchivalrously taped and subsequently released by Saddam, indicates a curiously complaisant American attitude in the face of his bellicose rhetoric. The U.S., Glaspie told him, took no position on Iraq's border dispute with Kuwait and wanted better relations with Iraq. On July 28, President Bush was briefed by William Webster, director of the CIA, on Iraq's threatening moves toward Kuwait. Saddam, Webster said, was going to invade Kuwait in order to seize the Rumaila oil field that straddled the border, as well as two islands, Warba and Bubiyan, that lie close to the Iraqi coastline. Bush's reaction was low-key. He cabled Saddam, saying that the U.S. was concerned about Iraq's threats to use force against its neighbors, but also reiterating that the U.S. wanted better relations with Iraq. On July 31, two days before the Republican Guard chased the Emir of Kuwait into temporary exile, Assistant Secretary of State John Kelly stressed to a congressional committee that the U.S. had no commitment to defend Kuwait.[6]

Once Saddam seized the whole of Kuwait, however, Bush became very energetic and decisive indeed. The U.S. mobilized the United Nations to denounce the invasion and to impose punitive sanctions on Iraq unless it withdrew. Simultaneously, the administration began to deploy an enormous military force to Saudi Arabia. The initial justification for sending troops to the desert was that Saddam was poised to attack Saudi Arabia itself. However, CIA officials have privately conceded that at no time was there any evidence that Saddam contemplated such a move. That was not the news given to the Saudi King Fahd by the administration when his permission was sought for the military buildup. Fahd was reportedly convinced by intelligence evidence handed to him by Defense Secretary Cheney that his realm was in mortal danger from Saddam's tanks.

The reaction from Israel toward Bush's sudden anti-Iraqi militancy was enthusiastic. Israeli spokesmen urged the president to show no mercy against Saddam. President Chaim Herzog even urged the Americans to use nuclear weapons. Opinion in the U.S. itself was divided on the desirability of war over Kuwait. There was a body of opinion that the U.S. was being pushed into a military confrontation in order to serve the needs of Israel. The right-wing columnist Patrick

Buchanan expressed this point of view most bluntly, and notoriously, when he observed on television that the only force pushing for war was "Israel and its amen corner here on Capitol Hill."

In fact, though the administration initially suggested that war would be a last resort and that UN trade sanctions would be given every opportunity to work, George Bush was fully as resolved as the Israelis that Saddam would have to be crushed. In the last hours of the war, in which Saddam's military power was indeed crushed, a former official with close ties to very senior White House officials confided that within four days of the seizure of Kuwait he had been informed of "exactly what they were going to do, through the buildup, rejecting any attempts by Saddam to settle it, right on to a war and where we are now. The problem was, I didn't believe it at the time. It all seemed too unlikely. None of us realized how determined George Bush was to do this."

There can be no doubts about President Bush's fixity of purpose, since events transpired exactly as forecast by his senior aide in early August 1990. It is the president's motivation that requires more explanation. What was it that made George Bush so determined to deal with Saddam, and Iraq, so mercilessly?

At the time, of course, the domestic political horizon looked somewhat unsettled from the point of view of the White House. The economy was sliding toward recession, while the epic scandal of the savings and loan debacle had become a focus of popular indignation, not least the fact that the president's son Neil was implicated in the downfall of one particular S&L. "We will bomb Iraq the day Neil Bush gets indicted," quipped one political commentator soon after the massive deployment to Saudi Arabia had begun.

Short-term domestic political considerations aside, there were very important institutional imperatives behind the push toward military confrontation in the Gulf. It was not just the men from Israel Military Industries who had seen the arrival of world peace as "apocalyptic." In April 1990 a seasoned Pentagon official lamented in casual conversation that the atmosphere at his place of employment was dire. "No one knows what to do over here," he sighed. "The [Soviet] threat has melted down on us, and what else do we have? The navy's been going up to the Hill to talk about the threat of the Indian navy in the Indian Ocean. Some people are talking about the threat of the Colombian drug cartels. But we can't keep a $300 billion budget afloat on that stuff. There's only one place that will do as a threat: Iraq." Iraq, he explained, was a long way away, which justified the budget for military airlift. It had a large air force, which would keep the United States Air Force happy, and the huge numbers of tanks in Saddam's army were more than enough to satisfy the requirements of the U.S. ground forces.[7]

In light of subsequent events, it was a prescient observation. The military buildup in Saudi Arabia, though respectfully referred to by the media as "Desert Shield," was more popularly referred to inside the Pentagon as "Budget Shield." Before the crisis, the U.S. military was due to spend just under $290 billion in the twelve months running from October 1990, the so-called Fiscal Year 1991. Thanks to the Shield, total U.S. military spending for the year, according to sources within the Defense Department, was projected to run at $341 billion, even before the war had ended. The threat of peace and consequent budget cuts had been dramatically staved off.

One more motivation for American actions must be taken into consideration. Ever since Franklin Roosevelt had met with King Ibn Saud of Saudi Arabia in 1945, the Saudi oil fields had been America's most vital strategic interest in the Middle East. As we have seen, Israel had been of great service in defending this interest by its actions against threats, principally from Gamal Abdel Nasser, to the feudal monarchy presiding over the oil fields. Though the Bush administration may have known full well on August 2 or 3 that Saddam had no intention of pushing on to Riyadh, an undisturbed Iraqi sequestration of Kuwait would put him in a position of commanding influence in the whole region and in a position to challenge the U.S. and Western position there. For the White House, that was unacceptable.

The problem for the Israelis was that although on the one hand the Americans seemed agreeable to confronting the only Arab leader with the resources to pose a serious military threat to Israel, on the other hand this task was being undertaken with a new set of strategic assets that did not include Israel, but that did include Egypt and, far worse, Hafez al-Asad of Syria. Israel was not used to being told that it was not wanted at the party, but the reasons for its ostracism were clear to all. America's new Arab alliance might not hold together if it involved fighting shoulder to shoulder with the IDF.

On one of his periodic visits to Washington in the fall of 1990, Defense Minister Moshe Arens complained to the president's national security adviser, Brent Scowcroft, that Israel was not being supplied with "real-time" intelligence on the dispositions of Saddam's Scud missile batteries. Why, asked Scowcraft, did Israel require such information. "So that we can preempt, if need be," replied Arens. "That is exactly why you are not going to get the intelligence," replied Scowcroft.

It is not clear whether or not the Israelis knew how very determined President Bush was to go beyond the liberation of Kuwait and to eliminate Iraq as a military and economic power in the Middle East for years to come. While continually pointing out that they were following American wishes and adopting a "low profile," they also periodically and loudly expressed the view that they feared an American double cross. On December 4, 1990, Foreign Minister David Levy threatened the American ambassador, William Brown, that Israel expected the U.S. to "fulfill all the goals it set for itself at the beginning of the Gulf crisis." If the United States did not attack Iraq, Levy reportedly told Brown, Israel would go ahead on its own.

It was at this time that the National Security Council ordered the U.S. intelligence community to undertake a full review of all intelligence on Israel's nuclear-war-fighting capability. "We knew pretty well what weapons they have," explained one former CIA official who had himself undertaken such exercises in the past, "but we have to check up on their procedures for using them."[8]

A few days after the delivery of this intemperate warning, Prime Minister Shamir arrived in Washington to meet with President Bush for the first time in over a year. The Israeli leader emerged from the encounter wreathed in smiles, expressing himself as "delighted" with what he had been told. The delight was for two reasons. Shamir finally came to understand that George Bush was fully determined to crush Saddam. In addition, he had, as Simcha Dinitz, the former Israeli ambassador to the U.S., explained to us later, come to understand at the meeting that differences of opinion over such matters as expanded Jewish settlements on the West Bank had been "postponed" until well into the future. This is not to say that the meeting went entirely smoothly. According to Washington sources privy to the discussion, Bush demanded that Shamir promise not to retaliate in the event of an Iraqi attack on Israel. Shamir refused. Bush then requested that Shamir submit any retaliation plan for American refusal. Shamir again balked at giving an explicit assurance, but was mollified by the president's willingness to push other matters, as Dinitz put it, "under the carpet."

It was an extraordinary reversal of the traditional way of doing things. Whereas formerly Israel had proved its worth as an asset through action, it was now to be rewarded for inaction.

It was not as if the American commanders had much need of Israeli forces, or even Israeli intelligence expertise. The American target planners did listen interestedly to Israeli advice that "the best way to hurt Saddam" was to target his family, his personal guard, and his mistress, as the U.S. Air Force chief of staff imprudently disclosed to reporters. Overall, however, Israeli intelligence was not highly regarded by its American peers. "They don't really have anything in the way of human intelligence [spies] in Iraq," explained one well-informed official early on in the crisis. "Their satellite intelligence is a joke, their analysis is rudimentary. They do have signals intelligence, but nothing approaching what we have. They basically rely on a bunch of academics reading the newspapers." (The Israelis had certainly scored no coups in intelligence regarding the actual invasion of Kuwait. Mossad had said it would not happen, and the chief of Military Intelligence was at his wedding party as the Republican Guard rolled south.)

In the past, the Israelis have always pointed to their expertise on Soviet weaponry, acquired through the periodic encounters with Arab forces, as one of their major intelligence contributions to the United States. But, in a telling example of what the end of the Cold War had brought about, the U.S. went straight to the source for such information this time. In an unprecedented transaction, which both parties strove to keep secret, the Defense Intelligence Agency approached the Soviet Ministry of Defense with a list of weapons that the USSR had previously supplied to Iraq. Without demur, the Soviets agreed to sell the United States (for a stiff price) samples of some of its most advanced weapons.[9]

So, the U.S. went to war without Israel. Saddam Hussein had perceived no less clearly than the White House that overt Israeli involvement would severely strain the Arab component of the coalition. Thus the Scuds were sent on their way to Tel Aviv.

George Bush reacted to Saddam's ballistic initiative, according to one observer in the White House, "like a politician on full afterburner." Any price was worth paying to keep America's Arab allies firmly in the anti-Iraq coalition. This point was made clear by Bush when he telephoned Shamir, a man he detested, on the night of the attack. A few months before, Bush had told a delegation of American Jewish leaders that dealing with the Israeli prime minister would drive a person to drink. Now, with his precious alliance under threat, Bush was ready to pay a high price for Israeli restraint. To make the message even more clear, the portly, chain-smoking figure of Deputy Secretary of State Lawrence Eagleburger appeared in Tel Aviv. After gravely inspecting the damage left by the Scuds, he slouched through the lobby of the Hilton in muddy boots, assisted by a cane. The Israelis were quick to put a precise dollar figure on their price for leaving the war to others: $13 billion. Three billion were for "war-related costs" and ten were for resettling the Russian immigrants. "What are we going to do," quipped one congressman when the amount was revealed in Washington, "put it on American Express?" At least the Patriots next to Hotel California had been taken out of existing U.S. stocks, already paid for.[10]

The Israelis were happy to find the Bush administration so accommodating. They understood very well that public announcements that their pilots could do better than the Americans at hunting down Saddam's Scud launchers were far from the truth. Asked what an Israeli bombing mission could accomplish beyond what the Americans were doing, Yalo Shavit, a retired Israeli air force general (who had flown in the first wave against the Egyptians on June 5, 1967), held up his thumb and forefinger and answered, candidly, "Zero." In fact, he frankly admitted, the Israelis might not even do as well, since they were not used to flying in the kind of weather being experienced by the Allied pilots.

The fact that the Americans were prepared both to deal with the Scud threat to Israel and to simultaneously pay the Israelis not to even try and help out was obviously a cause for satisfaction for the Israeli government, especially as opinion polls showed that ordinary Israelis had no desire at all for retaliation. It was, as former Military Intelligence chief Shlomo Gazit put it at the time, the Israeli military who were "trigger-happy," because they felt "bad that they are out of the war."

Whatever the Israeli people thought or desired, it was the trigger-happy faction that almost won the day. On February 11, Moshe Arens arrived in Washington to warn the administration that Israel had a "fully operational" plan to launch a ground assault by special forces into a large area of western Iraq, from where the Scuds were being launched, to physically eliminate the threat. This approach had been presaged by Yehoshua Saguy, the former Military Intelligence chief, who had told us in Tel Aviv two weeks before that the only way to deal with the problem was to "touch the missiles with your hand."

Arens complained to the American leadership that the Scud attacks, despite American bombing, showed no signs of stopping. The point was dramatically emphasized during his meeting with President Bush and other top advisers when a message came that another Scud had landed in Tel Aviv. What was not announced at the time was that the missile had landed in the wealthy suburb of Savion, one block from Arens's own house. Despite this personal touch, the Americans were appalled that the Israelis might actually send troops into Iraq, as well as irritated at Arens's suggestion that the Israelis could do the job and that the Americans had failed. The plan was rejected, although Arens indicated that Israel might go ahead anyway.

Two weeks later, the war was over, won without any help from the Israelis. Iraq lay in ruins. One hundred and sixty million pounds of Allied high explosives had sent the country if not back to the Stone Age, as had been once suggested as a suitable fate for Vietnam, at least back into a preindustrial state. Baghdad and most of the country were without electricity, fuel, sewage, medicine. Epidemics were on the rise. As many as a hundred thousand Iraqis had died.

Israel could hardly have hoped for more, and yet the American victory, like its victory in the Cold War, begged the question of what Israel's role was now to be. It had no covert wars against Soviet proxies to fight, no Soviet-sponsored Arab leader to humble on behalf of the Americans. The day the war ended, a mordant joke circulated in Tel Aviv: the campaign had presented a great opportunity for Israel. "Now we can sell the Iraqis replacements for all the weapons that the Americans destroyed." It was a new world. Shaul Hamelech would have to find a way to keep busy.

Source Notes

The observations recorded in this chapter were gathered in numerous trips by the authors to Israel, both together and separately in 1980, 1981, 1982, 1983, 1984, 1988, 1989, and 1991.

In the course of these trips we had the opportunity to interview the majority of the leading players. Many of these interviews, such as with David Kimche and Prime Minister Shamir, were videotaped.

1. *Ha'aretz*, 4/14/89.
2. The Hebrew-language press is an absolutely indispensable window into Israeli-Jewish society. Coverage of local politics and issues is far more hard-edged than most of what is carried in either the reports of the resident correspondents of the foreign English-language press or the English-language *Jerusalem Post*. Israelis themselves are conscious of this difference. An Israeli who immigrated from Poland in the 1950s recalled for us how his Hebrew teacher would give his class the exercise of translating the *Jerusalem Post* coverage of a particular event or issue into Hebrew and the *Ha'aretz* coverage of the same story into English. The class soon noted that the *Ha'aretz* coverage was invariably far more informative and critical than the *Post*, and pointed this out to the teacher. "You must understand the function of the *Jerusalem Post*," replied the teacher, "it is to give the American ambassador a happy breakfast!"
3. *Koterit Rashit*, 5/25/83.

4. On Israeli assistance to China on missiles sold to Saudi Arabia: *Israeli Foreign Affairs*, December 1987. Biographical details concerning Eisenberg: *Business Week*, 11/16/81.

CHAPTER 2

1. Amos Elon, *The Israelis* (Tel Aviv: Adam Publishers, 1981), p. 104.

2. Howard M. Sacher, *A History of Israel* (New York: Alfred A. Knopf, 1988), p. 157.

3. Avi Schlaim, *Collusion Across the Jordan* (New York: Columbia University Press, 1988), p. 17.

4. Tom Segev, *1949: The First Israelis* (New York: Free Press, 1986), p. 269.

5. Lenny Brenner, *Zionism in the Age of the Dictators* (Westport, CT: Lawrence Hill, 1983), p. 267.

6. David Hirst, *The Gun and the Olive Branch* (London: Faber, 1977), p. 118.

7. Uri Bialer, *Between East and West* (New York: Cambridge University Press, 1990), p. 13.

8. Stephen Green, *Taking Sides* (New York: William Morrow, 1984), pp. 58, 59.

9. Stephen Green, *Living by the Sword* (Brattleboro, VT: Amana Books, 1988), pp. 217, 218.

10. Bialer, op. cit., p. 15.

11. Ibid., p. 69.

12. "Lubricating expenses": Bialer, op. cit., p. 79. "Even the [Communist] Party": Segev, op. cit., p. 107.

13. Bialer, op. cit., p. 80.

14. Hank Greenspun, *Here I Stand* (New York: David McKay, 1966), pp. 75–167.

15. Teddy Kollek, *For Jerusalem* (New York: Random House), pp. 69–87.

16. Michael J. Stone, *Truman and Israel* (Berkeley: University of California Press, 1990), p. 61.

17. Ibid., p. 64.

18. Ibid., p. 70.

19. Ibid., pp. 168–70.

20. Ibid., p. 71.

21. Authors' discussion with the late Mr. Smith, September 1982.

22. Green, *Taking Sides*, p. 23.

23. On the Grunich story, see Segev, op. cit., pp. 273–79.

24. Segev, op. cit., p. 280.

25. Ibid., p. 281.

26. Bialer, op. cit., p. 49.

27. Ibid., p. 214.

28. Ibid., p. 213.

29. Ibid., p. 220.

30. On the Cabinet vote on Korea, see *Jerusalem Post*, October 17, 1988.

31. Bialer, op. cit., p. 222.

32. On Boris Guriel and the Anglo-American Commission, see Stewart Steven, *Spymasters of Israel* (New York: Ballantine Books, 1980), p. 34.

33. Schlaim, op. cit., p. 371.

34. Personal communication from Brian Urquhart.

35. On the Bernadotte assassination, see Green, *Taking Sides*, pp. 38–39.

36. Personal communication to author.

37. Letter to author, 12/10/84.

38. Anthony Cave Brown, *Wild Bill Donovan, The Last Hero* (New York: Times Books, 1982), pp. 701–2.

39. Christopher Simpson, *Blowback* (New York: Collier Books, 1989), pp. 40–46.

40. *Yerushalayim*, 6/29/90.

CHAPTER 3

1. On the background and early career of Harel, see Stewart Steven, *Spymasters of Israel* (New York: Ballantine Books, 1980), pp. 41–51.

2. Ibid., pp. 68–72.

3. Interviews with Harel, October 1989.

4. Uri Bialer, *Between East and West* (New York: Cambridge University Press, 1990), p. 251.

5. Meir Cotic, *The Prague Trial* (New York: Herzl Books, 1987), p. 87.

6. Stephen Green, *Taking Sides* (New York: William Morrow, 1984), p. 81.

7. Kenneth Love, *Suez: The Twice-Fought War* (New York: McGraw-Hill, 1969), p. 676.

8. Miles Copeland, *The Game of Nations* (London: Weidenfeld & Nicolson, 1969), p. 56.

9. Wilbur Crane Eveland, *Ropes of Sand* (New York: W.W. Norton, 1980), p. 103n.

10. Christopher Simpson, *Blowback* (New York: Collier Books, 1989), p. 249.

11. Bialer, op. cit., p. 262.

12. Ibid.

13. Livia Rokach, *Israel's Sacred Terrorism* (Belmont, MA: Association of Arab American University Graduates, 1980).

14. On Harel and Operation Mirage, see Isser Harel, *Security and Democracy* (Jerusalem: Edanim/Yediot Aharanot, 1989), pp. 389–91.

15. Donald Neff, *Warriors at Suez* (Brattleboro, VT: Amana Books, 1988), p. 33.

16. Love, op. cit., p. 80.

17. Ibid., p. 105.

18. Entry for 11/26/55.

19. Matti Golan, *The Road to Peace: A Biography of Shimon Peres* (New York: Warner Books, 1989), p. 31.

20. On who was really helping whom in Algeria, see Neff, op. cit., p. 162.

21. Sharett diary, entry for 10/19/55.

22. On the CIA search for the speech, see John Ranelagh, *The Agency* (New York: Simon & Schuster, 1986), p. 286. For the story of how the Poles put it into mass circulation in Warsaw, see Teresa Toranska, *Them: Stalin's Polish Puppets* (New York: Harper & Row, 1989), p. 174. Isser Harel's account of how he obtained the speech is told in Steven, op. cit., p. 116. Manor's contribution is detailed in Dan Raviv and Yossi Melman's *Every Spy a Prince* (New York: Houghton Mifflin, 1990), pp. 86–89.

23. Author interview January 1989.

24. Neff, op. cit., p. 433.
    Harel describes his altercation with Dulles after Suez in Harel, op. cit., pp. 405–6.

25. Harel, op. cit., p. 407.

26. Eveland, op. cit., pp. 292, 310.

27. Ibid., pp. 240–41.

CHAPTER 4

1. "their existence was classified": Author interview with James H. Conran, 6/13/89. Many details of the Conran story are drawn from author's interview. See also John Fialka, *Washington Star*, 3/28/78. The secret testimony of Carl Duckett was released by mistake under the Freedom of Information Act by the Nuclear Regulatory Commission in 1978. See Fialka, *Washington Star*, 8/3/78. It is interesting that another "top-secret" CIA document was released "by mistake" under FOIA that same year. The document, which the author included in a broadcast titled "The Nuclear Battlefield: The Defense of the United States," "CBS Reports," 6/81, gave the CIA assessment that Israel had produced nuclear weapons by 1974. Duckett appeared in an ABC News "Close-Up" produced by Chris Isham in April 1981 saying there was a "clear consensus" in the CIA that the "most likely case" was that Israel had diverted nuclear materials from NUMEC. "I believe that all of my senior analysts who worked on the problem agreed with me fully," Duckett told ABC News. See also *New York Times*, 2/25/78 and 5/1/81.

2. "terribly wrong": James H. Conran, Division of Safeguards, NMSS/ Nuclear Regulatory Commission, p. 6, "An Open Letter to the Nuclear Regulatory Commission," 4/4/77.

3. "the general public": TOP SECRET/DIVERT/TO DIRECTOR FBI FROM SAC/ Washington Field Office, document # 117–2564/117–273 (FBI), 5/14/76, Freedom of Information Office, FBI. A great many documents of interest can be found in the Washington Field Office 117–273 file. The General Accounting Office report citing eight key officials who had not been interviewed was titled "Nuclear Diversion in the US? 13 Years of Contradiction and Confusion," 12/18/78. The fact that Congressman Morris Udall regarded the NUMEC case as a scandal in the same league as Watergate, Koreagate, and My Lai is a quote from the House Interior Committee hearings of 7/29/77.

4. "atomic espionage": John Edgar Hoover/Memo for the Record, 2/10/69/SECRET/FBI/FOIA office, FBI. Paul Nitze was interviewed by the author in September 1990 in Washington. Peter Stockton was interviewed by the author in June 1989 in Washington. Duckett's secret testimony to the Nuclear Regulatory Commission, already cited, was released under FOIA in 1978.

5. "nuclear navy": Details of Shapiro's life from the *Congressional Record*, 5/14/79, and Raviv and Melman, *Every Spy a Prince* (New York:

Houghton Mifflin, 1990). The FBI lists were obtained by the author from a congressional source. Dr. X was cited in FBI memo to SAC Pittsburgh from Director FBI 3/4/69, U.S. Department of Justice/SECRET/ NOFORN/5/5/69/file 117–2564/FBI/FOI. The FBI memo notes: ". . . endeavor to ascertain whether the item was on the initiative of the newspaper or whether it was planted by some outside source. If the latter is the case, endeavor to ascertain who was responsible . . . [censored] Shapiro is head of Nuclear Materials and Equipment Corporation, Apollo, Pennsylvania [censored] and his company has classified AEC contracts . . ." Kissinger's interest in Shapiro is noted in "Memorandum of Record: Discussion with Henry Kissinger re Shapiro Case," 1/26/71, signed William T. Riley, Director, Division of Security. The memo was obtained by the author from congress but should be available through the Department of Energy FOI office. When the author interviewed Mort Halperin in June 1989, he added, "The Non-Proliferation Treaty never would have gone through under Nixon. The whole view in the White House was, who are we to stop responsible nations from having nuclear weapons?"

6. "saw things quite differently": Author interview with Peter Stockton, 6/89. For Starbird's 1978 statement see Fialka, *Washington Star*, 1/28/79. Also, according to an April 27, 1979 document (FOI/DOE) titled "Aug 8 1977 Numec-related Congressional Hearing," a July 29, 1977 ERDA briefing was "conducted by Theodore Shackley, who was the Associate Deputy Director of CIA Operations. The briefing was also attended by General Alfred D. Starbird . . ." Details of NUMEC financing can be found in FBI document "SECRET/NOFORN 117–2564–8/21/69"; also in "FBI Pittsburgh SECRET/6/13/68," a long document reviewing financing and NUMEC directors, with nine pages censored. Details of Lowenthal from "FBI Pittsburgh/SECRET/6/13/68" (FOI/FBI) and author interviews with Peter Stockton (Dingell Committee senior investigator) and with a confidential congressional source, and from an internal congressional report (unreleased).

7. "shut down the plant": Atomic Energy Commission Report, December 1, 1961. Other memos cited here: "Memo/SECRET/ JA Waters/AEC Division of Security/ 1/24/62; "AEC memo" from J. Badini, 8/1/63. The Waters/Betts AEC memo, 1/30/62, reports on the guest worker Baruch Cinai. Ephraim Lahav is the subject of a secret memo from JA Waters/ Atomic Energy Commission, Division of Security, 1/24/62. After the Badini inspection of the Apollo plant, William T. Riley of the Atomic Energy Commission wrote: "It was apparent during Mr. Badini's July 23, 1963 visit to NUMEC that the facility did not have positive controls for its

alien employees. . . ." (Letter to Mr. Georgi, 10/15/63). The matter of the metallurgist is addressed in a secret memo from JA Waters to AW Betts dated 2/27/62, cited in the internal congressional report of the Udall House Interior Committee investigation of NUMEC (unreleased) obtained by author from congressional source.

Authors interview with John Hadden, quoted here, 2/12/91. Author interview with Theodore Shackley, quoting his refusal to comment "one way or the other," 2/12/91.

8. "crying in the wilderness": See John Fialka, *Washington Star*, 8/28/77. The story of the Kimwipes comes from Memorandum for Chairman Seaborg (AEC), "Closing of Westinghouse Astro Nuclear Laboratory (WANL), Purchase Order No. 59–NP–12674, With Nuclear Materials and Equipment Corporation (NUMEC)," August 2, 1965, from Howard Brown, Assistant General Manager for Administration; also, "Memorandum for the Files," Atomic Energy Commission, 7/22/65, from Howard Brown. The internal memo prepared for the chairman of the AEC was dated 8/2/65.

The Mellon Bank loan was addressed by Congress in its internal investigation (unreleased), Udall Committee, p. 76: "NUMEC had borrowed, as of December 27, 1965, $1,125,000 under its arrangement with the Mellon Bank . . . The question of why the Mellon Bank would agree to make such loans in the face of NUMEC's unstable financial status became a matter of concern to JCAE [Joint Committee on Atomic Energy] staff." The skeptical comments of George Murphy are quoted in Howard Kohn and Barbara Newman, "How Israel Got the Nuclear Bomb," *Rolling Stone*, no. 235, December 1, 1977, pp. 38–40. The lack of experience in the "field of security" is a quote from the Udall Committee report on the NUMEC investigation (unreleased).

The white residue on the trees and bushes at NUMEC was quoted from FBI file 117–273 (FBI/FOI), Washington Field Office, 10/22/79. The hog wire fence and nuclear material on the floor are reported in FBI file 117–2564, filed office file 117–273/9-18-78/ DC Office, "Atomic Energy Act: Obstruction of Justice," and GAO Report "Nuclear Diversion in the US? 13 Years of Contradiction and Confusion," 12/18/78. On classified documents on NUMEC premises, see John Fialka, "The American Connection: How Israel Got the Bomb" as reprinted in the *Congressional Record*, 5/14/79, pp. S5739–S5740. The documents are also discussed in the internal congressional report on the NUMEC investigation (unreleased), which adds: "Suspicion of Shapiro and NUMEC centers on the following . . . Shapiro's relationship with persons involved in Israel's nuclear weapons program and other Israelis who were up to no good . . ."

9. "Israeli government": FBI/SECRET/NOFORN/Bureau file 117–2564, 9/18/78 (FBI/FOI). The FBI's inability to crack the code is discussed in the *Congressional Record*, 5/14/79, p. S5741. The description of NUMEC as sales agent for the government of Israel is in the J. Edgar Hoover letter dated 11/3/66 (FOI/FBI) from the Atomic Energy Commission. The export license issue was addressed in a letter from J. Walter Yeagley, Assistant Attorney General, Internal Security Division (AEC), to Ralph G. Mayer, Chief Violations Branch, Division of Security, October 1966, "RE: Dr. Zalman Mordechai Shapiro." For documents on ISO-RAD and experiments conducted in Israel, see FBI Report/Pittsburgh Office, 6/21/66 (FOI/FBI file 117–2564), and FBI Report/New York Office, 12/23/68 (FOI/FBI file 117–2564). Israel's efforts to solicit technical and financial assistance is quoted from an internal congressional investigation (unreleased) into the NUMEC affair by the Udall Committee in the House.

10. "just like Pollard": Author interview with confidential source, 6/89. AEC Director William Riley's threats that NUMEC was "bigger than they were" can be found in FBI/SECRET/"Atomic Energy Act"/"Obstruction of Justice"/ file 117–2564, 9/18/78 (FBI/FOI). Details of the security breaches at NUMEC are quoted from the following: FBI memo/King of Prussia Office/ file 117–174, 3/11/80; FBI memo/Pittsburgh Office/ file 117–108, 3/25/80; FBI memo/Washington Field Office, 3/17/78, 117–2564 (FBI/FOI); FBI/SECRET/NOFORN/ to Director FBI from SAC Pittsburgh, 11/20/68, 117–2564 (FBI/FOI).

11. "Ben-Gurion prevailed": Yigal Allon, *A Curtain of Sand (Massach Shel Chol;* Tel Aviv: Hakibbutz Hame'uchad Publishers, 1969). See also Amos Perlmutter, Michael Handel, and Uri Bar-Joseph, *Two Minutes Over Baghdad* (Cornwall: Vallentine, Mitchell, 1982), p. 27; Efraim Inbar, "Israel and Nuclear Weapons Since 1973," in Louis Rene Beres, ed., *Security or Armageddon?* (Lexington Books, 1986), pp. 65, 75; and Mark Gaffney, *Dimona, The Third Temple?* (Amana, 1989), p. 50. The quotes from Dr. Ernst Bergman and Shimon Peres regarding the nuclear program (as well as the Mapai party member) can be found in Yoram Nimrod, "L'eau, l'atome et le conflit," *Les Temps Modernes*, Paris XXII, 1967, no. 253, pp. 902–3; Gaffney, op. cit., pp. 50–51; and *Jewish Observer and Middle East Review*, July 9, 1965. French-Israeli nuclear cooperation is discussed in Fuad Jabber, *Israel and Nuclear Weapons* (London: Chatto & Windus, 1971), pp. 20–24. Author toured Saclay in January 1981 for CBS News, having been alerted by Defense Intelligence Agency sources that Israel would launch a conventional strike on the Osirak reactor (which occurred six months later, in June 1981). See "The

Nuclear Battlefield," "CBS Reports," 6/81. Author also interviewed General Shlomo Gazit (in Israel), who had just retired as chief of Israeli Military Intelligence, and Bertrand Goldschmidt (in Paris), regarded as a "father of the French bomb."

12. "three months after the Suez War": Wilbur Eveland quote from his book *Ropes of Sand* (New York: W. W. Norton, 1980), p. 309. CIA Director Allen Dulles's memo for Brigadier General Chester Clifton, military aide to the president, was dated 2/7/61 and titled "Memorandum Subject: Prime Minister Ben-Gurion's Resignation." The Director of Tahal, the Israeli water company, was quoted in the Israeli paper *Davar*, January 3, 1963. Ben Gurion's contention that Dimona was a pumping station or textile plant is cited in Stephen Green, *Taking Sides* (New York: William Morrow, 1984), pp. 153–54.

13. "sections 793 and 794": Letter from Lawton Geiger, AEC Division of Naval Reactors to Dr. Shapiro (NUMEC), February 13, 1962 (FOI/DOE). That document refers to another letter from Geiger as well, dated January 8, 1962, on the same subject. The Rickover reference is included in the unpublished internal report on NUMEC by the Udall Committee of the House of Representatives, p. 10. Other documents regarding NUMEC's French relationships include a letter dated November 3, 1966 from the AEC to J. Edgar Hoover (FOI/FBI) on NUMEC Instruments and Controls Corporation (NUMINCO), jointly owned by NUMEC and the Société d'Application Industrielles de la Physique (SAIP). The FBI Washington Field Office report file #117–2564/117–273 titled "Atomic Energy Act/Obstruction of Justice," dated 9/18/78 (FOI/FBI), states: "It seemed a bit odd [censored] that France, Israel, and NUMEC had an arrangement where they appeared to be very close in their operations. About six months after the incident became public concerning the missing materials at NUMEC in 1966, the French backed off from NUMEC and the Israelis went out of their way to avoid NUMEC. During the time preceding the official indication of unaccountable materials, there seemed to be a lot of contacts between the Israelis and NUMEC [censored]."

The physicist's story comes from an author interview with a confidential source in February 1989. The London *Sunday Times* series on Dimona ran on October 5 and October 12, 1986. The shipping of "textile machinery" and Perrin's comments on DeGaulle are detailed in it.

14. "highly distressing": Memo for Record, Anne Whitman file, Transition series, Memos of the Staff re Change of Administration, Dwight D. Eisenhower Library, 12/6/60. References to the Weizmann Institute research programs can be found in *Ha'aretz*, 12/21/60, the *London Times*,

12/20/60, and Sylvia Crosbie, *A Tacit Alliance: France and Israel from Suez to the Six-Day War* (Princeton: Princeton University Press, 1974), p. 162, as well as Green, op. cit., p. 151. The one-bomb-per-year estimate is cited in Crosbie, op. cit., p. 163, and Green, op. cit., p. 153. Eisenhower's discussion with Ben-Gurion comes from a memo of a conversation between Prime Minister Ben-Gurion and Eisenhower/SECRET/ 3/10/60/ Record of the White House Office, Office of the Staff Secretary/ Box 8/International Series/ Israel/ Dwight D. Eisenhower Library.

15. "possession of nuclear capability": Quotes from Sherman Kent are taken from CIA/Memo for the Director/SECRET/ 3/6/63/ Carrolton Press Declassified Documents Records System, 1978/49B. The conversation at the Kennedy/Ben-Gurion meeting is taken from Jabber, op. cit., p. 124, and Michael Bar Zohar, *Ben-Gurion* (New York: Adama Books, 1977), pp. 273–74.

16. Israel's "outside financial sources": TOP SECRET/CABLE TO U.S. EMBASSY CAIRO/ from George Ball/ 5/30/64/ Carrolton Press Declassified Documents Records System, 1976/184A. The quotes from John Hadden come from one of three interviews with the author on 2/12/91. Peres and the Hawk missiles are discussed in Matti Golan, *The Road to Peace: A Biography of Shimon Peres* (New York: Warner Books, 1989), pp. 71–75.

17. "a place on death row": See Green, op. cit., p. 174. The impermissible intelligence gathering activities are discussed in the internal congressional report on the NUMEC investigation/Udall Committee/House of Representatives/ unreleased/ p. 109. See also FBI/Memo to Director/file 117–2564/ (FOI/FBI) / 9/11/68/ from SAC/WFO. Subject: [censored] Atomic Energy Act. The Shapiro explanation that the airport meeting was convened to discuss a delinquent bill can be found on page 106 of the congressional report. The bureau for Israeli professionals is noted in Green, op. cit., p. 174. On the Home-to-Dimona drive, see the *Jerusalem Post*, 2/5/67. Shapiro's efforts to solicit advice from scientists is quoted in Fialka, *Washington Star*, 5/14/79. FBI reports on Avraham Hermoni include FBI/SECRET/WFO/2/13/69 and FBI/SECRET/ WFO/12/23/68. An internal congressional report on the NUMEC investigation (unreleased) says (p. 105): "On August 14th, 1969 Shapiro was interviewed in the AEC [Atomic Energy Commission] offices at 1717 H Street. One focus of the interview was a meeting held in Shapiro's Pittsburgh home attended by Avraham Hermoni [scientific counselor of the Israeli Embassy and possibly an Israeli intelligence officer] and eleven American scientists . . . Shapiro said the purpose was to discuss ways in which the people in attendance might assist Israel in solving

technical problems. Shapiro noted that much of the discussion centered on military activities and that people more experienced in such matters could have provided more detailed information. Shapiro indicated that he did not know why Hermoni had not requested information on these topics from the U.S. military." The purpose of the Eitan/Hermoni trip to Apollo being damage assessment is noted in Raviv and Melman, op. cit., p. 199.

18. "Duckett retired, citing reasons of health": Duckett's disclosure of the ten to twenty nuclear weapons assessment of the CIA is reported by John Fialka in the *Washington Star*, 1/29/78. See also George Bush's letter to the American Institute of Aeronautics and Astronautics dated March 16, 1976: "I recognize that the Agency [i.e. Duckett] was in error in respond-ing to certain questions at the AIAA session, and I have publicly accepted responsibility for that mistake." Shapiro's VIP treatment in Israel is recounted in the congressional report, op. cit. p. 3: "He was accorded the then rare privilege of a helicopter flight over the Sinai battlefield. He is alleged to have had a close relationship with Dr. Bergman, head of Israel's nuclear weapons program." Dr. Shapiro's fate after NUMEC is discussed in the congressional report, op. cit., pp. 110–11: ". . . circa October 1970, Atlantic Richfield notified Shapiro their relationship would be termi-nated as of October 15. Shapiro felt this was wrong . . . circa 1972 the clearance question arose at Westinghouse and then AEC Chairman Dixie Lee Ray intervened to help Shapiro by seeking his transfer to a less sensitive position."

19. "trigger off a nuclear holocaust": Vanunu is quoted in Gaffney, op. cit., p. 17. The quote from the Healey memoirs is in Dennis Healey, *The Time of My Life* (London: Michael Joseph, 1989), p. 315.

20. "leaking the story of the kidnapping to the London *Financial Times*": The story was leaked to Andrew Whitley, then *Financial Times* correspondent in Jerusalem. Vanunu's photographing spree is described in detail in Gaffney, op. cit., p. 44. Vanunu's presence at the PLO rally is cited in Louis Toscano, *Triple Cross* (New York: Birch Lane Press, 1990), p. 54.

CHAPTER 5

1. Wilbur Crane Eveland, *Ropes of Sand* (New York: W. W. Norton, 1980), p. 310.

2. Samuel Segev, *The Iranian Triangle* (New York: Free Press, 1988), p. 35.

3. Ibid., pp. 35–36.

4. Harel on the "peripheral" strategy: Isser Harel, *Security and Democracy* (Jerusalem: Edanim/Yediot Aharanot, 1989), p. 420.

5. The quotations from the CIA report on Israeli intelligence are taken from one of the volumes published by Iranian students who captured the U.S. embassy in Tehran. Document #11 from *Documents from the U.S. Espionage Den* is entitled "America: Supporter of Usurpers of the Qods" (Tehran: 1981); quotations on p. 28.

6. Eveland, op. cit., p. 322.

7. Uri Bialer, *Middle East Journal* 39 (Spring 1985).

8. James A. Bill, *The Eagle and the Lion* (New Haven: Yale University Press, 1988), p. 403.

9. *Davar*, 11/29/85. Sharon's description of Nimrodi appears there as well.

10. *Pike Committee Report* (Nottingham: Spokesman Books, 1977), pp. 195–98, 212–16.

11. Benjamin Beit Hallahmi, *The Israeli Connection* (New York: Pantheon Books, 1987), p. 11.

12. Ibid., p. 52.

13. "Chadian's Fall Marks End to War on Libya," *Israeli Foreign Affairs*, January 1991, p. 1.

14. On Lior's African trip, see Eitan Haber, *Today War Will Break Out: The Reminiscences of Brig. Gen. Israel Lior* (Jerusalem: Edanim/Yediot Aharanot, 1987), pp. 73–91. Lior was collaborating with Haber on his memoirs at the time of his death. Haber published the general's reminiscences under his own name.

15. Meyouhas is discussed in Stewart Steven, *Spymasters of Israel* (New York: Ballantine Books, 1980), p. 90, and in Beit Hallahmi, op. cit., pp. 60–61.

16. On Amin's rise to power, see Pat Hutton and Richard Bloch, *How the West Established Idi Amin and Kept Him There; Dirty Work 2: The CIA in Africa*, edited by Ellen Ray, William Schaap, Karl van Meter, and Louis Wolf (Secaucus, NJ: Lyle Stuart, 1979), pp. 171–80.

17. Matti Golan, *The Road to Peace* (New York: Warner Books, 1989), pp. 146–47.

18. For the story of Zimex, we are indebted to Murray Waas, a reporter who truly deserves the title "investigative," for turning over his files on Zimex and Amin. These included the Deposition of 11/30/77 by the SEC of Charles E. Hanner, who described the original arrangements between Page Airways, Mr. Ziegler, and Idi Amin, as well as the SEC Deposition of Vernon H. Phillips, one of the pilots involved in the military side of the

operation, on 12/19/79. See also *Washington Post*, 4/14/78; the *Wall Street Journal*, 4/8/80; and the *Democrat and Chronicle*, Rochester, NY, 4/20/80.

19. See John Stockwell, *In Search of Enemies* (New York: W. W. Norton, 1978), passim, for the American strategy; see also *The Economist*, 11/5/77.

20. *Israeli Foreign Affairs*, op. cit.

CHAPTER 6

1. See Michael Brecher, *Decisions in Israel's Foreign Policy* (New York: Oxford University Press, 1974), p. 322.

2. Richard Johns, *The House of Saud* (New York: Holt, Rinehart, & Winston, 1981), p. 248.

3. Jonathan Bloch and Patrick Fitzgerald, *British Intelligence and Covert Action* (Dingle, Ireland: Brandon Book Publishers, 1983), pp. 127–28.

4. Carl Von Horn, *Soldiering for Peace* (New York: David McKay, 1967), Chapter 21. The complicated story of the Israeli water project is told in Howard Sacher, *A History of Israel* (New York: Alfred A. Knopf, 1988), p. 522, and in Patrick Seale, *Asad: The Struggle for the Middle East* (London: I. B. Tauris, 1988), p. 119.

5. Seale, op. cit., p. 109. The views of the Israelis as communicated to Washington and endorsed by the CIA were confirmed in interviews with the authors by cognizant former intelligence officials, who also communicated their frustration at the lack of attention being paid to the situation in the Middle East by the rest of official Washington, which was obsessed by Vietnam.

6. Donald Neff, *Warriors for Jerusalem* (Brattleboro, VT: Amana Books, 1988), p. 52. For insights into Soviet foreign policy at this time we are indebted to Professor Richard D. Anderson of UCLA.

7. The story of the Samu Raid and the consequent pressures on King Hussein is told in Neff, op. cit., pp. 40–44.

8. Seale, op. cit., p. 127.

9. The issue of the Soviet warnings is discussed by David Hirst in *The Gun and the Olive Branch* (London: Faber, 1977), p. 215.

10. Weizman's revelation was carried in *Ot* (an Israeli weekly), 6/1/72.

11. See John Cooley, *Green March, Black September* (London: Frank Cass, 1973), pp. 160, 161.

12. Seale, op. cit., p. 137.

13. Ibid. The Israeli decision to attack on May 25 was recounted by Moshe Dayan in his *Story of My Life* (New York: William Morrow, 1976), p. 325.

14. Ezer Weizman, *On Wings of Eagles* (New York: Macmillan, 1976), p. 212.

15. Eitan Haber, *Today War Will Break Out: The Reminiscences of Brig. Gen. Israel Lior* (Jerusalem: Edanim/Yediot Aharanot, 1987), p. 194.

16. Robert Stephens, *Nasser* (London: Pelican, 1973), p. 479.

17. Dayan, op. cit., p. 335. The anger and frustration of the Israeli generals is vividly described in Weizman, op. cit., p. 214, and Haber, op. cit., pp. 194–98. Lior's book, which has unfortunately not been translated for publication, gives an extraordinary insight into the high-level maneuverings within the Israeli high command at this time. It is clear that Eshkol was a lot more clever than his warlords.

18. Neff, op. cit., p. 182.

19. Haber, op. cit., pp. 214–16. The phrase "break [Nasser] in pieces" is a translation of the Hebrew verb *pitzputz* and we are advised that the English phrase conveys the violence of the original.

20. Neff, op. cit., p. 50.

21. Neff, op. cit., p. 190. The account of Nasser's message to the Syrians about trapping Hussein and the reaction of U.S. embassy officials at his return along with Shukeiry and Riad, as well as the CIA warning delivered the night before the war, is based on personal information from American diplomatic sources.

22. Motti Hod boasted about the "plan" to Randolph and Winston Churchill after the war. His remarks are quoted in Kenneth Love, *Suez: The Twice-Fought War* (New York: McGraw-Hill, 1969), p. 677.

23. Neff, op. cit., p. 206.

24. Weizman's question to the cadets about Hebron was recounted in *Al Hamishmar*, 1/5/90. While commanding an air base in the 1950s he would excuse punishments to personnel on disciplinary charges if they could tell him a dirty joke he had not heard before. If he had heard the joke, the punishment was doubled.

25. Stephen Green, *Taking Sides* (New York: William Morrow, 1984), p. 203.

26. Neff, op. cit., p. 229.

27. Neff, op. cit., p. 233. The account of King Hussein's anguished complaint is based on personal information from former intelligence officials. The Israelis' use of napalm to speed the flight of Palestinians from the West

Bank has been attested to the authors by both Western observers and Palestinians still resident in the occupied territories.

28. For a graphic account by a survivor of the Liberty attack, see James M. Ennes, *Assault on the Liberty* (New York: Ivy Books, 1979). Ennes makes an unassailable case for the fact that the Israelis knew what they were doing, and that the U.S. government covered up the incident.

29. The *New York Times*, 8/21/82.

30. *Ha'aretz*, 3/20/72.

31. Peled made his claim that the notion that Egypt actually constituted a military threat was an insult to the Israeli army in the course of a lecture on the 1967 war. An account of his statements was carried in *Ma'ariv*, 3/24/72, some days after he had addressed the subject. Peled's remarks prompted Weizman's confirmation that there had been "no threat" in 1967. These refutations of the basic "David and Goliath" fable on the 1967 war were not generally publicized in the U.S., although Begin's invocation of the voluntary nature of the June 1967 choice was reported in the *New York Times*.

32. *Le Monde*, 2/29/68.

CHAPTER 7

1. Interview with author, June 1990. It may be of interest that Mr. Gal does not himself possess a copy of his famous gun. He asked me to keep his address and the town in which he lives confidential.

2. Matti Golan, *The Road to Peace: A Biography of Shimon Peres* (New York: Warner Books, 1989), p. 11.

3. Ibid., p. 20.

4. On Gardner's and Peres's views on arms sales, see Matti Golan, op. cit., pp. 79–82.

5. Pierre Pean, *Les Deux Bombes* (Paris: Fayard, 1982), p. 37.

6. *Davar*, 7/14/89.

7. Aaron Klieman, *Israel's Global Reach* (Washington, D.C.: Pergamon Brassey, 1985), p. 21.

8. Personal interview with Paul Nitze, September 1990. On opposition to the F-4 sale, see Stephen Green, *Living by the Sword* (Brattleboro, VT: Amana Books, 1988), p. 13.

9. *Christian Science Monitor*, 8/24/90.

10. Ze'ev Schiff, *History of the Israeli Army* (London: Sidgewick & Jackson, 1987), pp. 185–86.

11. Donald Neff, "Nixon's Middle East Policy: From Balance to Bias," *Arab Studies Quarterly*, Winter/Spring 1990, pp. 121–151.

12. *The Rabin Memoirs* (Boston: Little, Brown, 1979), p. 189.

13. On U.S. aid figures, see Congressional Research Service Issue Brief by Clyde R. Mark, "Israel: U.S. Foreign Assistance Facts," July 1990. See also R. D. McLaurin, "U.S. Military Technology Transfer and Second-tier Arms Exporters: A Case Study," *Pacific Review*, Summer 1985, which explores the growth of Israeli-U.S. military aid and technical cooperation.

14. The shortcomings of Israeli intelligence with regard to their Arab enemies are attested to by numerous intelligence officials with experience in the region. Archie Roosevelt's observations are in his memoirs, *For Lust of Knowing* (Boston: Little, Brown, 1988), p. 448.

15. Green, *Living by the Sword*, p. 82.

16. *Pike Committee Report* (Nottingham: Spokesman Books, 1977), p. 142.

17. The story of Fred Fear's bridges is attested to by former colleagues of his at the CIA. After the war Fear was promoted, as were the higher officials who had ignored his report.

18. Interview with Brian Urquhart, October 1988.

19. The ascription of 51 percent of the blame for the Yom Kippur intelligence failure to Mossad, which contradicts the general view that Military Intelligence was primarily to blame, comes from an interview in May 1989 with a former Israeli intelligence officer who knows as much as anyone about the intelligence background to the war.

20. Donald Neff, *Warriors Against Israel* (Brattleboro, VT: Amana Books, 1988), p. 105.

21. Lior's observations on Meir's dilemma are reported in Eitan Haber, *Today War Will Break Out: The Reminiscences of Brig. Gen. Israel Lior* (Jerusalem: Edanim/Yediot Aharanot), pp. 26–28. Kissinger's last-minute injunctions against an Israeli preemptive strike are also described by William Quandt (who was on the National Security Council Staff at the time) in his *Decade of Decision: American Policy Towards the Arab-Israeli Conflict, 1967–76* (Berkeley: University of California Press, 1977), p. 169.

22. Personal interview with National Security Council Middle East staffer William Quandt, October 1980. The consternation that news of the alert

caused at the White House is described in Green, *Living by the Sword*, pp. 90–92.

23. *Decade of Decision*, op. cit., p. 184. Stephen Green quotes the internal report from the DIA, which he obtained under the Freedom of Information Act in *Living by the Sword*, op. cit., p. 95. It must be borne in mind that there were two airlifts. The first, which began very soon after the Arab attack, was of essential items which were pulled out of U.S. military stocks in Germany and sent to the battlefield. The second, authorized by Kissinger to be given maximum publicity, began in the second week of the war and is the one Quandt discusses as having little relevance to the course of the fighting. Quandt's conclusion was confirmed directly to the authors by Israeli military sources. Quandt also says that the tonnage dispatched in the second airlift was arbitrarily fixed by Kissinger to equal or exceed the amounts being sent by the Soviets to the Arab countries.

24. GAO Report, April 16, 1975: Airlift Operations of the Military Airlift Command During the 1973 Middle East War.

25. *Aviation Week & Space Technology*, 6/26/67.

26. Interview with Lt. Col. Stolfi, January 1991. Other present and former Pentagon officials who prefer to remain anonymous attest to the unpopularity of his conclusions within the USAF.

27. *More Bucks, Less Bang*, published by the Project on Military Procurement, Washington, D.C., 1983, pp. 161–62.

28. Interview with former U.S. Air Force officer intimately involved with USAF antitank program, February 1990.

29. Aid figures are from a Congressional Research Service Issue Brief by Clyde R. Mark, "Israel: U.S. Foreign Assistance Facts," July 1990.

30. The story of the politics of Sparrows and F-15s is based on interviews with Colonel James Burton (November 1990) and Motti Hod (November 1988), as well as other U.S. and Israeli officials. The McDonnell Douglas representative in Israel, George Lavin, exclaimed to the authors during the 1982 Lebanon war: "Things are going great! We got six [Syrian Migs] today and GD [General Dynamics, makers of the rival F-16] only got one!" Even so, the F-16 emerged with a slightly higher score overall.

31. Eban, *An Autobiography* (New York: Random House, 1977), p. 460.

32. *New York Times*, 9/21/80.

33. Amnon Kapouliek Israel, *La Fin des Mythes* (Paris: Editions Albin Michel, 1975), p. 219.

34. The story of Jackson's politically profitable encounter with the issue of Soviet Jewish emigration has been chronicled in Ruth Stern's *Water's*

Edge: Domestic Politics and the Making of American Foreign Policy (Westport, CT: Greenwood Press, 1979).

35. For the origins of the JDL, and Kahane's involvement with the CIA, see Robert Friedman, *The False Prophet* (New York: Lawrence Hill, 1990), pp. 51–82.

36. Robert Friedman spent many years researching the instructive story of Meir Kahane. Our account of his recruitment by Geula Cohen and the ensuing JDL campaign against the Soviets is drawn from *The False Prophet*, op. cit., pp. 105–28. Golda Meir's pledge to abandon quiet diplomacy on behalf of Soviet Jews was reported in the *New York Times*, 11/20/69.

37. Friedman, op. cit., p. 107.

38. Dan Raviv and Yossi Melman, *Every Spy a Prince* (New York: Houghton Mifflin, 1990), p. 13.

39. Ruth Stern, op. cit.

40. The account of the joint debriefing center in Tel Aviv and the practice of extracting people under false documentation is based on interviews with cognizant Israelis and former U.S. intelligence officials.

41. Howard Sacher, *A History of Israel* (New York: Alfred A. Knopf, 1988), p. 737.

42. The memo from Pat Buchanan (the man who attracted some notoriety in 1990 by referring to Israel's "amen corner" on Capitol Hill) is reproduced in Bruce Oudes (ed.), *From: The President, Richard Nixon's Secret Files* (New York: Harper & Row, 1989), p. 468.

43. Podhoretz, *Breaking Ranks* (New York: Harper & Row, 1979), pp. 351, 353.

44. Thompson discussed his memories of the Coalition of the Present Danger in an interview in December 1990.

45. *Philadelphia Bulletin*, 12/6/77.

46. Cited in Noam Chomsky, *The Fateful Triangle: The United States, Israel and the Palestinians* (Boston: South End Press, 1983), pp. 14–15.

CHAPTER 8

1. "Collection of scientific intelligence in the U.S. . . .": "Israel: Foreign Intelligence and Security Services—March 1979, CIA," *Documents from the U.S. Espionage Den* (11), Tehran, 1981, p. 9. The authors attended Reuter's party on the invitation of the Sibat chief.

2. Kfirs to Ecuador: Bishara Bahbah, *Israel and Latin America: The Military Connection* (New York: St. Martin's Press, 1986), pp. 117–18. The dependence of Israeli weapons exports on U.S. components was discussed in the GAO report U.S. Assistance to the State of Israel, GAO ID 83–51, June 24, 1983, pp. 43–44.

3. F-15 fueltanks: Interview with Marvin Klemow, November 1981. The opposition to the F-15 sale is described in Edward Tivnan, *The Lobby* (New York: Simon & Schuster, 1987), p. 126.

4. Israelis charging U.S. for military mission and other details about the operation: *Washington Post*, 8/30/77. Ne'eman trying to tour Livermore: Dan Raviv and Yossi Melman, *Every Spy a Prince* (New York: Houghton Mifflin, 1990), p. 201. The career of Binyamin Blumberg is described in Raviv and Melman, op. cit., pp. 69–71.

5. The unedifying tale of Napco and the Israelis was laid out in the "offer of proof" entered into the record by the U.S. Attorney's Office in Albany, New York, when Napco pleaded guilty to exporting military-related commodities to Israel without a license on 11/24/87, Criminal No. 87–CR–240 in U.S. District Court, Northern District of New York.

6. Natti Sharoni and El-Op: Interview with Sharoni, December 1988. Most of the details of the El-Op story were carried in the *Chicago Tribune*, 11/17/86. We have confirmed and supplemented this account through private sources. The full story of the case of Stephen Bryen and his alleged passing of classified information to the Israelis is told in Michael Saba, *The Armageddon Network* (Brattleboro, VT: Amana Books, 1984).

7. Rafi Eitan and his relationship with Arik Sharon drew a good deal of coverage in the Israeli press. See *Yediot Aharanot*, 3/13/87; *Hoalam Ha'zeh*, 8/19/87; and *Ha'aretz*, 3/1/85. Sharon's efforts to meet Arafat are reported in Uzi Benziman, *Israeli Caesar* (New York: Adama Books, 1988), p. 194.

8. Pollard's early career and ATAC: Wolf Blitzer, *Territory of Lies* (New York: Harper & Row, 1989), pp. 35–70.

9. Israeli Air Force and Sella: Alex Fishman, *Hadashot*, 3/11/87.

10. Sella gets approval in writing: Blitzer, op. cit., p. 13.

11. "the countering of the Palestinian threat . . .": *The Third Option: An American View of Counterinsurgency Operations* (New York: Dell, 1981), p. 33.

12. "This is not a claim he can write down": *Koterit Rashit*, 3/25/87.

Chapter 9

1. "the Israel Defense Sales Directory": The information on the Spearhead Corporation in this section is drawn from author interviews with Klein, Shuali, et al, 10/31/88. See also Andrew and Leslie Cockburn, "Israel: The Covert Connection," PBS Frontline, 5/89.

2. "motivation and willingness to learn": Authors interview with Lieutenant Colonel Shuali, 10/31/88.

3. "operational experience": Authors interview with Dror Eyal, 10/31/88.

4. "detected the presence of Americans there": DAS/CONFIDENCIAL/ "Organización de sicarios y narcotrafficantes en el Magdalena Medio"/ July 20, 1988.

5. "Israel's admission to the UN": The large diamond is noted in Jane Hunter, *Israeli Foreign Policy* (Boston: South End Press, 1987), p. 138. The cash paid into Somoza's private account is discussed in Benjamin Beit Hallahmi, *The Israeli Connection* (New York: Pantheon Books, 1987), p. 92. On Somoza's friendship with Israel, see Jamail and Gutierrez, *It's No Secret* (Belmont, MA: Maple Leaf Press, 1986), p. 7.

6. "interwoven within the national creativity": Israeli Ministry of Defense, "Nahal Pioneering Fighting Youth," Tel Aviv, 1963. The Israeli civic action programs are cited in Bishara Bahbah, *Israel and Latin America: The Military Connection* (New York: St. Martin's Press, 1986), p. 90. The network of rural cooperatives is detailed in Hunter, op. cit., p. 99. The American strategy to counter radicalism is discussed in Beit Hallahmi, op. cit., p. 107. More on the exchanges between the Latin American military and the IDF can be found in Jamail and Gutierrez, op. cit., p. 11.

7. "unlike the gringos": Bernt Debusmann, "After Embassy Flap, a Look at Israel's Latin Arms Role," Reuters in the *Philadelphia Inquirer*, April 24, 1984. Haig and the Guatemalans are discussed in Beit Hallahmi, op. cit., p. 79, and General Peled is quoted in the same source, p. 78. See also authors interview with General Peled on PBS Frontline, "Israel: The Covert Connection," 5/89. The quotes from Spearhead's Dror Eyal come from authors interview, 10/31/88.

8. "making up death lists": Details of the computer system and the observations of the American priest can be found in Hunter, op. cit., p. 11. Beit Hallahmi, op. cit., p. 81, also describes the computer network. The *Ha'aretz* report on Uzis in Guatemala was dated 11/25/85. The Reagan administration source made his comments on Guatemala to the author in November 1988, while still deeply involved in Central American policy.

9. "clubs and fists in the village plaza": Victor Perera, "The Lost Tribes of Guatemala," *The Monthly*, Berkeley, CA, 11/85. The Guatemalan military commissioners are discussed in Nancy Peckenham, *Multinational Monitor*, 4/84. Rios Montt and the Roman Catholic Conference of Bishops are quoted in Simons, *New York Times*, 9/12/82. More on bullets and beans can be found in "Asesores Israelies se encuentran en Guatemala," AIP, Enfoprensa and Salpress in *El Día*, 6/23/83, and *Multinational Monitor*, 4/84. See also Hunter, op. cit., p. 118.

10. "modest seaside hotel": *Ma'ariv*, 12/13/85. Lieutenant Colonel Shuali's quotes on Ben Or and the Guatemalan military are drawn from author interview, 10/31/88, and Aluf Ben, writing in *Ha'ir*, 9/87.

11. "unilateral paramilitary action": National Security Decision Directive, November 23, 1981. The DIA reference is from the DIA Weekly Intelligence Summary, July 16, 1982. The fake end user certificate is noted in *Ma'ariv*, 12/13/85. Shapiro's 25-cent pen drawn from authors interview, 12/88. Shuali's quote on the gentiles comes from Aluf Ben, *Ha'ir*, 9/87.

12. "came to a violent end": The Sa'ada descriptions in Massachusetts come from two sources, both personal interviews with the authors, 11/88. Sa'ada's 17th-century adventurer quote comes from John Anderson, "Loose Cannons," writing in the Israeli magazine *New Outlook*, p. 14. Israel's ability to step in easily is quoted from Andrew and Leslie Cockburn, "Israel: The Covert Connection," PBS Frontline, 5/89. An account of Casey and Galtieri can be found in the *Los Angeles Times*, 3/3/85.

13. "I didn't renew their contract": Lopez quote from Anderson, op. cit., p. 26. The relationship of Battalion 316 and Gleser is described in Juan Tamayo, *Miami Herald*, quoted in Anderson, op. cit., p. 25. The association of drug trafficker Matta Ballesteros with the State Department is recorded in "Drugs, Law Enforcement and Foreign Policy: A Report of the Subcommittee on Narcotics, Terrorism and International Operations," Senate Foreign Relations Committee, April 13, 1989, Vol. 1, pp. 118–19. The Israeli trainer was interviewed about his relationship with the contras for the Jerusalem Television Service/ 11-28-86 (FBIS). The Latchinian quotes are drawn from a series of interviews with the authors in the spring of 1989. Latchinian's description of Gleser is quoted in Anderson, op. cit., p. 25. The Sales Directory entry for ISDS in the 1989 volume published by the Israeli Ministry of Defense is on page 363.

14. "east block arms from Israel for the contras": Wayne Smith cited in the *New York Times*, 8/10/85; *Guardian*, 10/11/85 and 4/16/86. Latchinian's relationship with Sherwood is described in *Ma'ariv*, 12/13/85. Sherwood is discussed further in Brogan and Zarca, *Deadly Business* (New York: W. W. Norton, 1983), p. 151. Latchinian's quotes on Gleser and Reuter

are taken from an author interview, 5/89. General Lopez is quoted in Anderson, op. cit., p. 26. Ricardo Lau's position with the contras is drawn from author interview with a confidential administration source, 6/85; his alleged involvement with the murder of Archbishop Romero is taken from the *New York Times*, March 22 and 23, 1985.

15. "millions of dollars' worth of weapons": Authors interview with confidential source, 5/89. The U.S. government stipulation cited is United States of America v. Oliver North/Criminal # 88–0080–02–GAG. The document is available from the National Security Archive, Washington, D.C. The Casey memo released in the North trial documents is CIA/SECRET/ Memo from William Casey DCI to Robert McFarlane, National Security Adviser/March 27th, 1984/ "Supplemental Assistance to Nicaragua Program." A copy can be obtained from the National Security Archive in Washington, the best archive for Iran-Contra documents.

16. "destabilize Central America": Reagan quote is cited in Edy Kaufman, "The View from Jerusalem," *Washington Quarterly* 7, No. 4, Fall 1984, p. 49, as well as in Bahbah, op. cit., p. 170. The *Jerusalem Post* quote on the Jewish community and the contras appeared there on 4/22/84. The quotes on Kimche, Teicher, and Israeli aid to the resistance are taken from the U.S. government stipulation, op. cit., p. 3. Porto Corinto is discussed in Leslie Cockburn, *Out of Control* (New York: Atlantic Monthly Press, 1987), p. 11.

17. "an international network with Israeli advisers": Cited in Anderson, op. cit., p. 24. The Edgar Chamorro references are taken from Anderson, op. cit., p. 23, and from a series of author interviews with Chamorro from 1985 to 1988. The Mercenario quote can be found in *El Día*, 11/6, 7/88. The fact that Sa'ada was named by Honduran military sources as a conduit for Israeli arms is reported in *Israeli Foreign Affairs*, 1/88, p. 5, and 7/87, p. 6. The authors' observations of Tegucigalpa are drawn from trips there on assignment for CBS News.

18. "all this counterinsurgency stuff": Deposition of General Robert Schweitzer, Senate Report #100–216, Appendix B, Vol. 24, pp. 359–60, Washington 1988. General Schweitzer's quotes in this section are all drawn from his deposition before the Senate on pages 331, 359, and 569. The GMT document referring to Nicaragua, Angola, Afghanistan, and Cambodia can be found in Senate Report #100–216, "Iran-Contra Affair," Appendix B, Vol. 24, p. 864, Washington, 1988.

19. "the cause of the Freedom Fighters": Deposition of General Robert Schweitzer, op. cit., Exhibit 11, p. 863. The remark about the arms ending up in the "Supermarket" is taken from the Deposition of General John Singlaub, Senate Report #100–216, "Iran-Contra Affair," Appen-

dix B, Vol. 25, p. 996, Washington, 1988. General Singlaub's quotes in this section are all drawn from his deposition on pages 926, 957, and 983. The discussion of the "vision" can be found in the Deposition of General Schweitzer, op. cit., p. 367.

20. "a representative of the government of Israel": Deposition of General Singlaub, op. cit., Vol. 25, p. 957, Washington 1988. Poland is cited in the *New York Times*, 5/2/87, and the *Jerusalem Post*, 5/6/87. The Iran trade question is raised in the General Schweitzer deposition, op. cit., Vol. 24, p. 461. Extending credit to Israel is discussed in Exhibit 11 of General Schweitzer's deposition, op. cit., Vol. 24, p. 866. U.S. arms reaching the hands of the Khmer Rouge was reported to the author by Nayan Chanda, editor of the *Asian Wall Street Journal Weekly* after author's ABC News documentary "Peter Jennings Reporting: From the Killing Fields" raised the questions in May 1990 of cooperation in the field between non-communist forces and the Khmer Rouge and gave evidence of same, including, according to Prince Sihanouk, sharing arms.

21. "napalm had been dropped on the civilian population": The reference to Dr. John Constable is in Hunter, op. cit., p. 101, and *Israeli Foreign Affairs*, December 1984. The Bustillo and Reagan administration sources comments on napalm are drawn from Beit Hallahmi, op. cit., p. 85, and author interviews with a confidential administration source, 1985–88. The civilian deaths are cited in Hunter, op. cit., p. 105. Israel settling into second place as an arms supplier comes from SIPRI report, Stockholm, 1981. The quote referring to the Salvadoran government's hopes of assistance from the pro-Israel lobby is taken from Ed Cody, "Salvador, Israel Set Closer Ties," *Washington Post*, 8/17/83. The quote on the mission of ISDS trainers in El Salvador is taken from the Jerusalem Television Service, 11/22/89.

22. "a thick carpet of buzzards": David Blundy, London *Sunday Times*, 2/22/81. Ochoa's involvement with a massacre in 1981 is taken from Chris Hedges, *Christian Science Monitor*, 9/26/84. D'Aubisson's Israeli training is cited in Hunter, op. cit., p. 98: from Hunter's interview with Guerra y Guerra, 2/83.

23. "chief of staff of Guatemala or Honduras": Kimche quotes in this section are taken from author interview with David Kimche, 12/88, also broadcast on PBS Frontline, "Israel: The Covert Connection," 5/89. The quote on Israeli vs. U.S. knowledge is taken from *Le Monde*, February 19, 1985, and authors interviews with Spearhead trainers, 10/31/88.

24. "occupied territories to some other country": The association of Katz with Gush Emunim is cited in *Davar*, 11/13, 14/79. Katz costing Israel contracts is alleged in *Davar*, ibid., and Moshe Lichtman, "Israel's

Weapons Exports," *Monitin*, July 1983. The Latchinian quote comes from an author interview, 5/17/89. On the U.S. Embassy cable concerning El Al planes in Nicaragua, see Department of State/U.S. Embassy Managua/ #5572. The $250 million dollars' worth of arms for Somoza is cited in NACLA, XXI, 2, p. 25. Katz's lucrative career in weapons is reported in *Latin American Regional Reports*, 2/19/87. The Katz party at the Pierre is mentioned in author interview with Shapiro, 5/89, Tel Aviv. The apartment listed under Brookdale Holdings was discovered by the author in the Essex House record of owners, 10/90, New York.

25. "Yeshiva University": author interview with Katz, 10/29/90. All of the Katz quotes in this section are drawn from author interview. Katz's standing in relation to Sa'ada is taken from the *Jerusalem Post*, 1/19/87. The mention of a Marcus Kritz in the Swiss bank records comes from the *Washington Times*, 12/16/86. Katz reported as a reinforcer of dictatorships is taken from the Mexico City newspaper *Excelsior*, 9/13/78.

CHAPTER 10

1. "including secret cables": Erlich and Me'iri, *Ma'ariv*, 8/25/89. Harari and Migdal are cited by Etti Hassid in *Ha'aretz*, 8/9/89. Harari's description of himself as a good friend of Manuel Noriega is taken from the *Wall Street Journal*, 3/7/90. The cartel lodgings at the Caesar Park Marriot are described in Kempe, *Divorcing the Dictator* (New York: Putnam, 1990), pp. 186–87. The Noriega adviser quote is from Joel McCleary, former political consultant to Noriega, to authors, 11/90. Harari's nickname Mad Mike is cited in *Yediot Aharanot*, 4/26/89. Harari and Mossad are discussed in the *Wall Street Journal*, 3/7/90. The general's retainer from the CIA is cited in Andrew and Leslie Cockburn, "Guns, Drugs, and the CIA," PBS Frontline, 5/88. Authors spent many hours discussing CIA payments with former Noriega adviser José Blandon, former CIA officials in the region, and Senate investigators. Noriega described as a lovely hooker is from Joel McCleary, cited in Kempe, op. cit., as well as in discussions with authors over a period of three years. Noriega's trip to Israel as a reward for providing end user certificates is reported in Kempe, op. cit., p. 187.

2. "our lives mean nothing to us": John Cooley, *Green March, Black September* (London: Frank Cass, 1977), p. 125. The quote about Harari and Zvi Zamir is taken from *Ha'aretz*, 8/9/89. The description of Harari's early Mossad years comes from *Ha'aretz*, 8/9/89.

3. "liaison with the Palestinian guerrillas": Bar-Zohar and Haber, *The Quest for the Red Prince* (London: Weidenfeld & Nicolson, 1983), pp. 215–21,

and Stewart Steven, *Spymasters of Israel* (New York: Ballantine Books, 1980), pp. 339–52. The description of the Moroccan waiter whose wife watched him die comes from Raviv and Melman, *Every Spy a Prince* (New York: Houghton Mifflin, 1990), p. 189. The flattened Lebanese taxi is reported in Cooley, op. cit., p. 129.

4. "a layer of banknotes": This description and the references to Rabbi Zion Levy are taken from *Yediot Aharanot*, 1/12/90. The description of Harari's apartment, driver, etc., is in the *Wall Street Journal*, 3/7/90. The routine approval of Harari's arms requests is cited by Uri Dan, *New York Post*, 7/11/88. The information about quantities of arms dispatched from Israel after Noriega had been exposed as involved with narcotics trafficking is taken from *Davar*, 12/22/89. The justification for the alliance as repayment of debts from 1948 is cited by Fishman, *Hadashot*, 1/12/90.

5. "they actually have money there": The Carlton testimony is from Senate Foreign Relations Committee hearings, March 1988, Subcommittee on Terrorism, Narcotics, and International Operations. Harari's profits are discussed in the *Wall Street Journal*, 3/7/90. The references to the Jewish community in Panama are from *Ha'aretz*, 1/12/90 and *Yediot Aharanot*, 1/12/90.

6. "they put together a complete business": The Blandon quotes in this section are from author interviews with José Blandon, 3/88. That same month, Blandon testified before the Senate Foreign Relations Committee in Washington.

7. "if someone else would put up the money": Robert Parry, *Newsweek*, 5/23/88. The North diaries are available from the National Security Archive in Washington. The Supermarket/drug money entry is dated 7/12/85.

8. "dismissed publicly as a secretarial error": The Watson memos on the resupply of the contras are on file at the National Security Archive in Washington, as is the Gorman memo to Pickering. Blandon quotes are drawn from authors interview, 3/88. Harari and the CIA are cited in the *Wall Street Journal*, 3/7/90. The SIBAT source on the forty million dollars' worth of arms and financing by interests related to the drug cartels is from *Hadashot*, 8/30/89. Gregg and Harari are discussed in Kempe, op. cit., p. 163. Authors were told Gregg and Harari had been met by Blandon, 3/88.

9. "U.S. military bases which are located in Honduras": Letter from Noriega released in Senate Foreign Relations Committee hearings, Subcommittee on Terrorism, Narcotics, and International Operations, 3/88. The ABC News report on the Harari operation was aired on 4/7/88. Blandon's

comments on drugs, Rodriguez, and Harari are taken from interviews with the authors, 3/88. For more on the relationship between Rodriguez and the Supermarket, see Leslie Cockburn, *Out of Control* (New York: Atlantic Monthly Press, 1987), pp. 226–27, quoting General Richard Secord, a principal in the North operation: "Felix was working for Ron Martin. I was also paying Felix . . . Martin bought Honduras . . . It only takes a few million dollars to buy Honduras. Martin had his supermarket down there [arms warehouses]. Martin expected Felix to promote his arms supermarket . . . I sent investigators to check it out. They thought some of the money was coming from drugs."

10. "He did plenty of damage to Panama": *Wall Street Journal*, 3/7/90. Harari's escape to Israel is also cited in the *Journal*. The Harari network as described by José Blandon comes from his testimony before the Senate Foreign Relations Committee, 4/88, Vol. 3, p. 18.

11. "Mossad-Noriega-Medellin tripartite relationship": *La Prensa*, 1/31/90. The documents and files being spirited out of Panama is cited in the *Washington Times*, 1/11/90. Harari's television interview was broadcast on Israeli television, 1/6/90, and on the BBC, 1/8/90. The letters of appreciation are cited by Eli Tavor in *Yediot Aharanot*, 4/29/89. Harari in Tel Aviv is cited by Etti Hassid, *Hadashot*, 4/29/89.

12. "the threat of the guerrillas": Author interview with Carlos Lemos Simmons in Cali, Colombia, 2/90, broadcast on PBS Frontline, Andrew and Leslie Cockburn, "Inside the Cartel," 5/90. Cartel details such as the wild animal dung are drawn from a series of author interviews in Colombia, October 1989–March 1990. There are some good references on the subject, notably "Los Jinetes de la Cocaina" by Fabio Castillo (Editorial Documentos Periodisticos, Bogota, November 1987); Mario Arango's *Impacto del Narcotrafico en Antioquia* (Editorial J.M. Arango, Medellin, 1988); and Mario Arango and Jorge Child's *Coca-Coca: Historia menejo politico y mafia de la cocaina* (Dos Mundos, Bogota, 1986). The figure of 82 massacres is taken from the *Miami Herald*, 1/23/89. Descriptions of Colombia, the Violencia, and violentology are drawn from authors' reporting in Bogota, Cali, Medellin, the Amazon region, and the Magdalena Medio in 1989–90. See Andrew and Leslie Cockburn, "Inside the Cartel," op. cit. References to Eitan in Colombia are drawn from Ron Ben-Yishai, *Yediot Aharanot*, 9/1/89, and *Israeli Foreign Affairs*, 5/87, p. 5. Harari and Rodriguez Gacha are discussed in the West German News Service, 4/19/90. The appearance of Mike in Puerto Boyaca is noted in *Newsday*, 5/23/90.

13. "very sophisticated machines of murder": Authors interviews with Carlos Lehder, 3/90. (All Lehder quotes are from those interviews.) MAS and

M-19 reporting comes from authors interviews with General Miguel Maza Marquez, Chief of DAS, Bogota, 12/89; interview with Lehder, 3/90; and testimony of Ramon Milian Rodriguez before the Senate Foreign Relations Committee, 3/88.

14. "an expert in security": Authors interview with General Miguel Maza Marquez, 12/89, Bogota. General Maza's description of the bombing of the DAS building in Bogota is also drawn from authors interview, 12/89.

15. "training the sicarios": DAS/CONFIDENCIAL/"Presence of Foreign Mercenaries in Colombia"/9-20/89. The $800,000-dollar figure and the sites for their guns are taken from *Yediot Aharanot*, 9/1/89. Ultimate Travel is reported in *Israeli Foreign Affairs*, 3/90. The little snake description comes from Ron Ben-Yishai, *Yediot Aharanot*, 9/1/89. The $250 million dollars' worth of Colombian contracts is reported by *Hadashot*, 8/30/90.

16. "training schools where the Israelis were working": Departamento Administrativo de Seguridad Central de Intelligencia/Organización de sicários y narcotraficantes en el Magdalena Medio/Confidencial/ July 20, 1988. DAS intelligence shared with DEA and CIA men is taken from authors interview with General Maza Marquez, Bogota, 12/89. The Israeli Ministry of Foreign Affairs comments are cited in *Hadashot*, 10/24/89. The discussion of Charry Solano is taken from the Gamez testimony to Senor Procurador General de la Nacion, 8/89. The sicario training film was obtained by authors in Colombia and broadcast on PBS Frontline, "Inside the Cartel," op. cit.

17. "bombarded, not the drug traffickers": Andrew Cockburn interview with refugee in Barranca Barmeja, 2/90, broadcast on PBS Frontline, "Inside the Cartel," op. cit. Father Flores Miro was interviewed by author 2/90, in Magdalena Medio. Michael Skol, Deputy Assistant Secretary for Latin America, was interviewed by authors 3/90, in Washington. Authors interviewed Professor Reyes 2/90, in Bogota.

18. "Caribbean island of Antigua": Royce, Eisner, Phelps, *Newsday*, 5/23/90. See also *Guns for Antigua*, Louis Blom-Cooper QC, "Report of the Commission of Inquiry into the circumstances surrounding the shipment of arms from Israel to Antigua and transshipment on 24 April 1989 en route to Colombia" (London: Duckworth, 1990). The weapons being Israeli Defense Force surplus was described in *Hadashot*, 8/29/89. The Cali celebration was witnessed by authors. The Gacha bank records were released by DAS 2/90. The Skol quotes are from author interview, 3/90, Washington.

19. "General Shachar's Miami bank account": See Blom-Cooper QC, op. cit., p. 27. Shuali named Ben Or in author interview, 10/31/88, broadcast on

PBS Frontline, Andrew and Leslie Cockburn, "Israel: The Covert Connection," 5/89. Shachar named as a Mossad agent and representative of IMI is drawn from the *London Independent*, 10/4/90, *Thames TV This Week*, 10/4/90, and Blom Cooper, op. cit., pp. 27–29. The fact that the end user certificate was faxed from Miami was reported in the *Washington Post*, 7/18/90, and confirmed in Blom-Cooper. The 90-man force, the payoff of $125,000, and the knowledge of Israeli officials was reported in *Newsday*, 5/23/90. Bruce Rappaport's involvement with the bank was investigated by Miami lawyer John Mattes and reported to the authors 10/90. For more on Rappaport, see Chapter 12.

20. "now they want to lynch me": Klein's explanation of events is taken from his interview with The Reporters, Fox Television, 9/89. The Colombian army providing intelligence for an attempt on the life of General Maza is taken from authors interview with General Maza, 12/89. Herrera's comment that Harari was behind "all of this" is reported in *Newsday*, 7/4/90, as is the labeling of weapons as machine parts, 5/23/90.

21. "Rabin called the Spearhead men mercenaries": Rabin quotes are from *Hadashot*, 8/31/89. Klein quote is from *Hadashot*, 8/29/89, and The Reporter, Fox Television, 9/89. General Bonnett was interviewed by authors in Cali, Colombia, 12/89.

22. "not something that we would give out anyway": *Washington Post*, 1/29/90. Afek and Klein details are from UPI, 1/27/90, and AP, 1/25/90, from the *Miami Herald*. The report of the CIA issuing a U.S. passport is from Associated Press, 1/26/90, and *Israeli Foreign Affairs*, 2/90. The report that Afek was cooperating with the CIA and U.S. Secret Services was in the *Miami Herald*, 1/27/90. The Israeli press identified Afek as a former intelligence officer in *Yediot Aharanot*, 1/26/90. Afek confided that he worked for Israeli military intelligence, according to the *New York Times*, 1/27/90. The Spearhead man's remark about Afek was taken from *Hadashot*, 8/31/89. Nahum Barnea's comments were in *Yediot Aharanot*, 9/1/89. Yossi Sarid commented in *Hadashot*, 8/29/89.

23. "in the past in covert operations": *Newsday*, 7/26/90. The charges against Klein were cited in the *Washington Post*, 7/29/90. Maza's views on the CIA and Medellin were expressed to authors in interview with confidential source, 2/90, Bogota. Klein's comment that they killed his best witness was taken from his interview for The Reporters, op. cit. The spokesman for the Secret Service was quoted in UPI, 1/27/90, and *Israeli Foreign Affairs*, 2/90. The status as seasonal migrant farm laborers was reported in AP, 1/26/90.

CHAPTER 11

1. "end of the century if not beyond": Quoted in *Washington Jewish Week*, 11/23/89. The Solarz quote is from *Ha'aretz*, 11/22/89. Randall Robinson's speech was on 4/4/87. The congressional meeting was reported in *Israeli Foreign Affairs*, 4/90. The congressmen's warning to the Israeli ambassador was reported in *Washington Jewish Week*, 3/15/90.

2. "ballistic missile designs to carry them": NBC News, 10/25/89, and *Washington Jewish Week*, 11/9/89. The description of the Arniston is taken from NBC News, 10/25/89. Israel sharing its design comes from the *New York Times*, 10/27/89. The increase of Israel's trade with South Africa was reported by Fred Francis, NBC News, 3/9/90. The J79 engines cable appeared in *Israeli Foreign Affairs*, 4/90. The *Jerusalem Post* report on existing contracts appeared on 1/5/90.

3. "in South Africa or abroad that they deserved": "Interagency Intelligence Memorandum"/CIA/SECRET/Dec 79/"The 22 September Event"/ (FOI/ CIA). The other CIA quotes in this section are taken from this memorandum. The conditions at the test site are cited in Green, *Taking Sides* (New York: William Morrow, 1984), pp. 118, 120, 125, 252. Green has more details on the Vela on pp. 111–12. The Bush taboo quote is taken from AP, 10/28/89. Declining comment on such intelligence matters was reported by AP on 10/27/89.

4. "might have been negotiable": CIA memorandum, op. cit., p. 10. The fission trigger is noted in the CIA report, p. 9. The London *Sunday Times* quote on thermonuclear weapons is dated 10/5/86. Turner is quoted in Green, op. cit., p. 130. The senior CIA official quoted comes from authors interview with confidential intelligence source.

5. "those are facts": General Hod interview with authors, 10/88, Tel Aviv. David Kimche's comments on South Africa come from authors interview, 12/88, Tel Aviv. The Urdan listing in the Israel Defense Sales Directory for 1988, Israeli Ministry of Defense, is on page 140. The fact that the caucus felt used was reported on National Public Radio, 10/27/89. The Pentagon leaks on the partnership of Israel and South Africa were reported on NBC News, 10/25/89, and by AP, 10/28/89.

6. "unconscionable use of our aid": the Congressional Black Caucus letter was dated 3/16/88. Congressman Crockett's statement was released 3/17/88. The comments on the Lavi lookalike come from the *Johannesburg Star*, 7/25/88. The *Yediot Aharanot* report was dated

11/3/87. The tankers' use as electronic warfare platforms is taken from *Israeli Foreign Affairs*, 9/88. The Kfir and Cheetah similarities are discussed in Benjamin Beit Hallahmi, *The Israeli Connection* (New York: Pantheon, 1987), p. 124. The U.S. permission quote from General Hod is from authors interview, 10/88, Tel Aviv.

7. "step up its exports to those countries": Matti Golan, *The Road to Peace: A Biography of Shimon Peres* (New York: Warner Books, 1989), p. 119. The IAI quote on the Lavi was reported in *Ha'aretz*, 7/17/88. The Cheetah-E was discussed in the *Johannesburg Star*, 7/25/88.

8. "solution for the Palestinian problem": *Yediot Aharanot*, 8/7/83. The Rabin quote on foreign-inspired instability is taken from *South African Digest*, 1976, p. 11. South Africa's maneuver schools was reported in Jane Hunter, *Israeli Foreign Policy* (Boston: South End Press, 1987), p. 25. South African assistance with spare parts is noted in Beit Hallahmi, op. cit., p. 117. Israel slapping South Africa in the face is taken from the South African Zionist Federation minutes, 3/21/62, and Hunter, op. cit., p. 25. The uranium for tanks exchange is noted in Beit Hallahmi, op. cit., pp. 111, 117, and in the SIPRI Report, Stockholm, 1975. The *Transvaaler* quote is dated 12/1/46. The Herman Cohen quote is taken from *Israeli Foreign Affairs*, 2/90, and *Southscan*, London, 1/19/90. The Canadian assistance is cited by confidential source in authors interview.

9. "people went to Israel for advanced training": *The Namibian*, 12/7/89. The Z team is noted in *Israeli Foreign Affairs*, 6/88. The ANC spokesman's quote is from the London *Sunday Times*, 4/10/88. Mossad and the letter bombs was reported in Foy, "The Grim Reality Behind South Africa's Ruthless Terror Team," *New African*, 10/82. Shabak's liaison with the South African security forces is noted in Beit Hallahmi, op. cit., p. 127. The Boyell case was reported by Andrew Cockburn, *New York Times*, 1985. The Tamuz relationship with President Sebe is described in *Ma'ariv*, June 29, 1984. The quote concerning no apartheid in Ciskei comes from *Hoalam Ha'zeh*, 6/11/86.

10. "restrictions on the white states": See *The Kissinger Study of Southern Africa* (New York: Lawrence Hill, 1976). The National Security Study Memorandum: NSC/SECRET/"Interdepartmental Group for Africa"/8-15-69. The green light from the White House was reported in *The Economist*, 11/5/77. The Uri Dan quote is from Dan, "SWAPO, Afrikaner, Bush-War," *Monitin*, 1/82. Sharon's pride at advising his South African counterparts is taken from author interview with Sharon, 12/81, Tel Aviv. The electrified wall was noted in the *Daily Telegraph*, 11/5/77.

11. "South Africa and the United States": James Adams, *The Unnatural Alliance* (London: Quartet Books, 1984), p. 128, quoting Les de Villiers, *Secret Information* (Capetown: Tafelberg, 1980), pp. 101–5. The $250,000 worth of South African government money was cited in Murray Waas, "Destructive Engagement: Apartheid's Target U.S. Campaign," *The National Reporter*, Winter 1985. For the Israelis and Sydney Baron, see *The Nation*, 4/14/79. Rhoodie's term psychological war can be found in Les de Villiers, op. cit., and Adams, op. cit., p. 128. For more on Kissinger, Angola, and the South African Defense Forces, see Adams, op. cit., p. 45. For the quote on South Africa's fight against the world, see Les de Villiers, op. cit.

12. "methods imported from Israel": Tavori, *Davar*, 4/1/86. Dayan and Israel's intention to ignore the resolution are in Golan, *Ha'aretz*, 11/9/77. Rabin's quote from the Vorster banquet was cited in the *Wall Street Journal*, 4/23/76, and Hunter, op. cit., p. 31. The warm reception by General Stroessner was reported in *Time*, 6/28/76, and the *Jerusalem Post*, 4/20/76. For more on the Gerald Ford contribution, see Adams, op. cit., p. 132, quoting from the Justice Department file of Smathers, Symington, and Herlong under Foreign Agents Registration Act as well as the Congressional Quarterly Almanac. South African money and *West Africa* magazine are cited in Hunter, op. cit., p. 29, and Bloch and Weir, *The Middle East*, 4/82.

13. "He didn't understand a thing about politics": Author interview with confidential source, 10/90. The Chaim Herzog quote was published in the *National Review*, 4/15/88. American-manufactured equipment arriving in South Africa is cited in International Defense and Aid Fund report, 1980. On the Barak naval missile, see Beit Hallahmi, op. cit., p. 123.

14. "He was playing literally with dynamite": Authors interview with confidential source, 10/90. The March 1982 Senate Report was titled "The Space Research Case and the Breakdown of the United States Arms Embargo Against South Africa." For more on the Elana case, see Adams, op. cit., pp. 53, 56, 58. The CIA's close liaison with BOSS and the Stockwell quotes are taken from Stockwell, *In Search of Enemies* (New York: W. W. Norton, 1978), pp. 187, 189.

15. "government operatives like Mr. Pollard": The "Al" network is reported in Victor Ostrovsky and Claire Hoy, *By Way of Deception* (New York: St. Martin's Press, 1990), p. 269. The exposure of CIA men in South Africa was cited in the London *Sunday Times*, 3/29/87. The cozy relationship with BOSS is noted in Stockwell, op. cit., p. 188. The Israel as proxy quote is from UPI, 8/17/81, "Israel Hoping to Double Its Arms Sales."

16. "orchestrating some of the violence": *Washington Post*, 10/17/90. The lobbyist quote from *Washington Jewish Week* was published on 11/9/89. See the *Tallahassee Democrat*, 6/23/89, for the city's antiapartheid policy. The Dellums quote is dated 6/8/89. On Iskor and Asoma, see *Ha'aretz*, 4/19, 20/89 and the *Jerusalem Post*, 5/31/89. The chairman of the board quote is from the *Jerusalem Post*, 5/30/89. The Tadiran in Tallahassee story was reported in *Israeli Foreign Affairs*, 5/89 and 6/89. Behrmann and the South African Embassy in Tel Aviv are cited in UPI, 11/16/89.

CHAPTER 12

1. "Organize forces in the U.S. and Israel": Matti Golan, *Shimon Peres* (New York: Warner Books, 1982), p. 194. Carter's reference to a Palestinian homeland is quoted in Edward Tivnan, *The Lobby* (New York: Simon and Schuster, 1987), pp. 102–3. The story of Mossad's role in provoking the resignation of Andrew Young is told by Victor Ostrovsky and Claire Hoy in *By Way of Deception* (New York: St. Martin's Press, 1990), pp. 278–83. President Carter's "fuck the Jews" remark was made in the presence of a number of senior campaign officials and political advisers, according to our informant, who was one of those present. A senior Carter administration aide informed us about the NSA report that inspired the President's rage.

2. "We bought the sands of the Sinai": George Ball's witticism is quoted in Patrick Seale's *Asad: The Struggle for the Middle East* (London: I. B. Tauris, 1988), p. 314. The figures for aid given to Israel and Egypt because of Camp David are taken from page 52 of the uncensored draft of the GAO report on aid to Israel. The figures were excised from the final version as officially published. The uncensored draft was leaked to an Arab-American organization. The figure of 2,000 people killed in the 1978 Israeli military operation in Lebanon is drawn from Robert Fisk, *Pity the Nation* (London: Andre Deutsch, 1990), p. 124.

3. Bani Sadr's intelligence on U.S.-Israeli-Iraqi planning for the war: Dilip Hiro, *The Longest War* (New York: Routledge, 1991), p. 71. Brzezinski's efforts to get an Iraqi move against Iran are examined in Christopher Hitchens, "Realpolitik in the Gulf, a Game Gone 'Tilt' " (*Harper's* magazine, January 1991). U.S. and foreign diplomatic sources attest to Saddam's successful solicitations of Arab support for the war against Iran. Samuel Segev gives the dates of the meetings in *The Iranian Triangle*, (New York: The Free Press, 1988), p. 120. Gary Sick refers to the U.S. consultations with the Israelis prior to the hostage rescue mission in *All Fall Down* (New York: Viking Penguin, 1986), p. 353, note 7.

4. Nimrodi's observations on the Israeli defense industry's need for jobs were carried in the *New York Times*, 2/1/87. The explanation that Israel's policy towards Iran was dictated by a ravenous hunger for profit was reported by Ze'ev Schiff in *Ha'aretz*, 11/28/86. The F-4 pilot who defected from Iran to Saudi Arabia was reported in *Newsweek*, 1/28/85. The estimate of $500 million a year in Israeli military sales to Iran was given in the London *Observer*, 9/29/85. The *New York Times* reported "at least $100 million a year in sales" on 3/8/82. David Kimche described his warm reaction to Reagan administration foreign policy in an interview, 11/89. The fact that Israel was already trading with Iran prior to the inauguration of Reagan was discussed by former Carter press secretary Jody Powell in an interview, 11/88.

5. "Somebody in the White House winked": Interview with Haig on PBS Frontline, 4/16/81. The statements of Sharon and Arens that Israel was selling arms to Iran with American permission were quoted in the *Washington Post*, 5/28/82 (Sharon) and the *Boston Globe*, 10/21/82 (Arens). On Operation Staunch and the discouragement of competition, see Murray Waas, *Village Voice*, 12/18/90.

6. "Ben-Gurion used to say . . ." Ze'ev Schiff and Ehud Ya'ari, *Israel's Lebanon War* (New York: Simon & Schuster, 1984), p. 31. Meridor appeal that "Israel will be your proxy in areas where you couldn't directly do it" was reported by United Press International, 8/17/81. "The kind of friendship we had with Jim [Angleton]" was stated by Saguy in an interview with the author, 5/89. The supply of intelligence data on Iraqi troop dispositions to the Israelis is discussed in the Tower Commission's Report of the President's Special Review Board (Washington: Government Printing Office, 1987), p. B-17. The provision of satellite reconnaissance by the CIA to Israel for the raid on the Iraqi reactor was reported by Bob Woodward in *Veil* (New York: Simon & Schuster, 1987), p. 160.

7. "Substantial move in Lebanon": Avraham Tamir, *A Soldier in Search of Peace* (London: Weidenfeld & Nicolson, 1988), p. 125; also extensive author interview with Tamir in Tel Aviv, 5/89. The invitation to the war from Sharon came while author Leslie Cockburn was on assignment for CBS News in Israel. Sharon could be rather impulsive. On one occasion he stopped his motorcade while traversing the West Bank in order to collect a dozen roses for the author at a nursery. David Kimche repeated Pierre Gemayel's observation that "The United States is a colony of Israel" in a taped interview with the authors, 12/88. Bashir Gemayel's "massacre of a rival's family" is reported in Avner Yariv, *Dilemmas of Security* (New York: Oxford University Press, 1987), p. 84. The fact that Bashir Gemayel was on the CIA payroll was reported in Woodward, op.

cit., p. 204. Ben-Gurion's intention to set up a state in Lebanon and "we shall sign a treaty with it" was quoted in the *Jerusalem Post* International Edition, 4/22/84, in a review of Ben-Gurion's diaries by Benny Morris.

8. Haig's statement that "the President knew that": *Boston Globe*, 3/2/83. Avraham Tamir discussed the meeting between Haig and Sharon in some detail in our interview of 5/89. The large increase in American arms supplies to Israel just prior to the war is noted in Yariv, op. cit., p. 138. Saguy's meeting with Haig in late February 1982 is discussed in Schiff and Ya'ari, op. cit., p. 68.

9. Sharon as "deceitful, crafty, uncouth . . . [with] little use for democracy and its values": Uzi Benziman, *Sharon: An Israeli Caesar* (New York: Adama Books, 1985), p. 263. The possible involvement of Saddam Hussein in the Argov shooting is discussed by Hiro, op. cit., p. 63. Sharon's trip to Rumania and Dracula's castle is described by Tamir in *A Soldier in Search of Peace*, pp. 126, 127. The fear of the Israeli government that the PLO "might agree in the future to a more far-reaching [peace] arrangement" was reported in *Ha'aretz*, 6/25/82.

10. The bombed school with the dead children "exposed, their legs splayed open, heads down" and Jonathan Randal's remarks to the Israeli major about paying taxes to "support your damn wars" come from Fisk, op. cit., pp. 245–47. Summary of General Gur's interesting reflections on how the Israeli army had always struck civilians "purposely" appeared in *Ha'aretz*, 5/15/78; cited by Noam Chomsky in *The Fateful Triangle* (Boston: South End Press, 1983), p. 181. The Israelis' military setbacks in the initial thrust into Lebanon and the fierce resistance from the Palestinians and the Shi'ite militia were analyzed by Dr. Emmanuel Wald (whose studies on the war were originally commissioned by the Israeli General Staff) in *Anatomy of a Military Failure*, excerpted in the newspaper *Al Hamishmar*, 10/3/86. The Pentagon briefing claiming that American tactics and weapons employed by the Israelis "can easily overpower current Soviet jets and missiles" was reported in the *Wall Street Journal*, 8/4/82.

11. "Screaming, looking for Bashir": Ran Edelist, "Profile of a Senior Mossad Executive," *Monitin*, June 1986. The account of the Mossad man dancing for joy appeared in the April 1983 issue of the same magazine, in an article by Haim Hecht.

12. "Hey, they wanted to stick their noses into this Lebanon thing . . .": Ostrovsky and Hoy, op. cit., p. 322. David Kimche described his relationship with "Bud McFarlane, who led this dialogue" in an interview, 12/88. The shelling of Lebanon by the Sixth Fleet and McFarlane's role in it are

described in David Martin's *Best Laid Plans* (New York: Harper & Row, 1988), pp. 119–24. McFarlane's pre-election meeting with the Iran emissary was reported in the *Miami Herald*, 4/12/87. Tamir described how for "Shultz, it was a cold shower" in an interview, 5/89. The death of Ali Salameh thanks to a "powerful car bomb" is described in Woodward, op. cit., p. 245. The dark suspicions among CIA personnel about a possible Israeli role in the Beirut embassy bombing were observed by the authors at the time. The official Israeli enquiry was the Kahane Commission. The Commission's report absolved the IDF from charges, attested to by many observers on the spot in West Beirut, that the massacre had been carried out within sight of Israeli watchposts, and that personnel from the Israeli-controlled forces of Major Sa'ad Haddad had been among those carrying out the massacre. General Amos Yaron, the Israeli military commander for the Beirut area, was criticized for having allowed the killing to go on after he had been informed of what was happening. Rafael Eitan's congratulations to the Phalangists at Sabra and Shatila were reported in the *New York Times*, 9/20/82; cited by Chomsky, op. cit., p. 365.

13. "Ben Menashe states . . .": Ben Menashe's observations were elicited in a series of interviews with the authors in Santiago and New York, in January and February 1989. Personal observation of Ben Menashe's connections in Santiago indicated that he did indeed have access to very high levels of the Chilean military and defense industrial complex. The letters of reference produced at his trial, which the Israeli Ministry of Defense admitted were authentic, were in English and dated from September 1987. They were fulsome in their description of Ben Menashe's talents. For example, Colonel Arieh Shur, who describes himself as Chief of External Relations, IDF (in fact a division of Military Intelligence), writes that "During Mr. Ben Menashe's service in the department, he was in charge of a task which demanded considerable analytical and executive skills. Mr. Ben Menashe carried out his task with understanding, skill and determination, managing to adapt himself to changing situations . . ."

The reference to Schwimmer giving "lots of money to Peres" is to be found in the Report of the President's Special Review Board, p. B-16. Marcus Katz's generosity toward the National Religious Party has been extensively reported in Israel; newspapers, including *Davar*, 11/13/79. The transition of Richard Fairbank from the State Department to lobbying for Iraq was detailed by Murray Waas in the *Village Voice*, 12/18/90. The administration's low-interest loan to Iraq was described in the *Manchester Guardian Weekly*, 1/23/90. The laundering of Chinese arms supplies through Israeli middlemen is reported both in Harvey Morris and

John Bulloch's *The Gulf War* (London: Methuen, 1990), p. 190, and in *Yediot Aharanot*, 7/27/87. Ostrovsky and Hoy, op. cit., give a detailed account of how Mossad, despite the instructions of Prime Minister Peres, declined to "pass on their best intelligence" about the American hostages in Beirut to the CIA. The observation regarding the "absolutely lunatic" American hostage rescue plans in Beirut comes from Anthony Haden-Guest, "The Unknown Hostage," *Vanity Fair*, 2/91.

14. The death of the "creative" insurance scheme, the NSC observation that "National security is our business," and the purging of Rappaport's CIA file, was reported in the *New York Times*, 1/31/88. The memo that suggested that "$65 million" would find its way to Labor Party funds (from the pipeline profits) "in return for a guarantee" and the dealings between Rappaport, Wallach, Meese and Peres are quoted and discussed in Marilyn Thompson, *Feeding the Beast* (New York: Charles Scribner's Sons, 1990), p. 212. Rappaport's business career, including the angry accusations from the governments of Gabon and Indonesia, were discussed in detail in *Hoalam Ha'zeh*, 10/19/88.

15. "When you do bad things, people are going to say bad things about you": Fisk, op. cit., p. 269. The accounts of the "Enterprise" were detailed in the ledger of Albert Hakim, released by the congressional Iran-contra committees as Exhibit OLN-17. Howard Teicher's employment with Shaul Eisenberg from an interview with a former employee of the Eisenberg organization, 5/89.

16. "Mirror the Israeli model . . .": North's testimony to the Iran-contra committees, July 10, 1987, as transcribed and published in *Taking the Stand* (New York: Pocket Books, 1987), p. 401. Boaz Evron's reflections on the fate of "servants whose services are no longer required" appeared in *Yediot Aharanot*, 11/28/86.

Chapter 13

1. "Four to twenty-four hours": *Ha'aretz*, 1/18/91. Israeli boots: Personal observation. Have Nap bombs: *Aviation Week & Space Technology*, 1/28/91.

2. Israel under the Scuds; Patriots and Russians: Author's personal observation and experience during Israeli sojourn January 20–28, 1991, on behalf of ABC News.

3. "First Saddam": Stated to Paul Roberts of *Toronto Star* during Arab summit, June 1990. "We are faced by the threat of peace": *Ha'aretz*, 11/14/89.

4. "We did not have any expectation . . .": Author interview, 1/24/91. "We will make fire eat up half of Israel . . ." is quoted in Judith Miller and Laurie Mylroie, *Saddam Hussein and the Crisis in the Gulf* (New York: Times Books, 1990), p. 14. The fact that this was a threat of retaliation against Israel usually goes unmentioned. The story of the back-channel communications between Saddam and Rabin was reported by Ze'ev Schiff in *Ha'aretz*, 11/5, 6/90. Saddam's remarks to Congressman Solarz were reported in the *Los Angeles Times*, 1/4/83. Saddam had followed his occasional practice of taping the meeting and then releasing the transcript.

5. There is no way of knowing whether Saddam had real intelligence about this attack plan. Saguy's concession that there was at least "a little bit of discussion" about such a raid came in a videotaped interview with one of the authors, 1/22/91. Tariq Aziz, the Iraqi foreign minister, for example, was specific on the subject of Israeli plans to attack Iraq in his press conference following his abortive pre-war meeting with James Baker in Geneva (*New York Times*, 1/10/91). Saddam's effort to surrender Kuwait without a fight—which he preambled with the complaint beginning "Ever since the United States, Zionism . . ."—was carried in the *New York Times*, 2/16/91.

6. The testimony of John Kelly and April Glaspie's talk with Saddam were carried for the first time on ABC News, 9/12/90. Murray Waas reported on the president's briefing by the CIA prior to the Kuwait invasion in the *Village Voice*, 1/22/91. The imbroglio over the kidnapped Shi'ite and the late Lieutenant Colonel Higgins were reported in the *Washington Post*, 11/11/90. Secretary Baker's little joke about "What do you do . . ." is based on personal information.

7. The perception in the Pentagon that Iraq was the only viable threat was communicated in a personal conversation in April 1990 with an official serving in the Office of the Secretary of Defense. Buchanan's famous "amen corner" remark was quoted in the *New York Times*, 8/25/90. President Herzog's observations on the proper use of nuclear weapons were quoted in the *London Times*, 9/5/90.

8. The review of all intelligence on Israel's nuclear warfighting: Personal information. Levy's threat to Brown was leaked to *Ha'aretz* and then reported in the *New York Times*, 12/6/90. Arens's request for "realtime" intelligence, and its denial by Scowcroft, comes from personal information. A CIA source asserts that at the time of the invasion U.S. intelligence had "no evidence" that Saddam was going to attack Saudi Arabia, and within a few days the agency knew absolutely that he was not intending to do so. Several Pentagon sources assert that the "evidence"

shown by Defense Secretary Cheney to King Fahd consisted of satellite intelligence photographs which the Saudi monarch was led to believe indicated the Iraqi forces poised for attack on Saudi Arabia, but which in fact did not indicate anything of the sort.

9. U.S. buys Russian weapons: Confidential information. The Air Force chief of staff, General Mike Dugan, outlined the bombing strategy for the "best way to hurt Saddam" in an interview with the *Washington Post* and *Los Angeles Times* which appeared on 9/16/90. His candor cost him his job. Dinitz, who is a former Israeli ambassador to the U.S., talked about matters unrelated to the war being pushed "under the carpet" in an interview with one of the authors on 1/23/91. Shamir's statement that he was "delighted" with the results of his meeting with Bush: *Washington Post*, 12/12/90.

10. The quip about putting the Israeli aid request "on American Express" was made in private conversation. It should be added that the congressman said he thought that he and his colleagues would probably vote the money. Larry Eagleburger's trip and the officially announced demand for the $13 billion were observed by one of the authors while in Tel Aviv.

A Note on Sources and Further Reading

In the end, of course, there is no substitute for talking to people. Over the space of ten years and numerous trips, we talked to hundreds of people in Israel, not to mention many more in the United States and in Latin America. We express thanks to all of those who gave us their time.

The literature on the U.S.-Israeli relationship is vast and growing by the month. Unfortunately, much of the most interesting material must be translated from the Hebrew. First and foremost in this category is the extraordinarily lively and, despite the constraints of censorship, informative Hebrew press, a treasure trove of information hidden from most of the outside world. It was this source, along with our personal encounters, that helped us to see the events we describe through Israeli eyes, and to understand such concepts as the "security system," familiar to every Israeli but unknown to outsiders.

Crucial parts of the history we discuss are also only to be found in Hebrew, unless privately translated. The diaries of Moshe Sharett, for example, have been only very partially translated. We were fortunate in having the services of Lia Nirgad, who translated otherwise unreachable sections of Sharett, as well as the works of Isser Harel and Israel Lior. The Israeli political literature that does appear in English consists for the most part of politicians' memoirs. These are well worth perusal, if only for the sometimes less than generous attitudes displayed toward former colleagues. Compare, for example, the sentiments expressed about Shimon Peres in the Rabin memoirs with the observations on Rabin to be found in Matti Golan's books on his friend Shimon Peres.

Two books are seminal in understanding the politics and foreign policy of Israel in the early years: Tom Segev's *1949: The First Israelis* and Uri Bialer's *Between East and West: Israel's Foreign Policy Orientation 1948–1956*. Avi Schlaim's *Collusion Across the Jordan*, while having little to do with Israel's relationship with the U.S., provides extraordinary insights into the characters and truths, as opposed to myths, of the founding of the state. Michael Brecher's *Decisions in Israel's Foreign Policy*, though somewhat out of date, is a very useful academic introduction to the topic. Howard Sacher's *A History of Israel* is an easily available general review of the subject. For anyone studying the tangled politics of the Middle East in the early 1950s, Kenneth Love's *Suez: The Twice-Fought War* is an indispensable source, as well as being a delight to read. The Warriors trilogy of Donald Neff, covering Israel's 1956, 1967, and 1973 wars, provides a certain guide through complex events. *Ropes of Sand* by the late Wilbur Eveland is hard to find, but provides an excellent overview of the CIA making its way in the region in the 1950s.

Patrick Seale's biography of Hafez al-Asad, though incidental to the main topic of this book, is a masterful guide to Middle Eastern events in much of the period under discussion. David Hirst's *The Gun and the Olive Branch*, for some reason very hard to find in the United States, is well worth the search for an insightful view of Israel's wars and their consequences.

All too little has been previously written concerning the defense and intelligence relationship between the United States and Israel, which may account for the proliferation of myth on the subject. However, Stephen Green's two works—*Taking Sides: America's Secret Relations with a Militant Israel* and *Living by the Sword: America and Israel in the Middle East*—are invaluable exceptions to the rule, especially because of the declassified documents unearthed by Mr. Green. No one attempting to read about the general topic of Israel and its relations with the United States can afford to neglect the works of Noam Chomsky, especially *The Fateful Triangle: The United States, Israel and the Palestinians*.

Literature on the CIA and the Middle East, let alone the CIA and Israel, is hard to find. The notable exception is Eveland's book, mentioned above. William Blum's *The CIA, a Forgotten History*; Christopher Simpson's *Blowback*; and John Ranelagh's *The Agency* are useful general guides to the subject. So far as Israeli intelligence is concerned, *Every Spy a Prince* by Dan Raviv and Yossi Melman has added a lot of knowledge to the previous best-known work on the subject, Stewart Steven's *Spymasters of Israel*. Victor Ostrovsky and Claire Hoy's *By Way of Deception*, the only one of these works to have been certified as authentic by the Israeli government, is also the only uncensored insider's work to have appeared to date. It is especially valuable for the light it throws on the attitudes and world views of Mossad functionaries, a topic that has otherwise tended to receive a somewhat rose-tinted treatment from the spy-fiction writers.

Israel's security relations with the Third World come under piercing scrutiny in Benjamin Beit Hallahmi's *The Israeli Connection: Who Israel Arms and Why* and Jane Hunter's *Israeli Foreign Policy*, both essential reading. In a specialized area, Bishara Bahbah's *Israel and Latin America: The Military Connection* and *It's No Secret: Israel's Military Involvement in Central America* by Milton Jamail and Margo Gutierrez add a lot of otherwise totally obscure information. Aaron Klieman provides a more mainstream overview in *Israel's Global Reach: Arms Sales as Diplomacy*.

So far as publications are concerned, *Israeli Foreign Affairs*, Sacramento, California, provides news on the subject drawn from an astonishing variety of sources. As we mentioned above, the language barrier shuts off access for most people to a lot of the best writing on general and particular subjects to do with Israel and America. However, *Translations from the Hebrew Press* by Professor Israel Shahak (available through *Washington Report on Middle East Affairs*, Washington, D.C.) offers an illuminating path through that barrier. No one should think he or she is getting simply an English-language version of the Hebrew press in the *Jerusalem Post* (described by one Israeli acquaintance of ours as being designed to "give the American ambassador a happy breakfast"), but it still provides an insight into Israeli affairs beyond what is to be found in the major American papers. *Washington Jewish Week* is a good source for news about Israeli diplomatic activities vis-à-vis the United States, as well as interesting digests of news from Israel. *Middle East International* is well worth the price for an insightful roundup of events in the region. For military-industrial affairs in general, *Aviation Week & Space Technology* and *Jane's Defense Weekly* belong on the coffee table of every weapons aficionado.

Thanks to diligent efforts on the part of the administration over the past ten years, the Freedom of Information Act is not what it used to be. When citing documents obtained under the act, we have given the pertinent information so that others can try and follow up. In this regard we must express our thanks to John Fialka of the *Wall Street Journal*, who opened to us his files of documents obtained under the act on the Israeli nuclear issue.

Index

About the Authors

Andrew Cockburn grew up in Ireland and was educated at Worchester College, Oxford. He is the author of *The Threat: Inside the Soviet Military Machine* and has won the George Foster Peabody Award for documentary television. Leslie Cockburn grew up in San Francisco and was educated at Yale and the University of London. She is the author of *Out of Control*. In the past year, she has won the George Polk Award, the Dupont-Columbia Award, and the Robert F. Kennedy Award for outstanding journalism. The authors live in Washington, D.C.